Reasoning and Discourse Processes

P250 Implicated assumption / conclusions —
parallel with inherent questions?
+ postponed coherence ??

Cognitive Science Series

Collections

1. Reasoning and Discourse Processes *T. Myers, K. Brown and B. McGonigle (eds), 1986*
2. New Directions in Semantics *E. LePore (ed.), 1986*
3. Language Perception and Production: Relationships between listening, speaking, reading and writing *A. Allport, D. G. MacKay, W. Prinz and E. Scheerer (eds), 1987*

Monographs

Agreement and Anaphora *P. Bosch, 1983*

Reasoning and Discourse Processes

edited by

TERRY MYERS

Centre for Cognitive Science and
Department of Psychology
University of Edinburgh
Edinburgh, Scotland

KEITH BROWN

Department of Language and Linguistics
University of Essex
Colchester, England

and

BRENDAN McGONIGLE

Centre for Cognitive Science and
Department of Psychology
University of Edinburgh
Edinburgh, Scotland

1986

ACADEMIC PRESS
Harcourt Brace Jovanovich, Publishers
London San Diego New York Berkeley
Boston Sydney Tokyo Toronto

ACADEMIC PRESS LTD
24/28 Oval Road
London NW1 7DX

United States Edition published by
ACADEMIC PRESS INC.
San Diego, CA 92101

Second printing (pbk only) 1987

British Library Cataloguing in Publication Data
Reasoning and discourse processes.—
(Cognitive science series)
1. Discourse analysis
I. Myers, Terry II. Brown, K.
III. McGonigle, B. IV. Series
415 P302

Library of Congress Cataloging-in-Publication Data
Main entry under title:

Reasoning and discourse processes.

Includes index.
1. Reasoning (Psychology) 2. Rhetoric.
I. Myers, Terry. II. Brown, K. (Keith),
III. McGonigle, B., Date-
BF441.R38 1985 153.4′3 85-9223
ISBN 0-12-512320-5
ISBN 0-12-512321-3 (Pbk)

Typeset by Composition House Limited,
Salisbury, Wiltshire.

Printed in Great Britain by St Edmundsbury Press Ltd
Bury St Edmunds, Suffolk

Contributors

Jens Allwood *Department of Linguistics, University of Goteborg, Erik Dahlbergsgatan 11B, S-411 26 Goteborg, Sweden*

Keith Brown *Department of Language and Linguistics, University of Essex, Wivenhoe Park, Colchester CO4 3SQ, England*

Margaret Chalmers *Department of Psychology, University of Edinburgh, 7 George Square, Edinburgh EH8 9JZ, Scotland*

Goran Hagert *Computing Science Department, University of Uppsala, Box 2059, S-750 02 Uppsala, Sweden*

Philip Johnson-Laird *MRC Applied Psychology Unit, 15 Chaucer Road, Cambridge CB2 2EF, England*

Ruth Kempson *Department of Linguistics, School of African and Oriental Studies, Malet Street, London WC1E 7HP, England*

Brendan McGonigle *Centre for Cognitive Science and Department of Psychology, University of Edinburgh, 2 Buccleuch Place, Edinburgh EH8 9LW, Scotland*

Terence Moore *Clare College, Cambridge CB2, England*

Terry Myers *Centre for Cognitive Science and Department of Psychology, University of Edinburgh, 2 Buccleuch Place, Edinburgh EH8 9LW, Scotland*

Jackie Stedmon *Department of Applied Psychology, University of Wales Institute of Science and Technology, Llwyn-y-Grant Road, Cardiff, Wales*

Keith Stenning *Centre for Cognitive Science, University of Edinburgh, 2 Buccleuch Place, Edinburgh EH8 9LW, Scotland*

Pieter Seuren *Filosofische Instituut, Katholieke Universiteit, Thomas Van Aquinostraat 3, 6500 HK Nijmegen, The Netherlands*

Dan Sperber *CNRS, 33 Rue Croulebarbe, Paris 75013, France*

Yvonne Waern *Department of Psychology, University of Stockholm, S-106 91 Stockholm, Sweden*

Deidre Wilson *Department of Phonetics and Linguistics, University College London, Gower Street, London WC1E 6BT, England*

Yorick Wilks *Computing Research Laboratory, New Mexico State University, Las Cruces, New Mexico 88003, USA*

Preface

The current volume in the *Cognitive Science Series* was planned with the aim of exploring the relationship between verbal reasoning and discourse, which are the major domains of language in use. The editors were motivated by their expectation that the project would not only lead to an increase in our understanding of reasoning and discourse but also contribute to the goal of constructing an adequate theory of natural language processing. Such an ambitious project required the mobilization of a range of expertise that now exists within the interdisciplinary community of cognitive scientists. The diversity of background is evident from the list of contributors. We take this opportunity to thank the contributors for their readiness to participate and their patience during the editorial process. We also thank the participants at the Second International Conference in Cognitive Science at Edinburgh (March–April, 1982),* entitled "Language, Reasoning and Inference". Their stimulating contributions provided the intellectual impetus necessary to get the project started.

The conference that stimulated the preparation of this volume was organized by the Centre for Cognitive Science (formerly School of Epistemics) and hosted by the Department of Psychology. We thank Professor Barry Richards, and the late Professor D. M. Vowles for their help and advice. Funding was provided by the Faculty of Social Sciences and the Centre for Cognitive Science: we are grateful for their support. Thanks are also due to colleagues at the Applied Psychology Unit, Cambridge, for the stimulating environment in which the introduction was prepared.

Edinburgh and Colchester
May 1986

T. Myers
K. Brown
B. McGonigle

*The first, held in July/August, 1979, was entitled: "The Cognitive Representation of Speech". The proceedings were published in 1981 by North-Holland Pub. Co., Amsterdam (Eds: T. Myers, J. Laver and J. Anderson).

Contents

Editors' Foreword

Cognitive science is the field of study marked off by the common concerns of artificial intelligence, linguistics, philosophy and psychology. The depth and richness of these mutual concerns suggest that certain issues may be essentially interdisciplinary. Nowhere is this clearer than at the intersection of cognition and language, where recent attempts to construct suitable formal theories have had to bring together different theoretical paradigms. The effect has been that the problems in one discipline have become those of another.

Cognitive science embraces a wide variety of topics, including parsing, discourse analysis, problem solving, language acquisition, concept formation, mental representation, semantics, cognitive modelling and visual processing. An interdisciplinary approach to these issues is committed to integrating, or perhaps synthesizing, relevant specialist theories with a view to revealing new horizons. The *Cognitive Science Series* aims to provide both a stimulus and a forum for relevant research. The intention is to encourage work which is either explicitly interdisciplinary or offers results likely to be of interdisciplinary interest. Since cognitive science is at an early stage of development, it is important to maintain the broadest possible perspective and hence, contributions to any aspect of the subject are invited.

Collections

To facilitate the growth of this multi-faceted subject the Series will include collections devoted to issues of topical interest. Since such issues will typically involve a wide spectrum of expertise, volumes of selected papers are likely to be particularly appropriate and useful. The Series will seek to publish thematic collections on a regular basis and would welcome proposals from prospective editors.

Monographs

As cognitive science matures, there will be an ever increasing need to meet the special concerns of the community. At the moment these concerns have yet to take a definite shape, and it is hoped that the Series will in the meantime provide a focus for enquiry. Speculative monographs would be entirely appropriate, as would more empirical studies. In general the objective is to canvas broadly and allow the field to impose its character on the Series.

Introduction: Representation and Inference in Reasoning and Discourse

T. MYERS

Centre for Cognitive Science and Department of Psychology
University of Edinburgh

K. BROWN

Department of Language and Linguistics and Cognitive Studies Centre
University of Essex

B. McGONIGLE

Centre for Cognitive Science and Department of Psychology
University of Edinburgh

A major goal of research in cognitive science is an adequate theory of natural language processing, one that will encompass the multi-sentence contexts of discourse and verbal reasoning. Such a theory would provide a formal characterization of those relationships both within and between sentences that are computed by the language user and the processes by which they are computed. This volume examines two related sets of problems that need to be resolved in the pursuit of such a theory. One concerns the forms of representation that seem to be required in accounts of reasoning and discourse; the other concerns the role of inference in such contexts of natural language processing. Both appear as closely interwoven themes that run throughout the volume. The principle behind the ordering of the chapters

ISBN 0-12-512320-5

derives, therefore, from two specific questions: (1) Is there a mental logic? and (2) What is the nature of coherence?

MENTAL LOGIC

The first six chapters address the question of whether rules of inference formalised in a logical calculus adequately characterize the deductive component of the verbal reasoning capacity. Johnson-Laird opens the debate by challenging what he refers to as the 'doctrine of mental logic', according to which the ability to draw valid inferences from a set of premises is attributable to the mental representation of a set of inference-rule schemas corresponding to logical formulae. Such a representation would constitute the syntax of a mental logic. Certainly, any theory of reasoning must provide an adequate characterization of validity. Johnson-Laird argues, however, that valid inference may be arrived at by following a general semantic procedure, and in the opening chapter he sketches an alternative theory of deductive reasoning based upon a 'semantic principle of validity'.

Johnson-Laird begins his argument by showing that mental logic is neither necessary nor sufficient as a basis for reasoning. He notes that the ability to reason depends on more than logic, because there must be constraints on spontaneous deductions that rule out trivial, though valid deductions. At the same time, the ability to reason need not depend on logic at all. Thus, valid deductions based upon propositional connectives, relational expressions or quantifiers can all be made without recourse to formal rules of inference. Indeed, a theory of reasoning could be founded on a knowledge of the truth conditions of such terms. Given a measure of semantic information, which the chapter outlines, spontaneous inferences can be characterized as yielding information that is not explicitly stated in the premises but that maintains their semantic content and conveys it parsimoniously. His theory assumes that there are three main steps in making deductions: reasoners interpret premises by constructing a 'mental model' of the state of affairs described; they formulate an informative conclusion that is true of the model, and they search for an alternative model of the premises that would render this conclusion false. If there is no such model, the inference is valid; otherwise, it is invalid. Johnson-Laird cites evidence supporting his theory from studies of reasoning with quantifiers, relational deductions, and common-sense inferences of daily life.

Moore (Chapter 2) considers the same theme from the position of the linguist. He observes that Chomsky, following Post, derived much of the inspiration for his hypothetico-deductive approach to syntax from logic. Similarly, theoretical linguists interested in the semantics of natural language have turned increasingly to logic, in particular to that concerned with deductive inference. Moore cautions against an over-emphasis on deduction, arguing that linguists should also pay attention to the *in*ductive processes of reasoning. Whereas deductive reasoning concentrates on the form of an argument at the expense of the meaning of its premises, in the case of inductive reasoning form cannot be separated from content; rather, the meaning of the premises and the bodies of knowledge to which they are related play a crucial role. Furthermore, inductive logics accept uncertainty and indeterminacy, which are primary characteristics of natural language.

Moore supports his position by reexamining and reinterpreting some of the data gathered by Luria from peasants in Uzbekistan, and by reporting on work by Cole and Scribner on Kpelle-speaking Liberian villagers. In both cases informants generally declined to restrict their inferences to the formal mode of deductive reasoning; rather, they interpreted premises according to their content and plausibility in light of the villagers' own first-hand experience and judgment. The result is often an apparent inability to argue 'logically'. However, Moore argues that given the appropriate modifications to the premises according to the way in which informants accept them, it is in fact possible to recast their reasoning as perfectly valid. Moreover, lest it should be assumed that inductive reasoning of this kind is characteristic only of peasant communities, he draws on the work of Tversky and Kahnemann to show that similar reasoning processes are at work among undergraduate students.

Moore extends his analysis by proposing an inductive solution to the problem of resolving the interpretation of anaphoric expressions, a subject that is taken up again later in this volume. In sum, a plausible account of the inferences involved in both reasoning and the resolution of anaphora can be framed in terms of an inductive probabilistic logic rather than a formal deductive logic. The conclusion of the chapter is that inductive inference may afford the more appropriate model for linguists who wish to explain how meaning emerges from the utterances of a language.

Allwood (Chapter 3) contends that parts of traditional logic can be used to describe the structure of analytic discourse and to explicate normative intuitions about how arguments should be structured. He demonstrates this notion by analysing the logical structure of two examples of spoken discourse, a debate and a discussion. Such an approach is clearly full of difficulties, since the logical structure of debates and informal discussion is often not readily discernible. Allwood identifies a number of ways in which such difficulties can arise. For instance, a 'textbook' example of a logically valid argument is often presented in the form of a set of premises followed by a conclusion, even though the logical relations they express may in fact be 'atemporal'. In conversation, however, premises and conclusions may be presented in any order, and are often shared among several speakers.

Allwood claims that speakers share a normative intuition about what the shape of an argument should be, and that this intuition follows the tenets of traditional logic. He goes on to argue that logical structures can have different scopes: Some may apply at a global level (throughout an extended piece of discourse), others at an intermediate level, and still others at the micro level of a single utterance. In all cases, however, Allwood sees the same kind of logical structuring principle at work. A further problem is that in conversation, the premises necessary to a logically valid argument are often, for a variety of pragmatic reasons, implicit rather than explicit. Allwood claims that in analysis these premises can legitimately be made explicit, but he does not discuss the problems involved in trying to do this. It is interesting to note that the type of data Allwood uses, and the kind of implicit premises he advocates supplying, are very similar to those used by Moore to argue that inductive rather than deductive logic is a more appropriate analytic tool.

In Chapter 4, Hagert and Waern focus on the question raised by both Moore and Allwood—namely, whether apparent errors in reasoning may be attributable not to faulty inference but to the introduction by the reasoner of implicit assumptions not immediately obvious to the observer. Their basic hypothesis is that content-independent rules of inference are employed by the reasoner and that these correspond to a subset of rules that can be found in logic (see Allwood, Chapter 2). Using a modelling procedure, together with protocol analysis of a single subject taken through a series of tasks, the authors try to show that apparently faulty reasoning is consistent with the operation of valid rules of inference if we accept the role of interpretational heuristics. These add assumptions to the propositional network (rather than model) in which the premises are encoded, and they take account of the strategies that not only govern attention and interpretation but also determine when inferences can be drawn. In the case of the subject under study, the authors reportedly observed a shift in emphasis from interpretational heuristics to an awareness of the logical structure of the task per se. This finding, they argue, shows that the subject was able to shift criteria and move from a pragmatic mode, where changes in background assumptions change the conclusion, to a specialized formal rule system where the conclusion drawn depends on the (formal) structure of the task rather than the semantic content of the premises.

This dichotomy between pragmatic and logical criteria in essence forms the basis of Stedmon's evaluation (Chapter 5) of how children come to understand the relationship between a class and its sub-classes. Drawing on one of Piaget's examples, let us suppose that a young child is presented with some flowers, of which more than half are primroses. The child is then asked, "Which are more, the primroses or the flowers?" What answer would we expect? Piaget found that it was not until about the eighth year, when they are said to have attained the level of 'concrete operations', that the children in his studies were able to give a whole-class response: "The flowers". Younger children typically answered: "The primroses". What Stedmon found, however, is that not only may children perform successfully in a class-inclusion task well before the eighth year, but also that such performance is sensitive to the choice of referential terms used in presenting the task. Her study, on children aged between five and six years, revealed a developmental shift in the functions they conferred upon the plural terms used to refer to the whole class. Thus the class-extension function, initially conferred upon expressions of the form 'every single X', was later transferred to expressions of the form 'all the Xs' and 'the Xs'. With that change in referential function came a corresponding shift to correct class-inclusion responses.

Although Stedmon suggests that her results indicate a significant role for language in the development of the reasoning capacity, it is by no means clear what the causal role of language could be in such a process. What are the origins of class inclusion if it is not controlled by linguistic *or* logical rules? From Stedmon's own work, it is clear that natural language quantifiers were understood by her subjects pragmatically. Thus the size of the set implied by the term 'all' can vary dramatically, as in her cutlery example where 'all the cutlery' can mean 'all the cutlery for the diners', 'all the cutlery which is nice' (e.g., made of silver), 'all of the cutlery in the canteen', and so on. The criteria used to determine the set (size) are often implicit in discourse situations, so background assumptions and background knowledge must play a vital role (albeit cued by logical particles). This view contrasts sharply, of course, with the purely logical form of the class-inclusion problem where the domain of the set implied by the universal quantifier is not subject to pragmatic manipulation. The logical case may be seen, in fact, as a highly specialized and restricted form of the pragmatic version used in natural language. Despite its exacting rule system, it is clear that the logical approach owes its origin to the concepts of relative inclusion which operate in many real-life situations and which are reflected in the language of quantification.

Relative inclusion is but one real-life concept with a counterpart within a formal logical system. Order relationships are another. Here too it is clear that there are many everyday situations which presuppose a grasp of such relationships from the dominance hierarchies of animals to the relative preferences of consumers within an economic system. An isomorph of such behaviour within a logical system is the linear, transitive inference commonly evaluated by psychologists through what is known as the '3/5 term series' problem. Thus subjects may be presented with the following problem: "Edith is fairer than Susanne; Edith is darker than Lilly: Which is the fairest, Edith, Susanne or Lilly?" As in the case of class-inclusion problems, the questions of genesis are similar: Is the logical case a specialised product of ordering behaviour which occurs naturally, or is a logical grasp of order relations presupposed when ordering behaviour occurs?

McGonigle and Chalmers take up these questions in Chapter 6. Based on evidence derived from experiments on adults, children and non-human primates, they claim that ordering devices which are used even by the most sophisticated of adult subjects to solve linear transitive inference problems are not constructions made by the subject as a consequence of logical procedures but owe their origins instead to prelogical forms of encoding. Rather than constructing a model of specific states of affairs, McGonigle and Chalmers argue that certain premises are mapped onto a prior (spatial) paralogical representation. This process is revealed by both protocol reports (in the case of adults) and decision time analysis (in the case of both human and non-human subjects).

One notable feature of such representational devices is that they do not permit the direct mapping of each and every logical or linguistic statement which can be understood by a subject. In the case of the comparatives 'bigger' and 'smaller', for example, the evidence suggests that psychological constraints operate on the *direction* of ordering, with subjects being more likely to form a series from big to small than vice versa (there are also constraints on the number and orientation of spatial vectors used to plot the items in cognitive space). As a result, the authors argue, a subject must devise procedures to convert and translate statements not immediately congruent with the core representational device into a form which can permit a more direct mapping. Their account distinguishes two levels at which these procedures are carried out: the first is a surface lexical level for conversion and translation; the second is a deep representational level for mapping and comprehension.

McGonigle and Chalmers conclude by specifying some of the factors extrinsic to logic and language which causally antedate linguistic competence. They contend that logic and discourse tasks have much in common. In both cases the subject must establish the nature of the bridge or the level of connectivity between successive statements, a process in which background knowledge plays a crucial role.

COHERENCE

A central requirement for any account of verbal reasoning and, more generally, of discourse processing is an adequate characterization of the relationships between premises and sentences that give rise to the phenomenon of 'coherence'. Unfortunately, the word is used differently in various discussions of these related domains. In the case of a reasoned, analytic argument it connotes the progression from a sequence of premises to a valid conclusion. However, the coherence of discourse is usually considered in terms of the accumulation of successive sentences into a consistent whole. Thus a reasoned argument may succeed in being coherent in both senses, and discourse may incorporate a deductive component (see Allwood, Chapter 3, and Wilson and Sperber, Chapter 10, this volume). We are therefore encouraged to speculate that the two kinds of coherence may bear at least some resemblance to one another. A clue to their kinship may lie in a shared form of representation, such as the mental model. Johnson-Laird describes the role of mental models in reasoning; in the same vein, Stenning describes a new line of research to examine their 'on-line' construction during text comprehension.

Stenning (Chapter 7) outlines an investigation of the processes by which models of simple texts are constructed, particularly the referential frameworks of such texts. These consist of small arrays of objects differing on a few property dimensions. Representation is achieved in part through the deployment of the logical particles of language. The construction process was probed by the ingenious technique of introducing transient indeterminacy into the texts and measuring the effect on reading time. A surprising result was the appearance of large processing delays, which occurred not at the point where indeterminacy was introduced but where it was resolved. Stenning interprets these delays as being occasioned by inferences that are required for integrating predicate information into a model of the text. Prior to resolution, the text is stored in a propositional format. He argues, with regard to his choice of method, that whereas texts of the expository type (such as those employed in his study) invite construction of a unique model, discursive text does not. Moreover, his texts enabled model construction to be examined more directly than would have been possible using, say, syllogistic reasoning tasks, which call for extra operations on the models once constructed.

A problem that has moved into the foreground of research on discourse understanding, and one that may hold a key to the explanation of coherence, is that of anaphora resolution, whereby a pronoun, for example, is related to an antecedent in a sentence or in the wider domain of discourse. In Chapter 8, Seuren describes an integrated theory of both internal and external anaphora and offers a general algorithm for interpreting pronouns of various kinds. Such interpretation begins with the semantic analysis of a sentence containing a pronoun. The results of this analysis constitute the input to an assignment procedure which provides the pronoun with the discourse address of its antecedent, whereupon both items may be said to 'denote' the same address. Thus anaphora is resolved when the 'co-denotation' of pronoun and antecedent has been determined.

Principles that have previously been invoked to accommodate pronoun anaphora have confronted some apparently intractable cases. Seuren shows how this problem may be greatly reduced by drawing clear distinctions among three major types of pronouns: reflexive (either morphologically marked or unmarked), bound variable and denoting. The 'primordial principle', according to which a pronoun must be either preceded or commanded by its antecedent, applies only to the denoting type, but there remain instances of this type that are themselves counter-examples to the principle.

Seuren argues that to capture all instances even of internal anaphora, a structural account may require supplementing in order to accommodate discourse phenomena such as topic and focus. Accordingly, he offers an amended principle. Further extensions are required, however, to handle the Bach–Peters paradox, whereby a sentence may contain one or two denoting pronouns so distributed that a grammatical characterization of their antecedents results in an infinite regress. This paradox is resolved by treating pronouns *as* pronouns in semantic analysis and by incorporating into the assignment procedure the means for making tentative discourse assignments, to be confirmed subsequently if consistency is achieved. Confirmation may be overruled if the resulting discourse is implausible, in which case one or both of the pronouns will take external antecedents. These are required only by denoting pronouns, when the antecedent may be either a definite noun phrase or an existentially quantified noun phase in the preceding sentence (or conjunct). In the first case, the pronoun takes over the denoting function of the antecedent noun phase; in the second, it denotes a new discourse address. So-called 'donkey sentences' provide instances of the second pronoun–antecedent relation.

Seuren's solution to the problem of relating pronouns to their antecedents requires the construction of discourse representations (to provide denotational addresses) which are not essentially different from the cognitive models envisaged by Johnson-Laird and by Stenning. A different comprehensive approach to the problem is taken by Kempson (Chap. 9). She offers a unified model–theoretic account which is enriched by the pragmatic theory of relevance presented by Sperber and Wilson (Chap. 10)

Kempson focusses on the distinction often drawn in the literature between bound variable anaphora, conventionally handled by a 'quantifying-in' mechanism, and discourse anaphora, which requires treating anaphors as referring expressions. She argues that these two types share many characteristics and should therefore be treated together. To this end, she adopts Sperber and Wilson's pragmatic theory of utterance interpretation, particularly their claims that natural language expressions are under-determined with respect to propositional content, that their interpretation is an inferential exercise which involves the construction of a contextual set of premises, and that natural language elements may involve the specification of their contribution(s) to context construction.

Kempson works out her proposal with a set of rules illustrated by a number of examples. The rules operate in two stages: The first provides a mapping from surface structures onto a government-binding style logical form, while the second involves a pragmatic relevance–driven rule of antecedent identification and produces a mapping from the first level of representation onto a standard predicate calculus formula containing no anaphors and no unbound variables. The consequence of this proposal is that the process of context construction and the resulting deduction of contextual implications are treated as integral parts of the theory rather than constructs of convenience, and that they are postulated for single utterances as well as sequences of utterances. Thus the proposal yields a unified account of anaphoric processes.

We owe to Grice, as much as anyone, the major insight that discourse understanding is achieved by drawing inferences both from what a speaker says and what may be assumed. He argues that these inferences, or 'conversational implicatures', must be capable of being worked out by listeners, although his own account of how listeners might do this is rather sketchy. The authors of the succeeding two chapters seek to repair this lacuna in the work of Grice. They focus on 'relevance', which is a pivotal construct in the analysis of implicature and, arguably, a primary source of coherence in discourse.

Wilson and Sperber's continuing work on relevance can be seen as an attempt to formalise the processes by which implicatures are worked out. The authors use a modified form of traditional deductive logic. Hence, their position is opposed to the inductive approach to this problem advocated by Moore (Chap. 2), and to that of many discourse analysts who propose various kinds of informal problem-solving strategies. In previous papers Wilson and Sperber have explored the deductive component associated with their theory of relevance, including the need to constrain inference rules and the possibility of quantifying relevance for any particular inference. In chapter 10, after summarising their approach to the problem, the authors consider the equally fundamental problem of forming the hypotheses in terms of which the deductive process is driven. These include contextual assumptions (and any relevant inferences that can be drawn from them), together with the probabilities that can be attached to such hypotheses and inferences. Within such a framework, utterance comprehension becomes a matter of hypothesis formation and evaluation, while deductive inference plays a central role in both processes.

Wilks (Chapter 11) presents a critical appraisal of previous work by Sperber and Wilson on which their chapter in this volume is based. He points up certain anomalies in their arguments, such as their slippage in perspective when considering speaker intention and listener processing, and various ambiguities in their treatment of context and processing cost. He then concludes that these difficulties stem from the conviction that there is an objectively 'right' context set of propositions, one that can be assumed independently of what speaker and listener believe, both separately and about each other's beliefs.

Drawing on his work with Bien, Wilks sets out an alternative account which addresses the problems raised in his critique. In the spirit of Grice, he assumes that a central requirement for any attempt to model discourse understanding is a means for drawing a formal distinction between the beliefs of the listener and the listener's beliefs about the speaker's beliefs, including those about the listener. A very general algorithm for the construction of belief spaces, or environments, is described which incorporates this formal requirement. The inner environment of the resulting belief space represents what the listener currently views as the speaker's beliefs. These may differ from the listener's own, especially when the speaker is, say, a novice talking to an expert, or a patient talking to a doctor. Nested, inner belief environments are therefore temporary structures assembled in real time during a conversation and dismantled when they are no longer required. They provide interim contexts in which pragmatic inferences are computed. In the end, it is the 'percolation' of the speaker's beliefs into the inner environment of the listener's belief space that ensures the relevance of the inferences drawn and the cost-effectiveness of their computation.

CONCLUSIONS

We began this introduction by considering whether reasoning and discourse processing require the mental representation of inference-rule schemas corresponding to a deductive logic. Johnson-Laird argues that mental logic is neither necessary nor sufficient to account for the way in which valid conclusions are reached in verbal reasoning tasks. Moore observes that common-sense reasoning, which draws heavily on knowledge and belief, often appears to be invalid when it is not; validity is restored on these occasions by taking into account the reasoner's implicit assumptions. Moore attributes such reasoning to the operation of inductive rather than deductive inferences and advocates inductive probabilistic logic as a model for characterizing them. However, he does not offer arguments that would compel acceptance of the doctrine of mental logic.

Hagert and Waern, as well as Allwood, find corroborative evidence of valid inferencing in common-sense reasoning, provided that the reasoner's implicit assumptions are taken into account. They attribute this ability to the mental representation of a part of traditional logic. However, faced with Johnson-Laird's demonstration that valid inferences may be drawn by means of semantic procedures, even in the case of abstract reasoning tasks, the burden of proof would seem to rest with the defenders of the doctrine. A further strategy available to its opponents is that of demonstrating an ability to draw valid inferences in pre-logical subjects, and this both Stedmon and McGonigle and Chalmers attempt to do. The designation 'prelogical' is, of course, question-begging in this context, but their findings do charge the other camp with the task of showing that the representational basis of reasoning ability in such experimental subjects is a part of mental logic. Our conclusion, meanwhile, is that the need to invoke mental logic to account for inference processes in reasoning and discourse has not been satisfactorily demonstrated.

A semantic account of verbal reasoning has the virtue of parsimony, in that reasoning may then be treated as a discourse genre. One advantage of this assimilation is the possibility of a unitary account of coherence. The unity may arise from a common form of representation—namely, what Johnson-Laird refers to as a mental model. Any discourse, and especially an analytic argument, will be coherent if it enables a single model to be constructed; otherwise, it will be indeterminate. Stenning provides experimental evidence which suggests that temporary indeterminacy of a text is resolved when the reader constructs a model of its referential framework. Such a model would seem to be required in Seuren's integrated account of internal and external anaphora involving denoting pronouns. It remains to be seen whether a rapprochement can be achieved between that account and Kempson's model-theoretic approach, which encompasses both bound variable and discourse anaphora.

The resolution of both determinacy and anaphora are two of the prerequisites for coherence. A third is the resolution of relevance. Wilson and Sperber show how a determination of the relevance of an utterance may be formalized using deductive logic. Thus they appear to espouse the doctrine of mental logic. Consequently, opponents of the doctrine will need to show that the computation of relevance is achieved by the operation of semantic procedures. In the meantime, it would appear that there may be problems with the Wilson–Sperber proposal. For example, as Wilks argues, it rests on the assumption that the computation of the context set of propositions by which relevance is determined operates independently of the beliefs of both speaker and listener; this would indeed be compatible with a mental logic account. However, Wilks demonstrates that the listener's representation of the speaker's knowledge and beliefs may play a crucial role in the determination of relevance. To conclude: Concerning coherence, mental models may provide the representational means by which semantic procedures resolve determinacy, anaphora and relevance. Such resolution, we suggest, is what gives rise to the coherence of both discourse and reasoning.

1

Reasoning without Logic

P. N. JOHNSON-LAIRD
MRC Applied Psychology Unit
Cambridge

INTRODUCTION

The psychology of reasoning should characterize both inferential competence—what the mind has to compute and why—and inferential performance—the mental processes underlying these computations. Unfortunately, there is no existing theory of what the mind computes in reasoning, and the resulting theoretical gap has been filled by logic. Psychologists suppose that since logic encompasses the set of valid deductions, it is reasonable to assume that ideal human competence is in accordance with logical principles. This assumption leads very naturally to the doctrine that the mind *contains* a logic, and to a theory of performance in which deductions are made on the basis of formal rules of inference, or inference schemata. Thus logic is implanted in the mind in much the same way that grammar is supposedly located there.

The doctrine of mental logic is highly plausible. It is embodied in the philosophical belief that laws of thought are nothing but laws of logic (Boole, 1854; Mill, 1874), and it is embraced by all current theories that assume that human beings are potentially rational (e.g., Beth & Piaget, 1966; Braine, 1978; Henle, 1962; Inhelder & Piaget, 1958; Osherson, 1975; Rips, 1983; Youniss, 1975). In addition, it was tacitly accepted by my colleagues and myself for many years (e.g., Johnson-Laird, 1975; Wason & Johnson-Laird,

ISBN 0-12-512320-5

1972). What I argue in this chapter, however, is that the doctrine is false. In my view, logic does not make a good theory of deductive competence, and theories of performance based on it are defective. It is necessary to give up, not the thesis that human beings are capable of rational thought, but the notion that what underlies this ability is logic. There *can* be reasoning without logic. Indeed, once the search for a logic of the mind is abandoned, it is possible to make better sense of the psychology of reasoning.

THE DOCTRINE OF MENTAL LOGIC

My first task is to examine the doctrine of mental logic in some detail, since it is important to make clear precisely what is at stake. Logicians formalize logic in many ways, but a crucial component of a formalization is the introduction of rules of inference, or inferential schemata. A typical rule of inference is *modus ponens*:

$$\begin{array}{l} p \\ p \rightarrow q \\ \hline \therefore q \end{array}$$

This rule stipulates that if there are premises of the form p, and p implies q, then the conclusion q is derivable.

A rule of inference can be applied to any set of premises, regardless of their contents, provided they have the appropriate logical form. Hence, according to the doctrine of mental logic, an individual makes the following deduction:

> The warning light is on.
> If the warning light is on, then the system is defective.
> Therefore, the system is defective.

by relying on an internalized representation of modus ponens. The first premise corresponds to p, and the second premise corresponds to $p \rightarrow q$, since 'if p then q' can be treated as an implication, and the conclusion corresponds to q. Proponents of mental logic assume that inferences are based on some such formal system, but they disagree among themselves about its precise nature (see, e.g., Braine, 1978; Johnson-Laird, 1975; Osherson, 1975; Rips, 1983).

The main virtue of mental logic is that it solves the otherwise profound riddle of how it is possible to reason validly. The question is puzzling because the invention of logic as an intellectual tool would seem to require the ability to reason soundly, and yet this ability would seem in turn to depend on a recourse to logic. The doctrine of mental logic resolves the riddle: people are able to reason validly because they have a logic in their minds, and the invention of formal logic depends on the 'externalization' of this inner system.

If one accepts the existence of mental logic, then a second riddle arises: How does it get into the mind in the first place? The puzzle here is that children might need to be able to reason validly in order to acquire a logic, but if they can reason validly, they might not need a mental logic. Some writers, inspired by Chomsky's theories, have drawn parallels between the acquisition of logic and the acquisition of language (e.g., Falmagne, 1980). Children may learn logic by encountering valid inferences in verbal guise, and by abstracting from them their underlying logical form in much the same way that grammatical rules are supposed to be acquired. The problem with this conjecture, at least as a complete explanation of the development of mental logic, is that it offers no account of how children recognise valid inferences when they encounter them. It is not as though adults engage in sustained demonstrations of valid deduction or take steps to instruct their offspring in the canons of logic. Consequently, there is a natural temptation to propose that logical competence is inborn (Fodor, 1980), just as the principles of 'universal grammar' are considered to be innate.

So far, this appeal to the powers of evolution has not been followed up by an account of how logic evolved. Indeed, the argument proceeds by default: there is no direct evidence for it, merely the lack of a convincing alternative. Piaget tried to escape the dilemma by arguing that logic is neither innate nor learned by the ordinary principles of reinforcement. He claimed that children 'construct' logic by internalizing their actions and by reflecting on each step in their operational development (see, e.g., Inhelder & Piaget, 1958). Unfortunately, it is unclear whether such a process could work, since it has never been formulated in an explicit algorithm. Nevertheless, the doctrine of mental logic—whether learned, innate, or constructed—remains appealing and has had no competitors. There are, however, three difficulties associated with it.

First, the existence of a mental logic would suggest that human beings are intrinsically rational. Yet experimental results, anecdotal observations, and the well-known 'budgets' of fallacies imply that few people have a secure grasp of the principles of valid inference. Proponents of mental logic explain such mistakes in the following way: they arise, not from faulty inferential principles, but from errors in the application of the rules, from misinterpreting premises, or from making unwarranted assumptions (see, e.g., Cohen, 1981; Henle, 1962; Revlis, 1975; Staudenmayer, 1975). Doubtless, people do misunderstand or forget premises; they do import extraneous or irrelevant considerations into their reasoning; and they do fail to stick to pure logic. But the trouble with this defence of reason is that it is hard to see how, in principle, any empirical findings could shake it. "I have never found errors which could be unambiguously attributed to faulty reasoning," remarks Henle (1978) characteristically. But it is always possible to provide alternative explanations for an error, and it is not usually clear how to decide which one is correct. The defence seems tendentious, as if it had sprung from a prior conviction that conscious thought is invariably rational.

Second, if there are formal rules of inference in the mind, they should apply regardless of the content of problems. However, there is evidence that human reasoners are affected by the content of premises (see, e.g., Wason & Johnson-Laird, 1972). The circumstances and the reasons for such effects remain highly controversial, but they undoubtedly occur and thus present an unsolved problem for the doctrine of mental logic.

Third, logic cannot determine which particular valid conclusions people draw spontaneously. A valid conclusion is one that must be true if the premises are true, and a complete logic sanctions all of the valid conclusions that follow from a set of premises. In fact, though, any set of premises implies an infinite number of different valid conclusions. For example, given the premises:

> If the warning light is on, then the system is defective.
> The warning light is on.

most people draw the valid conclusion:

> The system is defective.

But logic sanctions the following conclusion, too:

> The warning light is on, or if the warning light is on, then the system is defective.

and so on ad infinitum with any number of repetitions of the premises. Similarly, the rule of inference:

$$\frac{p}{\therefore\ p \text{ or } q}$$

sanctions such valid conclusions as:

> The system is defective or the government has abandoned monetarism.

No sane person would draw any of these conclusions, even though they are logically valid. Psychologists have therefore to specify a theory of competence that accounts for the inferences that people *do* make. This theory must embody principles that lie outside logic altogether, because they will determine which of a potentially infinite set of valid deductions the human inferential mechanism actually produces. Proponents of mental logic have had little, if anything, to say about this problem, probably because they have concentrated on experimental procedures in which subjects evaluate given conclusions or choose between a small set of different conclusions.

If there is a logic in the mind, then a major task for psychology is to discover which particular type of logic it is, how it is specified, and how it is acquired. Unfortunately, very little is known about these matters, and there is controversy about all of them. Still, these disagreements do not directly threaten the doctrine of mental logical. Indeed, there hardly appears to be a viable alternative to it, and it has seemed at times to be irrefutable (Cohen, 1981). Why, then, is the doctrine to be abandoned? The answer summarizes the main aims of the present chapter. It establishes three principal points:

1. Logic alone is not sufficient for a theory of competence. There must be extra-logical principles to account for spontaneous deductions.

2. Logic is not necessary for a theory of competence. All major types of deduction can be made without recourse to it or to formal rules of inference (or inferential schemata). This claim extends to types of deduction for which there are presently no formal calculi and to those for which there can be no complete calculi.

3. There is an alternative theory of competence that specifies which inferences people draw. It in turn leads to an alternative theory of performance that specifies the mental processes underlying inference. This theory, unlike those based on mental logic, ranges over all types of deduction. It is more parsimonious, and where the two approaches diverge, it is better supported by the experimental evidence.

In order to establish these three points in a convincing way, it is necessary to consider different sorts of inference. The chapter accordingly deals with all of the major types of inference that logicians and psychologists have traditionally analyzed. There are six main sections: First, it outlines a theory of semantic information, which is used to specify which inferences people draw spontaneously. Second, it considers the ways in which people reason with propositions and the connectives that can join them, and it contrasts the approach of mental logic with an alternative that makes no use of rules of inference. Third, it considers the same contrast for reasoning that depends on quantifiers (such terms as ‘all’, ‘some’, and ‘no’). Fourth, it demonstrates the advantages of abandoning mental logic in elucidating relational inferences. Fifth, it draws the same moral for the ‘common sense’ inferences of daily life. Finally, the chapter draws some brief conclusions in which an important limitation on the present approach—namely, its inability to account for deductions about infinite sets—is spelled out.

Table 1.1
A Truth Table Defining the Truth-Functional Sense of *p* and *q*, where *p* and *q* are Variables Ranging over Propositions

p	*q*	*p* and *q*
True	True	True
True	False	False
False	True	False
False	False	False

SEMANTIC INFORMATION AND INFERENTIAL HEURISTICS

Truth Tables and Truth-functional Reasoning

There are many words in English that can serve the function of interrelating clauses expressing propositions (e.g., 'and', 'or', 'if', 'because', 'before', 'when', and 'until'). A subset of them have meanings that can be treated as mapping the truth values of the clauses they connect onto a truth value for the sentence as a whole. 'And', for example, can be treated as yielding a true sentence if and only if the two clauses it connects both express true propositions. (There are obviously other senses of 'and' that cannot be analyzed in this way, as in "Charles and Diana are a splendid couple".) This way of talking about truth values is not appropriate when one is specifying formal rules of inference such as modus ponens, which should be thought of as purely syntactic formulae that allow one expression to be derived from others. It is appropriate, however, when one is defining the semantics of connectives by stating the conditions in which they are true and those in which they are false. It is crucial in what follows to bear in mind this contrast between the derivation of formulae in a quasi-syntactic way and the definition of their truth conditions.

A familiar device for defining 'truth-functional' connectives is the so-called 'truth table'. Table 1.1 defines the truth-functional sense of 'and'. The table shows that an assertion of the form *p and q* is true if *p* is true and *q* is true, but it is false for any other combination of truth values for *p* and *q*.

A formal logic for truth-functional connectives can be formulated using such rules as modus ponens; it is known as the propositional (or sentential) calculus. This calculus has been assumed by some psychologists to constitute the logic of the mind: "Reasoning is nothing more than the propositional calculus itself" (Inhelder & Piaget, 1958, p. 305). Other psychologists have merely assumed that certain inferences depend on truth-functional connectives and have tried to devise a psychologically realistic set of inferential schemata, following the idea of a 'natural deduction' system in which there are schemata for each connective (see Braine, 1978; Johnson-Laird, 1975; Osherson, 1975; Rips, 1983). No matter how the logic is formalized, a theory of competence still needs to place appropriate constraints on the deductive machinery in order to characterize the class of deductions that people draw spontaneously. Such principles can be developed from the concept of semantic information.

A Measure of Semantic Information

Psychologists are familiar with the statistical concept of information that derives from the work of Shannon and others; it is normally taken to have nothing directly to do with the meaning of messages (Shannon & Weaver, 1949). Nevertheless, a measure of semantic information can be developed from the plausible assumption that the more states of affairs that a proposition rules out, the greater the amount of semantic information it contains (see Bar-Hillel & Carnap, 1952/1964). This measure is particularly suitable for the analysis of propositional reasoning. Given a truth table, a proposition that eliminated half of its contingencies would be more informative than one that eliminated only a quarter of them. It follows that a categorical proposition such as "The warning light is on" is more informative than the inclusive disjunction, "The warning light is on or the system is defective (or both)", since the categorical eliminates half of the contingencies of any truth table into which it enters, whereas the disjunction eliminates only a quarter of the contingencies. Likewise, the conjunction, "The warning light is on and the system is defective," is more informative than a categorical proposition, since the conjunction eliminates three quarters of the truth table.

Most people have an intuitive grasp of the these differences. What may not be obvious at first glance, however, is that if the measure of semantic content is defined as the proportion of contingencies in the truth table that an assertion eliminates, then the measures above are independent of the number of contingencies in the table. A simple categorical premise always eliminates half of the contingencies, a conjunction eliminates three quarters of them, and a disjunction eliminates one quarter of them. Table 1.2 presents a number of such assertions and shows the contingencies they exclude. There is a simple way to compute the semantic information conveyed by any expression in the propositional calculus (see Johnson-Laird, 1983).

Table 1.2
The Relative Informativeness (I) of Different Sorts of Proposition[a]

Contingencies			Propositions and I Values						
a	*b*	*c*	*a* or *b* or *c* (0.125)	*a* or *b* (0.25)	(*a* & *b*) or *c* (0.375)	*a* (0.5)	(*a* or *b*) & *c* (0.625)	*a* & *b* (0.75)	*a* & *b* & *c* (0.875)
T	T	T							
T	T	F					X		X
T	F	T						X	X
T	F	F			X		X	X	X
F	T	T				X		X	X
F	T	F			X	X	X	X	X
F	F	T		X		X	X	X	X
F	F	F	X	X	X	X	X	X	X

[a] X indicates that a premise is inconsistent with the corresponding contingency.

Inferential Heuristics

No valid inference can yield a conclusion with a greater amount of semantic information than the premises on which it is based. Three constraints that characterize the valid inferences that people draw spontaneously can now be stated:

(1) Conclusions should not be based on throwing away semantic information from the premises. Thus, for example, given the premise:

The system is defective.

one should not expect anyone to draw the conclusion:

> The system is defective, or the government has abandoned monetarism.

since this conclusion, though valid, contains less information than the premise.

(2) Conclusions should express the semantic content of premises more parsimoniously; that is, conclusions should contain fewer occurrences of the connectives, relations, quantifiers, predicates, or atomic propositions contained within the premises. Thus, for example, given premises of the form:

If *p* then *q*

p

people do not normally draw the following valid conclusion, although it does maintain the content of the premises:

p, and if not-q then not-*p*, and *p*.

This conclusion is plainly less parsimonious than the premises.

(3) As a corollary of the previous heuristic, categorical premises should not be repeated as constituents of conclusions, since they can be taken for granted. Given such premises as:

John is lazy or he is rich. (*p or q*)
John is not lazy. (*not-p*)

then the conclusion:

John is not lazy and he is rich. (*not-p and q*)

is parsimonious and maintains the content of the premises. However, reasoners generally draw the simple conclusion:

John is rich. (*q*)

since they apparently find it unnecessary to repeat the categorical premise, not-*p* (see Johnson-Laird & Tridgell, 1972). Hence, this third principle should be taken to apply to the formulation of the conclusion rather than to its derivation. Likewise, given the relational premises:

Ann is taller than Bette.
Bette is taller than Carol.

the conclusion that subjects tend to draw (Johnson-Laird & Bara, 1983) is:

Ann is taller than Carol.

rather than the repetitious conclusion:

Ann is taller than Bette, who is taller than Carol.

Once a theory of competence has been developed, there are two ways in which to go about specifying a theory of performance. First, like Chomsky (1965), one can simply assume that the principles of competence are built directly into the mind. Thus, a knowledge of the heuristics outlined above might be part of the inferential system and act to filter out any deductions that fail to meet their constraints. Second, one can develop an independent theory of performance from which the principles of competence are emergent properties. That is, the performance algorithm abides by the competence principles even though it does not directly incorporate them. In what follows, I will show—beginning with propositional reasoning—that there is a plausible theory of performance of this second kind, which also illustrates how valid deductions can be made without recourse to formal rules of inference.

PROPOSITIONAL REASONING

A Simple Algorithm

There is a simple algorithm for propositional reasoning that does not rely on formal rules of inference but rather on the truth conditions of connectives (see Johnson-Laird, 1983). This knowledge is required in any case in order to understand or verify assertions containing the connectives. It is instructive to consider how the algorithm works before taking up the question of the extent to which it is independent of logic. Its first step, given such premises such as:

p and not-*q*, or *r*

q

is to determine which premise (if any) conveys most semantic information. Here, the second premise, *q*, conveys more information than the first. The algorithm then checks whether the more informative premise occurs elsewhere as a constituent of another premise. Since, in fact, the second premise occurs as a constituent of the first premise, the value 'true' can be substituted for its occurrence there:

p and not-true, or *r*

The truth conditions of 'not' in the propositional calculus are such that if a proposition is not true, then it is false; and if it is not false, then it is true. This semantics justifies the following substitution:

p and false, or *r*

The truth conditions of 'and' are such that a conjunction is false whenever one of its conjuncts is false. Hence, the conjunctive constituent of the premise can be simplified to false, with the result that the premise as a whole becomes:

false or *r*

The meaning of 'or' ensures that if a disjunction is true and one of its constituents is false, then the other constituent must be true. The application of this semantics to our example yields the conclusion, *r*.

This semantic procedure automatically ensures that no information is lost (the first heuristic in the competence theory) and that any forthcoming conclusion is more parsimonious than the premises on which it is based (the second heuristic). Since the algorithm operates on the premise into which the truth value is substituted, it does not repeat the categorical premise on which the inference is based (the third heuristic).

The general algorithm can be made completely explicit. To check its consistency, I implemented it in a computer program written in the list-processing language, POP-10. The program requires four steps:

(1) Find the maximally informative premise (of those that have not yet been tried as the basis for an inference) according to the measure of semantic content described above. Ordinary reasoners are unlikely to make anything other than an intuitive assessment of informativeness. If all the premises have been tried with no clear result, then no conclusion is drawn. If there is no single premise that is maximally informative, then a premise is chosen at random from the set of those that are maximally informative.

(2) If there is another premise that contains the one selected in the first step, then substitute in it the value 'true' for the one selected. If the first premise is negative and its unnegated proposition is a constituent of the second, then substitute the value 'false' for that constituent. If no substitution is possible, return to step 1.

(3) Use the semantics of the connective governing the substituted truth value to simplify the premise compositionally. If the result is a proposition that contains a truth value and a connective, then continue to carry out this step until the process can go no further.

(4) If the final result is a proposition that does not contain a truth value, then this proposition is the conclusion to be drawn. If the final result is the truth value 'true', then the premises are consistent but there is no conclusion of interest to be drawn. If the final result is the truth value 'false', then the premises are inconsistent.

A psychologically plausible algorithm should refrain from making trivial, though valid, deductions that are never drawn by human reasoners. This algorithm does indeed refrain from drawing trivial conclusions. For example, given premises of the form:

p
p or *q*

it substitutes a truth value for *p* in the second premise:

true or *q*

The semantics of 'or' in its inclusive sense then leads to the following simplification: true. This end-product merely establishes that the premises are consistent with each other, and therefore no conclusion is drawn. The same result occurs with premises of the form:

p
q

since the procedure is unable to make any substitution.

An algorithm for drawing conclusions spontaneously is obviously distinct from one for evaluating given conclusions. However, there is a simple way of extending the algorithm to deal with the evaluation of conclusions. It relies on the fact that an inconsistent set of assertions simplify to the truth value 'false'. If a putative conclusion has to be evaluated with respect to some premises, all that is necessary is to add its negation to the premises and then to determine what follows in the usual way. For example, suppose that the deduction:

not-*q*
p or *q*
∴ *p*

has to be evaluated. The negation of the conclusion is added to the premises:

not-*q*
p or q
not-*p*

The procedure substitutes 'false' for *q* in the second premise and simplifies it to *p*. This is a constituent of the negated conclusion, *not-p*, and the procedure substitutes the value 'true' for it:

not-true

which simplifies to false. This result shows that the negation of the conclusion is inconsistent with the premises. That is, the conclusion follows validly from the premises.

Not all propositional inferences derive from treating one premise as a constituent of another. The valid deduction,

p and *q*
not-*p* or *r*
not-*q* or *s*
∴ *r* and *s*

contains no premise that is a constituent of another. There is a very simple strategy at work here: Break down the maximally informative premise into its two constituents (*p*, *q*), use each of them as separate categorical premises in the procedure to yield separate conclusions (*r*, *s*), and join these conclusions by whatever connective was in the original premise (*r* and *s*). This method can be used recursively in order to break down a complex proposition into constituents that in turn need to be broken down, and so on. It is important, however, that the connectives are symmetrical. Since 'if *p* then *q*' is not symmetrical (i.e., it is not equivalent to 'if *q* then *p*'), conditionals must be translated into a symmetrical, truth-functional form: *not-p or q*, which is equivalent to *q or not-p*.

Truth Conditions Versus Rules of Inference

The algorithm for propositional reasoning relies on the truth conditions of connectives rather than on formal rules of inference. What is the difference, if any, between these two approaches? The algorithm needs access, in effect, to any row of the truth tables that define the meanings of the connectives. For example, it requires a representation of conjunction that is equivalent in force, though not necessarily in form, to the truth table in Table 1.1.

A system based on formal rules of inference (e.g., Braine, 1978; Johnson-Laird, 1975; Osherson, 1975; Rips, 1983) has no access to truth conditions but relies instead on rules of inference or inferential schemata such as

$$\frac{\begin{array}{l} p \\ q \end{array}}{\therefore\ p \text{ and } q} \qquad \frac{p \text{ and } q}{\therefore\ p} \qquad \frac{\text{not-}p}{\therefore\ \text{not } (p \text{ and } q)}$$

These rules can be used to derive a conclusion from premises without any knowledge of the truth conditions of the connective. They are part of the formal or syntactic formulation of a logical calculus, but truth tables and statements of truth conditions are part of a quite distinct enterprise—the formulation of a 'model-theoretic' semantics for the calculus. Validity is in fact a semantic notion, whereas derivability from formal rules is a syntactic notion. An important part of meta-logic is, indeed, to establish that the formal logic is complete (i.e., any inference that is valid according to the semantics is derivable within the formal syntactic system). A major logical discovery of the twentieth century is that certain calculi are incomplete, in that there is no way of framing formal rules that capture all and only the set of valid inferences (see, e.g., Boolos & Jeffrey, 1980).

An adherent of mental logic is likely to note that the rows of a truth table can be translated into formal rules of inference. For example, the first schema just shown corresponds to the first row of Table 1.1. Nevertheless, it does not follow that the two approaches are identical. This fact is readily grasped by logicians, who are familiar with the contrast between a formal calculus and a semantic model for it; however, 'mental logicians' often have difficulty understanding the contrast. The crux of the matter is that although a statement of truth conditions may be mapped unequivocally onto rules of inference, the converse does not follow. Once this point is grasped, the distinction between the two approaches becomes obvious.

Any formal calculus is open to more than one semantic interpretation. The propositional calculus, for example, has a different interpretation in which the connectives are given an 'intuitionistic' interpretation. Roughly speaking, instead of truth one talks of provability in a constructive way, and instead of falsity one talks of absurdity (see Kneale & Kneale, 1962). Likewise, to consider a more accessible case, if the variables *p*, *q*, and so on are taken to range over sets rather than propositions, then *p* can be taken to mean that the set *p* is not empty, and the connectives can be redefined. Thus '*p* and *q*' means that the intersection of the sets *p* and *q* is not empty; '*p* or *q*' means that the union of the sets *p* and *q* is not empty; and '$p \rightarrow q$', the formula for material implication, means that the intersection of *p* and the complement of *q* is empty. In other words, all *p* are *q*. The formal rule of inference, modus ponens, which together with a substitution rule and appropriate axioms, suffices for deriving all valid theorems in the calculus:

$$
\begin{array}{l} p \\ p \rightarrow q \\ \therefore q \end{array}
$$

means that given that *p* is not empty, and that all *p* are *q*, it follows that *q* is not empty.

The moral is clear: the meaning of a connective is not defined merely by specifying formal rules of inference for it. Admittedly, proponents of mental logic have usually stipulated that their systems are supposed to model reasoning with propositions, but any such stipulation merely smuggles some semantics in by the back door. My point is that semantics should be allowed in by the front door, because then formal rules can be thrown out of the house completely.

How can one decide which approach children adopt? Braine and Rumain (1981) argue that children acquire rules of inference for 'or' before they acquire the truth conditions of the connective. They base this claim on the fact that children are able to make inferences before they are able to evaluate the truth or falsity of disjunctive assertions. Although this finding is of considerable intrinsic interest, it fails to decide the issue. One must not beg the question either by assuming that inferences can be made only by relying on *rules* of inference (as opposed to a knowledge of truth conditions), or by assuming that failure in a verification task shows that the truth conditions are not known to the child.

It is difficult to establish that formal rules of inference are acquired prior to truth conditions, because it would be necessary to show that children make such inferences as:

John is lazy or John is rich.
John is not lazy.
Therefore, John is rich.

purely by virtue of their logical form:

$$
\begin{array}{l} p \text{ or } q \\ \text{not-}p \\ \hline \therefore q \end{array}
$$

and without knowing the truth conditions of the connective. Braine and Rumain's experiment does not, of course, demonstrate this point. In this regard, it is worth remarking that tests of comprehension often reflect a poorer grasp of meaning than does spontaneous speech (Braine & Rumain, forthcoming), and even four-year-olds understand that the command, "Do A or do B," is satisfied by carrying out one of the tasks (Johansson & Sjolin, 1975). Clearly, children may master some aspects of truth conditions long before they are able to make inferences.

A disinterested reader might suppose that I am making a fuss about a very minor distinction—the difference between formal rules and semantic interpretations—but the divergence between the two approaches increases as the chapter proceeds. Even within the domain of sentential connectives, the semantic approach has several advantages. It solves at a stroke the problems of which particular logic is in the mind, how it is mentally represented, and how children acquire it. These problems simply fail to arise, because there is no logic in the mind. Of course, it is necessary to explain how the truth conditions of connectives are acquired, but this task would still be necessary even if there were mental rules of inference, because children have to learn these truth conditions in order to determine the truth or falsity of assertions and to use the connectives appropriately.

A single, uniform semantics can be offered for 'and' (Gazdar, 1980) which embraces both its truth-functional use in connecting sentences and its other uses in connecting other constituents. This semantics suffices for the algorithm for propositional reasoning, whereas special and additional rules of inference are required to handle all of its uses within a formal calculus. Moreover, there are some sentential connectives, such as 'because' and 'until', which are clearly not truth-functional in their meanings, and for which there are no existing formal calculi. Perhaps these facts make it easier to grasp the point that children may initially acquire a knowledge of the truth conditions for these connectives before they acquire (if they do at all) the as yet unknown formal rules of inference for them.

Theories of mental logic and the propositional algorithm have a limited explanatory power. They are only as real as the phenomenon of truth-functional reasoning, and, as has been known for some time, people do not ordinarily think in this way. They are generally more interested in interrelating propositions within a model of causal or intentional relations. Wason and Johnson-Laird (1972, Chap. 7) show that when causal considerations conflict, as they often do, with those of truth-functional logic, subjects follow causality. This problem will be resolved later in the chapter by an account of a general semantic procedure that is applicable both to causal and propositional reasoning.

QUANTIFICATIONAL REASONING

Syllogisms

The validity of many deductions depends, not just on sentential connectives, but also on the internal structure of premises and on the occurrence within them of quantifiers (e.g., 'all', 'any', 'most', 'many', 'some', 'several', 'few', and 'none'). In this section I consider how people make these inferences, establish that the two approaches—the formal and the semantic—diverge from each other, and present some experimental evidence that supports the semantic approach.

Aristotle formulated a logic for a subset of quantified inferences that he called 'syllogisms', and they have been the focus of most psychological studies of reasoning with quantifiers. A syllogism consists of two premises and a conclusion. These assertions can occur in one of four 'moods':

All *X* are *Y*.
Some *X* are *Y*.
No *X* are *Y*.
Some *X* are not *Y*.

The arrangement of the terms in the premises can also occur in one of four 'figures':

A–B	*B–A*	*A–B*	*B–A*
B–C	*C–B*	*C–B*	*B–C*

Granted that there are four moods for each premise and four figures, there are 64 possible logical forms for the premises of a syllogism.

Although psychologists have studied syllogistic inference since the turn of the century (Störring, 1908), they have concentrated on explaining errors in evaluating one or more given conclusions (e.g., Chapman & Chapman, 1959; Wilkins, 1928; Woodworth & Sells, 1935) and have assumed that logic—and, strangely, the logic of the medieval Schoolman—characterizes human competence. It was not until recently that experiments were carried out in which subjects were asked to state in their own words what conclusion, if any, followed from syllogistic premises (Johnson-Laird, 1975; Johnson-Laird & Bara, 1984; Johnson-Laird & Steedman, 1978). A striking phenomenon emerged: some syllogisms almost always elicit a correct response, whereas others hardly ever do so. Here is an example of a pair of premises that almost always yields a correct response:

Some of the scientists are parents.	(Some of the *A* are *B*)
All the parents are drivers.	(All of the *B* are *C*)

Nearly everyone (90% of subjects) draws the valid conclusion:

Some of the scientists are drivers. (Some of the *A* are *C*)

and a few subjects (5%) draw the converse and equally valid conclusion:

Some of the drivers are scientists. (Some of the *C* are *A*)

The bias in the form of the response is an example of a general effect of figure. Given premises in the figure:

$$A\text{–}B$$
$$B\text{–}C$$

the vast majority of conclusions that are drawn take the form:

$$A\text{–}C$$

whereas given premises in the figure:

$$B\text{–}A$$
$$C\text{–}B$$

the vast majority of conclusions take the form:

$$C\text{–}A$$

The figural effect, which my colleagues and I have observed in every subject whom we have tested, was not previously noticed because experimenters relied on scholastic logic (which recognizes only conclusions of the form *C–A*) and on procedures requiring the evaluation of one or more given conclusions.

Here is an example of a pair of premises to which few subjects make the correct response:

All of the beekeepers are artists.
None of the chemists are beekeepers.

The responses of the subjects in a typical study (Experiment 2 of Johnson-Laird & Steedman, 1978) were as follows:

None of the chemists are artists.	(60% of subjects)
None of the artists are chemists.	(10% of subjects)
No valid conclusion	(20% of subjects)
Some of the chemists are not artists.	(10% of subjects)
Some of the artists are not chemists.	(0% of subjects)

The last of these responses, which was made by none of the subjects, is in fact the only valid conclusion. Clearly, a theory of deductive performance should account for the extreme and systematic range of difficulty of syllogisms.

Theories of the Syllogism

Theories of performance with syllogisms have only recently begun to be proposed. They have generally been based on well-known logical techniques, and they have been intended to account only for the evaluation of given conclusions. The most familiar technique for syllogistic inference is the method of Euler circles, which is often confused with the rather different method of Venn diagrams. Euler circles rely on diagrams in the Euclidean plane in which there is a different circle standing for each set referred to in the premises. A premise of the form, "All *A* are *B*," calls for two separate diagrams. In one, the circle standing for *A* lies entirely within the circle standing for *B* to represent the possibility that set *A* is wholly included within set *B*; in the other, the two circles lie on top of one another to represent the possibility that the two sets are co-extensive. Since 'some' is construed by logicians to mean 'at least some' and is accordingly consistent with 'all', a premise of the form, "Some *A* are *B*," needs four different diagrams: *A* overlapping *B*, *A* included in *B*, *B* included in *A*, and *A* co-extensive with *B*.

The Eulerian method depends on drawing the appropriate diagrams for each premise and then combining them. In order to guarantee that a conclusion is valid, it is necessary to check that it holds for all possible combinations of the diagrams for the two premises. This is a complex operation, because there is no simple algorithm for ensuring that all the combinations have been considered, and the total number of them is generally greater than the mere product of the numbers of separate diagrams for the two premises. For example, the reader may care to try to construct the set of combinations for the premise:

Some *A* are *B*.

which calls for four diagrams, and the premise:

All *B* are *C*.

which calls for two diagrams. In informal tests, I have not found anyone who has succeeded in constructing all of the logically distinct combinations (see below).

Erickson (1974) has proposed a theory of syllogistic inference based on the assumption that people form mental representations of the premises that are isomorphic to Euler circles. In order to deal with the embarrassing number of combinations, he assumed that subjects often fail to consider the full set of different ways in which an individual premise can be represented, and (in one version of his theory) that they construct only one of the many possible combinations of representations. Guyote and Sternberg (1981) devised a similar theory, based on strings of symbols corresponding to Euler circles, in which they limited the number of combinations that subjects consider to a maximum of four. Both theories accordingly view human beings as intrinsically illogical with respect to many syllogisms—including, of course, the easy one based on the two premises above. Both theories also rely on a fundamentally irrational mechanism, the production of conclusions that match the 'atmosphere' of the premises, in order to deliver valid conclusions for certain syllogisms. Hence, although subjects may reach the right conclusion, these theories imply that they hardly ever do so for the right reasons.

The major weakness of any theory based on Euler circles is that it is bound to make the wrong predictions about the relative difficulty of drawing the correct conclusion from different types of syllogistic premises. On the one hand, the easy problem that nearly everyone gets right, based on premises of the form:

Some of the *A* are *B*.
All the *B* are *C*.

requires 16 different Euler diagrams to be constructed. On the other hand, the difficult problem that hardly anyone gets right:

All the *B* are *A*.
None of the *C* are *B*.

requires only six different diagrams. If, following Erickson, we assume that premises of the form, "All *X* are *Y*," are represented by only one diagram (in which *X* is wholly included within *Y*), and that premises of the form, "Some *X* are *Y*," are represented by only two diagrams (one in which *X* and *Y* overlap, and the other in which *Y* is included in *X*), the position is hardly any better. The easy problem requires six different diagrams and the hard problem requires five. Evidently, the number of diagrams to be constructed bears no relation to the difficulty of the problems.

Euler diagrams have a further explanatory inadequacy: they cannot be used to represent inferences that depend on sentences containing more than one quantifier, such as:

Not all the critics liked all the pictures.
Therefore, some critic did not like some picture.

Thus the case against theories based on Euler circles seems to be overwhelming.

Proponents of mental logic will rightly reject any theory of syllogistic reasoning that is unable to account for the potential rationality of human beings. They have two options: They can either adopt a more tractable logical tool for syllogisms, or they can assume that mental logic consists of the standard (first order) quantificational calculus.

Newell (1981) chose the first option and put forward a psychological theory of syllogisms based on a symbolic equivalent of a superior topological technique—the method of Venn diagrams. Newell's theory, however, is more an account of competence in evaluating conclusions and an illustration of how such a theory can be expressed within his framework for problem-solving (Newell & Simon, 1972) than it is a full-fledged theory of performance. Thus, the theory makes no specific predictions about errors. Moreover, there is an alternative (and simpler) theory on the same general lines which depends on the close relation between Venn diagrams and truth tables (see the alternative interpretation of the propositional calculus, which I described earlier). For example, the premises:

Some *A* are *B*.
All *B* are *C*.

yield the following evaluations in the table of contingencies based on *A*, *B*, and *C*.

	A	*B*	*C*	
(first premise establishes	+	+	+	
one or other)	+	+	−	(eliminated by second premise)
	+	−	+	
	+	−	−	
	−	+	+	
	−	+	−	(eliminated by second premise)
	−	−	+	
	−	−	−	

The first premise establishes that the intersection of *A* and *B* is not empty, and the second premise establishes that the intersection of *B* and the complement of *C* is empty. Since the first contingency in the table is thereby definitely established, it is clear that "Some *A* are C." There are 16 different combinations of the Euler diagrams representing the premises, since they correspond to the possible ways of combining those four contingencies that involve the members of at least one of the three sets, and that may or may not be empty because they are neither established nor eliminated by the premises (rows 3, 4, 5, and 7).

The second option of building the predicate calculus into the mind has been implicitly adopted by linguists such as Chomsky (1977) for some time. They assume that assertions have a logical form that calls for the quantifiers and variables posited by the predicate calculus. The major difficulty with this assumption is the psychological implausibility of the rules of inference called for by the predicate calculus. There are, of course, different ways of formalizing the calculus, but they all rely on rules of inference that are not intuitively obvious.

The function of the rules is to get rid of quantifiers and then to reason propositionally, since the propositional connectives are part of the predicate calculus. The universal quantifier, 'for any *X*', is dropped by the rule of 'universal instantiation', which allows the quantifier to be replaced by any constant denoting an individual. This rule is readily grasped, since it merely formalizes the notion that if some predicate applies to everything, then it applies to, say, Fred. The rule of 'existential instantiation' for dropping the existential quantifier, 'there is at least some *x*', is not so obvious. It allows an existential quantifier to be dropped in favour of any constant denoting an arbitrary individual, provided that this individual has not been referred to in the argument. In other words, if a predicate applies to someone, then it is true of some particular individual, and we can assume that this individual is, say, Tom, provided that he has not been referred to anywhere else in the premises.

The notion of an arbitrary constant can cause trouble even to students of logic, and no psychologist is likely to assume that it, or the technique of dropping quantifiers, plays any part in ordinary reasoning. Unfortunately, the only way to avoid the rule of existential instantiation is to opt for a system based on a single rule of inference, the so-called 'resolution' rule, but this rule requires a very unnatural translation of assertions into a uniform disjunctive format in which existential quantifiers are represented by a special functional notation.

Although a mental logic based directly on the predicate calculus has not so far been explicitly advocated by any psychologist, Braine and Rumain (forthcoming) have constructed an ingenious set of inferential schemata that, in essence, build quantifiers into the required propositional rules. This theory, however, is primarily an account of rational competence; it makes few, if any, systematic predictions about errors in performance. Also, it cannot as yet account for the difference between the easy and the difficult syllogistic problems.

In summary, existing theories of reasoning with quantifiers divide into two main sorts. On the one hand, there are theories of performance which are based on logical techniques for the syllogism. These predict some of the errors that occur in performance but regard human beings as essentially irrational (Erickson, 1974; Guyote & Sternberg, 1981). On the other hand, there are theories of rational competence which are based either on techniques for the syllogism or the predicate calculus. These are often forced to assume psychologically implausible procedures and do not account for errors in performance (Braine & Rumain, forthcoming; Newell, 1981). All the theories, however, have one striking feature in common. There are simple inferences that they cannot, in principle, accommodate. For example, given the premises:

> More than half the teachers are men.
> More than half the teachers sing in the choir

even children can draw the valid conclusion:

> There is a man who sings in the choir.

Yet this deduction cannot be expressed in the first-order predicate calculus, because there is no way to capture the logic of the quantifier, 'more than half the *x*', in terms of quantification over individuals.

What is required is quantification over sets—that is, a higher order quantificational calculus (see Barwise & Cooper, 1981). Unfortunately there is a crucial problem with the higher order calculus: it is incomplete in that there is no way to specify rules of inference for it that will capture the complete set of valid deductions. Doubtless, a subset of the calculus can be formalized so as to allow the simple deduction above to be derivable from rules of inference. The fact that this problem arises with such a trivial deduction, however, should surely give pause to any advocate of mental logic. One way round it, together with a solution to marrying rational competence with errors in performance, is presented in the next section.

Reasoning as a Semantic Procedure

There is a general principle that governs all valid deductions: An inference is valid if and only if there is no way of interpreting the premises in which the conclusion is not true. This principle characterizes the semantics of validity, and all systems of logic are designed to capture it within their formal rules of inference. But not all systems, as we have just seen, can succeed completely in this task. In proposing an algorithm for propositional reasoning, I advocated a technique based on the semantics of connectives rather than on rules of inference for them, and elsewhere I have sketched a theory of syllogistic inference based on the semantics of a syllogism's premises (Johnson-Laird, 1980). I now intend to generalize the idea and to propose a theory of competence in which all deductions are made on the basis of the semantic principle of validity. What this assumption means in practice is that any deduction can be made using the following general procedure:

1. Construct a mental representation based on the meaning of the premises—that is, a model of the state of affairs that they describe.
2. Formulate, if possible, an informative conclusion that is true in all models of the premises that have so far been constructed. If none, then there is no relevant conclusion.

3. Try to construct an alternative model of the premises that renders the conclusion false. If there is such a model, abandon the conclusion and return to step 2. If there is no such model, then the conclusion is valid.

Where a conclusion has to be evaluated rather than drawn spontaneously, all that is required is a simplified version of step 3: If an alternative model can be constructed that renders the given conclusion false, then it is invalid; otherwise, it is valid.

The concept of a mental model is a subtle one that is of relevance to comprehension in general (see Johnson-Laird, 1983). Here I shall illustrate it only with respect to inferences with quantifiers. The algorithm, which I will describe informally, has in fact been implemented in the programming language LISP-80 (a dialect of LISP).

The way in which an individual can represent the state of affairs described by the premise:

Some authors are book-keepers.

is by imagining an arbitrary number of authors and then mentally tagging them in some way to indicate that they are book-keepers. Such a model may take the form of a vivid image or, alternatively, it may be outside conscious access. Regardless of its phenomenal content, however, it has a structure that can be mapped one-to-one onto an actual state of affairs in which, indeed, some authors are book-keepers:

author	=	book-keeper
author	=	book-keeper
author	=	book-keeper
(author)		(book-keeper)

This model represents five individuals: three authors who are book-keepers, a possible author (as indicated by the parentheses) who is not a book-keeper, and a possible book-keeper who is not an author. Since the model is no more than a representative sample from the set of possible models of the premises, the system that constructs and interprets it must in this instance appreciate that the numbers are arbitrary, that is, the procedures for constructing the model can recursively revise the numbers of entities that it contains.

The information conveyed by a second premise:

All the book-keepers are cardplayers.

can be added to the model of the first premise. It is merely necessary to locate each individual who is a book-keeper and to add a further tag indicating that the same person is also a cardplayer:

author = book-keeper = cardplayer
author = book-keeper = cardplayer
author = book-keeper = cardplayer
(author) (book-keeper = cardplayer)
(cardplayer)

The final parenthesized token represents the possibility that there may be cardplayers who are not book-keepers. At this point, step 1 in the deduction procedure has been completed: a model of the state of affairs described in the premises has been constructed. The second step calls for the formulation of an informative conclusion. The inferential heuristics described earlier in the chapter require that if the premises relate A to B, and B to C, then an informative conclusion should relate A to C. The maximally informative assertion about this relation is:

Some authors are cardplayers.

or its converse, Finally, step 3 requires us to search for a model of the premises that falsifies this conclusion. There is no need to make pointless manipulations of the number of individuals in the model, since validity in a syllogism does not depend on particular numbers. Since any mental model contains only a finite number of individuals, there will always be only a finite number of ways of re-arranging the elements in the model in ways consistent with the premises. In the present case, there is no falsifying model, since there is no way of destroying the links between the end terms that does not also violate the truth conditions of the premises. Thus the conclusion is valid.

In the case of premises of the form:

All A are B.
All C are B.

the initial model may consist of:

$$
\begin{array}{c}
a = b = c \\
a = b = c \\
(b) \\
(b)
\end{array}
$$

which yields the informative conclusion: "All A are C," or its converse. A search for a model of the premises that falsifies this conclusion will, if properly conducted, yield the model:

$$
\begin{array}{lll}
a = & b & \\
a = & b & = c \\
& b & = c \\
& (b) &
\end{array}
$$

On returning to the second step, it is possible to formulate a conclusion that is consistent with both models: "Some *A* are *C*," or its converse. A search for a falsifying model of this conclusion should yield:

$$
\begin{array}{l}
a = b \\
a = b \\
\quad\;\; b = c \\
\quad\;\; b = c
\end{array}
$$

Step 2 now fails to yield any conclusion interrelating *A* and *C* which holds over all three models, because in the first model *A* and *C* are co-extensive, whereas in the third model they are wholly disjoint. There is therefore no informative conclusion to be drawn from these premises.

The algorithm readily generalizes beyond syllogisms to deductions that depend on multiple quantification or non-standard quantifiers. Hence, the premise: "More than half the teachers are men," yields a model of the form:

teacher = man
teacher = man
teacher = man
teacher (man)

and there is no way in which to incorporate the premise, "More than half the teachers sing in the choir," that does not identify at least one teacher as both a man and a singer in the choir.

It should be clear that the use of the general semantic procedure as a method of inference is very different from the use of a mental logic. The semantic procedure contains no formal rules of inference; it relies instead on the ability to construct models of premises, to formulate conclusions that are true of them, and to search for models that falsify those conclusions. The ability to construct models and to describe them, however, is presumably what underlies the production and comprehension of discourse. The only addition called for by deduction is a knowledge of the semantic principle of validity and the ability to put it into practice in the search for counter examples. Hence, the theory of reasoning without logic is certainly more parsimonious than the theory of mental logic, because it does not require any rules of inference. Is it, however, the correct theory of human inferential performance?

Evidence in Favour of the Semantic Procedure

It is difficult to choose between the formal and the semantic approaches to reasoning on the basis of empirical observations of propositional reasoning. The results from experiments with syllogisms are more clear-cut, and they plainly support the semantic theory. There are three crucial observations:

(1) The errors that occur in syllogistic reasoning are proportional to the number of models that have to be constructed in order to make the correct response (Johnson-Laird, 1982). This result is to be expected on the reasonable assumption that the greater the number of models to be constructed, the greater the load on working memory and the more likely that a model will be overlooked. The difference between the easy and the difficult syllogistic problems presented earlier can indeed be explained in this way. The easy problem:

Some of the *A* are *C*.
All of the *B* are *C*.

has only a single model of the form:

$$\begin{array}{ccccc} a & = & b & = & c \\ a & = & b & = & c \\ (a) & & (b) & & c \\ & & & & (c) \end{array}$$

which yields the conclusions:

Some of the *A* are *C*.

or its equally valid converse. The difficult problem:

All of the *B* are *A*.
None of the *C* are *B*.

yields three models:

$$\begin{array}{cccc} & (1) & & \\ c & & & \\ c & & & \\ \hline & b & = & a \\ & b & = & a \\ & & & (a) \end{array} \qquad \begin{array}{cccc} & (2) & & \\ c & & & \\ c & = & & a \\ \hline & b & = & a \\ & b & = & a \\ & & & (a) \end{array} \qquad \begin{array}{cccc} & (3) & & \\ c & = & & a \\ c & = & & a \\ \hline & b & = & a \\ & b & = & a \\ & & & (a) \end{array}$$

where the horizontal barriers are a notational convention for representing the premise that none of the *C* are *B*.

(2) The erroneous conclusions that occur fit the assumption that subjects overlook the possibility of certain models. Thus, in the previous example, subjects who construct only the first model will respond:

No *C* are *A*. (60% of responses)

Subjects who succeed in falsifying this conclusion by constructing the second model will respond:

Some *C* are not *A*. (10% of responses)

And subjects who succeed in falsifying this conclusion by constructing the third model are likely to respond:

No valid conclusion. (20% of responses)

Only if subjects succeed in constructing all three models and in evaluating them in the opposite direction to the figural bias will they appreciate that the conclusion:

Some of the *A* are not *C*. (0% of responses)

holds over all the models of the premises. The predictions are stated here together with the percentages of spontaneous conclusions cited earlier (from Johnson-Laird & Steedman, 1978). These data are wholly typical in that the theory predicts the vast majority of responses that are made, and there are no responses made in significant numbers that are not predicted by the theory.

(3) The main effect of the figure of the premises is to create a bias towards certain conclusions, which is contrary to Revlis's (1975) hypothesis that subjects invariably make illicit conversions of the premises. The bias can be explained in terms of the operations required to construct a model of the two premises. It is necessary to form a model of one premise and then to incorporate within it the information from the second premise. The hinge on which the process depends is, of course, the term that occurs in both premises—the so-called middle term. William James (1890) pointed out that it was easy to integrate two relational assertions of the form *aRb* and *bRc* because the two middle terms occurred continguously. Hunter (1957) expands on this notion by introducing two mental operations that would be required to bring the middle terms into contiguity with premises in other figures. This idea can be extended to the integration of mental models. With premises in the figure, *A–B*, *B–C*, the process of integration can occur immediately. Working memory evidently operates on the principle that the first information into memory is the first information out of it (see Broadbent, 1958. p. 236). Hence, subjects will in this case be biased towards conclusions of the form *A–C*. With premises of the form *B–A*, *C–B*, an immediate integration is impossible, but if the initial model is based on the second premise, *C–B*, the information from the first premise, *B–A*, can then be integrated. The 'first in, first out' principle dictates that subjects will now be biased towards conclusions of the form *C–A*. With premises of the form *A–B*, *C–B*, the initial model can be based on either premise, but it is necessary to carry out a major operation—switching round the

interpretation of the other premise in order to bring the middle term into contiguity with its representation in the model. With premises in the figure *B–A*, *B–C*, the initial model cannot be fruitfully based on either premise. It is first necessary to switch round the interpretation of a premise and then to recall the other premise. Hence, the complexity of the mental operations required to form an integrated model increases over the four figures, and this increase is mirrored both in the latencies to one-model problems (for which there are sufficient correct responses to assess the reliability of the trend) and in the decline in correct valid conclusions to all the premises permitting them (see Johnson-Laird & Bara, 1984).

The semantic theory does not rule out the possibility that subjects may misinterpret or illicitly convert premises, forget them, or bring to mind irrelevant considerations. Nevertheless, the major causes of error in syllogistic reasoning appear to be, first, the need to construct alternative models of the premises, and, second, the effects of figure. The theory therefore appears to be superior to any current explanation based on the doctrine of mental logic.

RELATIONAL INFERENCES

Many deductions in daily life depend on simple relations. The following deduction, for example, depends on grasping a variety of temporal and geographical relations:

> John will stand in the local elections in Camden.
> Camden is a borough of London.
> London has its annual borough elections on Tuesday.
> Therefore, John stands in the elections on Tuesday.

A proponent of mental logic would argue that such deductions are drawn on the basis of formal rules of inference. Such rules, however, have yet to be formalized within any existing logic. Thus, for instance, although there are so-called 'tense logics', they are relatively remote from the logical properties of English tenses and modal auxiliaries. Nonetheless, it is clear how, in principle, a theory based on mental logic would account for the ability to make relational inferences. It would do so by analogy with the explanations of performance in three-term series problems, which are the type of relational inference that have received the most attention in the psychological literature.

Here is a typical three-term series problem:

> Anne is taller than Bertha.
> Bertha is taller than Charles.
> Therefore, Anne is taller than Charles.

The main puzzle that psychologists have sought to resolve is the nature of the mental representation of the premises and the mental processes by which the conclusion is derived. There has been considerable controversy over whether those representations and processes are primarily verbal or visual (see, e.g., Clark, 1969; Huttenlocher, 1968). Many experimental results suggest that different subjects may employ different strategies and that they can be induced to change strategies (see, e.g., Egan & Grimes-Farrow, 1982; Mayer, 1979; Ormrod, 1979; Sternberg & Weil, 1980). A crucial aspect of such inferences, regardless of the nature of their mental representation, is how reasoners grasp their logical validity. Advocates of mental logic are forced to argue either that there is a general schema of trasitivity:

For any x, y, and z, if xRy and yRz, then xRz.

to which particular relations such as 'taller than' are linked (Johnson-Laird, 1975), or else that specific schemata or 'meaning postulates' are acquired for each transitive relation (Kintsch, 1974):

> For any x, y, and z, if x is taller than y, and y is taller than z, then x is taller than z.

The semantic approach suggests a different way in which such deductions are made. Reasoners build a model of the state of affairs described in the premises, generate an informative conclusion on the basis of that model, and then search for an alternative model of the premises in which the conclusion is false. The ability to construct models plainly depends on a grasp of the truth conditions of the premises—that is, a knowledge of the states of affairs in which the premises are true in principle. This knowledge, in turn, depends on grasping the contribution to these truth conditions of the meanings of relational expressions such as 'taller than'. Earlier in the chapter, a distinction was drawn between the truth conditions of propositional connectives and the rules of inference governing them. The same contrast can be drawn between the meanings of relational expressions and the schemata characterizing their logical properties. Since such relational expressions as 'taller than', 'greater than', 'kinder than', and their cognates are all transitive, asymmetric, and irreflexive, it follows that the differences in meaning between them cannot be distinguished merely by specifying their logical properties. Hence, a proper grasp of their meaning must depend on a knowledge of their truth conditions.

Although there is no need for inferential schemata once the truth conditions of an expression have been acquired, it might be argued that such schemata are useful and play a role in the psychology of inference. It is impossible to rule out this hypothesis in general, but there are domains where one can be certain that it is false. One such domain concerns spatial relations.

The spatial relation, 'on the right of', has two similar meanings (Miller & Johnson-Laird, 1976, Sec. 6.1.3). One meaning refers to the relation between objects from a particular point of view (usually the speaker's), as in the assertion:

The boulder is on the right of the road.

The other meaning depends on the fact that people (and many other entities) are conceived of as having an intrinsic right- and left-hand side:

St. John is on the right of Jesus in *The Last Supper*.

The first meaning plainly gives rise to transitivity. However, the second meaning has a very interesting property: In some cases, it is transitive; in others, it is intransitive; and in still others, it has a limited transitivity over a finite number of individuals. An example of the last sort arises with people seated round a circular table. It may then be valid to argue:

Arthur is on Guinevere's right.
Guinevere is on Lancelot's right.
Therefore, Arthur is on Lancelot's right.

But the seating arrangement may render transitivity over four or more individuals out of the question (for example, the fourth individual may be sitting directly opposite the first).

It is very difficult to define the logical properties of such relations using inference schemata because it is necessary to specify an infinite number of schemata ranging over all possible degrees of transitivity. A sensible way to proceed would be to postulate a meta-schema that allows the required degree of transitivity to be determined from information about the circumstances referred to in the premises. To concede this point, however, is to concede too much. If information about the situation were to be used in this way, then it would be better to abandon altogether the inferential schemata that mediate between one expression and another, and to rely instead on meanings that directly relate language to mental models of situations. Indeed, it is a simple matter to specify such a semantics for " on the right of" by defining the appropriate direction in a Cartesian framework: Increment the value of one horizontal co-ordinate whilst holding the other one constant. If the horizontal co-ordinates are those of a spatial layout as seen from a particular point of view, then these truth conditions yield transitivity as an emergent property of the relation. If the horizontal co-ordinates are centred on a particular individual in order to make an intrinsic interpretation, the same truth conditions yield transitivity over a collinear arrangement. Otherwise, as with a circular arrangement, transitivity may break down. In particular, *A* may be on *B*'s right and *B* on *C*'s right, but *A* may not be on *C*'s right because the line specifying those points on the right of *C* goes off at a tangent from the circle and clearly misses *A*, who is, say, nearly opposite to *C*.

COMMON-SENSE REASONING

Perhaps the most important purpose served by inference is to produce new knowledge. Suppose, for example, that I want to get my car, a Renault, serviced, but that I do not know a good garage. Someone may tell me that some of the people in the linguistics department own Renaults. I am then likely to try to contact these individuals. My behaviour is motivated by a simple deduction in which one premise is the assertion by my informant, and the other is a piece of general knowledge:

> Anyone who owns a Renault is likely to know where Renaults can be serviced.

The conclusion provides me with new information:

> Some of the people in the linguistics department are likely to know where Renaults can be serviced.

This use of deduction places constraints, which we have already encountered, on practical inference: conclusions should be informative—that is, they should establish relations between terms that are not explicitly related in the premises, and these relations should contain at least as much semantic information as is conveyed by the premises.

Another major function of inference is to serve the process of comprehension. Because people can make inferences, it is often unnecessary for speakers to spell everything out in detail; they can leave certain information unstated and rely on their listeners to infer it. Very often, however, this missing information can be filled in only by default. It can be assumed only because there is nothing to the contrary. The conclusion is not valid, since it may be overruled by subsequent information. Consider the following discourse:

> When I returned to my house last night, I discovered that I had lost my keys. There was no one there and the door was locked. I broke the glass and turned the lock from the inside. Someone heard the noise and came running.

In order to understand this passage, the reader will have drawn a series of inferences by default:

> The keys the speaker lost included the key to the door of his house.
> There was no one *in his house*.
> The door that was locked was the door to his house.
> He broke a pane of glass in the door to his house.
> He reached in through the resulting hole and unlocked the door.
> Someone (not in the house) heard the noise of the breaking glass and came running to investigate its cause.

Each of these inferences helps to tie the discourse together and enables the reader to construct a mental model that integrates the information from the separate sentences. None of these inferences, however, is valid; each of them could have been contraverted by subsequent information. For example, the passage might have made it clear that the speaker lost his car keys and had to break into his car by smashing a window.

Workers in artificial intelligence have suggested that certain default inferences depend on 'scripts'—that is, representations of the typical sequences of events that occur in certain stereotyped situations, such as dining in a restaurant (see, e.g., Schank & Abelson, 1977). Scripts, however, do not embrace all default inferences, as shown by some of the examples above, and they lack any explicit machinery for revising conclusions in the light of subsequent information. Attempts have accordingly been made to devise so-called 'non-monotonic' logics. Orthodox systems of logic are monotonic in that when a conclusion follows validly from a set of premises, it still follows validly if any additional premise is added to the set. However, if we reason by default, we draw a conclusion that a subsequent assertion may force us to abandon. Non-monotonic logics are designed to formalize this notion (see, e.g., McDermott & Doyle, 1980). Unfortunately, formal rules of inference run into apparently insurmountable problems with the underlying semantics of reasoning by default (Davis, 1980).

The whole point of the semantic approach is to marry reasoning with comprehension. Comprehension depends on the construction of mental models and is in fact akin to the process of maintaining a consistent database. It is necessary to make inferences from input information, and to be able to revise the database if such conclusions conflict with subsequent information.

Any particular assertion is interpreted by constructing an appropriate mental model or an appropriate addition to an existing model. Of course, an assertion may conflict with the current model of the discourse, perhaps because a default inference has been made earlier. Clearly, in the case of a conflict, an attempt should be made to construct an alternative model that is consistent with the discourse as a whole. Where there is such a model, the assertion conveys new semantic information; where there is no such model, the assertion is genuinely inconsistent with the previous discourse. This process is complementary to the semantic approach to deduction in which an attempt is made to construct an alternative model of the discourse that renders an assertion (the putative conclusion) false. Where there is such a model, the assertion does not follow validly from the previous discourse; where there is no such model, the assertion is a valid deduction from the previous discourse. Hence, both deduction and the revision of a default inference depend on recursive processes that search for alternative models.

There is one further hiatus between formal logic and the inferences of daily life. Suppose that the following evidence is presented at a murder trial:

> The victim was stabbed to death in a cinema.
> The suspect was travelling on a train to London when the murder took place.

Even children appreciate that this evidence provides a good alibi for the suspect. This conclusion is not valid, however, and so it cannot be drawn simply on the basis of a mental logic.

In some informal tests, I asked small groups of subjects what follows from these premises. They concluded that the suspect was indeed innocent, and when I inquired why, they pointed out a number of unstated assumptions:

> One person cannot be in two places at the same time.
> There are no cinemas on trains to London.
> Trains don't pass through cinemas.

When I queried whether the subjects were absolutely certain about their conclusion, an interesting phenomenon occurred: they began to try to construct scenarios in which the suspect *was* guilty. They argued that perhaps he left the cinema and boarded the train, that he might have thrown the knife, and so on. When I ruled out these hypotheses, the subjects suggested further possibilities, such as the use of a confederate, a spring-loaded knife in the seat, or a radio-controlled robot.

The only way to guarantee the validity of a conclusion is, of course, to eliminate all possible counterexamples. Logic is a formal machine designed to achieve this goal. In this case, however, logic cannot ensure that one has considered all the different ways in which the murder might have been accomplished. Like most everyday problems that call for reasoning, the explicit premises leave most of the relevant information unstated. Indeed, the real business of reasoning in these cases is to determine the relevant factors and possibilities, and it therefore depends on a knowledge of the specific domain. Hence, the construction of putative counterexamples calls for an active exercise of memory and imagination rather than a formal derivation of one expression from others. Yet the process is deductive: reasoners are trying to find an interpretation of the premises from which there is an informative conclusion that must be true.

Even if there were a complete logic for all utterances in natural language, it would still be necessary to spell out explicitly all the unstated assumptions that people rely on in making such inferences. Reasoning itself is largely concerned with the exploration of the tacit assumptions that flesh out the explicit premises. Reasoners draw a tentative conclusion and then seek to become aware of what they have assumed in order to ascertain whether it is necessarily true. Psychologists would have appreciated this aspect of practical reasoning long ago if they had not examined deductive performance through the distorting lens of formal logic.

CONCLUSIONS

Reasoning without logic consists of three simple steps: Interpret the premises by constructing a model based on their truth conditions, formulate an informative conclusion, and check the conclusion by searching for different models of the premises. Nevertheless, such reasoning is also very powerful. Any of the deductions that people are ordinarily able to make fall within its scope, and it is not necessary to devise different theories of reasoning for propositional connectives, quantifiers, and relational terms. Similarly, it is not necessary to formulate special theories for sentential connectives such as 'because' and 'if', which are used in senses that are not truth-functional. Once the truth conditions of a sentence have been grasped, they can be used as a basis for reasoning.

In the past, psychologists have assumed the doctrine of mental logic without argument. What they have argued about is different versions of the doctrine—no one ever collected data to investigate whether the doctrine itself was correct, and even to this day there are theorists who regard it as irrefutable (Cohen, 1981). In fact, however, we can now see that logic is neither necessary nor sufficient to account for rational competence, and that the experimental evidence favours a theory based on truth conditions. The semantic theory offers a superior account of syllogistic inference, relational deductions, and the common-sense and default inferences of daily life. Theories of performance based on mental logic should therefore be abandoned.

This step has three important consequences: First, it follows that current conceptions of children's intellectual development are wrong; children do not learn, construct, or inherit a mental logic. On the contrary, they acquire the truth conditions of words, and they use them to construct models of premises and to search for alternative models in accordance with the semantic criterion of validity. Second, the concept of 'logical form'—the form of a sentence as captured by a system of logic—has no role to play in accounting for deductive competence. In other words, there are no terms, such as the connectives 'and' and 'or' or the quantifiers 'all' and 'some', that have to be treated specially by the theory of reasoning. People need only to know the truth conditions of these terms in order to make deductions, just as they need only to know them for other so-called non-logical terms. Psychologists and linguists should give up the notion of logical form along with that of mental logic. Third, formal logic as an intellectual discipline does not depend on externalizing an inner system of logic. Rather, it is an attempt to formalize systematic rules that capture syntactically a class of deductively valid inferences that are initially grasped intuitively, incompletely, and unsystematically through the pre-theoretical manipulation of mental models.

There is one class of deductions that the semantic theory, in common with all other psychological analyses, cannot explain: inferences concerning infinite sets. There is obviously no way in which an infinite number of entities can be directly represented in the mind. Hence, it is plausible to assume that these inferences are made possible by the invention of formal logic and mathematics. A primary motive for this invention is indeed our limited ability to reason. Too often, we make invalid inferences, not because we have forgotten the premises or distorted their meaning, but because our working memories are too overloaded for us to consider all the possible models of the premises. Logic is a consequence of our limited ability to reason, not the fundamental machinery on which this ability is based.

ACKNOWLEDGEMENTS

The work reported in this chapter was supported in part by a grant from the S.S.R.C. (G.B.) to Jane Oakhill and the author. I am particularly grateful both to Jane Oakhill and to Bruno Bara for help, ideas, and criticism. I am also grateful to Martin Braine, the doyen of the 'mental logicians', for stimulating discussions on the theory of inference.

REFERENCES

Bar-Hillel, Y., & Carnap, R. An outline of the theory of semantic information. In Y. Bar-Hillel, *Language and information.* Reading, MA: Addison-Wesley, 1964. Reprinted from Technical Report No. 247, MIT, Research Laboratory of Electronics, 1952.

Barwise, J., & Cooper R. Generalized quantifiers and natural languages. *Linguistics and Philosophy*, 1981, **4**, 159–219.

Beth, E. W., & Piaget, J. *Mathematical epistemology and psychology.* Dordrecht: Reidel, 1966.

Boole, G. *An investigation of the laws of thought.* London: Walton and Maberly, 1854.

Boolos, G. S., & Jeffrey, R. C. *Computability and logic* (2nd ed.). Cambridge: Cambridge University Press, 1980.

Braine, M. D. S. On the relation between the natural logic of reasoning and standard logic. *Psychological Review*, 1978, **85**, 1–21.

Braine, M. D. S., & Rumain, B. Development of comprehension of "or": Evidence for a sequence of competencies, *Journal of Experimental Child Psychology*, 1981, **31**, 46–70.

Braine, M. D. S., & Rumain, B. Logical reasoning. In J. Favell & E. Markman (Eds.), *Carmichael's Manual of Child Psychology* (4th ed.). New York: Wiley, forthcoming.

Broadbent, D. E. *Perception and communication.* London: Pergamon, 1958.

Chapman, I. J., & Chapman, J. P. Atmosphere effect re-examined. *Journal of Experimental Psychology, 1959,* **58**, 220–226.
Chomsky, N. *Aspects of the theory of syntax*. Cambridge, MA: MIT Press, 1965.
Chomsky, N. *Essays on form and interpretation*. Amsterdam: North-Holland, 1977.
Clark, H. H. Linguistic processes in deductive reasoning. *Psychological Review, 1969,* **76**, 387–404.
Cohen, L. J. Can human irrationality be experimentally demonstrated? *Behavioral and Brain Sciences*, 1981, **4**, 317–370.
Davis, M. The mathematics of non-monotonic reasoning. *Artificial Intelligence*, 1980, **13**, 73–80.
Egan, D. E., & Grimes-Farrow, D. D. Differences in mental representations spontaneously adopted for reasoning. *Memory and Cognition*, 1982, **10**, 297–307.
Erickson, J. R. A set analysis of behavior in formal syllogistic tasks. In R. L. Solso (Ed.), *Theories in cognitive psychology: The Loyola symposium*. Potomac, MD: Erlbaum, 1974.
Falmagne, R. J. The development of logical competence: A psycholinguistic perspective. In R. H. Kluwe & H. Spada (Eds.), *Developmental models of thinking*. New York: Academic Press, 1980.
Fodor, J. A. Fixation of belief and concept acquisition. In M. Piatelli-Palmarini (Ed.), *Language and learning: The debate between Jean Piaget and Noam Chomsky*. Cambridge, MA: Harvard University Press, 1980.
Gazdar, G. A cross-categorial semantics for coordination. *Linguistics and Philosophy, 1980,* **3**, 407–409.
Guyote, M. J., & Sternberg, R. J. A transitive-chain theory of syllogistic reasoning. *Cognitive Psychology*, 1981, **13**, 461–525.
Henle, M. On the relation between logic and thinking. *Psychological Review*, 1962, **69**, 366–378.
Henle, M. Foreword. In R. Revlin & R. E. Mayer (Eds.), *Human reasoning*. Washington, DC: Winston, 1978.
Hunter, I. M. L. The solving of three-term series problems. *British Journal of Psychology*, 1957, **48**, 286–298.
Huttenlocher, J. Constructing spatial images: A strategy in reasoning. *Psychological Review*, 1968, **75**, 550–560.
Inhelder, B., & Piaget, J. *The growth of logical thinking from childhood to adolescence*. London: Routledge & Kegan Paul, 1958.
James, W. *The principles of psychology* (Vol. 2). New York: Holt, 1890.
Johansson, B. S., & Sjolin, B. Preschool children's understanding of the coordinators "and" and "or". *Journal of Experimental Child Psychology*, 1975, **19**, 233–240.
Johnson-Laird, P. N. Models of deduction. In R. J. Falmagne (Ed.), *Reasoning: Representation and process in children and adults*. Hillsdale, NJ: Erlbaum, 1975.
Johnson-Laird, P. N. Mental models in cognitive science. *Cognitive Science*, 1980, **4**, 71–115.
Johnson-Laird, P. N. Ninth Bartlett memorial lecture: Thinking as a skill. *Quarterly Journal of Experimental Psychology*, 1982, **34A**, 1–29.
Johnson-Laird, P. N. *Mental models*. Cambridge, MA: Harvard University Press, 1983.
Johnson-Laird, P. N., & Bara, B. Syllogistic inference. *Cognition*, 1984, **16**, 1–61.
Johnson-Laird, P. N., & Steedman, M. J. The psychology of syllogisms. *Cognitive Psychology*, 1978, **10**, 64–99.
Johnson-Laird, P. N., & Tridgell, J. M. When negation is easier than affirmation. *Quarterly Journal of Experimental Psychology*, 1972, **24**, 87–91.
Kintsch, W. *The representation of meaning in memory*. Hillsdale, NJ: Erlbaum, 1974.
Kneale, W., & Kneale, M. *The development of logic*. Oxford: Clarendon Press, 1962.

Mayer, R. E. Qualitatively different encoding strategies for linear reasoning problems: Evidence for single association and distance theories. *Journal of Experimental Psychology: Human Learning and Memory*, 1979, **5**, 1–10.
McDermott, D., & Doyle, J. Non-monotonic logic, I. *Artificial Intelligence*, 1980, **13**, 41–72.
Mill, J. S. *A system of logic* (8th ed.). New York: Harper, 1874.
Miller, G. A., & Johnson-Laird, P. N. *Language and perception*. Cambridge, MA: Harvard University Press, 1976.
Newell, A. Reasoning, problem solving, and decision processes: The problem space as a fundamental category. In R. Nickerson (Ed.), *Attention and Performance* (Vol. VIII). Hillsdale, NJ: Erlbaum, 1981.
Newell, A., & Simon, H. A. *Human problem solving*. Englewood Cliffs, NJ: Prentice-Hall, 1972.
Ormrod, J. E. Cognitive processes in the solution of three-term series problems. *American Jounral of Psychology*, 1979, **92**, 235–255.
Osherson, D. N. Logic and models of logical thinking. In R. J. Falmagne (Ed.), *Reasoning: Representation and process in children and adults*. Hillsdale, NJ: Erlbaum, 1975.
Revlis, R. Two models of syllogistic reasoning: Feature selection and conversion. *Journal of Verbal Learning and Verbal Behavior*, 1975, **14**, 180–195.
Rips, L. J. Cognitive processes in propositional reasoning. *Psychological Review*, 1983, **90**, 38–71.
Schank, R. C., & Abelson, R. P. *Scripts, plans, goals and understanding*. Hillsdale, NJ: Erlbaum, 1977.
Shannon, C., & Weaver, W. *The mathematical theory of communication*. Urbana: University of Illinois Press, 1949.
Staudenmayer, H. Understanding conditional reasoning with meaningful propositions. In R. J. Falmagne (Ed.), *Reasoning: Representation and process in children and adults*. Hillsdale, NJ: Erlbaum, 1975.
Sternberg, R. J., & Weil, E. M. An aptitude-strategy interaction in linear syllogistic reasoning. *Journal of Educational Psychology*, 1980, **72**, 226–239.
Störring, G. Experimentelle Untersuchungen über einfache Schlussprozesse. *Archiv für die gasamte Psychologie*, 1908, **11**, 1–127.
Wason, P. C., & Johnson-Laird, P. N. *Psychology of reasoning: Structure and content*. Cambridge, MA: Harvard University Press, 1972.
Wilkins, M. C. The effect of changed material on the ability to do formal syllogistic reasoning. *Archives of Psychology*, 1928, **16**, No. 102.
Woodworth, R. S., & Sells, S. B. An atmosphere effect in formal syllogistic reasoning. *Journal of Experimental Psychology*, 1935, **18**, 451–460.
Youniss, J. Inference as a developmental construction. In R. Falmagne (Ed.), *Reasoning: Representation and process in children and adults*. Hillsdale, NJ: Erlbaum, 1975.

2

Reasoning and Inference in Logic and in Language*

TERENCE MOORE

Department of Linguistics
University of Cambridge

INTRODUCTION

As theoretical linguistics has become more formal in character, so have linguists seen in logic a natural source of insight into techniques for modelling aspects of language. When, in the 1950s, Chomsky was developing his hypothetico-deductive approach to syntax, he took a good deal of his early inspiration from logicians. His conception of grammars not as descriptive statements but as devices, in the form of rewrite rules, for synthesising or generating the sentences of a language, was borrowed (as he acknowledges) from E. Post's work on the properties of combinatorial systems used in symbolic logic. Similarly, as theoretical linguists have become increasingly interested in the semantics of natural language, they have turned once again to logic, this time to the various calculi developed by logicians to explore the character of deductive reasoning.

In using logical systems as a basis for characterising reasoning and inference in natural language, however, linguists face a very real danger: that of taking too narrow a view of their subject matter. Logicians, with quite

* The author would like to thank Christine Carling for helpful comments and constructive criticisms.

ISBN 0-12-512320-5

different ends in view compared with those of linguists, have largely concentrated on one type of logic: deductive logic, devised to allow for the study of necessarily valid inference. This is not surprising given that the primary interest of logicians is with the forms that valid inference can take. What is more surprising is that linguists, in seeking to understand reasoning and inference in natural language, should have assumed that deductive logic is the appropriate type of logic for their purposes. One introductory textbook for linguists entitled *Logic in Linguistics* considers only deductive logic on the grounds that it "provides the most interesting insights into the structure of language" (Allwood, Andersson, & Dahl, 1977, p. 16). Inductive logic is expressly excluded. Nevertheless, this branch of logic, though formally much less developed, is more likely to provide insight into natural language inferencing processes, since it deals with *probably* rather than *necessarily* valid inference.

The aim of this chapter is therefore twofold: first, to argue that deductive logics are too narrowly based to provide appropriate and revealing models of reasoning and inference in natural language; and second, to show how a better understanding of inductive inference is essential if linguists are to gain useful insight into natural language operation.

DEGREES OF VALIDITY

To point up the limitations for the linguist of deductive logics, consider the following example:

Premises:	If Max is hungry, he is ratty.
	Max is hungry.
Conclusion:	Max is ratty.

Here, if the premises are true, then given the appropriate form, the conclusion is necessarily true. Thus deductive inference is an all-or-none affair, its arguments either completely valid or completely invalid, with no degree of partial validity. Compare this with an example of inductive inference:

Premises:	When Max is hungry, he is usually ratty.
	Max is hungry.
Conclusion:	Max is ratty.

In this case, we cannot have perfect confidence in the conclusion. To be able to quantify the degree of probability that should be assigned to the conclusion, we would need to assign a value to 'usually'. Unlike deductive inference, inductive inference *does* admit of degrees of validity, its conclusions are only probably, not necessarily valid.

Consider a further example of deductive reasoning:

Premises:	Every mammal has a heart.
	A cat is a mammal.
Conclusion:	A cat has a heart.

For a non-logician, what is striking about this conclusion is that it tells us nothing new. It states nothing that has not already been stated, in effect, by the premises. This conclusion, like all valid deductive arguments, states explicitly, or reformulates, knowledge already given in the premises. It is not, and must not be, innovative.

Compare this example with a similar inductive case:

Premise:	Every cat that has been examined has a heart.
Conclusion:	Every cat has a heart.

Here the premise refers only to cats that have been examined, while the conclusion refers, boldly, to all cats. In this case, the conclusion affirms a statement that goes beyond the information given in the premise. It is necessarily innovative, a jump not altogether in the dark. Of course, the additional content of the conclusion, pace Hume, might be false, thus rendering the conclusion as a whole false. An inductive inference is thus able to extend the content of the premises, but at the cost of introducing uncertainty. By contrast, a deductive inference achieves absolute certainty, at the cost of sacrificing innovation.

THE TRUTH ABOUT LOGIC

It is essential for linguists tempted to use logical systems in the characterisation of the semantics of natural language to keep in mind the rigid, non-innovative nature of deductive logics, as well as the fact that logicians interested in deductive logics are interested primarily in the form, not the content, of deductive arguments. Natural language sentences are of concern only insofar as they can be converted into the kind of representations required by deductive logics. Nor do there even exist effective translation procedures for converting ordinary language into the required logical form. Logicians have tended to acknowledge this problem and then set it aside. For them, the issue is whether or not the form of an argument justifies the conclusion. Form matters, because the right forms (and the right forms only) justify their conclusions. Logic is not about truth but rather the justification of conclusions. Justification is all.

Consider the following stylised argument, which serves to illustrate the implications of the logician's approach:

This man has a wide forehead.
People with wide foreheads have large brains.
People with large brains are highly intelligent.
Therefore, this man is highly intelligent.

The final statement is the conclusion of an argument with three premises, each intended to provide evidence for the conclusion. When evidence is offered as a justification for a conclusion, two questions arise in the mind of the non-logician: First, is the evidence true? Second, is the evidence properly related to the conclusion? If the answer to either question is no, the conclusion, while it may or may not be true, cannot be said to be justified on the basis of the evidence. However, in the mind of the logician, only one of the two questions matters: Is the evidence properly related to the conclusions?

Deductive logic deals with the relation of premises to conclusions, not at all with the question of the truth of premises. It would thus be wrong to call an argument logically fallacious because it contained one or more false premises. Proof must not be confused with truth. Our stylised argument from forehead width to intelligence, for example, is logically valid in spite of the dubious nature of our premises. The question this raises is not why logicians do what they do, but rather whether such an approach has anything to offer linguists interested in understanding meaning and inference in natural language.

This question becomes all the more pressing if a different type of example is studied. Consider one of the valid forms of syllogistic inference:

No P are M.
Some S are M.
Therefore, some S are not P.

We may insert in this schema any propositions of the permitted form, regardless of their content:

No linguists are diagonal.
Some poems are diagonal.

and arrive at the logically valid conclusion:

Therefore, some poems are not linguists.

An example of this sort brings out the divergence between the concerns of logicians and linguists. Too often, the examples used in syllogisms are persuasive either by covert links with other knowledge (e.g., the well-worn example: All men are mortal; Socrates is a man; therefore, Socrates is mortal) or by being as neutral and bland as possible with respect to our perception of the world.

PREMISES AND PERCEPTIONS

The simplifying assumption that the syllogism requires is in part a restriction of complex ordinary utterances to unrepresentative forms, and in part an emphasis on form at the expense of meaning. But suppose we try to look afresh at typical syllogisms. What are called 'premises' are series of words in a certain order. A hearer given a set of premises and asked to speculate on what follows can take one of two paths: He can pay attention to the words and interpret them in relation to his overall perception of the world, in which case there are a range of responses open to him. He may, for example, deny the main premise as implausible and refuse to draw any conclusions; he may deny the minor premise as implausible; or he may ask for more information. The other path he may follow is to produce the logically 'correct' inference—a more likely choice if he has had some previous schooling. This training would have involved his learning that it is unnecessary to attempt to evaluate the plausibility of sentences in order to draw logically valid inferences.

Suppose we look more closely at the first of these paths. In the thirties, Luria carried out an extensive series of tests on a variety of cognitive processes: perception, generalisation, abstraction, reasoning and problem solving, and deduction and inference. Particularly relevant to the question of the appropriateness of deductive reasoning as a model for reasoning and inference in natural language are the data that emerged from Luria's experiment with schooled and non-schooled peasants from the remoter regions of Uzbekistan. Quite inadvertently, these data tell us a great deal about natural language reasoning and inference. Luria reports his subjects as living "in a backward economy based mainly on the raising of cotton. The kishlak (village) dwellers displayed remnants of a once-high culture together with virtually complete illiteracy, and also showed the pronounced influence of Islamic religion" (Luria, 1976, p. 13).

Luria presented two sorts of syllogism to his subjects: One consisted of premises whose content was easily relatable to the subjects' immediate practical experience; the other involved premises whose content was divorced from such experience. In the latter case, Luria believed that inference could be made only by logical deduction. Of the 30 subjects who took part in the experiments, 15 were peasants from remote regions who had spent little time in large cities and who had no education. A comparison group included 15 collective-farm activists and young people who had received short-term (one or two years) school education. Luria notes that the data obtained from this comparison group were so uniform that enlarging the study group seemed pointless.

An example of a syllogism containing premises familiar to the subjects from their own practical experience was the following:

> Cotton grows well where it is hot and dry.
> England is cold and damp.
> *Question*: Can cotton grow there?

An example of the second sort of syllogism (containing material unfamiliar to the subjects) was:

> In the Far North, where there is snow, all bears are white.
> Novaya Zemlya is in the Far North.
> *Question*: What colour are the bears there?

According to Luria's interpretation of his results, those of his subjects living under the most backward conditions refused to make any inferences, even from syllogisms containing material generally familiar to them. They usually declared that they hadn't been to England and therefore didn't know whether cotton grew there. Only under prolonged questioning and repeated prompting ("What do my words suggest?") did they sometimes agree to draw a conclusion. One example of an apparently grudging response was: "From your words, it should be that cotton can't grow there if it is cold and damp; when it is cold and damp, cotton doesn't grow" (Luria, 1976, p. 107).

Luria reports that the unschooled peasants refused even more decisively to draw inferences from the syllogisms whose premises were divorced from their direct experience. Typically, many refused to accept the major premise, declaring that they 'had never been in the North and had never seen bears', and proposing that 'to answer the question you would have to ask people who had been there and seen them'. Frequently, they completely ignored either the major or the minor premise and replaced the deductive inferential process by inferential considerations of their own. For example, they would comment, "There are different kinds of bear; if one was born red, he will stay that way," or "The world is large, I don't know what kinds of bear there are." Furthermore, they would introduce what Luria calls 'rumour-based' opinions about bears but in each case resolutely avoided, Luria claims, solving the deductive inferential task.

A re-analysis of his data, however, shows a considerably more complex and illuminating position than Luria appears to have noticed. Consider the following exchange after presentation of the syllogism containing unfamiliar material about the colour of bears in the Far North:

> *Subject*: Abdurakhm, age 37, from a remote Kashyar village in Uzbekistan, illiterate.
> Q: What colour are the bears in Novaya Zemlya?
> A: We always speak only of what we see; we don't talk about what we haven't seen.

After repeated questioning and considerable prompting, Abdurakhm replied:

"If a man was sixty or eighty and had seen a white bear and had told about it, he could be believed, but I've never seen one and hence I can't say. That's my last word. Those who saw can tell, and those who didn't see can't say anything."

At this point, Luria reports that a young Uzbek volunteered the comment: "From your words, it means that bears there are white." The interviewer then asked Abdurakhm:

> Q: Well, which of you is right?
> A: What the cock knows how to do he does. What I know, I say and nothing beyond that.

Luria comments on this exchange in the following passage:

> We could scarcely find a better example of how the theoretical operation of inference from syllogisms is dealt with than the responses of this subject. . . . [He] refused to discuss any topics that went beyond his personal experience, insisting that 'one could speak only of what one had seen', and failing to accept the premises presented to him. [Luria, 1976, p. 110]

Yet an altogether different interpretation of Abdurakhm's cognitive capabilities is possible. While it is perfectly true that he appeared unwilling and indeed impatient with playing the deductive syllogism game in the form that Luria presented it, he shows unmistakably, though covertly, the ability to argue and infer deductively when he sees some point in doing so. Consider his comment beginning, "If a man was sixty or eighty..." Extractable from that, though not presented in the standard logical form, is a perfectly valid conditional argument called 'denying the consequent', or 'modus tollens':

If I could tell, I would have seen
I did not see.
Therefore, I cannot tell.

This has the schema:

If p, then q.
Not-q.
Therefore, not-p.

Abdurakhm also expresses himself in more complex patterns of the form:

Everybody who didn't see can't say anything.
I didn't see.
Therefore, I can't say anything.

Thus, despite Luria's comments, it appears that although Abdurakhm may understandably be impatient with playing logic games and indeed perform badly at them, there is no convincing evidence that he cannot, when he chooses, argue deductively.

Luria goes on to contrast the results of his experiments on the illiterate and non-schooled with his control group who had received some schooling. This group had no difficulty whatsoever in completing the deductive inferences 'correctly'. In fact, Luria (1976, p. 116, Table 8) reports 100 percent success for the control group in completing the syllogisms of both types.

In conducting his experiments on the responses of the schooled and the non-schooled to deductive inference problems, Luria was not concerned with the light that might be shed on reasoning and inference in natural language. Rather, his interest was to test a hypothesis of Vygotsky's—namely, that specific characteristics of mental development, particularly the ability to infer deductively, depend on the conditions of social life and practical activity found in a particular community. Luria interpreted his results as showing quite clearly that the acquisition of new modes of thought such as deductive inference depend on socio-historical development. The Abdurakhm example, however, suggests that Luria's conclusion may have been an overly hasty one, and that deductive reasoning may not have the special 'advanced' status he accords it.

Additional studies have been done on how people in a range of cultures with clearly different states of knowledge, belief and expectation respond to tests of verbal reasoning in the form of syllogisms. Cole (1977) and Scribner (1977), for example, like Luria, presented the same series of logic problems to two distinct groups: a literate, schooled group and a non-literate, non-schooled group.

Consider one representative example of the verbal reasoning of a non-schooled, non-literate Liberian Kpelle-speaking villager. The syllogism went as follows:

> All people who own houses pay a house tax.
> Boima does not pay a house tax.

The conclusion that was sought was an answer to the question, "Does Boima own a house?" (Scribner, 1977, p. 489). The non-literate Kpelle villager answers unequivocally that yes, Boima owns a house. When pressed for his reasoning, it went as follows: "Boima has a house, but he is exempted from paying house tax. The government appointed him to collect the house tax, so they exempted him from paying it."

This investigation found that across cultures, using many examples of this sort, the non-literate, non-schooled overwhelmingly supported their inferences by appeals to what they held as fact, belief or opinion. They responded to the content, not the form, of the syllogism. Similarly, in arriving at a meaning they drew, as they had to, on their knowledge and experience of the world as they perceived it.

With comparable consistency, the literate, schooled groups in the various communities answered the same questions in the logically 'correct' way. It is significant that seven-year-old children in school systems noted for emphasising rote learning rather than the development of critical thinking gave, in a high preponderance of cases, the logically 'correct' answer. In discussing the cross-cultural evidence for the responses of the non-literate group, Cole concludes that the particular verbal context and content dictated their responses, rather than the arbitrarily imposed relations among the elements in the problem.

The difference in responses to verbal reasoning tests does not, of course, indicate that the unschooled group was unable to reason and infer. On the contrary, Scribner (1977, p. 487) gives an example of an elegant piece of reasoning from a verbal logic problem by a non-literate Kpelle farmer. The investigator explains:

> If Sumo or Saki drink palm wine, the Town Chief gets vexed. Sumo is not drinking palm wine, Saki is. Is the Town Chief vexed?
>
> Kpelle farmer: The Town Chief was not vexed on that day.
> *Investigator:* What is the reason?
> Kpelle farmer: The reason is that the Town Chief does not love Sumo.
> *Investigator:* He doesn't love Sumo? Go on with the reason.
> Kpelle farmer: The reason is that Sumo's drinking means a hard time. That is why when he drinks palm wine, the Town Chief gets vexed. But when Saki drinks palm wine, he will not give a hard time to people. He goes to lie down and sleep. In that way people do not get vexed with him. But people who drink and go about fighting, the Town Chief cannot love them.

While this is the 'wrong' conclusion to this particular logico-linguistic puzzle, it is nevertheless clearly reasoned. The Kpelle farm rejects one of the disjuncts (namely, that if Saki drinks palm wine, the Town Chief gets vexed) of the major premise. He also brings in additional evidence relating to the varied effects of palm wine on Sumo and Saki. In other words, he declines to restrict himself to the 'closed' world of the deductive reasoning exercise; he interprets the premises inductively according to their content and its plausibility, not simply their form, and comes up with a response which, while lacking the certainty of a valid inference, is innovative. Furthermore, within the overall inductive framework, he includes a set of statements which demonstrate his capacity to perform deductive reasoning. Scribner (1977, p. 488) then recasts them in a more conventional syllogistic form:

Explicit premises:	Sumo's drinking gives people a hard time.
	Saki's drinking does not give people a hard time.
Universal:	All people do not get vexed when they are not given a hard time.
Implicit premise:	Town Chief is a person.
Conclusion:	Town Chief is not vexed.

The main difference between the groups has therefore not to do with ability in deductive reasoning but with ability to separate form from content. The responses of the non-literate strongly suggest that in their effort to understand, they are seriously bringing to bear complex frames of reference and states of knowledge, belief and expectation that have been accessed by the words of the syllogism and the order in which they are arranged. Processes of reasoning and inference are used to fill in gaps and establish links between frames of reference representing the subject's accumulated and categorised experience of the world. Thus they appear to construct meanings and draw conclusions. These active, constructive processes may well involve rejecting 'absurd' premises or importing new, more convincing evidence in order to draw plausible inferences. In brief, their desire to understand leads them to draw conclusions that are congruent with their overall image (in Boulding's sense) of the world. Their reasoning may include deductive inference, but only if this is congruent with their knowledge and experience of the world.

The literate, schooled group differed in their responses to the same words in the same order in that in their quest for understanding they appear to have acquired an ability to virtually disregard the frames of reference set in motion for the non-literate. For the literate, the words are thus largely inactive, inert, neutralised. Instead, they concentrate in their responses almost entirely on the syllogism as a form of expression.

For this group, the processes of reasoning and inference set in motion by words are of an altogether different order. They require, for example, in a categorical syllogism, minimally recognising which terms are distributed and which are not. If the syllogism is in the form of a universal affirmative (e.g., All linguists are students of language), they must recognise that the subject term is distributed but the predicate is not. If the categorical syllogism is in the form of a universal negative (e.g., No spiders are insects), they must recognise that both the subject and the predicate terms are distributed. It is not, of course, necessary for the solver of a deductive logic problem to understand the concept of distribution of terms; it is only necessary to remember *how* such terms must be distributed for a deductive inference to be valid. One must learn, that is, to acquire the skill of recognising patterns between arguments and conclusions, whatever the world is like.

UNDERSTANDING ANAPHORS

Such exercises are perfectly appropriate within their own domain, but they are not characteristic of most reasoning and inference in natural language. Language users do not reason and infer merely for the sake of doing so. Rather, they reason and infer about some subject, some matter of concern to them. Their conclusions are only occasionally 'necessarily valid'; most of the time they reason within an inductive framework, bringing to bear their beliefs and experience and arriving at conclusions which go beyond the content of premises, which are uncertain, at best 'probably valid', but innovative. They do, in other words, largely what the non-schooled and illiterate illustrate: They follow a pattern of valid deductive reasoning when the content of the premises appears to warrant it. Otherwise, they reason inductively, making a judgement on the appropriateness of the observations expressed in the premises and arriving at conclusions which go beyond the premises.

As an illustration of the close relation between natural language processing and inductive inference, consider the processes involved in the interpretation of anaphoric expressions. Typical examples are pronouns and 'pro-verbs'. The problem in understanding an utterance or text containing these expressions is to establish what they refer to, their antecedents. Despite the popular view, pronouns do not simply 'stand for nouns'—thus the problem of establishing antecedents is often not at all straightforward. Consider a comparatively simple case:

A: An alsatian bit me.
B: They are vicious beasts.

B's response contains an anaphoric expression, *they*, whose referent A will recognise as most probably being the class of alsatians, although there is no explicit reference to this class anywhere in the exchange. The referent of *they*, however, cannot be established beyond any doubt as being the class of alsatians. Rather, depending on the context, and on A's knowledge about B's views on dogs, A might consider as a more likely interpretation of *they* either the class of dogs or, possibly, a particular group of alsatians—or even the class of dogs with alsatians in particular. Thus the interpretation of anaphoric expressions involves uncertainty.

But how does A arrive at an interpretation of the antecedent of *they* as, say, the class of alsatians? The answer, it would appear, is by a form of inductive reasoning which recognises that speaker B has linked the reported case with her general belief about the propensity of alsatians to attack without cause. Note that B is unlikely to be able to offer any very conclusive evidence for her statement about the viciousness of alsatians. Speaker A will nevertheless be able to interpret *they* as probably referring to the class of alsatians, regardless of the validity of B's claim. He can do this because he is familiar with the process, common in everyday reasoning, of generalising from a minute sample. Thus, in resolving the anaphor, A has at the same time had to call upon information not directly involved in the exchange.

Such an example shows that interpreting anaphoric expressions may require bringing to bear information not explicit in a text or exchange; the understander arrives at the most probable, rather than the 'correct', interpretation of the anaphor. Both of these factors—the introduction of new information and the uncertainty associated with the conclusion—are, as we have seen, characteristic of inductive inferencing. Looked at in this way, anaphoric expressions do not refer to elements in an utterance but to 'mental categories' that the hearer constructs as the utterance, in the course of being processed, connects with his or her existing frameworks of knowledge, belief and experience. On this view, the fact that the antecedent to an anaphoric expression cannot necessarily be identified with any degree of certainty does not constitute a problem. Indeed, the relation between an anaphoric expression and its antecedent may have to be induced. The conclusion reached is not formally valid but is the most plausible in the context given.

To see this point more clearly, consider the following, more complicated examples:

(1) Pick your next resort with care if you're holidaying on home shores this summer. They're not likely to mention it at the local tourist office ... but raw sewage is dumped in the sea at more than 100 beaches around England and Wales.

Because we bring to bear knowledge about the practices of tourist offices, it is not difficult to infer the referent of *they* as most probably being the information officers working in local tourist offices. It is important to note, however, that we can go no further than identifying the most plausible referent. We cannot prove conclusively that the referent of *they* is this group of tourist office workers. Once more, in arriving at a referent we go beyond the information we are given directly in the text. As we innovate on the basis of our knowledge and experience, we accept a degree of uncertainty in our conclusion.

As for *it*, probably the most elusive and variable of all anaphors, we find no precisely identifiable referent —for example, the explicit *raw sewage*—but rather something less well-defined, a situation or state of affairs: the fact that raw sewage is dumped in the sea.

(2) Suppose cracks are appearing on the outside of your house. Your surveyor finds that the cause of the trouble is inadequate foundations put in when the house was built 10 years ago. It will cost £5000 to put right.

Here the most plausible candidate as antecedent for *it* is not the plural form 'cracks' or even 'inadequate foundations', but the more general problem of house repair that the reader constructs for himself on the basis of the particulars specified in the text, coupled with his or her own accumulated and categorised experience of house repair and maintenance. Once again, arriving at the antecedent requires using information not made explicit in the text; the most plausible antecedent is not a precise noun phrase but a situation or state of affairs.

(3) In the U.S.A. you can read off the shampoo packaging what it contains.

The referent we construct for this anaphoric *it* depends crucially on what other evidence is available. If the sentence is part of an article or discussion on the ingredients used in shampoos, the most probable antecedent for *it* is the first element of the nominal compound *shampoo packaging*. If, however, it appears in an account of the *Journal of Packaging* on the need to declare the materials used to package objects, then it will pick out the second element of the nominal compound. In resolving the anaphor, the reader thus brings to bear in quite subtle ways additional evidence cued by the text.

These examples begin to show the way in which resolving anaphors in natural language involves complex inductive reasoning and inference processes that leave room for uncertainty and indeterminacy. Nor are the inductive processes involved in establishing the antecedents for anaphoric expressions a special limited case of a type of process required in understanding the utterances of natural language. The understanding of deictic expressions (e.g., I, you, here, there, now, then) also requires the hearer/reader to construct a spatio-temporal viewpoint momentarily shared with his or her interlocutor. The deictic verbs in the following pair, for example,

May we come in?
May we go in?

locate the addressee in quite different positions in relation to some enclosed space. The addressee must bring to bear previous knowledge and experience of the situation in which the exchange takes place in order to arrive at the most probable interpretation of either question. There still may be an area of uncertainty; for example, "May we go in?" spoken at the entrance to a vault may or may not mean that the speaker wishes to go into the walk-in safe.

There are, of course, differences between deixis and anaphora. Deictic elements may be viewed as cues enabling a hearer to use both context and other accumulated experience to construct a specific set of spatio-temporal relations. By contrast, anaphoric expressions serve to initiate complex processing mechanisms aimed at constructing a representation that makes sense of the anaphora—that is, giving it an interpretation congruent with the understander's view of the world. Anaphora and deixis are best viewed as typical cases of ill-understood processes that are ubiquitous—and inescapable—in coming to understand any utterance of natural language. As Whitehead (1948, p. 73) remarks: "There is not a sentence which adequately states its own meaning. There is always a background of presupposition which defies analysis by reason of its infinitude." The interpretation of anaphora and deixis requires the activation of some of this 'background of presupposition'.

THE CENTRALITY OF INDUCTIVE REASONING

Given this widespread dependence of natural language processing on inductive reasoning and inference, it is all the more odd that linguists should have almost invariably looked for models of reasoning and inference in deductive logics. It is possible that, as in the case of Chomsky's earlier borrowing of grammars of formal languages to be used in the formulation of grammars of natural languages, the reasons are in essence threefold: They were there, they were formally precise, and they were reasonably well-understood. As a general rule, inductive reasoning in anaphora, deixis and natural language processing appears to be done informally, almost casually, on the basis of beliefs and impressions formed, with little if any reference to evidence. Yet logicians interested in inductive reasoning have begun to formally characterise those forms of inductive argument that provide grounds for more confidence in the soundness of a conclusion than, let us say, our earlier example about the viciousness of alsatians. Some of the more sophisticated cases of this type of induction involve the testing of both scientific hypotheses and the validity of inductive generalisation involving possibly insufficient or biased samples.

Tversky and Kahneman have studied the ways in which educated people arrive at their beliefs and judgements involving probabilities. They report that we are likely to perform on certain inductive reasoning problems at the same level at which Luria's non-schooled, illiterate Uzbekistan peasants performed on their deductive logic problems. Tversky and Kahneman (1977) asked subjects to answer a question, given certain data, that would involve their inductive reasoning powers. Consider a typical example:

> A certain town is served by two hospitals. In the larger hospital about forty-five babies are born each day and in the smaller hospital about fifteen babies are born each day. As you know about 50 per cent of all babies are boys. However, the exact percentage varies from day to day. Sometimes it may be higher than 50 per cent, sometimes lower.
>
> For a period of one year, each hospital recorded the days on which more than 60 per cent of the babies born were boys. Which hospital do you think recorded more such days.
>
> (p. 329)

Most of the schooled and literate subjects, undergraduates, judged the probability of obtaining more than 60% boys to be the same in both hospitals. But as Tversky and Kahneman (1977, p. 329) emphasise: "Sampling theory entails that the expected number of days on which more than 60 per cent of the babies are boys is much greater in the smaller hospital than in the larger one, because a large sample is less likely to stray from the 50 per cent." It is evident that a basic concept of statistics was not part of the framework of knowledge brought to bear in solving this inductive reasoning problem. Thus, a statistically sophisticated outsider investigating the undergraduates' inductive reasoning powers would be bound to report unfavourably on them, much as Luria did on the deductive capabilities of the Uzbekistan peasants.

There is a difference, however. Once an individual learns the basic concepts of sampling theory, these will form part of a framework of knowledge and belief which can be called upon in the solution of subsequent related problems. There is thus no standard technique for performing exercises in inductive logic. Instead, since it depends on one's knowledge and experience of the world, groups with different frameworks of knowledge and belief will be adept at handling inductive inference for different bodies of knowledge.

For the linguist interested in natural language processing, what is particularly striking about inductive reasoning is, first, the importance of the content of the sentences that form the premises of an inductive argument. Form cannot be separated from content; thus the meaning of the premises and the bodies of knowledge to which they are related play a crucial role—as they do in much natural language processing. Second, linguists are concerned with the extent to which, unlike deductive logics, induction involves uncertainty and indeterminacy, both primary characteristics of natural language. This factor strongly suggests that inductive reasoning provides the more appropriate model for linguists wishing to explain how meaning emerges from the utterances of a language. Progress in understanding how natural language works is therefore likely to go hand in hand with progress in understanding the processes of inductive reasoning.

REFERENCES

Allwood, J., Andersson, L-G., & Dahl, O. *Logic in linguistics.* Cambridge: Cambridge University Press, 1977.

Boulding, K. E. *The Image.* Ann Arbor: University of Michigan Press, 1961.

Cole, M. An ethnographic psychology of cognition. In P. N. Johnson-Laird & P. C. Wason (Eds.), *Thinking.* Cambridge: Cambridge University Press, 1977.

Luria, A. R. *Cognitive development.* Cambridge, MA: Harvard University Press, 1976.

Scribner, S. Modes of thinking and ways of speaking. In P. N. Johnson-Laird & P. C. Wason (Eds.), *Thinking*. Cambridge: Cambridge University Press, 1977.
Tversky, A., & Kahneman, D. Judgment under uncertainty, In P. N. Johnson-Laird & P. C. Wason (Eds.), *Thinking*. Cambridge: Cambridge University Press, 1977.
Whitehead, A. N. *Essays in science and philosophy*. London: Rider and Company, 1948.

3

Logic and Spoken Interaction*

JENS ALLWOOD

Department of Linguistics
University of Göteborg

INTRODUCTION

One of the long-standing questions in Western theorizing about language and thought is the question of how logic relates to thinking, on the one hand, and to actual discourse and argumentation on the other (see Aristotle's discussion in De interpretations). In this chapter I attempt the beginning of an answer to the second part of this question while dealing only indirectly with the first part.

My position is that significant parts of traditional logic play an important role in how the discourse of many types of spoken interaction is structured. The term 'traditional logic' is used to distinguish it from mathematical logic and is meant in principle to include, for example, those parts of logic that have been formalized in propositional and predicate calculus, as well as various types of so-called philosophical logic (tense, modality, and so on). I say 'in principle' since it is unclear whether logicians sometimes have not been forced to make finer distinctions than are ever used in ordinary discourse.

More specifically, I argue that traditional logic explicates a kind of normative competence that participants in spoken interaction exhibit both

* This study has been presented in seminars at the Universities of Edinburgh, Sussex and Urbino. I thank the participants of those seminars for valuable criticism. I would also like to thank Merrick Tabor, Carl-Martin Allwood and Dag Westerståhl for discussion and comments on an earlier version of this chapter.

ISBN 0-12-512320-5

collectively and individually. The formalizations of traditional logic provide us with a number of shorthand formulae which in an abstract and idealized manner explicate at least some of our intuitions about what an argument should be like in order to preserve truth. Another way of putting this is to say that the formulae characterize, in an abstract way, normatively idealized goals to which the result of our arguments should correspond, if our desire is to preserve truth.

METHODOLOGY

From a methodological point of view, the arguments in this chapter are a compromise between a rationalist and an empiricist approach. They do not rely exclusively on invented illustrative examples, as is the practise in those traditions within linguistics, philosophy and artificial intelligence that have been inspired by rationalism. Nor do they rely on the results of statistically analyzed and ascertained data, as is demanded by the traditions in the behavioural sciences that have been influenced by empiricism.

Instead of a statistical analysis of a representative sample of discourse in which the risks would be great that the coding procedures would hide all doubtful cases, excerpts from a debate and a discussion are presented. This is done so that the reader can get a feeling for the complexity involved. The use of data from spoken interactions which have actually occurred also provides more of a guarantee of contact with empirical reality than would invented illustrative examples. The excerpts used here have been chosen so as to be typical of a range of similar debates and discussions. Of course, such a judgement of typicality has to be taken on trust and cannot replace proper sampling and statistical treatment. Therefore, from an empiricist point of view the study can be regarded as exploratory.

The chapter is also exploratory from a rationalist point of view. It makes suggestions about the conceptual components of a possible way of relating parts of logic to discourse, but it does not attempt to formalize those suggestions in a manner that is currently acceptable within the traditions that have been influenced by rationalism.

Even if the approach taken in this chapter is exploratory both from the empiricist and the rationalist points of view, I believe that the study of spoken interaction can benefit greatly from this type of approach. Otherwise, there is a risk that using an empiricist approach, both theory and data may be over-simplified and that using a rationalist approach, they may be too constrained. In an empiricist approach, great energy has to be spent on reliable coding and statistical treatment. This rarely leaves time for in-depth consideration of the rather subtle issues involved in the semantic and pragmatic aspects of spoken interaction. By contrast, a rationalist approach is threatened by too many formal constraints being imposed prematurely. This can lead to artifactual problems being raised by the formalism. Another drawback is that certain substantive questions might be overlooked or disallowed because the formalism is incapable of handling them.

TWO EXAMPLES OF SPOKEN INTERACTION

In order to familiarize the reader with the kind of data being discussed, the two excerpts mentioned earlier are now presented in both translated and original versions. The first excerpt is an initial sequence from a debate between two persons that was arranged as an exercise in a course on argumentation. The two debators were instructed to take positions for or against day care centers. The second excerpt is an initial part of a discussion between three persons who have been instructed to discuss environmental problems. The discussion was arranged as part of a study on people's attitudes toward natural resources. Two slashes (//) indicate a pause, one slash (/) a shorter pause, a bracket ([) two simultaneous speakers, dots (....) that something cannot be heard on tape and italics that something is emphasized.

Debate on Day Care Centres (English Translation)

S1: Well // I am for day care centers for eh different reasons // *and first* I think that society today which is very private and eh // families live very isolated // and that means then that one does not have many contacts with other families with children // which leads to isolation and loneliness for those who // have children home // and secondly I think that children need possibilities to meet other children // since it is in interaction with other children that they get a picture of themselves // and a child in a day care center learns to cooperate and // since there is trained staff // they learn different techniques to express emotions // to learn to create with different materials // which a single person at home does not have strength or time to do // those are the arguments I have for day care centers.

S2: Well I don't want to counter directly now but rather I would like to bring up the arguments which I have *Against* day care centers and that is // that I above all believe in the *Family*.

Debate on Day Care Centers (Swedish Original)

T1: Ha // jag är alltså för daghem av eh olika skäl å för de första så tycker ja att samhället i dag // som // allså e väldigt privatiserat och eh //

familjer lever väldigt isolerade // å de gör då att man inte har många kontakter med andra barnfamiljer // vilket leder till isolering å ensamhet för dom som // har barn hemma // å för de andra så anser ja att barn behöver möjlighet att träffa andra barn // för att de e i samspel me andra barn som dom får en bild av sig själva // å ett barn på daghem lär sej att samarbeta å // i å me att de finns utbildad personal så // lär dom sej olika tekniker för att uttrycka känslor // för lära sej å skapa me olika material // vilket en ensam människa hemma inte har ork eller tid att göra // de e dom argumenten som ja har // för daghem.

T2: ja ja vill inte bemöta direkt nu utan ja vill snarast ta upp dom argumenten som jag har *Mot* daghem å de e // att ja tror framför allt på att på *Familjen.*

Discussion of Environmental Problems (English Translation)

A: I have not understood this with the rivers really I don't understand this with the rivers right // this they are protesting against is that electr/ they are going to construct electricity out of the rivers // [it can't be for the sake

B: [mm

A: of the *Fish* can it?

C: No.

B: No but there is a lot of other stuff with the balance of nature there are there are some animals who always have to cross these / rivers there and when they constructh / expand these *then* these animals can't cross there and *then* there is something which / influences the whole balance of nature so I have read but I don't know [very much

A: [.....

B: about it either // should we care more about these animals than people then?

C: The construction eh // also causes that eh // the rivers become completely // they become totally waste.

A: mm dry

C: They become only they become only little trickling brooks // for example [and furthermore they put giant areas under water

A: [*but that is because*

C: these dams that they then must put the water in many miles big dams in nature they flood agricultural areas areas which have been farming land and where there has been houses and ....

Discussion of Environmental Problems (Swedish Original)

A: ja har inte fattat det där med älvarna faktiskt ja fattar inte de med älvarna va de här dom protesterar mot ä de elektr / dom ska bygga ut elektriciteten ur älvarna // de kan ju inte va
B: mm
A: för *Fiskarnas* skull va?
C: nä.
B: nämen de e mycket annat med naturbalansen de finns de finns några djur som ska alltid korsa di här / älvarna där när dom bygger / byggerh / ut di här då kan inte di här djuren korsa där å då blir de nånting som / påverkar hela naturbalansen de har ja läst fast ja vet inte [heller mycke
A: [.....
B: om de att // skall vi tänka mera på di här djur än människor då?
C: utbyggnaden ä / orsakar ju också att ä / älvarna blir helt / dom blir helt ödelagda.
A: m torra
C: de blir bara de blir bara små strilande bäckar / till exempel [å dessutom lägger de jättestora arealer under vatten
A: [men de e för a
C: dessa dammar som dom då måste anhopa vattnet i flera mil stora dammar i naturen dom svämmar över ä kanske brukningsbyggd byggd som har varit jordbruksland å där de har vart bebyggelse å.

IS LOGIC RELATED TO SPOKEN INTERACTION?

After reading these two excerpts, the first question one might want to ask is whether there is any relationship at all between logic and spoken interaction. A negative answer to this question could claim that logic is a branch of mathematics dealing with certain types of relations between abstract elements which have nothing to do with spoken interaction and ordinary thinking. In spoken interaction, people think and talk about concrete things and events, and their thinking is guided by the properties of those events and things. They do not use and have no need for the abstract relationships that are studied in logic. Arguments which are close to this position have been suggested by researchers who have studied illiterate people with no knowledge of Western abstract thinking (see, e.g., Fuglesang, 1983; Scribner, 1979; Vygotsky, 1978). However, similar claims have also been made in relation to the ordinary reasoning of people who have been through Western schooling. An example is provided by the way in which people cope with certain types of inferences involving quantifiers (see Johnson-Laird, 1975).

Another type of negative answer would deny the relevance of logical inference on the grounds that feelings are more important than logic when people question, convince and persuade each other. Positions of this type have sometimes been taken by people studying rhetoric (e.g., Lindhart, 1975). A third negative answer would claim that there is a lot of inference in ordinary spoken interaction, but that such inference is not logical. Rather, it is inference by association, induction or analogy.

An answer which is much more positive regarding logic is given by certain researchers within artificial intelligence, who affirm the relationship between logic, thinking and spoken interaction with arguments like the following: We find logical inference everywhere, but this does not mean that it is necessarily conscious or marked in speech. The analogy between the mind and a computer shows that so much information must be processed, and at such a rapid speed, that most mental processes cannot be conscious or marked in speech. Further, in working with computational problem solving, logical control structures can be shown to be very convenient (see Kowalsky, 1979). Might they not be just as convenient for the brain in regulating its reasoning processes? This approach seems at least to resemble what the proponents of the so-called 'computational hypothesis' of cognitive processing have argued (see Hagert & Hansson, 1983).

My position cannot be identified with either of the two preceding positions. In some ways it is a compromise, but it also contains new elements not present in either of these. In order to present this position, I first consider some of the factors which influence the kind of logical structures found in spoken interaction.

FACTORS INFLUENCING THE LOGICAL STRUCTURE APPARENT IN SPEECH

The Order of Premises and Conclusions

Logical relations are atemporal. However, they are easier to grasp if a temporal order is imposed on them. Thus, in most text books on logic (e.g., Allwood, Andersson, & Dahl, 1977; Hodges, 1977; Resnick, 1970, Thomason, 1970), the idea of a logically valid argument is usually introduced by giving premises first and then a conclusion. In handbooks on rhetoric, the opposite order (conclusion first and then premises) is sometimes suggested. In both cases, one attempts to attain increased perspicuity by using temporal order to indicate what is supposed to follow from what. But as anyone knows who has followed a course on logic, the pedagogical order is not the order in which one actually proceeds, as, for example, in trying to find a proof. What goes on is closer to what seems to be going on in spoken interaction, since premises and conclusions can come in any order. For example, first a few premises, then the conclusion, then some additional premises for the same conclusion. If speakers are logical, they will be able to keep track of logical relationships without the aid of a pedagogically prescribed order.

Distribution of Premises and Conclusions Among Several Speakers

Regarding the pedagogical presentation of logic in textbooks, another difficulty is that more than one speaker seems to be able to contribute to an argument. Very often, an argument is the result of a collective effort. Premises and conclusions can be contributed by several speakers. One speaker contributes a premise, a second speaker draws what perhaps is a hasty conclusion and a third speaker therefore contributes another premise for the conclusion. Such patterns have not, in general, been noticed in traditional handbooks on argumentation and rhetoric, since these books have often concentrated on written language or on the speech of a single speaker.

If speakers use logic, they therefore seem to be able to handle both the lack of pedagogical order and the fact that contributions affecting logical relationships can be made by several speakers. Both of these elements must naturally be taken into account by any analyst who wishes to relate logic to spoken interaction.

Implicit Information

One feature which might cause problems for the analyst of logical inference patterns in speech is the fact that normally in spoken interaction, much information is implicit. Speakers do not spell out everything that is needed for an argument because they take many things for granted as shared background assumptions. To mention this information explicitly would be uneconomical, boring and tedious. As a rule, spoken interaction will therefore not contain all the information which, strictly speaking, would be necessary for a logically valid inference. Rather, it will contain only the information that speakers consider to be new or otherwise necessary to activate other implicit and presupposed information.

An additional reason for the pervasiveness of implicit information in ordinary discourse is that it makes language more flexible; thus it can be used for many purposes. Implicit information allows words to have vague and indeterminate meanings out of context. By supplementing intra- and extra-linguistic contextual information—that is, inplicit information—different meanings which are more determinate can be actualized in different contexts.

Through this ongoing interaction between what is given by linguistic convention and what is given as understood by context, the linguistic expressions can be used for new types of information and their flexibility is increased. Language itself does not have to bear the whole burden of information. It is aided continuously by understood information which in each context can help to make the meaning as determinate as is required by the purpose at hand.

For example, if a speaker says 'my wife', we will usually assume that the woman referred to is the speaker's wife at the time of the utterance and not at some earlier or later time. Further, in a monogamous society we will usually assume that the speaker has no other wives, which we would probably not do in a polygamous society. However, all of this information would have to be implicit and not conveyed by the expression 'my wife' when it is considered out of context.

Leaving shared information implicit enables speakers to make increased use of limited linguistic resources. It also makes most communication easier and more efficient for speakers. But it makes it harder for an analyst to determine whether arguments really display evidence of logical inference. In order to obtain valid inferences from what is actually said, analysts usually have to fill in the additional information that speakers have assumed.

An additional difficulty for the analyst is that speakers (consciously or subconsciously) sometimes exploit the fact that information can be left implicit. For example, they may suppress or hide incorrect, unreasonable or detestable assumptions which may be necessary for the validity of their conclusions. They may also be careless and make mistakes regarding both the assumptions they make and the way in which they infer their conclusions. Since much of their reasoning is implicit, it is not immediately clear how one should check whether a certain piece of reasoning contains harmless implicit assumptions, illicit assumptions or assumptions which are simply a mistake. However, even if the filling in of information runs the risk of becoming ad hoc, it should still be attempted, since the alternative of adopting some simpler and more reliable measure will almost certainly fail to do justice to the phenomenon under study.

The Multifunctionality of Discourse

A fourth factor to be taken into account when studying logical inference in spoke interaction is the fact that most utterances are multifunctional. For example, an utterance can be a description, an attempt to persuade, an expression of sorrow and a warning all at the same time (see Austin, 1962; Bühler, 1934). This multiplicity of functions can arise because, on the one hand, the speaker may have several intentions in making an utterance and, on the other hand, no matter what the speaker's intentions were, the listener can interpret the utterance as having several functions on the basis of his or her assumptions about the background and the setting.

For some purposes, such as the wish to amuse or persuade, logic might not be very helpful or relevant. Thus, in order to find the logical structure inherent in ordinary conversation, we have to disregard those parts and aspects of an utterance which serve other purposes than truth-preserving inference. This in turn means that logic might not be relevant to a certain piece of discourse, or that it might be relevant to some aspects of an utterance, but not all.

Other Types of Inference

A fifth factor of relevance, one which has already been mentioned, is that discourse can contain other types of inference besides logical inference. It is important to distinguish between 'new' types of inference and certain assumptions which are accepted as reasonable only by some speakers. Proverbs or quotes from some authority are accepted by many speakers as very strong support for a conclusion, but the same evidence may be totally rejected by other speakers. This does not mean, however, that the two sets of speakers are following different rules of inference. Rather, it means that they disagree about the reasonableness of the premises.

Inference means here simply a way to generate new information from old information. The question is, then, whether there are any ways of doing this over and above the ways described in logic. The answer to the question is to some extent dependent on the meaning of the word *information.* In order not to prejudice the case, by defining *inference* so that it means generating information while preserving truth, i.e. logical inference, I will use *information* to mean (cognitive) content of a mental act. The information does not need to be true or to stand in a causal reference relation to any object in the external world. An association from one perceived object to another could be an inference, if the type of association could be made systematic. However, the discussion below will show that it is difficult to find any other type of inference than logical inference which can satisfy the requirements of systematicity and certainty that we probably want to put on the inference relation.

The candidate traditionally proposed as an alternative to logical inference is induction, the kind of reasoning used to derive a general conclusion from particular instances. The status of induction, which has been much debated since the days of Hume, need not concern us here. It is enough to say that it undoubtedly does occur in ordinary discourse and that it does not seem to be reducible to logical or deductive inference. Thus, for example, it is not possible to reduce induction to deduction by introducing a premise which allows induction, or by introducing probabilities in the premises and then proceeding to a conclusion also containing these probabilities. In the first case induction is not reduced since it is being presupposed and in the second case induction is, in fact, never used. The inductive leap itself, that is, the leap from the particular to the general, remains unanalyzed.

Another proposal is reasoning by analogy, an example of which is:

> A brain is like a computer, so it (probably) contains both a central processing unit and peripheral memories.

However, in this case one can more plausibly argue that the inferential step in this argument is not due to analogy but rather to standard logic. The structure of the argument could be stated as:

> *If* a brain is like a computer and a computer contains both a CPU and peripheral memories, *then* a brain must contain both a CPU and peripheral memories.

The premises begin with a statement about a computer being like a brain. This can be analyzed as being a statement to the effect that certain relevant properties are identical between a brain and a computer. The second premise is implicit and states only that a computer has a CPU and peripheral memories. The conclusion then states that this is one of the relevant properties shared by a computer and a brain. The insertion of 'probably' in the conclusion indicates that it is unclear if the similarity between a brain and a computer is strong enough to warrant the conclusion. On this analysis, the argument can be said to involve both identity of properties and instantiation, both of which have been investigated in traditional logic. On this view, analogy would not be a type of inference but rather a method of discovering similarities and identities between two phenomena. If a perceived analogy is correct, it can be used as a premise for a logical deduction where properties of one entity are attributed to another.

It should be noted that this argument against counting analogy as a type of inference is not intended to be an argument against the use of analogy as such. On the contrary, analogy is probably one of the most important methods both of discovering the world and of making it more coherent by bringing together what is similar.

I turn now to a third type of nonlogical inference based on the suggestion that all reasoning is concrete and dependent on the inherent properties of our mental models of the world (see Johnson-Laird, 1975). An objection that can be raised to this suggestion is that it ignores the abstract, normative nature of logic. Logic was never intended as a direct description of how people think. If one takes the abstract nature of logic into account, concrete reasoning, when correct, can be thought of as an instantiation of the more general and abstract patterns studied in logic. Another way of putting this is to say that correct concrete reasoning is compatible with logical inference if a number of restrictions are introduced to allow for the nature of mental models.

Even if analogy and reasoning with mental models are not alternatives to logical inference, they nevertheless point to factors which have to be taken into account in attempting to understand the contribution of logic to spoken interaction. In addition, there may be still other species of inference which are genuine alternatives to logical inference.

LEVELS OF ANALYSIS OF SPOKEN INTERACTION

Before we turn to the excerpts to see which logical structure can be found in view of the phenomena just discussed, a few words must be said about my approach to the study of spoken interaction. The main tenets of this approach can be seen as a development of some of the ideas behind Wittgenstein's notion of a language 'game' (see Wittgenstein, 1953). The central idea of this approach is that linguistic interaction is seen as an aspect of interpersonal activity of a more or less extra-linguistic variety. In some cases, linguistic interaction is essential to this activity, as in teaching, debating or discussing. In other cases it is less essential, as in hunting, harvesting or playing tennis (see Allwood, 1980, 1982; Goldkühl, 1982, Levinson, 1979).

However great or small the role of language for such an activity, for both its linguistic and nonlinguistic aspects we can distinguish among traits of the activity which pertain to its global nature, traits which pertain to its more limited sequences and, finally, traits which pertain to individual behavior, In terms of linguistic interaction, we can say that the first two types usually concern the collective features of an interaction, whereas the third type concerns individual utterances. Examples of the first two types are patterns of turntaking, feedback and spatial positioning. Examples of the third type are one's choice of words and the intonation or grammatical structure of a single utterance.

We can also look at the factors that determine these different features. Whatever the scope of a feature, we can ask why it occurs. Again, it is possible to distinguish among factors which seem to determine a certain discourse globally, factors which have more intermediate effects and factors which only affect a single utterance. For example, in considering factors which have a global or intermediate effect, the purpose of the activity is especially important, as are the roles taken by participants and the external setting of the activity. Among the factors which determine single utterances, current topic and current communicative intention are both important.

To summarize, the approach taken here to spoken interaction claims that we can identify discourse structures with the following different types of scope:

1. global—relevant for the entire discourse or interaction;
2. intermediate—relevant between the local utterance level and the global level; and
3. local—relevant for single utterances only.

LOGICAL STRUCTURE IN SPOKEN INTERACTION

Bearing in mind what has just been said, I now would like to return now to some questions of methodology concerning ways to locate logical structure in transcripts of spoken interaction. I will do this by considering separately properties with different scope. We first consider global structures, followed by intermediate and finally structures which can be found only in single utterances. The same procedure can also be used for monologic discourse, provided that we make the smallest local unit something different from utterances (e.g., tone groups, phrases or sentences).

One way to find properties with global scope is to consider the purpose of an interaction. Very often, an a priori consideration of the purpose of an entire interaction will reveal that the purpose is connected with certain requirements which have to be met if the interaction is to be successful. The requirements can often be met only if a certain structure is imposed on the interaction. In cases where the interaction involves inference, this structure can be based, at least in part, on logical considerations. Thus, logic can be used to complete the interaction successfully. There may also be global properties which are not related to the purpose but rather to other determining factors of the activity.

Likewise, some of the properties which have intermediate scope can be predicted a priori by considering the purpose of the entire interaction. For example, in a trial certain things have to be said initially and others towards the end. At least to some extent, both types of things can be brought out by considering the purpose of the trial.

Other intermediate structures belong to a set of conversational practices which can be employed across different types of spoken interaction—for example, a question-and-answer sequence or a proposal–reject/accept sequence. Since such practices have purposes which are similar to the global purposes we have discussed earlier, aspects of their structure can also be predicted through a priori contemplation. Finally, of course, there are intermediate structures which are developed contingently in a particular interaction.

If it is possible to ascribe a purpose and to use this purpose to hypothesize certain structural consequences, the next task is to check whether the consequences are actually realized. An illustration of this procedure, applied primarily to global and intermediate sequences of discourse, is given below. However, in single utterances the suggested procedure is more problematic.

Purposes can often be correlated with structural properties. A question, for example, can be realized syntactically only in a limited number of ways. But the predictive value of a purpose is then diminished, since the features that can be predicted are usually the same features as those on which the ascription of the purpose is based in the first place. This problem also arises for global and intermediate structures, but since the scope of the prediction is larger for these structures, there is only a partial overlap between the features that are the basis of the ascription and those that are predicted. This allows a predictive value to be maintained.

Another problem, one which is more acute for single utterances than for larger structures, is that of an utterance's argumentative status. Is the utterance at all relevant for a logical inference? And, if it is, does it contain a full argument in itself, or is it to be regarded as a contribution to an argument which is being constructed jointly by a group of speakers?

The first of these questions actually has three parts:

1. Is there an inference?
2. Is the inference logical?
3. Is the inference valid and reasonable?

These questions might be reformulated as:

1. Does the utterance seem to use information to derive other information?
2. Can the derivation be supposed to aim at truth preservation?
3. Is the derivation in fact truth preserving, and are its premises and conclusions true and reasonable?

If we answer these questions intuitively, we find a number of logical inferences in many types of discourse, but as yet we cannot give operational procedures to answer them. One of the difficulties is that the answers require us to consider not only a particular utterance but also the whole context in which it occurs. This is the case if we want to decide in what way a certain utterance contributes to an argument involving several utterances and if we want to decide what implicit information an argument presupposes.

Particular linguistic expressions such as 'reason', 'cause', 'then', 'because', 'since', 'as', 'therefore', 'must', 'follows', 'consequently', and so on are often used by speakers to mark an inference. However, it does not seem possible to point to a finite closed list of such expressions, since new ways are sometimes found of expressing inferential relationships. Similarly, we cannot give any operational criteria for distinguishing logical inferences from inferences in general. As we have hinted earlier, the problem is that it is not theoretically clear what a non-logical 'inference' would be like. Could an inference which did not preserve truth or reference really be counted as an inference?

If we try to decide whether an argument is valid or reasonable, the problem of implicit assumptions faces us. Hardly any arguments found in spoken interaction contain sufficient information to allow a logically valid conclusion; unspoken, implicit assumptions are nearly always needed. But how are these implicit assumptions to be assigned? Following is an outline of the method followed in the present chapter.

We assume of a certain utterance that it contains a logically valid argument. We then check what implicit assumptions would be needed to make the argument valid strictly speaking. If it turns out to be impossible to supply premises that are relevant and necessary, or if the necessary premises turn out to be incorrect or unreasonable, then this is evidence either that the argument is not valid or that the argument is valid but lacking in empirical applicability or reasonableness. In many cases it is, of course, impossible to make any decision and the case has to be left undecided.

Even if reasonable premises can be found, we still have a problem. Can those premises reasonably be attributed to the speaker in question? In the present framework, an affirmative answer is given to this question if the attribution can be given some independent motivation. Such independent motivation can, for example, be of the following four types:

1. Consistency with other parts of transcribed text;
2. Factual information about the particular speaker at hand;
3. General information about the speaker's culture, activity and role; and
4. Construction of the speaker as a motivated, rational agent.

It might be thought that the approach just presented is circular. We claim that speakers are logical and then, as evidence, and in (4) we make them logical by attempting to construe them so. However, the circularity is only apparent. There are conditions under which the assumption that speakers are logical can be shown to be wrong—for example, if they never show any interest in truthpreserving arguments, or if their attempts at such arguments are always incoherent. Similarly, speakers can be shown to be unreasonable if the (implicit or explicit) premises which are necessary for their arguments always turn out to be unreasonable. The impression of circularity results only if one does not realize that an attempt to construe a speaker as logical or reasonable need not succeed.

Even if the method is not circular, one might still wonder why one should try to perceive speakers as logical and reasonable in trying to interpret what they say. My suggestion is that we do so because it constitutes a fundamental part of the ways in which we understand other people. There is a sense in which other people become incomprehensible if their actions are irrational and their utterances contradictory. We can feel empathy with such behavior or causally explain it, but we cannot understand it as the product of a motivated, rational agent (see Allwood, 1976).

Attributions of motivation, rationality and intention are the fundamental ingredients of an understanding of (especially) the linguistic behavior of other people. These ingredients are, in fact, so fundamental that something essentially human is detracted from another person if we find no reason, motivation or intention behind his or her behavior. We try to view other people as possessing these qualities even when the evidence is scant. We also expect others to construe our utterances the same way, which has the effect that we normally leave a lot of information out. Why should a rational person repeat what everybody takes for granted?

On this view, interpretation as logical construction plays a role for both the listener's comprehension and the speaker's production. This is so because speech production is viewed as a process in which, among other things, the speaker attempts to adjust his or her speech to the audience. In some circumstances, this means that the speaker will attempt to make his or her speech more logically coherent.

If logical construction does indeed play the role suggested here, then it also provides the answer to the question why, in looking for logical inference in spoken interaction, we should perceive speakers as logical. We use this method because it recaptures the conditions under which the speakers originally thought they would be interpreted. The method thus increases the ecological validity of the interpretation.

THE GLOBAL STRUCTURE OF THE DEBATE

Let us turn now to the debate and compare the role which can be given to logic from an a priori point of view with what actually occurs in the excerpt. The global purpose of the present debate was to take sides for or against day care centers in order to see which position was most reasonable. This was also the instruction given to a pair of debators who then had to choose one side each.

If one is for day care centers, one is likely to argue that day care centers are good. In fact, on a subjectivist theory of ethics, *X is good* is supposed to mean *I like X*. At any rate, a good reason to be for *X* is that *X* is good. Similarly, a good reason to be against day care centers is that they are not good. The debate's global purpose thus gives rise to two propositions: *Day care centers are good* and *day care centers are not good*. Each debator tries to show that one of these propositions is true. Both of them cannot be true, since each proposition is the negation of the other. This means that on a global level, the two propositions make up a disjunction. One or the other might be true, but we do not know which.

We can now reformulate the debators' task as follows: Their task is simply to increase information by eliminating the disjunction in favor of a single proposition. This can be done in two ways:

1. The debators can try to show that only one of the disjuncts is true by simultaneously providing positive evidence for one and negative evidence for the other.
2. They can try to show that both disjuncts are false in favor of a third proposition which is identical to neither of them but implied by both of them.

The second way is unusual and is reminiscent of the move from thesis to antithesis and finally to synthesis.

If we look at the excerpt from the debate, we find that it does conform to these a priori expectations. In their initial remarks, both debators show evidence of having chosen the first strategy—that is, to eliminate the disjunction by arguing simultaneously that one disjunct is correct and the other one incorrect. S1, who argues for day care centers, starts by arguing against the lack of day care centers, which she says leads to isolation, lack of contact and loneliness. She then continues her argument by saying that the centers lead to contact, self-development and cooperation among children. She also says that day care centers have trained staff who can teach children to express emotions and to create using different materials. Finally, she points out that single persons at home generally do not have the time or the strength to teach children such things. This circumstance functions as S1's final argument against the lack of day care centers.

If we take as out point of departure the disjunction which globally characterizes the debate, we can summarize the first speaker's argument by saying that first she argues against the disjunct that her opponent is defending (i.e., *not day care centers are not good*). She then gives positive arguments for the disjunct that she herself is defending (i.e., *day care centers are good*). In her last remark she gives an extra argument against her opponent's thesis. The result is that S1's argument seems to fit very well the logical requirement that we saw could be associated with the overall purpose of the debate.

S2 is supposed to argue against day care centers and can do this legitimately by arguing for the lack of day care centers, which she, like S1, implicitly assumes to mean arguing for the family. In her long speech, of which I have quoted only the opening lines, she develops such an argument. It is interrupted by a short argument against day care centers in which she claims that they do not give children a chance to wash up, clean and shop, and that therefore they give children an unrealistic view of life.

S2's position can be summarized the following way: She argues mainly that *not day care centers is good*, which, in her case, means arguing that *the family is good*. Her argument is interrupted briefly by an attempt to say that *day care centers are not good*. Thus, S2 concentrates her main efforts on trying to provide support for the negation of the disjunct that S1 is defending. She supports only briefly the disjunct that she is supposed to defend. Her argument therefore exhibits the logical features that it would if it were produced in line with the proposed analysis.

THE GLOBAL STRUCTURE OF THE DISCUSSION

Just as for the debate, we will first use an a priori analysis of the purpose of the discussion to see if there are any implications of a logical kind regarding its macrostructure. A discussion is normally less constrained than are those in the debate described above. In fact, the debate can be seen as a discussion in which the constraint has been imposed that all participants have to choose sides for or against a certain topic. This means that, in a discussion, a participant can present information both for and against a certain topic. The only restriction is that the information should be of mutual interest. It is commonly presented through such communicative activities as describing, asserting, judging, explaining and giving evidence.

In the discussion excepted here, the task of the participants was to discuss environmental problems. This task can be achieved in at least two ways. Either participants can discuss environmental problems on a general level (e.g., comparing them with other problems) or they can discuss particular environmental problems. If they choose the latter route, they have to find problems which they all can agree are environmental problems. Initially, we can therefore expect arguments about whether a certain problem is an environmental problem or not. Each such argument can be seen as originating in a disjunction scheme which, relying on the law of the excluded middle, claims that every problem proposed either is or is not an environmental problem. The discussants are then faced with the task of eliminating this disjunction by arguing for one of the disjuncts and against the other, just like in a debate.

If we look at the excerpt quoted here, we find that the three speakers do indeed choose the second route—that is, they choose to discuss particular environmental problems. Consequently, their first task is to find problems which are acceptable to all of them as environmental problems. Not surprisingly, we find that the ensuing discussion conforms to the expected logical pattern.

Speaker A proposes 'rivers' as a problem but says that he is uncertain—that is, the disjunction is not eliminated. In favor of rivers being a problem, he mentions that people protest, but at the same time he notices that the protest concerns electricity, something which is desirable for humans. He also expresses doubts as to whether fish are important enough to be a subject of protest, all of which makes him unable to eliminate the disjunction.

B comes to A's aid by pointing out that rivers are connected with the balance of nature and that construction in the rivers leads to animals not being able to cross them. This latter fact, he believes, influences the balance of nature. B also expresses a lack of knowledge and plays with the idea that the protesters are more concerned with animals than with humans, which again makes it difficult to eliminate the disjunction.

Next, C tries to show that rivers are environmental problems by saying that the planned constructions devastate the rivers. A clarifies this by pointing out that the rivers become dry, and C comments that they become 'little trickling brooks'. C continues by saying that both agricultural and inhabited areas are flooded by the construction of dams across rivers.

In summary, the initial steps of the discussion seem to have the following structure: The set task of discussing environmental problems is carried out by adopting the strategy of trying to find concrete instances of environmental problems. However, this strategy sets a second task of finding concrete instances which everybody can agree on. This task is carried out in turn using the law of the excluded middle: Every problem that is suggested either is or is not an environmental problem. A particular problem is found by attempting to strengthen the disjunction so that only one disjunct remains true.

It is important to notice that this is not the only possible procedure. The participants in the discussion do not need to presuppose that a given candidate for being a problem, in fact, is or is not a problem (i.e. presuppose the law of the excluded middle). It might be impossible to settle the problem. However, the participants do not use this option but seem to presuppose the law of the excluded middle.

The first problem proposed is that of rivers, but no conclusive evidence is found. The second speaker therefore shifts the topic to construction in rivers, but he is also unable to argue conclusively. The third speaker then contributes to the unfinished argument set up by the second speaker, offering better evidence that construction in rivers must be an environmental problem. The discussion thus exemplifies how, as in the debate excerpted here, speakers can use logic in structuring of discourse, not only individually but also jointly.

LOGICAL STRUCTURE ON INTERMEDIATE LEVELS

The logical structure that we have considered here did not really have global scope. Rather, it was a structure of an initial and intermediate kind used by the discussants to establish an example which would be compatible with the global purpose of the discussion. Another example of an intermediate structure, this time of even more limited scope, is provided when the discussants try to show that constructions in a river are a problem. Speaker C ventures the general statement that constructions in rivers lead to waste. Speaker A supports and exemplifies C's general statement, saying "Mm, dry." Speaker C is then able to come back, saying that rivers become trickling brooks. Thus, what we have here is a general conclusion made by C and supported by a concrete instance contributed by A and C together.

It is not difficult to point to other, similar examples of intermediate scope. A striking feature of many of them is that one structure is often nested into another, as in this case.

LOGICAL STRUCTURE WITHIN SINGLE UTTERANCES

I have mentioned earlier some of the problems connected with establishing the presence of logical inference in an utterance. Due to the difference in expectations generated by the purposes of the discussion and the debate, fewer of these problems are perhaps present in the debate than in the discussion. I therefore choose as an example speaker B's utterance in the discussion.

B begins by stating the conclusions he wants: 'another connection with the balance of nature'. In so doing, he leaves three assumptions implicit: (1) that he wants the connection in relation to rivers; (2) that he needs another connection, since the first one (the fish) was inconclusive; and (3) that such a conclusion would allow him to show that rivers are connected with an environmental problem. His arguments are as follows: There are animals who must cross rivers. When constructions are put in the rivers, the animals cannot cross and this influences the balance of nature. He continues by realizing that this argument would fail for the same reason as the first: Animals would become more important than humans, which would mean that even though the balance of nature were threatened, it might not be an environmental problem (implicitly for humans).

Schematically, the argument has the following form:

Premise 1:	Some animals must always cross these rivers.
Premise 2:	construction, expansion (of dams)
Conclusion 1:	The animals cannot cross.
Conclusion 2:	influence on the balance of nature
Conclusion 3:	environmental problem (implicit)
Premise 3:	think more about animals than humans
Conclusion 4:	no environmental problem (implicit)

We can now address the questions that were raised earlier. Is this an example of inference? I think it is. One indication of this is that when a step to a conclusion is to be taken, the word 'then' (*då*) occurs. A further question is whether the inference is of a logical kind (i.e., whether the conclusions are supposed to be true given that the premises are true. Again, I think the answer is clearly yes. We can also claim that B intends that both premises and conclusion should, in fact, be true. The description is intended not merely to preserve the truth of the premises (if there is any) but also to contain premises that are actually true.

The last question—whether the inference is valid as it stands—must be answered negatively. It needs implicit premises of the following type to become valid:

Explicit premise 1:	Some animals must always cross these rivers.
Explicit premise 2:	They are constructing dams in these rivers.
Implicit premise 1:	These dams prevent the animals from crossing.
Explicit conclusion 1:	The animals cannot cross these rivers.
Implicit premise 2:	If we are going to have a balance of nature which is uninfluenced, the animals must be able to cross.
Explicit conclusion 2:	The balance of nature is influenced (by the dams).
Implicit premise 3:	If something influences the balance of nature, then it is an environmental problem.
Implicit conclusion 1:	The dams are an environmental problem.
Implicit premise 4:	Environmental problems should concern humans.
Explicit premise 3:	We are concerned more with animals than with humans (in the dam problem).
Implicit conclusion 2:	Only if we care more about animals than humans is dam construction an environmental problem .... thus it is not an environmental problem.

By assuming four implicit premises, it thus seems possible to make B's argument more or less valid. The reader will note that the argument is still not fully explicit. Inserting implicit information only reduces indeterminancy but very seldom removes it totally. Since none of the explicit or assumed premises can be rejected as totally unreasonable, we can conclude that if we give the argument a charitable reading, it is neither incoherent nor unreasonable. Further, the assumptions made do not rely on any specific information pertaining to speaker B's background. Rather, they are generated merely by the wish to provide B with a valid argument that is as short as possible and yet more or less within the bounds of common sense. They therefore qualify as what was earlier called an attempt to perceive another speaker as a rational, motivated agent.

LOGIC AS NORMATIVE COMPETENCE

Let us return now to the question of what the relationship is between logic and spoken interaction. Significant parts of the formalizations of traditional logic provide shorthand formulae which, in an abstract and idealized way, characterize and clarify our intuitions about what the end result of an argument should be like in order to be truth-preserving. These intuitions about what an argument should be like to be valid, can be used not only to evaluate arguments but also to guide our reasoning when we want it to preserve truth.

The intuitions form an important part of what can be called the normative competence that individuals seem to possess with regard to logic. This competence is what makes them able, at least to some extent, to make judgements about whether a certain argument is logically valid or not. Because of it, they are also able to correct both their own and other people's arguments in order to increase the logical validity of the arguments. This does not mean that truth in itself is a normative concept. The normative element does not concern truth directly, but our attempts through mental or linguistic action to discover and preserve truth.

In other words, to claim that people have a logical normative competence is not to claim that they always argue logically. (As we have seen, they are often interested in other things besides logical argument, or they simply make mistakes.) Rather, it is merely to claim that people assent to logical norms when they are pointed out to them and that they spontaneously attempt to follow such norms when they are relevant.

I believe that a logical competence of this kind can be found in all human societies. It is hard to image human life in any of its present forms without some form of truth-preserving (i.e., logical) inference. The fact that some researchers (e.g., Fuglesang, 1983; Scribner, 1979; Vygotsky, 1978) seem to claim the contrary is, I think, a result of neglecting the factors I have mentioned earlier which, besides logic, influence actual argumentation.

However, saying that logic plays a role in spontaneous argumentation in no way precludes the notion that, through schooling and other types of training, we can improve our intuitions about logical validity, as well as our ability to see and follow the logic of an argument. On the contrary, whether logical competence is rooted in our genetic makeup or merely a very basic cultural product, there is no reason to deny the role of schooling as a means to learn to focus on logical abilities. What perhaps is not least important is that such training can make us willing to consider the logical structure of an argument as a relevant focus of attention.

In my opinion, it is primarily the lack of training in focussing on logical structures per se which shows up in the results obtained by the above-mentioned researchers. If supplementary studies were made of indigenous argumentation, with due attention to the factors mentioned earlier, I am sure the results would show plentiful use of logical inference (cf. Franker, 1983). At the same time, the view of logic as normative competence is largely compatible with the view that people use mental models in their thinking. In fact, the views become totally compatible if we regard both logic and mental models as ways of making reasoning isomorphic with reality. The only difference is that traditional logic operates on a more general and abstract level than the mental models approach.

Reasoning with a mental model can be viewed as a concrete application of an abstract logical pattern. The pattern itself need not become manifest for the person who is following it, at least not as long as it is being followed. But if he or she is concerned with truth preservation and deviates from what is logically sound and, furthermore, becomes aware of the deviation, then he or she, if I am right about the pervasive normative status of logic, will then wish to correct his or her reasoning.

What I am claiming is that people are oriented toward logical norms, and what I intend by this concept can be operationally characterized as follows:

1. *Conformity with the norm.* Whenever it is relevant, people can be expected to use inferential structures which are compatible with logical requirements.
2. *Normative judgements of deviance.* Whenever it is relevant, people can be expected to be able to judge everyday arguments as correct or incorrect from a logical point of view.
3. *Self- and other-correction.* Whenever it is relevant and possible, people can be expected to correct logical errors (or to be so inclined) that they recognize in their own or other people's arguments. An important restriction, especially on correcting others, is that the correction should not prevent the speaker from attaining goals he or she might value more highly than logical coherence. For example, one would hesitate to tell one's boss that he or she was illogical even if one thought so.

These criteria are also applicable to other types of claims to a normative orientation, such as grammatical or ethical claims. The expression, 'orientation toward a norm', is used rather than the expression 'follow a norm' in order to eschew any suggestion that logical rules could be part of the actual mechanism whereby inference and arguments are produced in spoken interaction. The only claim that is made is that logical norms provide goals with which speakers want the end result of their arguments to be compatible. The term 'orient' is also used to indicate that sometimes logical norms are not followed. Mistakes are made, and if they are discovered, both judgements of deviance and self- and other-correction play an important role. This term is also used to indicate that following logical norms is a context-sensitive process, since logical inference is not always relevant. For example, in certain types of jokes or in highly emotional discourse, the preservation of truth can be almost irrelevant. Finally, 'orient' has been chosen to indicate tacit disagreement with those who want to give logical inference an even stronger position than the one for which I have been arguing in this chapter. We can make connections and associations which are not based on logical inference, and we can sensibly make use of such connections in spoken interaction with other people. I see no reason to believe that all such connections are actually based on logical inference, even if this probably is the case if one wants a guarantee that new information with certainty can be generated from old. To derive something with certainty is not the same thing as meaningfully connecting two pieces of information.

CONCLUSIONS

The claims in the present chapter can be summarized in the following points:

(1) Significant parts of traditional logic explicate normative intuitions about what an argument should be like in order to be truth-preserving. Valid formulae are seen as representing, in an abstract and idealized way, some of the semantic properties of ordinary language that are relevant for truth preservation. The formulae can also be seen as idealized versions of logical goals that speakers make use of in judging and correcting both their own and other speakers' arguments. I have argued that the ability to carry out operations of this kind is a consequence of a logical normative competence that humans in general possess.

(2) In studying spoken interaction, the logical structure of an inference is not directly discernible. Truth preservation is normally only one of several concerns that a speaker has to express, which means that some parts of the discourse might be irrelevant from the point of view of logical inference. It also means that the same expression will sometimes have both an inferential and a non-inferential function. Finally, it means that the order in which an argument is presented is often different from the order which is used in elementary textbooks on logic. Another source of opaqueness is the fact that speakers rely to a great extent on implicit information in making inferences.

(3) The logical structures which are relevant to spoken interaction have different scopes. Some structures have global scope—that is, they are relevant to the whole interaction. Other structures can be found on various intermediate levels, and still others cover only a single utterance or part of an utterance. When an argument or an inference structure is relevant to more than a single utterance, it is often contributed to by several speakers, so that it becomes in effect, a collective achievement. The same logical structure can thus serve as an orientational standard for several speakers, either in jointly building up an argument or in finding relevant arguments against each other. In this sense, logical norms function as a sort of invisible hand for the inferential aspects of spoken discourse.

(4) The logical structure of an argument can often be related to the purpose of the argument. Hence, if the purpose is known, it is sometimes possible, by a priori analysis, to predict what type of inference pattern should be used. For argument patterns which have a global scope, we might therefore be able to predict differences in overall logical structure between different types of spoken interaction. For argument patterns of a less global scope, we will probably find that they recur as constituents of arguments from one type of spoken interaction to another.

REFERENCES

Allwood, J. *Linguistic communication as action and cooperation* (Gothenburgh Monographs in Linguistics No. 2). Göteborg: University of Göteborg, Department of Linguistics, 1976.

Allwood, J. Power and communication. In J. Allwood & M. Ljung (Eds.), *Alvar—A Festschrift to Alvar Ellegård.* Stockholm: University of Stockholm, Department of English, 1980.

Allwood, J. Finns det svenska kommunikationsmönster? In *Vad är svensk kultur?* (Papers in Anthropological Linguistics No. 9). Göteborg: University of Göteborg, Department of Linguistics, 1982.

Allwood, J., Andersson, L. G., & Dahl, Ö. *Logic in linguistics.* Cambridge: Cambridge University Press.

Franker, G. *Syllogismer.* University of Goteborg: Department of Linguistics, 1983.

Fuglesang, A. *About Understanding.* Uppsala: The Dag Hammarsköld Foundation, 1983.

Goldkühl, G. *Informationssystem och bergreppet formellt verksamhetsspråk.* Stockholm: Stockholm University, Institute för ADB, 1982.

Hagert, G., & Hansson, Å. Logic modelling of cognitive reasoning. In *Proceedings of the Eighth International Joint Conference on Artificial Intelligence,* Vol. 1. Karlsruhe, West Germany, 8–10 August 1983.

Hodges, W. *Logic.* Harmondsworth: Penguin.

Johnson-Laird, P. N. Models of deduction. In R. C. Falmaque (Ed.), *Reasoning: representation and process.* Hillsdale, NJ: Erlbaum.

Kowalsky, R. A. *Logic for problem solving*. North Holland: Elsevier, 1979.
Levinson, S. Activity types and language. In *Linguistics 1979*, Vol. 17. The Hague: Mouton, 1979.
Lindhart, J. *Retorik*. Copenhagen: Berlingske, 1975.
Resnick, M. *Elementary logic*. New York: McGraw-Hill, 1970.
Scribner, S. Modes of thinking and ways of speaking. In *Culture and logic reconsidered: New directions in discourse processing*. New York: Norwood, 1979.
Thomason, R. H. *Symbolic logic*. London: Macmillan, 1970.
Vygotsky, L. *Mind in society*. Cambridge, MA: Harvard University Press.
Wittgenstein, L. *Philosophical investigations*. Oxford: Blackwell, 1953.

4

On Implicit Assumptions in Reasoning

G. HAGERT
Computing Science Department
Uppsala University

Y. WAERN
Department of Psychology
University of Stockholm

INTRODUCTION

Studies of human reasoning processes have a long tradition in psychology, and formal logic has provided the major model of the human mind's ability to reason and make inferences. Nevertheless, several authors have questioned the relationship between human reasoning and formal logic. Their major concern has been to raise such issues as: Is formal logic (in some version) a plausible model of the human mind's ability to draw and check inferences? Can logic be used to model *any* aspect of human reasoning? Naturally, such general questions address several other aspects of reasoning besides logic. For instance, can a reasoning process be described in terms of the application and use of syntactical, domain-independent rules of inference? Can a human reasoner understand a logical connective, such as ($\wedge$), in the way a truth table postulates? Evidently, there are many specific issues that could be (and have been) addressed.

There is a very straightforward and simple answer to the first general question regarding formal logic. It is *no*. That is, logic is not a plausible

ISBN 0-12-512320-5

model of cognitive reasoning, at least not if we only consider different types of performance measures such as yes–no answers. Such measures do not, of course, contain any information about how the particular answer came about.

A plausible, but maybe too simple, interpretation of observations using these basic measures is that our minds are not equipped with anything that has the same characteristics as formal logic. Alternatively, it might be possible to hold the view that either logical rules of inference do not exist or that premises are understood in a manner quite incongruent with the logical demands of a given task. These two approaches to the problem were first pointed out by Henle (1962). Although Smedslund (1970) argues that it is impossible to determine whether the rules are missing or the understanding of premises differs, this reasoning is valid only for a certain kind of empirical data—namely, those produced by subjects who either judge a set of premises or produce conclusions from them. Henle (1962) and Evans (1972), among others, have tried to avoid this circularity by designing experiments in such a way that information about these factors is obtained. They found that subjects interpreted premises in different ways. For a valid conclusion, however, only one interpretation (defined by the experimenter) was acceptable.

There is still no consensus about where to place logic in human thinking, but the current trend seems to favour an approach based on our understanding of premises. One example of this 'non-logical' trend is the work of Johnson-Laird (1980, 1981) and his associates. On the basis of their studies on syllogistic reasoning, spatial reasoning, and other task domains, they propose that domain-independent rules do not exist. These authors also claim that a propositional format is (in any case) an inadequate characterization of the representational processes involved in human cognition. Instead, they propose that reasoners develop a mental model of a task when confronted by a set of premises. On this view, inferences are then generated by manipulating the model, but not according to rules which are independent of content or domain.

In this chapter we do not use the notion of a mental model in the way proposed by Johnson-Laird and his associates. Instead, we shall explore the notion of a propositional model. Briefly, such a model corresponds to the activated part of a propositional network (see Anderson, 1976) that can be manipulated by different types of operations, including a subset of formal rules of inference. Thus, our basic hypothesis is that there exist domain-independent rules of inference which correspond to a subject of rules that can be found in formal logic. However, inferences are generated both from the sentences making up a task and from the sentences and assumptions introduced by reasoners themselves through the process of encoding and understanding. If these implicit assumptions are not made explicit to an observer, they can change the reasoning process in such a way that the resulting inference might look incorrect. An elaboration of this idea can be found in Hagert, Waern, and Tärnlund (1982).

In the present study we focus on some theoretical and empirical work on conditional reasoning, In particular, we will discuss a task in which three premises are presented. Two of them are conditionals, and one is a factual premise. The task is to generate inferences from this set. The following example is shown in sentential form

$$p \rightarrow q$$
$$r \rightarrow s$$
$$\neg s$$

where $\neg$ means negation and $\rightarrow$ means material implication. This is the type of task that we will analyze and discuss. However, we want to emphasize that the basic hypothesis to be examined and illustrated can be applied to other reasoning tasks as well (see Hagert & Hansson, 1983).

There are five remaining sections in this chapter. The first contains a simple and rather informal example of the main ideas that will be explored in detail. The reasoning domain is presented in the second section. In the third section we present steps towards a production system that operates according to the basic ideas in the particular domain we have chosen. A preliminary empirical study on human reasoning in this task domain is given in the fourth section to provide the simulation model with some psychological background, and to show how it could be developed further. Finally, we offer a few summarizing remarks.

AN INFORMAL ILLUSTRATION

In this section we introduce a few general aspects of the concept under study. We begin with a simple example, followed by a hypothetical line of reasoning. Consider the following set of premises concerning a Swedish tennis player named Borg:

> If Borg plays against Connors in Wimbledon, he will win. If he plays against McEnroe, he will lose. As we know, he lost. So, what can be said?

This example has a similar structure to that given earlier—that is, two conditional sentences and one factual premise. Now consider the following two inferences:

Borg did not play against Conners.
Borg played against McEnroe.

It is obvious that this task contains a lot of semantic information that needs to be interpreted. But let us continue the informal illustration. Suppose you cannot remember what happened that year, or suppose you do not know anything about tennis. You then have to do some reasoning. Which inference would you prefer? Are they both valid?

If losing is the negation of winning, then the first inference is valid. The second inference, however, is known as the fallacy of affirming the consequent (Wason & Johnson-Laird, 1972). But what is wrong with the following line of reasoning?

> Borg lost, and losing means not winning. Well, suppose that he played against Connors or against McEnroe and we know that it is impossible to both win and lose. Then he obviously didn't play against Connors, so therefore he played against McEnroe. That's all.

This approach generates both of the inferences given above. As we noticed there, only the first inference was valid. However, a closer look at this short line of reasoning shows that the second inference is also valid, given the details of the line of reasoning just presented. Let us rewrite the task in simple sentential format and then try to show that both inferences are equally valid:

$$p \rightarrow q \tag{1}$$
$$r \rightarrow s \tag{2}$$
$$s \tag{3}$$

Let q stand for 'Borg wins' and s for 'Borg loses'. The reasoner first notices that losing implies not winning:

$$s \rightarrow \neg q \tag{4}$$

The reasoner then introduces the assumption that either Borg plays against Conors (denoted by p), or he plays against McEnroe (denoted by r). If we use $\vee$ to mean a disjunction, we can represent this assumption as:

$$p \wedge r \tag{5}$$

Let us use three simple inference rules. They are sometimes called *modus ponendo ponens* $((p \wedge (p \rightarrow q)) \rightarrow q)$, *modus tollendo tollens* $((\neg q \wedge (p \rightarrow q)) \rightarrow \neg p)$, and *modus tollendo ponens* $((\neg p \wedge (p \vee q)) \rightarrow q)$. Using the sentential representation and these rules of inference, we can reproduce the line of reasoning as follows:

	Reason	*Premise*
1:	(3)	s
2:	(4)	$s \rightarrow \neg q$

3: modus ponendo ponens on 1: and 2:	$\neg q$
4: (1)	$p \rightarrow q$
5: modus tollendo tollens on 3: and 4:	$\neg p$
6: (5)	$p \vee r$
7: modus tollendo ponens on 5: and 6:	r

We have thus shown that $s \rightarrow r$, or, if we make a substitution, "If Borg lost, he played against McEnroe." We have also shown that by this line of reasoning, the apparently invalid inference was made valid, because the reasoner introduced additional premises.

In short, our thesis is that there can be a number of implicit assumptions in a reasoning process that can give rise to a line of reasoning quite different from what can be expected if only the set of external premises is taken into account. Thus, such implicit assumptions have to be considered before one can tell if an inference is valid or not. Two more aspects worth mentioning from this illustration are that (1) each premise was understood correctly, and (2) each step in the reasoning process was produced by a valid rule of inference.

DEMARCATION AND ANALYSIS OF A REASONING DOMAIN

In the following section we define a reasoning task which we will use to develop further the ideas in this section and the next. In particular, we will exemplify the notion of a propositional network and the spreading of activation (see Anderson, 1976). We will continue to use a type of reasoning task in which a set of three premises is given one of which is a factual premise. The other two premises are constructed as material implications. The goal is to draw one or more inferences from the set of premises.

The content of the tasks that we examine in the rest of this chapter is based on concepts that people use to describe football matches—concepts like playing at home, playing as visitors, winning, and losing. An example of this domain is:

> If A plays as visitors against B, A will lose. If A plays at home against C, A will not lose. A did not play as visitors against B.

We can rewrite this text in a predicate form that we will use from now on (IMP means →, or materials implication):

C1	(IMP (PLAYVISI A B)(LOSE A B))
C2	(IMP (PLAYHOME A C)(NOT (LOSE A C)))
C3	(NOT (PLAYVISI A B))

We call C1 and C2 premises. A premise is composed of at least two propositions which are related by a connective. Thus, the premise C1 is composed of two propositions (PLAYVISI A B) and (LOSE A B), which in turn are connected by IMPlication. Hence, C3 is a proposition. It is also the case that two premises that are related by a predicate or a connective—for example, (OR C1 C2)—also constitute a premise.

In short, propositions are units of representation. They can be interrelated to each other by either (1) predicates or arguments, or (2) connectives. These connections in turn form a propositional network. We can summarize this representational scheme as follows:

1. A proposition is a knowledge structure of the form (predicate argument1 argument2 . . .). Examples: (PLAYVISI A B or LOSE A B).
2. A premise is a knowledge structure of the form (connective proposition1 proposition2 . . .) or (connective premise1 premise2). Examples: (IMP (PLAYVISI A B)(LOSE A B)) or (OR (IMP (PLAYVISI A B)(LOSE A B))(IMP (PLAYHOME A C)(NOT (LOSE A C)))).
3. A propositional network is a knowledge structure in which propositions and premises are interrelated through common predicates and arguments.

We will also use the following convention: Suppose that P1 is the proposition (PLAYVISI A B) and P2 is (LOSE A B). We can then make C1 (IMP P1 P2). Thus, (OR C1 C2) is equivalent to a premise connecting two other premises, C1 and C2, and C1 is equivalent to a premise connecting two propositions, P1 and P2. Figure 4.1 gives a graphical example of the notation we have chosen. As can be seen, each proposition corresponds to a node, and the links to relations between the nodes.

The reason for constructing this rather complex set of propositions was that we wanted to study the interaction between propositions in the text and

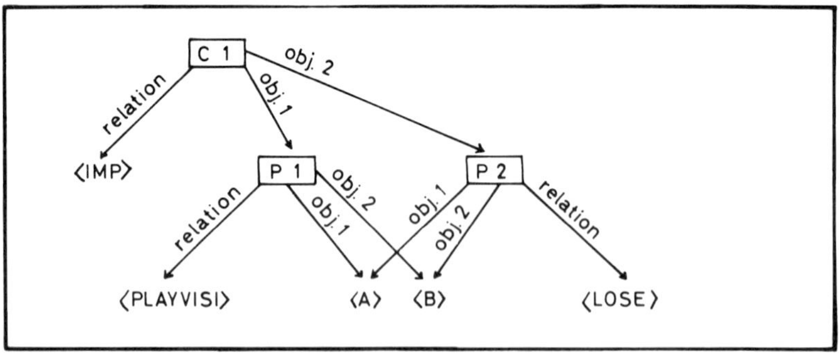

Figure 4.1. A propositional network based on sentence C1.

the network activated in and from long-term memory. In particular, we wanted to study and analyze whether and how reasoners create additional assumptions when confronted with a reasoning task. Making the task complex with respect to its semantic content can increase the possibility that these processes will show up. We also wanted to propose a reasoning task that would make it possible for the process of reasoning to last for at least a couple of minutes. A detailed task analysis can be found in Hagert et al.

FORMULATING THE HYPOTHESES IN A PRODUCTION SYSTEM

In order to specify and test our hypotheses, we now present a number of steps that we have taken towards constructing a computer model. As a means for doing so, we used a production system language (Newell, 1973) to test a propositional network. This approach is in line with work by Anderson (1976), in the form of the Act theory, and with the Prism language developed by Langley and Neches (1981) for simulating learning processes.

Let us briefly review the basic characteristics of production systems (Newell, 1973). A production is a rule of the form:

$$\text{Condition} \rightarrow \text{Action}$$

meaning that if the condition is satisfied, the action can be performed. A set of productions is stored in production memory. The condition side is matched against information held in a second memory that corresponds to an activated portion of a propositional network. A production is applicable if all of its conditions are satisfied by the activated network. Thus, the model we are building consists of a production memory, a working memory, and a propositional network. The production memory holds the procedural knowledge in the form of production rules, whereas the network contains the declarative knowledge (Anderson, 1976), of which the working memory is an activated part. The rules in the production memory only modify information that is in the working memory—that is, the active portion of the network. This structure is similar to that of the Act and Prism production system languages.

One of the reasons for choosing this type of production system architecture is that it allows for a distinction between declarative and procedural knowledge (the latter for manipulating the former). As was clear from the informal illustration given earlier, we claim that reasoning is a process in which knowledge plays a crucial role. The reasoner's personal knowledge and beliefs are introduced through implicit assumptions about the premises that make up a task. We propose that such knowledge is encoded in a declarative manner and brought into the line of reasoning by means of rules that are encoded procedurally.

Other aspects of this production system architecture will be brought into the discussion as we present more details about the model. We will discuss three parts of the design. They concern issues about three components of the reasoning process that we find especially important:

Interpretational Issues

In the preceding section we defined a reasoning domain and gave a format for representing tasks in that domain. In developing the model, we shall focus on other issues related to representation. For instance, what knowledge is available for a human reasoner, and how can it be brought into the reasoning process?

Imagine a reasoner who has the following propositions stored in long-term memory:

```
B1        (EQUIV (PLAYVISI TEAM1 TEAM2)
                 (PLAYHOME TEAM2 TEAM1))
B2        (EQUIV (WIN TEAM1 TEAM2)
                 (LOSE TEAM2 TEAM1))
B3     (OPPOSITE (PLAYVISI TEAM1 TEAM2)
                 (PLAYHOME TEAM1 TEAM2))
B4     (OPPOSITE (WIN TEAM1 TEAM2)
                 (LOSE TEAM1 TEAM2))
```

EQUIV is a connective that denotes an equivalence (or iff). B1 is a belief or knowledge structure that states: A team (or someone) is playing as visitors against another team (TEAM2) if and only if that team (TEAM2) is playing at home against the first team (TEAM1). B4 is a belief that states: The opposite of winning is losing. These knowledge structures could be available for a human reasoner. Notice that the predicate OPPOSITE is not a connective in the formal sense.

In Figure 4.2a, we depict the belief embedded in B1. If the reasoner now reads the first premise in the example text, it could be related to the belief structure in B1 as follows (see also Figure 4.2b): When propositions P1 and P2 are read, they are encoded and stored in working memory. When common elements are identified, P1 and P2 are assimilated. These processes (encoding and assimilating) are generated by a spreading activation mechanism. That is, knowledge in the propositional network is activated if the encoding process generates propositions that share elements with that knowledge structure. In our example, the propositions share the predicate PLAYVISI.

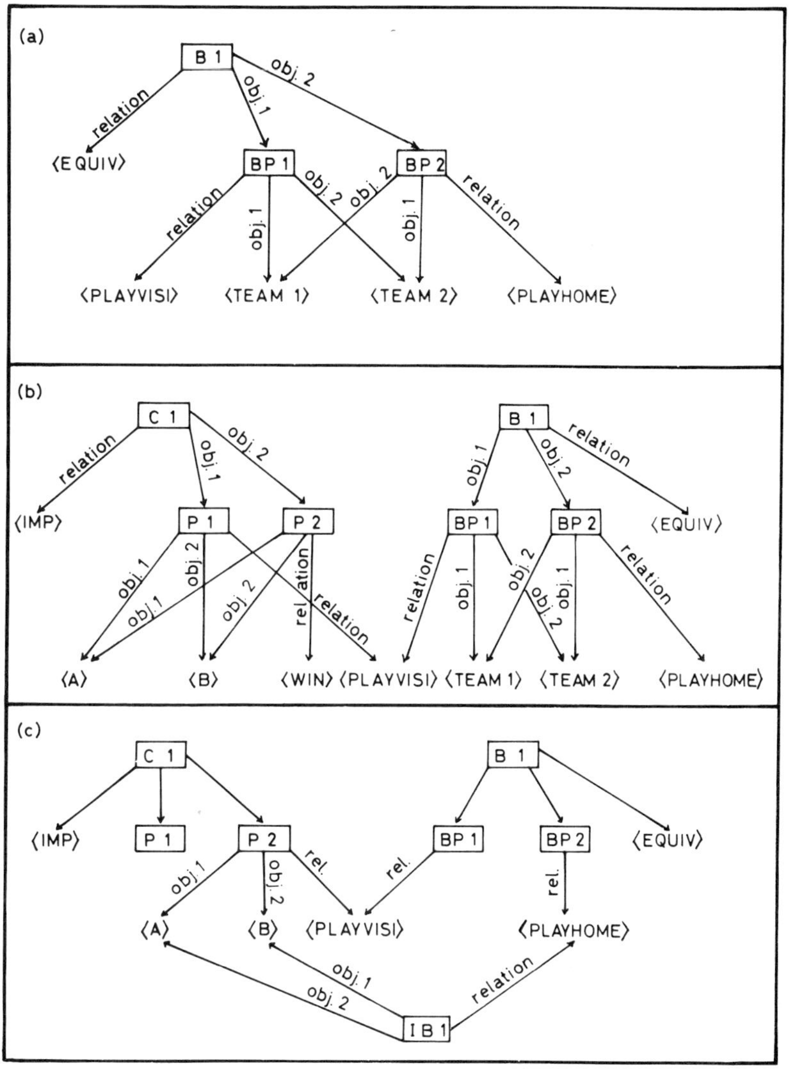

Figure 4.2. (a) A propositional network showing the relation between playing at home and as visitors. (b) A network in which the first premise, C1, has been encoded. (c) The resulting network if rule 1 is applied to (b).

Suppose further that there is a heuristic available that can use the activated portion of the network. This heuristic is encoded as a production rule. Each symbol beginning with '=' is a variable that can be bound to any symbol structure that has the same syntax as the symbol in which the variable is found. We give the rule in English:

> Interpretational Rule 1
>
> IF
> There is a proposition (=predicate1 =arg1 =arg2), and an activated premise that says that the proposition is EQUIValent to another proposition (=predicate2 =arg3 =arg4), and there are common elements in the proposition and the premise, and the goal is to make an interpretation,
> THEN
> Add to the network a new proposition in which the old proposition is modified according to the premise.

We call this type of heuristic 'interpretational rules', since they try to relate available knowledge to the new information in the task. Panel Figure 4.2c shows how the network in 4.2b is modified if Rule 1 is applied in that knowledge state. Thus, the process of assimilation consists of the activation (Figure 4.2b) and creation (Figure 4.2c) of the propositional network.

One of the conditions in this rule is the goal of making an interpretation. This goal concerns a particular proposition that has been encoded and related to others and that is now about to be further assimilated through, for example, a heuristic like Rule 1 or like the rule that follows (we return to the goals in the subsection on strategies):

> Interpretational Rule 2
>
> IF
> There is a negated proposition (NOT (=predicate1 =arg1 =arg2)), and an activated premise that says that (=predicate1 =arg3 =arg4) is OPPOSITE to another proposition (=predicate2 =ar35 =ar46), and there are common elements in the proposition and the premise, and the goal is to make an interpretation,
> THEN
> Add to the network a new proposition (=predicate2 =arg1 =arg2).

This rule is somewhat different from Rule 1. The difference is that this one has a condition in which a proposition is negated. For example, suppose there is a proposition, (NOT (PLAYHOME A B)), in the net. There should also be a belief active in working memory, (OPPOSITE (PLAYHOME TEAM1 TEAM2)(PLAYVISI TEAM1 TEAM2)), in order for the rule to be satisfied. Applying Rule 2 in a situation where this information is active (and given the right goal) would create the proposition (PLAYVISI A B). Other ways of interpreting a negation are discussed in Hagert et al. (1982).

The goal of making an interpretation means that an encoded proposition and activated knowledge are related. Another type of goal concerns a set of propositions, as in a premise, for example. This goal means that an assumption is introduced on the basis of an encoded premise and stored beliefs. The following is an example of such a heuristic:

Interpretational Rule 3

IF
There is a premise (IMP (=predicate1 =arg1 =arg2) (=predicate2 =arg3 =arg4)), and two activated premises saying that =predicate3 is the OPPOSITE to =predicate1 and =predicate4 is the OPPOSITE to =predicate2, and the goal is to make an assumption,
THEN
Assume and add to the network a new premise (IMP (=predicate3 = arg1 =arg2)(=predicate4 =arg3 =arg4)).

Suppose that the network contains the following propositions:

C1	(IMP (PLAYVISI A B)(LOSE A B))
B3	(OPPOSITE (PLAYVISI TEAM1 TEAM2) (PLAYHOME TEAM1 TEAM2))
B4	(OPPOSITE (WIN TEAM1 TEAM2) (LOSE TEAM1 TEAM2))

If the current goal is to make an assumption, Rule 3 could be used to generate:

(IMP (PLAYHOME A B)(WIN A B))

which is a premise containing the opposite propositions to the ones in C1. Thus, given "If A plays as visitors against B, they will lose" and the beliefs B3 and B4, it might be assumed that "If A plays at home against B, they will win."

Following is another example of a heuristic that can be used given the goal of making an assumption about a set of propositions. This rule makes an assumption about the task as a whole. It introduces a premise which says that at least one of the antecedents must be true if they have common elements:

Interpretational Rule 4

IF
There are two active premises such that each connect two propositions through an IMPlication, and with the

propositions =prop1 and =prop2 as antecedents, respectively,
and =prop1 and =prop2 have common elements, and the goal
is to make an assumption,
THEN
Assume and add to the net the premise (OR =prop1 =prop2).

For example, given the two premises C1 and C2, this rule would create the following new premise:

(OR (PLAVISI A B)(PLAYHOME A C))

In short, interpretation issues concern the way in which different sources of knowledge can be related to the text through a process of understanding or assimilation. We suggest that propositions and premises in the text are encoded and related to knowledge in long-term memory. It is also possible to create new propositions and premises during this process of understanding. The heuristics for doing this are readily available. Of course it should be emphasized that individual differences exist in terms of both knowledge sources and interpretational heuristics.

Inferential Capabilities

As stated earlier, we propose a small set of classical rules of inference. In the design so far, we have been experimenting with three simple rules. The best known is given below:

Inference Rule 1

IF
There is a premise (IMP =proposition1 =proposition2),
and =proposition1 is known to be true, and a goal
(GOAL MAKE INFERENCE),
THEN
Infer and add to net that =proposition2 is true.

This rule is also known as modus ponens. Its goal is discussed in the next paragraph.

It might be objected that there is no obvious difference between understanding a premise and drawing an inference from it. As we have presented these processes, however, there are differences. The process of understanding involves both the activation of knowledge in a propositional network and heuristics for relating that knowledge to the encoded text. Although this process also involves heuristics for creating assumptions about the text, nothing is actually done to the truth-value of the assumptions. Inference rules, by contrast, try to generate propositions (or premises) that can be regarded as true or false, given a certain interpretation. As exemplified, these rules are independent of content, whereas interpretational heuristics sometimes contain conditions that refer to content, so that their utility depends on the knowledge and beliefs that a particular reasoner has acquired. The two processes that we have discussed so far should not be regarded as serial; rather, they interact during a reasoning attempt much as Hayes and Simon (1974) propose in the UNDERSTAND program.

Strategic Issues

Two reasoners who share the same knowledge and the same inference rules, and who understand a particular text in the same way, may nevertheless process inferential tasks differently. The reason is that they may not share the same strategy. In this type of task, strategy is conceived of as a set of rules about how to read, interpret, and make inferences from a given text. For example, is the factual proposition read first, or are the propositions encoded from the beginning of the text? Are assumptions introduced during reading, or after the whole text has been read? When is an inference made? These are all questions that concern the reasoning strategy.

We suggest that it is possible to capture some of these differences in terms of goals. Thus, we regard a reasoning strategy as composed of a set of goals to be resolved. These goals can contain subgoals that concern either the text or interpretations of it. Since the task consists of making inferences, the primary goal is (GOAL MAKE INFERENCE). This goal can be attained in several ways. We now briefly describe two quite different strategies.

Consider the following abstract goal structure:

```
1   (GOAL MAKE INFERENCE)
2     (GOAL MAKE ASSUMPTION)
3       (GOAL MAKE INTERPRETATION)
4         (GOAL READ TEXT)
4         (TEXT ENCODED)
3       (PREMISE ADDED-TO-NET)
2     (PREMISE ASSUMED)
1   (INFERENCE MADE)
```

The first goal has already been mentioned. The second and third goals refer to processes in which interpretational heuristics are applied. The difference corresponds to that between interpreting a proposition and making an assumption about a set of propositions. Finally, all of these goals depend on the fact that the text has to be read and encoded.

The subgoals described here can be utilized in different ways. As they appear above, they correspond to a strategy that corresponds roughly to a backward, or means–ends, method. That is, to make an inference, one needs to assume something. First, however, the text has to be interpreted, and this can only be accomplished when a premise has been read.

Another way of setting goals is:

```
1    (GOAL MAKE INFERENCE)
4       (GOAL READ TEXT)
4       (TEXT ENCODED)
3       (GOAL MAKE INTERPRETATION)
3       (PREMISE ADDED-TO-NET)
2       (GOAL MAKE ASSUMPTION)
2       (PREMISE ASSUMED)
1    (INFERENCE MADE)
```

This strategy is forward-oriented. Its first goal is to read a premise rather than make an assumption. As can be seen, the goals are executed in the same order, but they are not established in the same order.

Goal-structures refer to the interaction between text, knowledge, and inferences. However, the process also depends on how a reasoner utilizes the premises in a text. We can therefore describe a reasoning strategy as being composed of an inference strategy (such as the two examples shown earlier) and an attentional, or reading, strategy. That is, a reasoner might attend to different parts of the text in trying to derive an inference.

To read a text, a reasoner must first choose a premise:

```
4    (GOAL READ TEXT)
5       (GOAL READ PREMISE)
5       (PREMISE READ)
4    (TEXT ENCODED)
```

One example of choosing among sentences is:

```
6    (GOAL READ FACTUAL-PREMISE)
6    (FACTUAL-PREMISE READ)
7    (GOAL READ FIRST-PREMISE)
7    (FIRST-PREMISE READ)
8    (GOAL READ SECOND-PREMISE)
8    (SECOND-PREMISE READ)
```

We have discussed the interaction between reading, interpreting, and inferring in strategic terms. This discussion leads to a brief analysis of both inference and reading strategies. It should be emphasized that our analysis is abstract—that is, we have not discussed how the strategies can be executed, nor how the goals of inference and reading interact.

This section has presented some of the design issues being developed in our model. A preliminary program that is able to reason according to the ideas presented here has been constructed. Its mechanisms are sufficient for producing a line of reasoning in which several propositions are introduced. Thus, a number of implicit assumptions underlie its inferences.

PSYCHOLOGICAL RELEVANCE: PROTOCOL ANALYSES

The purpose of this section is to illustrate the hypotheses we have discussed so far by analyzing a few protocol fragments obtained from one subject performing different tasks. The subject was a psychology student with no prior experience in working with tasks of logic. All of the tasks had the structure presented earlier (p. 95) but differed in content. The premises presented to the subject contained the names of Swedish football teams. In the following we use the symbols A, B, and C instead of the names. The subject was asked to 'think aloud' during the reasoning process.

We will analyze some fragments of the think-aloud protocols in order to illustrate our suggestions for interpretations, inferences, and strategies. We have chosen protocols which contain information about the processes behind the inferences (not all protocols do) and which illustrate the use of some different interpretation rules and inference strategies. Some of these fragments are discussed in a different frame of reference in Hagert et al. (1982).

Observation 1

The following excerpt constitutes the basis for the first observation in the list below.

F1	if A plays as visitors against B
F2	then A loses
F3	if A plays at home against C
F4	then A won't lose
F5	A didn't play as visitors against B
F6	didn't play as visitors against B
F7	yes according to the first sentence
F8	A would probably win then
F9	if they play at all
F10	if A plays at home against C
F11	then A won't lose
F12	that has nothing to do with this

This excerpt indicates a strategy in which each conditional premise is considered in isolation, together with the factual premise.

There are two inferences in these fragments. They are found in comments F8 and F12. A tentative explanation of the process behind the first inference could be that the subject had interpreted the material implication in F1 and F2 as an equivalence. In that case, the subject should have generated something like "A should not have lost against B." Instead, he says, "According to the first sentence, A would probably win," which is not in accordance with an explanation based on equivalence.

Let us suppose that the subject understood the connective as a material implication. If the subject has interpreted the first and third sentence and rejected the second, his understanding might have been:

1:	(IMP PLAYVISI A B)(LOSE A B))	F1 and F2
2:	(NOT (PLAYVISI A B))	F5 and F6
3:	(IMP (PLAYHOME A B)(WIN A B))	Assumption
4:	(OR (PLAYHOME A B)(PLAYVISI A B))	Assumption

This could be a rough picture of the subject's understanding in this protocol. It is also important to consider how such an understanding can be established. Is there any evidence for processes involving interpretational heuristics? As can be seen in the protocol, there are no direct fragments in which an interpretation is made. Nevertheless, the process behind the understanding could have been composed of a few states that we now describe briefly.

Suppose that when the propositions in 1: and 2: were encoded, they activated the following:

(OPPOSITE (PLAYHOME TEAM1 TEAM2)
(PLAYVISI TEAM1 TEAM2))
(OPPOSITE (LOSE TEAM1 TEAM2)(WIN TEAM1 TEAM2))

If the goal is to make an assumption and Rule 3 is used, it will create, on the basis of these beliefs:

(IMP (PLAYHOME A B)(WIN A B))

and Rule 4 will create:

(OR (PLAYHOME A B)(PLAYVISI A B))

The inference follows naturally from this understanding. That is, from the set of premises in which two additional assumptions (3: and 4:) have been introduced, the inference, "According to the first sentence, A would probably win," is perfectly valid and understandable. Of course, this explanation differs from the one based on a misunderstanding of the connective. It should be pointed out that the data in the think-aloud fragment are too meager to support each step suggested.

We turn now to the second inference. F9 indicates a questioning of the result arrived at so far. This can be interpreted as a shift in attention toward the next premise, which is then attended to in F10. Comment F12 gives further support to the interpretation that the subject considers only one premise at a time. Thus, the second premise becomes relevant only if the first premise is no longer being considered.

Observation 2

The first sentence to read in this task is, "If A does not play as visitors against B, then B would not win." The following excerpt shows a protocol generated by the same subject:

F1 if A doesn't play as visitors against B
F2 okay we can remake that into
F3 A plays at home against B
F4 then B won't win
F5 but then A wins

This segment is a clear illustration of Rule 2. We can give two simple instantiations of that rule. The first is:

```
if
(NOT (PLAYVISI A B))
(OPPOSITE (PLAYVISI TEAM1 TEAM2)
                    (PLAYHOME TEAM1 TEAM2))
(GOAL MAKE INTERPRETATION)
then
(PLAYHOME A B)
```

The second instantiation is:

```
if
(NOT (WIN B A))
(OPPOSITE (WIN TEAM1 TEAM2)(LOSE TEAM1 TEAM2))
(GOAL MAKE INTERPRETATION)
then
(LOSE B A)
```

The final interpretation in F5 is then generated through Rule 1:

```
if
(LOSE B A)
(EQUIV (LOSE TEAM1 TEAM2)(WIN TEAM2 TEAM1)
(GOAL MAKE INTERPRETATION)
then
(WIN A B)
```

The subject has thus created a completely new premise than can be compared to the first sentence above: "If A plays at home against B, A will win." Notice, however, that this premise was created in quite a different manner than that in the first protocol. In the present protocol, the new premise was introduced by an interpretation of the negation. In the first protocol, the new premise was introduced through an assumption.

It is interesting to note that in both of the protocols discussed here, the subject shifted attention between reading, interpreting, and assuming. In the first task, the subject read through the text before any interpretation showed up. In the second task, however, he started immediately to interpret the first proposition.

Observation 3

The protocol in the following excerpt is an example of a strategy in which the conditionals are treated one at a time. In F6–F9, the first premise is processed together with the factual one. In F10–F17, the second premise is considered together with the factual one.

F1	if A plays as visitors against B
F2	then B loses
F3	if C plays at home against B
F4	then B won't lose
F5	B didn't lose
F6	A plays as visitors against B
F7	then B loses
F8	okay then you may say that
F9	A plays at home against B
F10	B plays as visitors
F11	then it might happen that they don't lose
F12	C plays at home against B
F13	B plays as visitors against C
F14	then B won't lose
F15	that's clearly written
F16	but again you don't really know
F17	it says nothing about that

The first inference is found in F9. There is no further information in the fragment which can tell how the subject arrived at that inference. However, it is interesting to note how it was formulated. The formulation, "A plays at home," is not the same as that in the text ("A plays as visitors"). This formulation might have been derived through the following simple steps:

A does not play as visitors (modus tollendo tollens on premises 1 and 3).
A plays at home against B (Interpretational Rule 2).

F10–F15 contain evidence about an interpretational process, while F12 and F13 can be regarded as resulting from Interpretational Rule 1. It is interesting to note how definite the result of this rule appears to the subject in F15 ("that's clearly written").

It should be noted that the protocols show how the subject changes his reasoning both within and between tasks. The order of tasks in the presentation given here corresponds to the order in which the tasks were solved. Compared to the first excerpt, this one is much more sophisticated. However, the basic mechanisms in terms of heuristics do not change as much as the strategy.

Observation 4

It clear that the subject considered larger parts of the text in these fragments than in the earlier ones. To give an account of that observation, let us present a final protocol from the subject.

F1	if A plays as visitors against B
F2	A will win
F3	if C plays at home against A
F4	A will win
F5	A did not win
F6	yes then it isn't true that
F7	A plays as visitors against B
F8	maybe that A plays at home against B

First, note the direct inference that the subject did not verbalize in the preceding protocol—namely, the negation of the antecedent in the first sentence. An instantiation of the corresponding inference rule is:

if
(IMP (PLAYVISI A B)(WIN A B)
(NOT (WIN A B))
(GOAL MAKE INFERENCE)
then
(NOT (PLAYVISI A B))

Thus, F1–F7 show that the subject then made an inference without interpreting and assuming additional premises. This development is also evidence of changes in strategy rather than heuristics.

Second, in F8 the subject again uses Rule 3, as was the case in the preceding protocol. The interpretational heuristics are still used, but it is clear that their use has become much more restricted.

DISCUSSION

Our two main endeavours have so far been successful: We have shown that it is possible to specify a model of people's understanding in a reasoning task in terms of a propositional representation and production rules which operate on that representation. We have also shown that the assumptions put forward in the design of this preliminary model are supported by empirical observations. We now discuss the theoretical model and its psychological support.

We have shown how the general idea of 'understanding' in a reasoning task can be specified in several steps. We started with the general idea that text and prior knowledge interacted. This interaction was found to lead to new assumptions, which were then added to the interpretation of the text. Finally, we suggested a model which can produce a line of reasoning containing interpretations as well as inferences. In a working model, it is necessary to specify various details. In Table 4.1 we summarize these requirements and our specifications and discuss some of them further.

The specifications of text and prior knowledge are based on work in text processing (e.g., Miller & Kintsch, 1980) and human memory (e.g., Anderson, 1976). The heuristic interpretational rules in our model are new, compared with the other ones. As we have implicitly argued, it is unplausible to suppose that the representation of a text in working memory has a one-to-one correspondence with the text as it appears on paper. Instead, a reader or reasoner constructs his or her own interpretation of the text, which thereby assume quite a different meaning from that intended by the author or the researcher. We conceptualized this through the notion of assumptions which were added to the text. This idea of interpretation and its specification in terms of domain-dependent heuristics, along with domain-independent inference rules, is seldom found in research on text processing and reasoning.

Even though much prior research has acknowledged the existence of different strategies for solving tasks, no one has yet specified the strategic issues involved. We have suggested that two such issues are especially important: how one's attention is directed toward premises, and how the inference process is governed. These issues have been described through the use of subgoals.

Finally, it might be questioned whether or not it is necessary to postulate general inference rules. We have chosen to do so, since some rules seem

TABLE 4.1
Requirements of a Model for Reasoning and the Specification Chosen

Requirement	Specification
From text to internal representation	None
Representation of text	Propositions and premises
Representation of prior knowledge	Propositional network
Utilization of prior knowledge	Activation of network
Interpretation and assumptions	Interpretational heuristics
Inference	General rules of inference
Coordination of processes	Reasoning strategies
From thought to speech	None

psychologically plausible (particularly the modus ponens rule). However, it should be emphasized again that these general rules are included in addition to those that are more domain-specific, such as the interpretational heuristics which make the resulting model both logical and non-logical.

We turn now to the issue of supporting the model with psychological data. We have shown that the specifications chosen are sufficient to generate inferences of the type that were illustrated by the four examples given here. However, if psychological data consisted only of inferences or judgments of inferences, several models could describe the data equally well. In fact, at any level of data, many different explanations are always possible (see Anderson, 1976, 1978).

Our data do not consist only of inferences; we have also collected verbal protocols. These can tell us something about the processes behind the inferences reached. Of course, the protocols do not cover all of the details in the reasoning process, as was evident in our examples, and it is impossible to predict which points in the process will be omitted in the protocol. Therefore, the think-aloud data cannot be used as a strict test, for the absence of comment need not imply the absence of a proposed operation or representation. Nevertheless, the mention of particular procedures by subjects may indicate aspects of the reasoning process which have to be considered in any model. In our data, one such aspect emerged clearly: The subject was found to actively interpret the premises. This interpretation was evident in the protocols as a rewording of the premises. Also, there are indications that the rewording was done consciously. Thus, our assumption is supported that the reasoning process consists not only of making inferences but of interpretational processes as well.

The protocols indicate that reasoners' strategies have to be taken into account in a model of reasoning. Although our own attempt to develop such a model was rather weak, we have tried to illustrate, both theoretically and empirically, some of the aspects concerning different strategies. Indeed, there were a few interesting strategic characteristics that showed up in the protocols. For instance, the subject directed his attention to one conditional premise at a time. This attentional heuristic has an obvious consequence for what inference is made and when. This aspect of the strategy can, of course, be attributed to the limited capacity of working memory. Another characteristic is revealed by the changes in the reasoning process observed across different tasks. In particular, the subject seemed to use interpretational heuristics more cautiously in the later tasks than in the earlier ones. This trend indicates that the subject did not change the understanding of logical connectives, nor did he acquire any new inference rules. Instead, the strategic change corresponded to a change in the use of interpretational and inferential heuristics.

To conclude, we would like to suggest that the non-logical behaviour of human reasoners does not preclude the possibility that human reasoners use a subset of domain-independent rules in their reasoning. As we have tried to show, the apparently faulty reasoning can be understood by basically two assumptions: (1) that interpretational heuristics are used, whereby additional assumptions are added to the propositional network, and (2) that strategies are used which govern attention, interpretation, and inferencing. We have presented examples which show that these hypotheses are sufficient for simulating at least some aspects of a human reasoning process.

REFERENCES

Anderson, J. R. *Language, memory and thought.* Hillsdale, NJ: Erlbaum, 1976.

Anderson, J. R. Arguments concerning representations for mental imagery. *Psychological Review,* 1978, **85**, 249–277.

Evans, J. S. T. B. T. On the problems of interpreting reasoning data: Logical and psychological approaches. *Cognition,* 1972, **70**, 121–126.

Evans, J. S. T. B. T. Current issues in the psychology of reasoning. *British Journal of Psychology,* 1980, **71**, 227–239.

Hagert, G., & Hansson, Å. *Logic modelling of cognitive reasoning.* Paper presented at the International Joint Conference on Artificial Intelligence, Karlsruhe, West Germany, 1983.

Hagert, G., Waern, Y., & Tärnlund, S-Å. Open and closed models of understanding in conditional reasoning. *Acta Psychologica,* 1982, **52**, 41–59.

Hayes, J. R., & Simon, H. A. Understanding written problem instructions. In L. W. Bregg (Ed.), *Knowledge and cognition.* Ptomac, MD: Erlbaum, 1974.

Henle, M. On the relation between logic and thinking. *Psychological Review,* 1962, **69**, 561–566.

Johnson-Laird, P. N. Mental models in cognitive science. *Cognitive Science,* 1980, **4**, 71–115.

Johnson-Laird, P. N. *The form and function of mental models.* Paper presented at the third annual Conference of the Cognitive Science Society, Berkeley, CA, 1981.

Langley, P., & Neches, R. *PRISM user's manual.* Carnegie-Mellon University, Department of Computer Science, 1981.

Miller, J. R., & Kintsch, W. Readability and recall of short prose passages: A theoretical analysis. *Journal of Experience Psychology: Human Learning and Memory*, 1980, **6**, 335–354.

Newell, A. Production system: Models of control structures. In W. G. Chase (Ed.), *Visual information processing*. New York: Academic Press, 1973.

Smedslung, J. Circular relation between understanding and logic. *Scandinavian Journal of Psychology*, 1970, **11**, 217–219.

Wason, P. C., & Johnson-Laird, P. N. *Psychology of reasoning: Structure and content*. Cambridge, MA: Harvard University Press, 1972.

5

More than 'All'? Children's Problems with Plural Judgements

J. A. STEDMON

Department of Applied Psychology
University of Wales Institute of Science and Technology
Cardiff

GENERAL INTRODUCTION

Suppose you were asked to fetch 'the cutlery' from a drawer, a common enough occurrence. Immediately, one has to decide which cutlery the speaker has in mind. Perhaps just sufficient items are required to set the table for a known number of diners, or the entire drawer of cutlery might be due for a clean and polish. In either case, the listener must be able to solve the prior determining problem by relying on presuppositions which are shared with the speaker before proceeding with the task at hand. Indeed, it would not necessarily be more helpful to request 'all the cutlery' unless both interlocutors had reached agreement about the temporary purpose of the search, for this phrase also might be taken to refer to only a sub-class of the cutlery in the drawer.

In the absence of any evidence as to the speaker's purpose, one could adopt a default convention always to search exhaustively and so empty the cutlery drawer. Assuming that the listener is able to decide on a boundary for the cutlery-gathering exercise, there will be a variety of quantifying strategies available to complete the search. A rather tedious approach might be to check that each separate item belonged to the admissible list of cutlery, be it a

ISBN 0-12-512320-5

knife, fork or spoon. A less cautious approach would be to gather the knives, forks and spoons together in separate bundles. Either strategy—cumulating individuals or summing across sub-totals—should yield the same grand total if the quantifying procedure is implemented accurately.

One can now appreciate that an act of reference can fail for a number of reasons. A listener might not be able to agree on the purpose of an act and so focus on the wrong set of items. This would be a problem of underdetermination. A related problem would occur if the listener simply failed to recognize that an unusual item (say, a sweetcorn fork) was to be included. At the same time, the gathering operation itself might be prone to faulty implementation; it is conceivable that collecting each sub-class separately, rather than making an assiduous check for each item, might lead one to overlook some sub-sets entirely. Thus procedural errors can occur too, with failure due to faulty quantification over the total set. Here I rest the case; it should now be clear that the first step toward a proper diagnosis of reference failure with plural sets must be analysing the determining and quantifying information available to the listener about the referents which require integration.

In this chapter I investigate a case of reference failure which occurred with children in an experiment designed to test their logical competence. Drawing on a distinction commented upon by Miller and Miller (1979), I argue that a prior logical analysis needs to be balanced by an equally detailed analysis of the psychological semantics of all referential language used in the test situation. In the first half I note that plural terms need not have a logical status in everyday language but rather should be accorded a pluri-functional status. Therefore, I propose to adopt a functional, rather than a form-based, analysis of plural reference. This approach provides the theoretical framework for analysing children's referential problems in Piaget's class inclusion test and leads to a re-evaluation of Piaget's claims. It thus becomes an empirical issue whether or not the functional analysis of reference leads to a re-interpretation of children's acquisition of logico-cognitive skills.

A PLURIFUNCTIONAL ANALYSIS OF DETERMINERS AND QUANTIFIERS

The term 'quantifier' is used by linguists to group together such words as 'all', 'some', 'each', 'every' and 'any' (as well as 'many', 'few' and 'several') which, in certain contexts, function in much the same way as logical quantifiers. As Lyons (1977, p. 454) reminds us: "The term quantifier is used by logicians to refer to particular operators . . . whose function it is to bind the variables which come within its scope." Indeed, the operators of universal and existential quantification remain the modern logician's favourite quantifiers (McCawley, 1982, p. 98). Roughly speaking, the universal quantifier corresponds to the English words 'all', 'every', 'any' and 'each', while the existential quantifier corresponds to certain uses of the terms 'some' and 'any'. However, it would be a category mistake to treat natural language quantifiers as if they always behaved like their logical counterparts.

The chief source of confusion which arises with quantifiers is that they overlap in both distribution and function with linguistic determiners. The latter refer to a class of words which includes the definite and indefinite articles ('the' and 'a'), the demonstrative adjectives ('this', 'that', 'these' and 'those') and possessive adjectives (e.g., 'your' and 'my'). One clear example of the equivalent function of a determiner term as a quantifier term is the general use of the definite article in English. In the sentence, "The tiger is a fierce beast," the definite article has the force of a universal quantifier, for it binds the class of all admissible tigers within its scope. The intersubstitutability of quantifier and determiner terms in such contexts precludes a purely form-based linguistic analysis of plural referential terms, as Stedmon and Freeman (1983) argue in detail. Instead, the use of quantifiers and determiners in natural language should be analysed according to the referential functions they serve for interlocutors. This approach provides us with the tools needed to expose the implicit assumptions about the role of language which underlie many tests of children's logical competence.

Strawson (1950) suggests that the speaker must forestall two questions to identify plural referent sets linguistically. They are "Which ones?" and "How many?" Lyons (1977) sustains this intuition when he distinguishes between the determining and the quantifying functions. In short, determiners forestall Strawson's first question, and quantifiers forestall the second. Formally stated, "Determiners are modifiers which combine with nouns to produce expressions whose reference is thereby determined in terms of the identity of the referent; quantifiers are modifiers which combine with nouns to produce expressions whose reference is thereby determined in terms of the size of the set of individuals" (Lyons, 1977, pp. 454–455).

On the basis of Lyons' observation it seems that an appropriate functional test for deciding whether a plural term is operating as a determiner or a quantifier would be to check the referential information it conveys against Strawson's two questions. When one attempts this approach, it becomes apparent that even conventional quantifier terms can function as determiners. At one extreme, quantifiers can formally head noun phrases, as in "Many tame tigers exist," by standing in the determining position of the sentence. More subtly, Lyons (1977) points out that a child may quite truthfully answer the question, "Which sweets do you want?" by retorting "All of them!" However, in this case the determining use of the quantifier 'All' may well depend on prior agreement by the interlocutors that a predetermined referent set is available for further quantification. Indeed, Strawson (1976) makes the formal claim that universal quantification technically presupposes the existence of an admissible referent set. He uses this argument to explain why it would sound absurd to claim: "All tame tigers exist." There is no need to explore here the conditions under which quantifiers may serve a primary determining function; rather, I simply note that the psychological status of the referents might be a privileged one.

So far, an analytic distinction has been drawn between determining and quantifying terms. This distinction will shortly be applied to a practical example. In the next section I outline the conditions under which both types of terms can be used by a speaker to serve an identifying function for a listener. Returning to Strawson's questions, it is clear that for a listener to be able to identify the plural referent set intended by the speaker, both determining and quantifying information is required. The modus operandi of each type of term is described in detail in Karmiloff-Smith's (1979) functional analysis of reference, which I summarize for the present purpose. Karmiloff-Smith (1979, p. 46) distinguishes between two main functions of both quantifier terms and determiner terms:

> The *descriptive* function is defined as follows: a word is used by the speaker to give additional information about a referent already implicitly or explicitly under focus of attention by speaker and addressee. The *determiner* function is defined as follows: a word is used by the speaker to enable the addressee to pick out a referent among other potential candidates. Thus the *determiner* function defines a relationship between the referent and its extralinguistic context (the concrete situation) or its intralinguistic context (the temporary universe of discourse). The *descriptor* function is centred on the attributes of the referent and not on its relationship with other potential referents.

For our present purpose, the major focus of analysis of reference has to be the antecedent-*determining* or -*identifying* function of language rather than the consequent opportunities for employing the descriptive function. I want to concentrate here on the identifying function of quantifier terms. Returning to the cutlery example, I pointed out earlier that there are a variety of quantificational procedures available to a listener. The next task is to analyse the precise quantifying functions which can be conferred on plural terms. At a very general semantic level, plural referential terms can be classed together according to their most primitive function—to mark plurality linguistically. However, this function alone would serve only to inform a listener that more than one referent was to be identified, without specifying the procedure for carrying out the search.

Karmiloff-Smith analyses further the operation by which a listener is assumed to quantify over a referent set. She distinguishes between three quantifying functions: those of plurality, totality and class extension. The empirical work here can serve to test how far this analysis helps to explain children's referential errors concerning plural sets. To bring the theory to bear on the data which follows, one needs to examine the difference between the totalising and the class-extension functions. A plural term has a totalising function if it directs the listener to cumulate referents up to an identifiable set boundary. The listener is thus expected to stop the search for referents at some boundary. There may be a problem, however, in that a cumulative search procedure will not necessarily guarantee that the listener is able to distinguish between a sub-total and a grand total. This problem will be even more acute if the sub-total has been linguistically specified. I argue later that this is the case in class-inclusion tests. Presumably, some plural terms will have been developed within the language system to serve a more powerful function—namely, to direct the listener to sum over sub-totals cumulatively in order to complete an exhaustive search for referents. This is what Karmiloff-Smith calls the class-extension function. The listener is expected to continue cumulating across any sub-class boundary.

The class of intensifier terms in English serves an emphatic function. For example, the expressions 'every single', 'each and every', 'absolutely all' and 'very many' are linguistic intensifiers. However, functional equivalence may cut across their modus operandi at the psychological level. Thus, in the sentence, "John is very good", the intensifier term serves a dual role—that of focusing on the predicate expression and of strengthening its degree of instantiation. By contrast, quantifier terms like 'every single' and 'each one' serve a particularizing function to mark *distributive predication.* They can also serve an intensifying function by re-directing one to consider individual cases separately. Therefore, a particularizing term differs from the universal quantifier 'all' with respect to the relation which holds between the bound variables and their predicates. The quantifying function of the former is to distribute predicate expressions across individuals, whereas for the latter it is to totalize predication across a class of entities, thereby implying the collectivity of a class. Thus, 'every single' focuses on individual class members, while 'all' focuses on the total class. As Vendler (1967) notes, this difference in the meaning of words is reflected in the grammatical use of 'all' to modify plural noun-phrases, and of 'each' and 'every single' to modify singular ones. It is an empirical question whether the difference in quantifying operations signalled by the plural terms may have real psychological consequences for children. Indeed, this question has formed the basis for some experimental work.

Using this functional framework, one can now analyse plural terms in English. It is possible to refer economically to a plural set using a plural definite noun phrase of the general form, 'the *X*'s'. Although there is no explicit quantifying term in the referential expression, by convention the listener is expected to proceed with an exhaustive search of the referent domain. As Hawkins (1977) points out, exhaustive search is in fact the only quantifying procedure which guarantees a unique solution for plural definite reference.

Karmiloff-Smith's work demonstrates children's problems when they try to master plural reference. In her studies, children were shown two parking lots, with one belonging to the child (to distinguish it lexically from the other). Various items, such as blue closed cars and red open cars, were in both lots. When 4-year-old children were asked to put 'The red cars' into a garage, they failed to cross the boundary to collect all the cars, stopping short at a sub-class boundary. Performance improved only up to 20% correct when the quantified expression, 'all the red open cars,' was used instead. Karmiloff-Smith concluded that young children do not yet understand the totalizing function of 'all' and interpret it weakly to mean 'a lot'. Although 6-year olds experience a problem when the definite article is used alone, from 7 years onwards most children accurately interpret such definite references. Nevertheless, an experiment on children's production of plural references in an identical context showed that it is not until around 9 years of age that children cumulate exhaustively over all admissible items referred to in a plural noun phrase, thus reliably summing across sub-classes. At this stage they reserve an intensifier function for the quantifier 'all', using it to emphasize the totalizing function and to signal class extension. Karmiloff-Smith's thesis is that the shift in function which children confer on referential terms is achieved via the solution of specifically intra-linguistic problems. They must spontaneously come to recognize the equivalence of inter-substitutable plural terms by experience with concrete examples.

These studies concentrate on the exophoric function of referential language—to pick out referent sets in the extra-linguistic context. Further work has shown that intra-linguistic functions such as anaphoric or generic reference are not mastered until later. To clarify this position theoretically, Stedmon and Freeman (1983) identify three possible search domains for holding the potential alternative referents: the physical, contextual and universal. The physical domain contains referents in the real world, whereas the contextual domain is a mentally constructed 'holding file' for representing referential entities. Both the physical and contextual domains contain tokens and are subsets of the universal domain, which contains a specification of the properties of types and their relationship to one another—that is, the 'intensional' specification of the words which denote the types. This segment completes the theoretical framework for re-examining children's problems with class inclusion.

THE ROLE OF LANGUAGE IN CLASS INCLUSION REASONING

Piaget's account of class inclusion is contained in three studies (Inhelder & Piaget, 1964; Piaget, 1952, 1977). He claims that pre-operational children lack the ability simultaneously to compare part of a class with the whole. The standard test is a verbal request for children quantitatively to compare the larger of two subclasses with the whole in which it is included. Failure is usually due to children mistakenly comparing the two excluded sub-classes, thus translating the reference to the whole class into one for the small sub-class (Shipley, 1979; Trabasso, Isen, Dolecki, McClanahan, Riley & Tucker, 1978). For Piaget, failure at the performance level is taken to index the absence of underlying logical competence (see Broughton, 1981), and it is this assumption that I want to challenge. Since one cannot do justice to Piaget's theory of mental logic here, my argument is focused on the role of language in the test designed to access the child's knowledge of intensional class relations.

Piaget adopts a nominalist position on language. He asserts that children age 8 and younger do not differentiate between word and referent, and so treat language as if it were a property of the object which it names. From a psychological point of view, language is reduced to the level of object knowledge, so there is no room for further analysis of referential variables within Piaget's theory. This assessment is supported in the following quote, cited by Elliot and Donaldson (1982), which is a covert statement of the 'cognition hypothesis' (Cromer, 1974): "Children assimilate the language they hear to their semantic structures, which are a function of their level of development" (Inhelder & Piaget, 1964, p. 3). With tasks involving exophoric reference, this position necessarily blurs the sense/reference distinction. As such, Piaget accords conceptual knowledge a prior status compared with linguistic knowledge.

As a consequence of Piaget's view of language as dependent on the child's general level of cognitive development, Elliot and Donaldson (1982, p. 157) suggest that he is in danger of making two types of errors: "First, he might wrongly assess the role of language in the development of thinking; and, second, to the extent that he uses language in his own experiments, he might misinterpret his findings by failing to take due account of how the linguistic component is affecting the outcome." Similarly, I argue that Piaget may commit both erros in his analysis of the class inclusion test. Karmiloff-Smith's functional analysis of reference will be used to criticize Piaget's implicit assumptions about language.

In the class inclusion task, children will succeed only if the referential expressions used for both the part and the whole class serve an identifying function. Piaget assumes that children can interpret the key plural terms used in the extensional class inclusion task context in strict accordance with their logical, intensional meaning only when they have grasped the logical operation of class inclusion. This approach entails that children have already mastered the logical relation between the terms 'some' and 'all':

> In order to study the additive composition of classes, i.e. the inclusion of partial classes in a wider class, in as close connection as possible with the problem of conservation of quantities, it was necessary to examine the logical relationship between the terms "some" and "all" in order to bring out the element of quantification inherent in any addition either of classes or number. [Piaget, 1952, Chap. 7.]

Piaget makes this point explicitly in his rejection of the notion that reasoning with semantic hierarchies is in any way related to true class inclusion competence, and in his use of a variety of different category-level terms in his own experiments. He did not consider that the precise language used could, in principle, affect the outcome because he believed that language can only be interpreted by children in terms of their pre-existing logical structures. Therefore, he rejects the possibility that linguistic knowledge can be a source of knowledge about class structure. In addition, he accords a privileged status to quantifier terms as formal logical operators, without considering their other uses in natural language.

Karmiloff-Smith's (1979) functional analysis of quantifier terms challenges Piaget's strictly logical analysis for two important reasons. First, the functional theory accords a plurifunctional status to quantifier terms, so there is more scope for interpreting children's referential errors than in a logical theory. Second, in Karmiloff-Smith's theory, quantifiers are related at an intra-linguistic level, so one must take into account the referential functions which children confer on related terms. Thus one can raise the following objections to Piaget's logical analysis:

(1) A plurifunctional theory distinguishes between the generic use of quantifier terms to refer to abstract classes in the universal search domain and their exophoric use to refer to referent sets in the physical search domain. Piaget's theory assumes that the exophoric function coincides with the generic function. Therefore, he fails to analyse the special difficulties which might arise when children try to identify physical referent sets rather than abstract mental classes. Karmiloff-Smith suggests that exophoric search skills developmentally precede the generic use of plural terms. This is a special difficulty for all uni-functional theories.

(2) Although 'some' and 'all' can both be logical operators, they cannot be categorized together within a referential theory. Only the universal quantifier 'all' can be used to serve an identifying function, whereas the existential quantifier 'some' is generally non-specific when used exophorically. In the class inclusion test, the experimenter intends to make identifying

reference to both the sub-class and the whole class. Therefore, the exophoric use of the referential expressions used in the class inclusion problem is not identical with the intensional sense of the key logical terms in the idealised problem. Furthermore, Piaget does not use the terms 'some' and 'all' in the class inclusion question. We know from Karmiloff-Smith's work that little words can make a lot of difference to the referential function which children confer on a description. Piaget's assumption that the surface form of referential expressions does not contribute significantly to children's logical interpretation is thus a serious weakness.

(3) Quantifier terms can serve either a descriptive or an identifying function. For example, the quantifier 'all' functions descriptively as a numerical operator, semantically encoding the features of plurality and totality. It serves a powerful identifying function only when it additionally signals 'class extension' to children, and when they can successfully locate the outer boundary of a referent set, as discussed earlier. Karmiloff-Smith argues that children may acquire one function at a time, whereas Piaget's theory treats the acquisition of the logical meaning of quantifier terms as an all-or-none process. We now re-examine the class inclusion test from the former point of view.

IDENTIFYING LANGUAGE IN THE CLASS INCLUSION TEST

I want to consider the conditions under which referential language serves an identifying function in the class inclusion test for a whole class. It will be argued that children must co-ordinate both the determining and the quantifying functions by (1) categorizing the referents at the higher class level and (2) proceeding to search exhaustively across the entire class, respectively. I first consider evidence that children have difficulty with the determining function of language in class inclusion problems. This examination will subsequently be balanced by an equally detailed analysis of the quantifying function, leading directly to the experimental hypotheses under study.

Whenever exophoric reference is made to referent sets, a child must work out the mapping rules for relating universal semantic categories to the physical search domain. Children must learn that the correct approach is to search exhaustively for the referents at the level of categorisation specified by the speaker. Eventually, they must elevate sets in the physical domain to the status of classes in the universe-of-discourse in order to arrive at an understanding of the necessity of class inclusion relations. This process entails that the structure of a particular search episode is related to the structure of long-term semantic memory. In fact, there is an abundance of evidence that preoperational children can utilise knowledge about the hierarchical structure of semantic classes well before they can reason inclusively (see Mandler, 1982, for a recent review). Thus, by relating children's problems with exophoric search to their ability to categorise discourse referents at the appropriate level, one can link referential language to class inclusion reasoning.

A number of authors (Barrett, 1982; Bowerman, 1976; Brown, 1978; Rosch, Mervis, Gray, Johnson, & Boyes-Braem, 1976) have argued that children must construct natural categories of objects around prototypical instances in order to learn the correct range of extension for each referential term. Harris (1982) suggests that the child has difficulty in working out the correct extension of terms because:

> he or she is engaged in constructing categories at several levels of abstraction. ... Therefore, supplied with a term of reference such as "dog", the child does not know whether the adult is referring to the dog as a member of the category of collies, of dogs, or of animals, and therefore has difficulty in knowing the correct range of extension.

A subtle finding, the 'typicality effect' reported by Carson and Abrahamson (1976), shows that the solution to the referent categorization problem is in a fine state of balance for children. In a class inclusion test, they found that children are more likely to categorize referents as members of the whole class when they are highly typical exemplars having a privileged access to the higher level of categorization. If there is a wide gap between the typicality of referents represented in the temporary search domain as members of a particular class and the speaker's choice of the linguistic level for categorizing the referents within the universal hierarchy of classes, then children may not accept the speaker's intended level of categorization. Thus the correct solution entails that the level of categorization for sets in the physical search domain corresponds to the structure of classes in the universal domain, which the child has been actively reconstructing in semantic memory.

The peculiarity of class inclusion questions can be appreciated by all; the referential expressions used for the part and the whole class are asymmetrical with respect to the level of categorization of the referents. By convention, the context usually determines the appropriate level for categorizing the referents (see Karmiloff-Smith, 1979; Olson, 1970; Stedmon & Freeman, 1983). That is, a speaker will select a linguistic term which encodes the referents at the level of categorization that discriminates them from potential alternatives in the search domain. As a consequence, all the referents will tend to be categorised at the same level, which need not be the basic level described by Rosch et al. (1976) and, later, Brown (1978). For example, a set of dogs may be called 'dogs' in contradistinction to 'cats', 'animals' in contradistinction to 'birds', and perhaps 'collies' to differentiate them from poodles, but for each pair the chosen linguistic levels of categorisation are symmetrical.

Empirical evidence confirms that young children find it very hard to compare referent sets when the judgement questions are referentially asymmetrical. Grieve and Garton (1981) show that this is a problem for 4-year-olds concerning both included and excluded set comparisons, so the linguistic difficulty is not restricted to the class inclusion test per se. McGarrigle, Grieve and Hughes (1978) also reported a bias by young children to compare referent sets at the same level of categorization. Shipley and Kuhn (1983) go even further and suggest that class inclusion errors are due entirely to the level-of-categorization problem. I hope to redress the balance by providing both theoretical and empirical support for the importance of quantification processes in class inclusion questions.

So far, it has been argued that children encounter a determining problem when interpreting descriptions used for whole classes. Descriptions which use class nouns are inherently ambiguous insofar as they are semantically appropriate for both parts and whole classes. (A similar difficulty with the totalizing component of the universal quantifier will be discussed later). One test for under-determination, when one suspects that children cannot answer the question, "Which ones?" is to check for a facilitation effect upon the addition of qualifying information about the referents. Several studies provide corroborative evidence for such an effect when the description for the whole class is furbished with extra referential information about the identity of set members (Dean, Chaubaud & Bridges, 1981; Markman, 1973; Markman & Siebert, 1976; McGarrigle et al., 1978; Shipley, 1979; Shipley & Kuhn, 1983; Wilkinson, 1976; see also Stedmon, 1983, for a critical review). I now examine the quantifying function of the language used to refer to the whole class, which has previously been overlooked. This discussion will provide a focus for the empirical work.

I argued earlier that children must learn to implement the quantifying procedure of exhaustive search in order to identify correctly the whole class in class inclusion tests. In fact, children may be highly sensitive to the quantifying function of related plural terms. Thus, a good test for faulty quantification, when one suspects that children cannot answer the question, "How many?" is to check for a facilitation effect when additional quantifying information about the referents is provided. In the case of class inclusion, one would predict a null result for such a test if children's difficulty with the determining function of language were the limiting factor. The point is that whenever there is a prior problem over locating set boundaries, it would be inappropriate to evoke an explanation in terms of faulty quantifying procedures.

Freeman, Sinha and Stedmon (1982) provide one such extreme example. They re-analyse a case of reference failure with plural sets discussed by Donaldson and Lloyd (1974) and show the difficulty to be one of deciding which referents to quantify over. The task was to answer the question, 'Are all the cars in the garages?' for a mismatched paired array. The children were prone to make both under-exhaustive and over-exhaustive search errors; either they ignored an extra item, or they recruited an extra item relative to the referent set intended by the experimenter. It turned out that they were using information about the putative discourse topic to infer the size of one of the referent sets, which was consequently either under- or over-extended. Therefore, although they failed to locate the outer search boundary intended by the experimenter, they were nonetheless competent at searching up to the wrong set boundary. The problem thus seemed to be one of under-determination rather than faulty quantifying procedures. This might turn out to be the case in the class inclusion test if children's problems with co-ordinating the quantifying and determining functions of language were heavily weighted towards the latter. So far, I have not presented firm evidence to the contrary. However, there are data available which indicate children's sensitivity to quantifying information when it is provided in class inclusion questions.

Upon close examination, certain differences in children's performance with the quantifier 'all' do show up across studies. For example, while Grieve and Garton (1981) found only a slight facilitation effect when the quantifier term 'all' was used relative to definite reference, Shipley (1979) claims that this same term cued older children into the logical structure of the task. This observation fits well with the functional account proposed earlier, for there may be differences in the referential status of the quantifier terms across the subject groups which the authors failed to analyse. The aim of the remainder of this chapter is to formulate a rigorous set of hypotheses out of the functional analysis of plural terms and to test them empirically.

I have argued that children must learn to implement an exhaustive search procedure in order to identify an entire class in a class inclusion tests. The search-directing function of the plural terms used must therefore serve a powerful totalizing function, prompting the child to cumulate over sub-totals and to admit items up to the outermost search boundary. Returning to Karmiloff-Smith's arguments, outlined earlier, the functions which children confer on plural terms will be due in part to their level of referential competence. This hypothesis can now be tested empirically. For example, plural expressions can be scaled together intra-linguistically according to a single criterion—the extent to which they signal the powerful class extension function (Stedmon & Freeman, 1983). The results of this study will provide the rationale for selecting plural terms to use in the class inclusion study which follows.

I am suggesting that children's class-inclusion competence is related to the referential functions which they confer on plural quantifier terms. My hypothesis is that children solve the problem of èxophoric search via mastery of the powerful function of plural terms to direct searches across sub-class boundaries. At first, children will reserve the class extension function for those terms which serve an intensifier function. Gradually, however the class-extension function will come to be conferred even on definite plural noun phrases. This occurrence would be indexed by differential performance between plural terms in the class inclusion test. The experiment which follows provides a critical test. Of course, there is a null hypothesis: Varying the quantifying information provided about the whole class will have no effect on children's class inclusion performance at any level of competence. Accordingly, one can now proceed with a rigorous test of the functional hypotheses.

SELECTING PLURAL REFERENTIAL TERMS TO SCALE INTRA-LINGUISTICALLY

The language-directed search task which follows is a partial replication of Karmiloff-Smith's (1979) experiment with English-speaking children as reported in Stedmon and Freeman (1983). The task is to identify plural referent sets which are divided into sub-classes from linguistic descriptions. This allows one to scale together intra-linguistically inter-substitutable plural terms according to whether they signal totality to children, thus prompting them to search exhaustively across the sub-class boundary. Following the results of Stedmon and Freeman (1983), three types of plural expressions were used. *Definite reference* of the form 'the *X*'s' served the weakest identifying function and accordingly set a base line for interpreting the rest of the data. *Universal quantification* of the form 'all the *X*'s' re-directed nearly all of the children to search exhaustively, as did the *intensified* expression, 'every single *X*'. Accordingly, these three terms can be scaled together for single set quantification. Next, using the identical experimental context, the same expressions can be re-scaled for the class inclusion test. However, taken alone, the language-directed search task will not show up the class extension function, as children are not forced to confront the problem of deciding between a sub-total and a grand total—the main difficulty in the class-inclusion test, as just noted. Karmiloff-Smith (1979, p. 198) also argues that the ability to sum across sub-classes for single set quantification is present in pre-operational children and does not by itself imply that children are using class inclusion concepts.

If the totalising function alone were a sufficient condition for class inclusion, then one might expect that language-directed search errors would underlie class inclusion errors. Instead, I am predicting that quantitative differences in error level between language-directed search and class inclusion will be found. Therefore, the referential function of each plural term will be analysed by integrating the results for the two tasks. The quantitative differences between the tasks will then be explained in terms of the qualitative differences in the psychological status of plural terms for children.

THE EXPERIMENTAL WORK: LANGUAGE-DIRECTED SEARCH AND CLASS INCLUSION

Subjects

There were 70 subjects in all, with equal numbers of each sex and a mean age of 5.7 years (standard deviation = 2.5 months). Following the data analysis, an intermediate group of 36 experimental subjects was found to have a mean age of 5.8 years (standard deviation = 2.8 months). For the 25 children who failed class inclusion, the mean age was 5.6 years (standard deviation = 2.6 months). For the 9 children who passed class inclusion, the mean age was 5.7 years (standard deviation = 2.6 months).

Apparatus

The physical array comprised two 'lots' constructed with white plastic 'fencing' on a table surface. One lot was assigned to the experimenter, the other to the child. Three sets of toy farm animals, tractors and scarecrows were divided between the two lots in a 4:3 sub-class ratio (see Figure 5.1).

Method

The Language-Directed Search Task

Children were seated next to the experimenter, with both facing the two lots. Each subject was told that one lot belonged to the experimenter, the

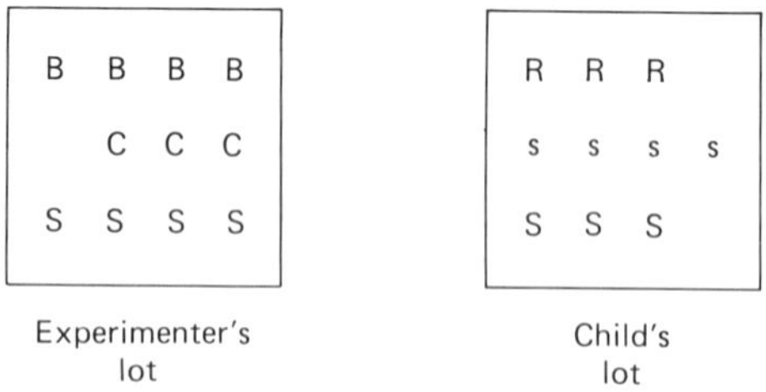

Figure 5.1. Experimental context for the language-directed search task and the class-inclusion task. B, blue tractor; R, red tractor; C, cow; s, sheep; S, scarecrow.

TABLE 5.1
Referential Expressions Used in the Language-Directed Search Task and the Class Inclusion Test

Trial Number	Referential expression	Type of expression	Type of class
1	The blue tractors		Sub-class
2 (1)[a]	The tractors	D.R.	Whole
3 (2)	All the tractors	U.Q.	Whole
4 (3)	Every single tractor	I	Whole
5	Your sheep		Sub-class
6 (4)	The farm animals	D.R.	Whole
7 (5)	All the farm animals	U.Q.	Whole
8 (6)	Every single farm animal	I	Whole
9	My scarecrows		Sub-class
10 (7)	The scarecrows	D.R.	Whole
11 (8)	All the scarecrows	U.Q.	Whole
12 (9)	Every single scarecrow	I	Whole

[a] Class inclusion trial numbers appear in parentheses. D.R., definite reference; U.Q., universally quantified reference; I, intensified reference.

other to the child. He or she was instructed to remove each referent set as requested by the experimenter and place it on the table. Table 5.1 shows the referential expressions used to refer to either a sub-class or a whole class of referents. No feedback was given.

The Class Inclusion Test

The class inclusion test was administered immediately after the language-directed search task, using the same apparatus. The class inclusion question was of the general form, "Which are more? The/all the/every single *X*'s or the/my/your *X*'s?" where the first option refers to the whole class and the second to the sub-class. Order of mention of sub-classes and whole classes was randomized within subjects. Table 5.1 also shows the referential expressions used to refer to whole classes for the nine class inclusion trials. Each subject received all of the trials in both tests.

Results

Individual Response Strategies

The children were first classified according to the strategy they used in the class inclusion test. The data for both the language-directed search task and the class inclusion test were then analysed separately for three groups of

TABLE 5.2
Language-Directed Search Errors as a Function of Referential Expressions

Trials	Reference to whole class	Non-includers ($N = 25$)	Language-sensitive ($N = 36$)	Includers ($N = 9$)	Totals
2, 6, 10	The *X*'s	22	14	1	37 (77%)
3, 7, 11	All the *X*'s	5	1	0	6 (12.5%)
4, 8, 12	Every single *X*	4	1	0	5 (10.5%)
		31	16	1	48

children. Individual responses were categorised into the following strategy groups:

1. *Class-includer*: 9 subjects answered all of the class inclusion questions correctly.
2. *Non-includer*: 25 subjects failed all of the class inclusion questions.
3. *Language-sensitive*: 36 subjects showed an intermediate number of errors in the class-inclusion test, indicating that these subjects might be sensitive to the referential variables.

(Two children who were 'yes' and 'no' responders were dropped from the data analysis.)

Language-directed search

Although there were only 58 errors altogether, all but three of these were due to under-exhaustive searches for a whole class, as predicted. Subjects failed because they identified sub-classes only. Table 5.2 shows that of these errors, 77% occurred when a definite reference was used, compared with only 12.5% and 10.5%, respectively, for the quantified expressions, 'all the *X*'s', and the intensified term, 'every single *X*'.

For a language-directed search, the definite article used alone has only a weak identifying function relative to both the universal quantifier and the linguistic intensifier. I shall account for this difference shortly.

The Class Inclusion Test

It is only appropriate to analyse the referential variable for the intermediate subjects in the language-sensitive group, because floor and ceiling

TABLE 5.3
Correct Responses for the Language-Sensitive Group as a Function of References to a Whole Class[a]

The *X*'s	All the *X*'s	Every single *X*
46 (43%)	47 (44%)	74 (69%)

[a] Maximum score = 108.

TABLE 5.4
Individual-Level Analysis of 'The *X*'s' and 'All the *X*'s' Used to Refer to a Whole Class[a]

No. of subjects showing no difference	No. of subjects better with the *X*'s	No. of subjects better with All the *X*'s
All *X*s/All the *X*'s Both ✓ or Both ×	The *X*'s ✓ All the *X*'s ×	The *X*'s × All the *X*'s ✓
80	13	15

[a] Based on three comparisons per subject ($N = 36$); $p =$ n.s.

effects entail that subjects confer an equivalent function on the three plural expressions. Table 5.3 shows the distribution of correct responses for this group as a function of the particular expression used to refer to a whole class.

Upon inspection, performance is better for the linguistic intensifier (69%) than for the universal quantifier (44%) or the definite article (46%). Thus the quantifier 'all' does not serve a more powerful identifying function than a definite reference alone. Next, the data were tested at the individual level. The comparisons in Tables 5.4 and 5.5 are based on inter-trial differences for each subject and each type of material (each subject yielded three comparisons). Table 5.4 shows that there is no significant difference between definite and quantified references. By contrast, Table 5.5 shows a significant difference between definite and intensified references.

Summary of Results

Taken together, these two experiments confirm the hypothesis that referential variables are crucial to children's class-inclusion performance. To summarize, the important findings are:

1. The children who failed class inclusion did not always treat the definite article as a totalizer signalling an exhaustive search in the language-directed search task.

TABLE 5.5

Individual-Level Analysis of 'The *X*'s' and 'Every single *X*' Used to Refer to a Whole Class[a]

No. of subjects showing no difference	No. of subjects better with the *X*'s	No. of subjects better at Every single *X*
All *X*s/All the *X*'s Both ✓ or Both ×	The *X*'s ✓ Every single *X* ×	The *X*'s × Every single *X* ✓
68	7	33

[a] Based on three comparisons per subject ($N = 36$); $p < .01$.

2. The referential function of definite plural descriptions for the language-sensitive group was equivalent to the function of universally quantified expressions for the non-includers.
3. The language-sensitive subjects reserved the class extension function for intensified expressions, yet they treated the universal quantifier and the linguistic intensifier as referentially equivalent, indicating set totality, in the language-directed search task
4. The referential function of both the universal quantifier and the definite article for the class-includers was equivalent to the function of intensified expressions for the language-sensitive group.

The pattern of responding for individual children across the two tasks, language-directed search and class inclusion, was distinct for the three groups of children identified. It is thus clear that the interpretation of plural referential terms does not have the same cognitive status for children at different levels of class inclusion competence. Using these results, one can work out the referential functions which children conferred on the plural terms. We can then analyse the qualitative differences in linguistic competence among children who show quantitative differences in their level of class inclusion reasoning.

Consistent with Karmiloff-Smith's (1979) account, the weakest function, plurality, is assigned to plural terms which do not always serve a totalizing function in language-directed searches. A plural term is assigned a totalizing function here only if it directs a child to search across the sub-class boundary in the language-directed search task. The class extension function is reserved for terms which, in addition, direct exhaustive search in the class inclusion test. The modal responses of subjects in the three groups can be taken as evidence for the function they confer on the plural terms, as shown in Table 5.6.

TABLE 5.6
Referential Functions Conferred on Related Plural Terms

Plural term	Class-inclusion failures	Language-sensitive group	Class-includers
The	Plurality	Totality	Class extension
All the	Totality	Totality	Class extension
Every single	Totality	Class extension	Class extension

FINAL DISCUSSION: THE ROLE OF LANGUAGE IN LOGICAL DEVELOPMENT—A PROCEDURAL ANALYSIS OF THE QUANTIFYING FUNCTION

Piaget argues that class inclusion competence logically entails the co-ordination of the intensional specifications of the existential and universal quantifiers 'some' and 'all'. This problem formally resembles a comparison between unspecified plurality and the extension of an entire class insofar as the 'some/all' comparison does not force one to construct a sub-total for the extended referent set. In contrast, I have argued that the linguistic instructions in the class-inclusion test refer the child to two conflicting operations. *At the same time* as they are told to search cumulatively beyond the sub-total to identify the total class, children are also referred to the misleading sub-total. Thus they find it hard to respond at first and only succeed when a linguistic intensifier is used. I now explain the facilitation effect reported when the intensifier 'every single' is used, compared with the quantifier 'all', in terms of the relationship between referential language and Piaget's intensional class problem. A workable approach is to view children as (1) developing skills in exophoric reference, (2) operating with plurality, totality and class extension (in that order), (3) grasping the inclusion relation between the extreme functions of plurality and class extension and (4) applying this relation to the totalizing function. My argument against Piaget's account therefore concentrates on the quantifying operations which children confer on specific plural terms, and not on their general logical abilities.

When children first start to solve the class inclusion problem correctly, they succeed when the linguistic intensifier 'every single' is used but often fail with the universal quantifier 'all'. I want to make the claim that the plural term 'all' does not at first serve a class extension function for children in the class-inclusion task because it is especially misleading. Perhaps the role of the totalizing function (between plurality and class extension) is a special case, since linguistic realisation of this function will provide a source of miscue for the child. I suggest that the totalizing component of 'all' concentrates children on finding a referent set boundary which need not coincide with the extended class. Whenever there is a prior problem with the determining function, children may well be encouraged to focus on the wrong set boundary with respect to the speaker's intentions. In the case of class inclusion, I have argued that young children do experience difficulty with the determining function of language, which biases them towards mistakenly identifying the sub-class. The totalizing component of 'all', which simply directs search up to some boundary, could therefore encourage young children to concentrate on identifying the psychologically privileged set boundary, thereby powerfully miscuing them to fix on the sub-total. It would seem that children who have not yet fully grasped the exhaustive quantifying power of the term 'all' are unable to overcome the prior determining problem in the class inclusion test. Yet I have shown that these same children, who are sensitive to referential variations, can operate successfully with class extension, but only when the intensifier 'every single' is used. To understand this, one must concentrate once again on the procedure of quantification in relation to the determining problem.

The intensifier 'every single' may powerfully signal class extension because it takes the emphasis away from the sub-total to concentrate children on cumulating individuals. In this way, the particularising function of 'every single' to distribute the predicate across items may avoid the sub-totalising problem in the same way as the logical comparison between 'some' and 'all'. Of course, an alternative is that the intensifier function of 'every single' (rather than the quantifying function) may encourage children to adopt a strategy either of summing across sub-totals or of deleting the sub-total in favour of a true inclusion relation. There is a logical argument against this explanation, for in both cases children would first have to focus on the sub-class *before* carrying out additional quantifying procedures on it. Thus children would still have to confront the sub-totalising problem which, as I have already shown, they cannot readily overcome for universal quantification. With hindsight, it is regrettable that the expression '*absolutely* all' was not included for comparison, since it would have allowed the intensifier function to be disassociated from the quantifying function of distributive predication.

To summarize, I suggest that children do not necessarily fail to grasp the operation of class extension in class inclusion problems, but rather that the totalizing component of the universal quantifier can be a powerful source of miscuing. The differences in children's class inclusion performance can be explained in terms of the relative strength accorded to the determining and quantifying functions of language, which must be co-ordinated for the identification of the extended class. Therefore, I am arguing that children do not fail class inclusion because they lack the necessary quantificational skills, but because they are unable to co-ordinate determining and quantifying information and thus wrongly accord priority to the former.

My account can be related back to Piaget's theory. His concept of idealised class inclusion competence entails the ability to quantify and compare over universal classes. The problem must be represented as a comparison between the intensional meanings of the logical quantifiers 'some' and 'all'. This is equivalent to an understanding that the concept of plurality is necessarily entailed by the concept of class extension. Yet the extensional inclusion problem which children have to solve requires them to compare a sub-total within an extended class. Therefore, it is the sub-total/class extension relation, rather than the plurality/class extension functions, which children have to master empirically as a prerequisite to class inclusion competence. I strongly suggest that the totalizing function is a developmental advance needed to attain mastery over class inclusion and, at the same time, an obstacle to implementing the logical abstraction of the relations between existential and universal quantification. The linguistic intensifier facilitates inclusive reasoning because it enhances a direct mapping from plurality to class extension, thus enabling children to construct an analogue of Piaget's logical problem. By contrast, 'all' focuses on the sub-total and presents an additional problem for children until they learn that the entailment relation between totality and class extension takes priority over the contrast between the two.

To conclude, I am not claiming that children in the language-sensitive group understand the logical necessity of part—whole relations in the sense intended by Piaget (see Smith, 1982). Rather, I am using a detailed analysis of the conditions for early success at class inclusion to shed new light on the linguistic pre-conditions for the achievement of deductive class inclusion competence. This leads to a re-evaluation of the role of language in logical development. The theory proposed here is that the shift to correct class inclusion responses depends on a corresponding shift in the referential functions that children confer on related plural terms. This process is driven by an internal re-organization of the language system, in that a function which was previously reserved for one modifier is transferred to another. Therefore, purely intra-linguistic processes play a role in driving logical development. It would take a massive research program to test this formulation longitudinally and to expose the lexical mapping rules at each functional level, for one would need to calibrate the determining and quantifying functions against one another. Within such an endeavour, the class inclusion paradigm would have no special status but would be one among many tools for investigating the determining and quantifying functions of referential language in relation to logico-cognitive competence.

REFERENCES

Barrett, M. D. Distinguishing between prototypes: The early acquisition of the meaning of object names. In S. A. Kuczaj III (Ed.), *Language development, Vol. 1, Syntax and Semantics.* New Jersey: Lawrence Erlbaum Associates, 1982.

Bowerman, M. Semantic factors in the acquisition of rules for word use and sentence construction. In D. M. Morehead & A. E. Morehead (Eds), *Normal and deficient child language.* Baltimore: University Park Press, 1976.

Broughton, J. M. Piaget's structural developmental psychology. *Human Development,* 1981, **24**, 195–224.

Brown, R. A new paradigm of reference. In *Psychology and biology of language and thought: Essays in honour of Eric Lenneberg.* New York: Academic Press, 1978.

Carson, M. T., & Abrahamson, A. Some members are more equal than others: The effect of semantic typicality on class-inclusion performance. *Child Development,* 1976, **47**, 1186–1190.

Cromer, R. The development of language and cognition: The cognition hypothesis. In B. Foss (Ed.), *New perspectives in child development.* Harmondsworth: Penguin, 1974.

Dean, A. L., Chaubaud, S., & Bridges, E. Classes, collections and distinctive features: Alternative strategies for solving inclusion problems. *Cognitive Psychology,* 1981, **13**, 84–112.

Donaldson, M., & Lloyd, P. Children's judgements of match and mismatch. In F. Bresson (Ed.), *Problems actuels en psycholinguistique.* Paris: Presses Universitaires de France, 1974.

Elliot, A., & Donaldson, M. Piaget on language. In S. Modgil & C. Modgil (Eds.), *Jean Piaget: Consensus and controversy.* New York: Holt, Rinehart & Winston, 1982.

Freeman, N. H., Sinha, C. G., and Stedmon, J. A. The allative bias is almost proof against task naturalness. *Journal of Child Language,* 1981, **8**, 283–296.

Freeman, N. H., Sinha, C. G., & Stedmon, J. A. All the cars—which cars? From word meaning to discourse analysis. In M. Beveride (Ed.), *Children thinking through language.* London: Edward Arnold, 1982.

Grieve, G., & Garton, A. On the young child's comparison of sets. *Journal of Experimental Child Psychology, 1981,* **32**, 443–458.

Harris, P. L. Cognitive prerequisites to language. *British Journal of Psychology,* 1982, **73**, 187–195.

Hawkins, J. The pragmatics of definiteness, I & II. *Linguistische Berichte,* 1977, **47**, 1–27; **48**, 1–27.

Inhelder, B., & Piaget, J. *The early growth of logic in the child.* London: Routledge & Kegan Paul, 1964.

Karmiloff-Smith, A. *A functional approach to child language: A study of determiners and reference.* Cambridge: Cambridge University Press, 1979.

Lyons, J. *Semantics,* Vols. I & II. Cambridge: Cambridge University Press, 1977.

Mandler, J. M. Representation. In P. Mussen (Ed.), *Manual of child psychplogy,* Vol. 2. New York: Wiley, 1982.

Markman, E. M. The facilitation of part-whole comparisons by use of the collective noun 'family'. *Child Development,* 1973, **44**, 837–840.

Markman, E. M., & Siebert, J. Classes and collections: Internal organisation and resulting holistic properties. *Cognitive Psychology,* 1976, **8**, 561–577.

McCawley, J. D. *Everything that linguists have always wanted to know about logic* (*but were ashamed to ask).*Oxford: Blackwell, 1982.

McGarrigle, J., Grieve, R., & Hughes, M. A contribution to the study of the children's cognitive and linguistic development. *Journal of Experimental Child Psychology,* 1978, **26**, 528–550.

Miller, G. A., & Miller, K. Critical notice—John Lyons on 'Semantics'. *Quarterly Journal of Experimental Psychology,* 1979, **31**, 711–736.

Miller, L. K., and Barg, M. D. Comparison of exclusive versus inclusive classes by young children. *Child Development,* 1982, **53**, .

Olson, D. Language and thought: Aspects of a cognitive theory of semantics. *Psychological Review,* 1970, **77**, 257–273.

Piaget, J. *The child's conception of number.* London: Routledge & Kegan Paul, 1952.

Piaget, J. *Recherches sur l'abstraction reflechissante,* I. Paris: Presses Universitaires de France, 1977.

Rosch, E., Mervis, C. B., Gray, W., Johnson, D., & Boyes-Braem, D. Basic objects in natural categories. *Cognitive Psychology,* 1976, **8**, 382–439.

Shipley, E. F. The class-inclusion task: Question form and distributive comparisons. *Journal of Psycholinguistic Research,* 1979, **8**, 301–331.

Shipley, E. F., & Kuhn, I. F. A constraint on comparisons: Equally detailed alternative. *Journal of Experimental Child Psychology,* 1983, **35**, 195–222.

Stedmon, J. A. Children's Problems with Plural Reference. Doctoral dissertation. Bristol: Bristol University, 1983.

Stedmon, J. A., & Freeman, N. H. When reference fails: An analysis of the use and misuse of quantifier terms to make identifying reference. In J. Allwood & E. Helmquist (Eds.), *Foregrounding background.* Stockholm: Doxa, 1983.

Strawson, P. F. On referring. *Minds,* 1950, **59**, 320–344.

Strawson, P. F. Identifying reference and truth values. *Theoria,* 1964, **30**, 96–118.

Strawson, P. F. Is existence never a predicate? *Critica,* 1976, **1**, 5–15.

Trabasso, T., Isen, A. M., Dolecki, P., McLanahan, A. G., Riley, C. A., & Tucker, T. H. How do children solve class-inclusion problems? In R. S. Siegler (Ed.), *Children's thinking: What develops?* Hillsdale, NJ: Erlbaum, 1978.

Vendler, Z. *Linguistics in philosophy.* Ithaca, NY: Cornell University Press, 1967.

Wilkinson, A. Counting strategies and semantic analysis as applied to class-inclusion. *Cognitive Psychology,* 1976, **8**, 64–85.

6

Representations and Strategies During Inference

B. McGONIGLE

Centre for Cognitive Science and Department of Psychology
University of Edinburgh

M. CHALMERS

Department of Psychology
University of Edinburgh

INTRODUCTION

What is the role of deductive inference in understanding language? Are such inferences ever drawn (where they can be drawn at all) by the average language user? And on those (frequent) occasions when we seem to have gone 'beyond the information given' by the language per se, what is the nature of the process? Is it also a form of inference? A contextual one? And, if contextual, how is this form of inference to be characterised and explained? Such are the issues hotly debated by many contemporary linguists and logicians. The moment seems to have arrived, therefore, for the psychologist to offer his wares. And yet, almost perversely, the majority of psychological studies on inference have been devoted to an analysis of deductive reasoning processes alone. It might therefore seem wrong to lead with evidence based on such studies. Nevertheless, research on deductive inference has opened a window on a range of important cognitive activities, many of which seem to be heavily implicated in understanding language. This development is not

ISBN 0-12-512320-5

altogether surprising, for the task of subjects in classical reasoning tasks as traditionally used by psychologists (e.g., the three-term series problem as in Clark, 1969) could be described as requiring the integration of two statements such that the product of the enterprise is greater than the information derivable from the statements considered independently. That is, the subject must be informed by one statement when interpreting the other. Language requires similar acts of inter-sentential binding and integration.

In the case of both inference and language, theorists have been divided as to whether the mechanisms of such binding can best be explained by linguistic and logical theories or psychological ones. According to Clark (1969), for example, adults' solutions to (transitive) inference problems are to be understood in terms of a linguistic deep structural account in which premises and questions are thought to be decoded into their underlying base strings. Thus, premise information of the form 'A is better than B; B is better than C' will be decoded as 'A is good + ; B is good and C is good – '. While this form will thus be congruent with the question, "Who is best?" (i.e., 'most good'), it will not readily afford an answer to the question, "Who is worst?" (i.e., 'most bad'). In these circumstances, Clark argues, the subject must reformulate the question to read, "Who is least good?"

In contrast to this account, there are a number of models of both language comprehension and logical performance which seek to specify in more psychological terms the procedures which allow correct interpretations to be made of text (see, e.g., Schank, 1975) and inferences to be drawn from purely logical statements (Johnson-Laird, 1983). In language, these models generally conform to those which seek to use the state of world knowledge or background information of a subject, together with those hypotheses or expectancies he or she may have about the nature of the task under review, as important causal determinants of what is understood when lexical input is processed. For Minsky (1975), Schank (1975), Sanford and Garrod (1981) and others, the frame, scenario or expectancy of what is about to be processed materially affects the disambiguation of linguistic information, controls inferences and maintains coherence.

Such models imply top-down processing in which it is assumed that the subject accesses a resource which is historically prior and, from an informational point of view, more extensive than the input interrogated from moment to moment. Thus Johnson-Laird's (1983) claim that we use words in a sentence "as cues to build a *familiar mental model*" seems to imply that language understanding is fundamentally a recognition problem. Although Brown and Yule (1983) point out that the word 'familiar' "is rather smuggled into the description without any account of what 'being familiar' is based on", one reasonable interpretation of Johnson-Laird's account seems to be that in order to be understood, language must somehow 'map' onto a model of reality already established. Trabasso endorses this position in the context of deductive inference when he suggests that a linear representational device may be used by subjects when encoding premise information (in transitive reasoning tasks) such that "end-anchors (of the series) are *mapped* onto a spatial dimension and the pairs are first ordered and entered into the array" (Trabasso & Riley, 1975, p. 394, emphasis added).

And yet there is confusion and conflict here, for claims have also been made which suggest that the quality of the linguistic input per se is the sole determinant of whether or not a mental model will be constructed. For example, Mani and Johnson-Laird (1982) claim that an entirely arbitrary state of affairs can be modelled so long as the input is determinate. On this view, the intrinsic properties of statements are held to be both necessary and sufficient to establish a mental model. Where determinacy is violated, the argument runs, no such model is possible; instead, subjects code the statements into a propositional form "close to the surface form of the sentence" (Trabasso & Riley, 1975, p. 185). And Trabasso (despite endorsing an apparently conflicting interpretation, as cited above) appears to conjure with a similar process when he describes premise-encoding as "*constructing* linear orders from pairwise ordered information" (Trabasso & Riley, 1975, p. 407, emphasis added).

It would thus appear that two rival positions compete for dominance in both logic and linguistic theories. In one, a mental model is used as an explanatory construct to account for language understanding; in the other, the form of the linguistic input is taken as the crucial determinant of the model itself. Given this dilemma, we shall explore the issue of mapping versus constructivism with special reference to the transitive inference (deductive) task. Using a variety of experimental paradigms and subjects—human adults, children and non-human primates—we shall introduce evidence to support the thesis that logical tasks (of the linear transitive inference sort, at any rate) are understood by subjects through a mapping of the premises (whether determinate or indeterminate) onto cognitive structures which causally predate logical and linguistic competence.

THE NATURE OF THE IMAGE: MAPPING VERSUS CONSTRUCTIVISM IN LOGICAL THEORIES

Although causal relationships are unclear, there is a growing consensus among investigators that adults frequently form spatial images when solving transitive inference problems of the sort, "Tom is smaller than Bill; Tom is taller than Jack; Who is the tallest?" Typically, "S arranges the items described in the first premise, starting at the top or left of his imaginary space. . . . After constructing an array from the first premise, S uses the second premise to add the third item to his construction" (Huttenlocher, 1968, p. 558). A protocol from a recent study of our own (Chalmers & McGonigle, 1983) with 9-year-old children illustrates the use of a similar device by younger subjects when solving these problems: "I see a picture in my head and the names are written underneath them. . . . If you say Gill is bigger than Linda, Gill comes in and then Linda comes in" and after some practice:

> If you say Eve is bigger than Polly and Marion is bigger than Eve, I put Marion at the beginning, Eve in the middle and Polly at the end—left to right, biggest, middle, smallest. That was how I was doing it today. In the beginning I was doing it in my head; they were different sizes but they all looked the same . . . all just girls and they stood the way you say them. Now when you said them all I turned them round . . . left to right.

Although it is clear that subjects literally go beyond the information given in constructing these models, it is also the case that severe constraints operate on the spatial vectors realised in the image or model of the state of affairs represented by the premises. As de Soto, London, and Handel (1965, p. 520) put it:

> People are good at thinking of elements as ordered because they can readily arrange them appropriately on an axis—ordinarily the vertical axis—in their cognitive space. But this space is in a sense one-dimensional. It does not provide other axes; even the left–right axis seems relatively unavailable. And the space is certainly not an n-dimensional cartesian coordinate system in which an element can have different values on different dimensions, nor can an element simultaneously occupy different positions on the one axis.

Not only are the axes constrained in this way, but the direction of working within the axes is likewise restricted, with top to bottom and left to right being the preferred ones (de Soto et al., 1965; Huttenlocher, 1968).

Despite the wide consensus established for image use (see Jones, 1970; Egan & Grimes-Farrow, 1982), the emphasis varies, among investigators as to the particular aspects of the imaginal representation they see as crucial. For some, the constraints on the direction of working are critically related to the polarities implied by the relational terms themselves, which in turn influence the vector of encoding that subjects may use. According to de Soto et al. (1965, p. 515), for example, "People learn an evaluative ordering more readily from better to worse than from worse to better." The authors also report: "The tie to the vertical axis we have found for better–worse relations seems to exist for the three major dimensions of meaning reported by Osgood, Suci and Tannenbaum" (de Soto et al., 1965, p. 520). For others (e.g., Huttenlocher, 1968, p. 560), the relational terms are not as important as the spatial constructions of the subject, "since problems which are laid out left to right are frequently easier than those using the terms 'left' and 'right.'"

Instead, as mental operations are carried out with imaginary objects "which can be picked up and moved", it is the grammatical relationship between subject and object which is seen as central in determining the assembly of objects into a progression in a rightwards direction.

Thus there are two main characteristics of logical problem-solving which emerge from the analysis of protocol reports. The first is a privileged direction of encoding where the dimensional polarity implied by the terms is paramount in determining the relative congruity of the premises; the second is the use of a spatial paralogical device. Here, premise order and subject/object order are the crucial determiners of congruence. If these features of the mental model are causal to the subject's understanding of the premises (and we shall present evidence later that they are), then a major implication of the first notion is that only some statements of relation can be mapped directly onto a model of the state of affairs implied by the premises; in the case of non-congruent statements, conversion and translation will be required. For some statements, therefore, an extra cost is incurred in their decoding. This cost should be registered in terms of extra processing time.

Compelling as this notion is, there exists little evidence in its favour (see, e.g., Foos, 1980; Potts & Scholz, 1975). One reason is that the locus of congruity is unclear within the logical paradigm as it is used conventionally. This is due to a difficulty endemic to the conventional transitive inference paradigm insofar as the experimenter is required to provide information to the subject before asking any questions of him. Thus the experimenter must decide which form and direction to use in the premises and the question. In these tasks, therefore, the possible sources of congruity lie between the language of the premises, the language of the question and the underlying representation.

A major psychological implication of the second (spatial paralogic) feature of the image is mental distance. Items can be considered as more or less remote (spatially) from one another in a series laid out, say, from left to right along an imaginary horizontal axis. Such a concept implies that the more remote the items to be compared 'in the mind's eye', the less confusable, and hence the faster, inferential decisions become. Such counter intuitive results have, in fact, been well established by Trabasso in a series of experiments (Trabasso & Riley, 1975). However, it is by no means clear what these phenomena imply for the nature of mental representation. On the one hand, they may signify merely the use of an optional mnemonic aid calculated to reduce retrieval difficulties but playing no major causal role in the subject's understanding and integration of the premises themselves. Alternatively, they may be indexical of important *pre*logical structures without which the logic of serial order would be impossible (see Berlyne, 1971). Trabasso reflects this dilemma in his own accounts, as Breslow (1981) observes. Given that all subjects who have shown these effects thus far have been logically competent, the causal role of the spatial paralogical device remains obscure. However, if similar devices are found in subjects lacking logical skills, the issue might be readily resolved.

It can be seen that neither representational congruity as a concept nor the causal role of the spatial paralogical device has been clearly established. In an attempt to resolve these questions, we employed two main strategies. First, we dealt with the congruity issue using an alternative paradigm concerned essentially with our natural mode of ordering information in memory. This type of research, known as 'internal psychophysics' (after Moyer, 1973), normally requires subjects to decide as rapidly as possible, say, the relative sizes of well-known objects from memory alone. Thus subjects might be confronted with, for example, a pair of names of animals such as 'hen' or 'elephant' and asked to denote the larger by pressing a switch below the panel bearing the printed name (pictures are also used, scaled to appear of equal size). As the knowledge representation is assumed to be established prior to the task, the problem of congruity endemic to the logical task can be eliminated. Now there is no basis for ambiguity. The degree of mapping achieved has to be between the question and the representation, and not between the question, the informing statement, and the representation. Second, we investigated the causal role of the spatial paralogical device using younger subjects, whose failures in logical tasks have been documented (e.g., Inhelder & Piaget, 1964) and monkeys (not well-known for their logical skills). We report our findings in the following sections.

REPRESENTATIONAL CONGRUITY AND THE SYMBOLIC DISTANCE PARADIGM

In our study using this paradigm (McGonigle and Chalmers, 1984), we required 6- and 9-year-old children to compare familiar items in the physical world (animals) using the conventional pictorial and lexical methods as described here. The finding usually obtained with adults is that the time taken to compare symbols varies inversely with the distance between the referents on the dimension being judged (e.g., Moyer, 1973; Paivio, 1975). Thus, the time taken to judge the relative size of 'cat' versus 'whale' is less than that required to determine the relative size of 'cat' versus 'fox'. This effect is known as the 'symbolic distance effect', and it is analogous with the effects described by Trabasso (Trabasso & Riley, 1975). In addition, we required subjects to verify statements of relation pertaining to the items (e.g., 'Is a cow smaller than a cat?'). Thus, in this latter condition, subjects were confronted with four question forms, as illustrated in Table 6.1.

Our results were quite clear. First, significant overall distance effects were obtained, particularly in the conventional comparison condition, analogous to those reported by Trabasso and Riley (1975); see Figure 6.1. Second, the

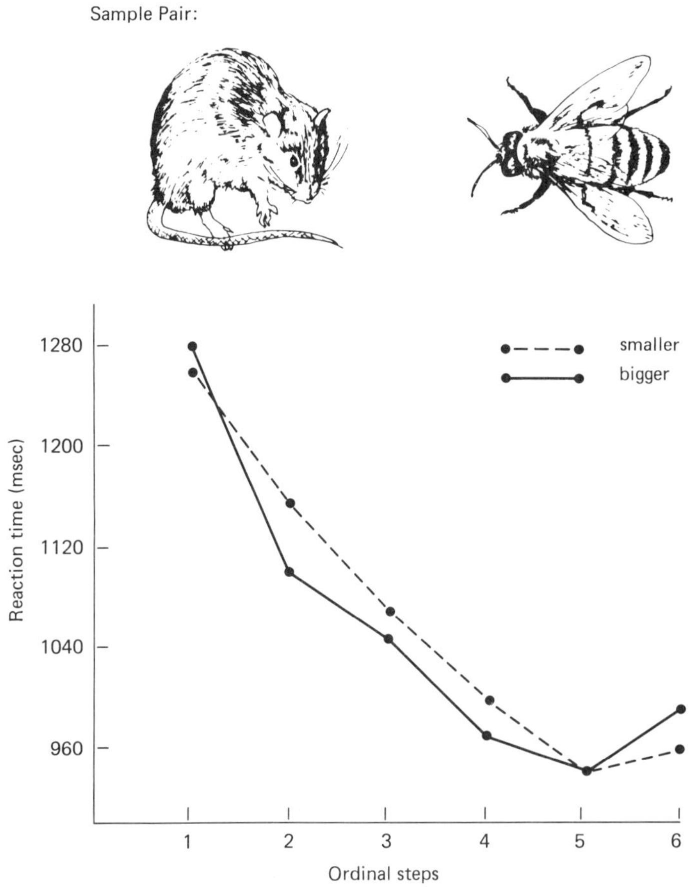

Figure 6.1. Symbolic distance effects produced by 6-year-olds making animal size comparisons.

type of question asked in the verification condition significantly affected the overall performance profile, in terms of both choice, accuracy and decision time. Consistent with a strongly directional codification, smaller 'true' questions were answered significantly less accurately and significantly more slowly (when correct) than the other three forms of question. Table 6.1 summarises these effects.

Although an intuitive interpretation of directional effects might suggest a clean split between smaller and bigger questions in favour of both question types feature the 'unmarked' comparative (bigger), the model articulated below (Figure 6.2) shows how simple strategies designed to map relational statements with a very definite subject–object relationship onto a directional representation of the sort we hypothesise can lead to success with three forms

TABLE 6.1

Accuracy and Decision Times of 6-year-olds on Four Question Forms

	True		False	
	% correct	msec	% correct	msec
Bigger	75	3590	87	3830
Smaller	58	4320	87	3908

of question (bigger 'true', bigger 'false' and smaller 'false') and failure with one (smaller 'true'). In contrast, 9-year-olds were able to answer all forms of question correctly. Their reaction-time profiles, however, reflect a selective difficulty with the smaller 'true' question. This question form was not only answered more slowly than any of the others (see Table 6.2) but was also the only one which failed to show a distance effect when these were computed separately for each question form. Nevertheless, 9-year-olds did succeed in answering this question correctly.

While these data are open to the interpretation that a second, if weaker, polarity has been established by older subjects to enable them to cope with

Assumption: Subjects retrieve knowledge of animal size relations in 'bigger than' statements only and then match it against the given question.

Thus:

(a) Bigger 'true'—e.g., "Is a cow bigger than a cat?"
Strategy: given information—'cow big'
retrieved information—'cow big'
Therefore *Direct confirmation*

(b) Smaller 'false'—e.g., "Is a cow smaller than a cat?"
Strategy: given information—'cow small'
retrieved information—'cow big'
Therefore *Direct disconfirmation*

(c) Bigger 'false'—e.g., "Is a cat bigger than a cow?"
Strategy: given information—'cat big'
retrieved information—'cow big'
Therefore *Indirect disconfirmation*

(d) Smaller 'true'—e.g., "Is a cat smaller than a cow?"
Strategy: given information—'cat small'
retrieved information—'cow big'
No basis for match or mismatch

Given the above assumption, (a), (b) and even (c) may be answered correctly, but (d) should result in failure.

Figure 6.2. Model of verification procedures based on unidirectional processing assumptions.

TABLE 6.2
Accuracy and Decision Times of 9-year-olds on Four Question Forms

	True		False	
	% correct	msec	% correct	msec
Bigger	87	1510	93	1710
Smaller	84	1770	88	1660

smaller 'true' questions, (albeit more tardily), we believe the more parsimonious interpretation to be that they convert descriptions such as '*X* smaller than' into '*X* is not bigger than' and thereby add a further operation to the decision-making process. Not only would this account for the fact that smaller 'true' questions, while answered correctly, are still the slowest, it would also square with the fact that the order of difficulty of the three other forms of question is as predicted by the model summarized earlier. Thus, smaller 'false' is faster than bigger 'false' because one involves direct, and the other indirect, disconfirmation. But smaller 'true', while indirectly confirmed (e.g., 'cow bigger'; 'cat not bigger') will be slowest of all owing to the extra operation required in this case. Similar results following the only analogous tests on adults we found reported (see Holyoak, Dumais & Moyer, 1979) suggest that the 9-year-olds' profile was not merely a transitional phase of development.

Taken as a package, we interpret these results as an endorsement of the distinction between representation and strategy suggested by much of the work on inference reviewed earlier. Whatever the particular details of individual models, there appears to be almost universal support for the notion that subjects prefer a particular form of statement (Clark, Carpenter & Just, 1973), premise order (Hunter, 1957), direction of working along a spatial vector and/or vector orientation (de Soto et al., 1965; Huttenlocher, 1968). If such predelictions imply some 'ideal' form of representation, it follows that strategies will be elaborated which are dedicated to the processing of incoming information to make it congruent with that ideal or 'image of achievement'. What has not been clear thus far, however, is the extent to which such processing characteristics are strategic or otherwise in origin. In contrast, our results with 6-year-olds, showing a collapse of performance when the subject was forced to process in the 'wrong' direction, indicate unequivocally, we would argue, a basic design or computational constraint on representation.

In general, the case for separating representational from strategic influences seems to be supported by the research. Yet given that the verification tests have themselves been linguistic, the possibility cannot be ruled out that

TABLE 6.3
Decision Times (msecs) Obtained Under Various Input Conditions

Question form	Bigger		Smaller		Overall Mean
	True	False	True	False	
Perceptual	2520	2710	2910	2890	2758
Memorial (pictorial)	2980	2970	3299	2960	3028
Memorial (lexical)	3590	3830	4320	3890	3908

the selective congruity effects that we have recorded here are endemic to a purely linguistic form of representation. To counter this difficulty, we included in our study (McConigle & Chalmers, 1984) tests in which the items were represented by pictures. Similar congruity effects were also observed, however, as Table 6.3 shows.

Picture symbols are usually compared faster than lexical items, although the superiority of pictorial over lexical input has been the subject of recent controversy. For Paivio (1978, p. 42), the effect implies that "the linguistic system per se does not contain the perceptual or semantic information that corresponds to our knowledge of the world. . . . Instead, the verbal system can retrieve such information only by probing the nonverbal representational system." The implication of Paivio's view is that language needs to be converted or mapped into a form of representation which is essentially non-linguistic before it can understood—hence the temporal disadvantage of lexical input. In contrast, Banks (1977) believes that such effects are best understood as being due to a form of encoding which is essentially semantic and symbolic. Contrary to Paivio's explanation, Banks accounts for the mode effects merely in terms of the differences in time that it takes subjects to categorise the items used in the test. Once these differences are taken into consideration, he argues, no further mode differences remain.

In line with both positions, we first report a highly significant mode effect using pictures scaled to appear of equal size. The performance of 6-year-olds viewing the pictures was almost as good as if the actual sizes were shown. The inferior lexical performance is all the more striking, as the tests were oral, not written (as in the case of Paivio's (1978) tests with adult subjects). These results are summarized in Table 6.3.

When categorisation tests were run, however, the absolute differences in performance found as a function of mode were too small to fully account for the mode differences obtained in the comparison condition. Thus our results appear to support Paivio's position rather than Banks'. In addition, in comparing the time it took subjects to classify items (both lexical and pictorial) as 'big' or 'small', there was a striking asymmetry in favour of the 'big' category. When making 'small' category judgements, subjects appeared

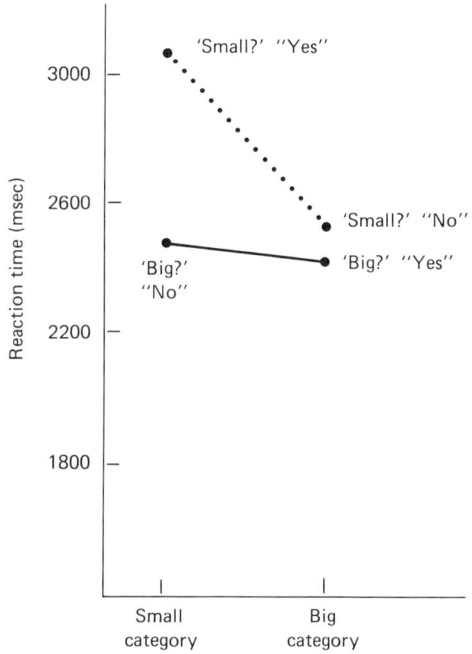

Figure 6.3. Reaction time profile produced by 6-year-olds verifying animal size.

to use 'not big' rather than 'small'. Asked to determine, by means of a simple verification task, whether individual items were 'big' or 'small', 6-year-olds provided the profile shown in Fig. 6.3.

As in the previous verification conditions, these results show a strong polarity effect. It was easier for subjects to negate 'false' statements made about small items (e.g., "Is a rat a big one?") than to affirm 'true' statements concerning their smallness, especially for lexical items. The reverse was true for items judged to be 'big'. Although there was a significant difference in categorisation time in favour of the pictorial condition, the absolute differences between these times do not account in any way for the mode differences obtained in the comparison tasks.

Overall, the results show strong directionality effects as a function of term polarity. Such results are fully consistent with those which have emerged thus far in the context of experiments on inference. These are indexed by the selective impact of question form, best explained (we would argue) as a consequence of the mapping relationship between the form of the input and the natural mode of representation of the subject—a representation which, judging by the strong mode effects we obtained, is essentially non-linguistic in character. Further, the performance profile of the older (9-year-old) subjects seems to suggest the development of a strategic factor permitting ostensibly incongruent forms of input to be understood through conversion and translation. Finally, we have shown clear distance functions which are analogous with those found in the context of experiments on inference. These suggest the early development of a mental metric or set of codes which allow for the representation of order with respect to some reference point or pole.

The mode effects reported earlier notwithstanding, we would find it hard to rule out purely linguistic, rather than representational, factors as causal to the effects we report here. As Richards (1979) points out, culturally induced biases alone may be responsible for any antonymic asymmetry effects found; certainly the role of language is difficult to exclude, even in ostensibly non-linguistic tests. In addition, there are problems of interpretation and extrapolation, for the distance effects we uncovered within the context of the symbolic distance effect paradigm may not be at all analogous to the (symbolic) distance effects obtained during the course of inference tasks. In these latter conditions, the subject deals ostensibly with arbitrary objects whose attributes are known merely by repute. In the former conditions, by contrast, it is reasonable to suppose that most if not all of the objects have been experienced directly. In the former case, therefore, it could be said that the subject simply accesses memory for the data as stored, whereas in the latter case the subject constructs the ordinality using logical operators. To eschew difficulties of interpretation, we would need to have a group of subjects with no known logical competence, confront them with inference tasks as they are conventionally given, and then compare their performance profile with, say, adult subjects.

Although 6-year-olds have been found to use non-logical strategies in transitive inference tasks (Chalmers & McGonigle, 1984), their status in this respect is somewhat controversial (see Breslow, 1981). However, no such controversy surrounds the monkey as a logical subject (see McGonigle & Chalmers, 1977), and the linguistic skills of non-human primates seem rudimentary (see McGonigle, 1980). Should analogous tests provide similar results when given to these subjects, the implication would be that the main features of mental models for transitive inference-taking (direction and distance) are prelinguistic and prelogical in origin and play a causal role in the (later) understanding of both linguistic and logical terms of relation. We summarize the results of such experiments in the following section.

DIRECTION AND DISTANCE PHENOMENA WITHOUT A LOGICAL SUBJECT

Direction

To assess this effect, we carried out a study with five squirrel monkeys. The animals were required to learn a series of conditional size discriminations such that within a series of size objects (ABCDE), they had to choose the larger or largest one of a pair or a triad if, say, the objects were black; if white, they had to choose the smaller/smallest one (McGonigle & Chalmers, 1980). Testing continued for several months, during which performance was generally perfect; decision times were recorded for all trials, and the monkeys were tested on 10 pairs and 10 triadic permutations derived from the five size stimuli using both instruction conditions.

Three findings of considerable relevance to the human case emerged from the decision time profile. First, there was a significant and consistent effect of direction of processing such that decisions following the 'instruction', "Find the bigger," were made faster than those made in response to the other comparative, 'smaller'. Through practice, the animals became progressively faster, and yet the absolute difference between the instruction conditions remained invariant. Finally, there was a significant effect of ordinal position such that a beneficial interaction occurred between the categorical status of the items at the 'big' end of the series and the instructions congruent with those items (e.g., "Take the bigger/biggest"). No such congruity effects occurred for the small end of the continuum. Figure 6.4 summarizes the results for congruity and direction and compares them with those obtained for children under the memorial (lexical) conditions described earlier.

Combined with the selective congruity effects just reported, distance effects observed indicate that monkeys also use a reference point or pole analogous to that alleged to be used by adults in logico-linguistic tasks. However, the effects we have described, while decisive with respect to the issue of directionality, are less so with respect to the distance effects obtained, based as they are on purely perceptual computations remote from the formal reasoning tasks described earlier. However, we have developed a symbolic analogue for use with monkeys (McGonigle & Chalmers, 1977), the results of which we now report.

'Symbolic' Transitivity and Distance

Based on a modification of a five-term series problem given to very young children by Bryant and Trabasso (1971), we tested monkeys on transitive inference tasks as follows: Eight squirrel monkeys were trained to solve a series of four discrimination problems (see Table 6.4 for design schema). Each monkey was first confronted with a pair of differently coloured containers that also varied in weight ($A > B$). When B was chosen reliably over A, the monkey moved on to the next problem ($B > C$, where C must be chosen), and so on until the entire series was performed correctly. Only two weight values were used throughout the series, so no specific weight could be uniquely identified with stimuli B, C or D. The problems were presented in random order until subjects achieved a high level of performance on all four training

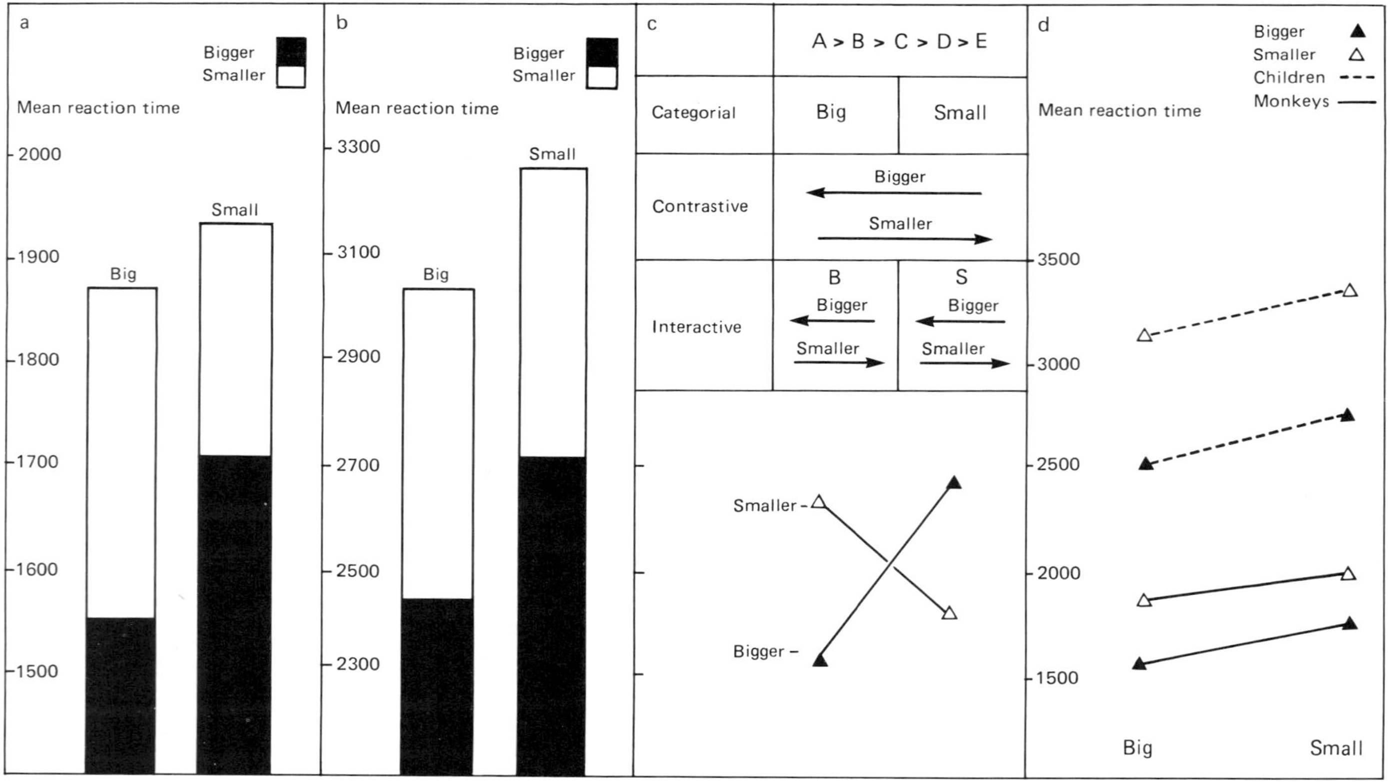

Figure 6.4. Categorical and contrastive effects in monkeys (a) and children (b); symmetrical category with contrastive interaction (c); (d) interactions obtained in monkeys and children.

TABLE 6.4
Five-Term Series Training Paradigm Given to Monkeys

Series identification		1		2		3		4	
		A	B	B	C	C	D	D	E
Pair	4 subjects	Light	Heavy	Light	Heavy	Light	Heavy	Light	Heavy
Weight	4 subjects	Heavy	Light	Heavy	Light	Heavy	Light	Heavy	Light
Color (for (example)		Yellow	Blue	Blue	Green	Green	Red	Red	White

pairs, regardless of presentation order. On subsequent tests of transitivity, novel pairings represented all ten pairings derivable from the five-term series were presented. No further training was given.

The results are recorded in Table 6.5. They show an impeccable transitive profile, of special significance in the case of comparisons involving terms *B* and *D*, each of which had been specified as both heavier than and lighter than its neighbour within the training series. Our data for monkeys are indistinguishable from those of 6-year-old children as reported by Bryant and Trabasso (1971).

The monkeys also showed strong serial position effects (i.e., pair asymmetry, with the end pairs being easier to learn than the middle pairs, *BC* and *CD*), regarded by Trabasso (1977) as a "sine qua non of linear representation". Preliminary decision time analysis showed a significant distance

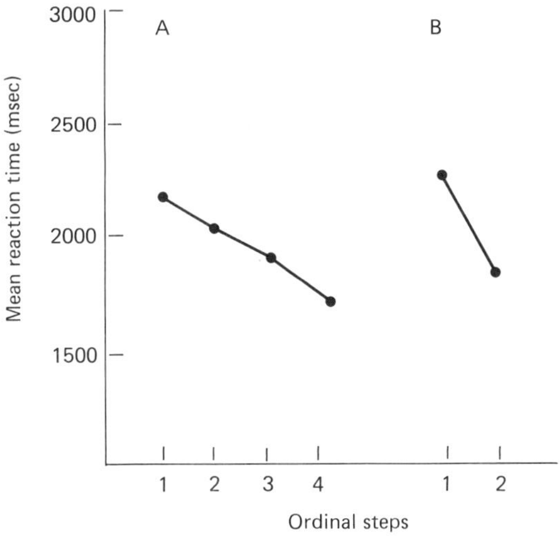

Figure 6.5. Symbolic distance effect in monkeys: (a) all comparisons, and (b) non-end-anchored comparisons.

TABLE 6.5
Performances by Monkeys and 6-year-olds on Five-term Series Tests
(% transitive choice)

	Monkeys				Children[a]			
	B	C	D	E	B	C	D	E
A	98	100	100	100	99	99	100	100
B		93	90	76		94	92	99
C			89	87			98	100
				97				100

[a] Data reported in Bryant and Trabasso (1971).

effect in which the decision times for non-adjacent comparisons (the transitive inference tests) were significantly shorter than those for solving the training pairs (embedded within the tests of transitivity)—the crucial evidence in Trasbasso's experiments for a spatial paralogical device. This effect is illustrated in Figure 6.5.

On all major points of comparison, the monkeys were identical in performance to young humans. Even the non-verbal nature of their task cannot be used to distinguish their performance, as similar profiles in 6-year-old children, using both non-verbal and verbal forms of the same task, have also been reported (Chalmers & McGonigle, 1984). As that same study shows, the performances of both species are indistinguishable and, taken together with the monkey data, indicate that neither species nor task factors play a substantial role here.

Are monkeys logical, however? Have the profiles we recorded been produced as a result of the co-ordination of premise information? Unlike conventional studies, we tested both monkeys and 6-year-old children on explicit tests of co-ordination within the same study. Here we confronted subjects with three items, derived from the five-term series. Thus *B*, *C* and *D* were given, for example, on the same trial, and the decision profile compared with the binary test profile. Our hypothesis was that subjects would select, say, *D* exclusively, had co-ordination been an operator in the binary test situation. In fact, they did not, as Table 6.6 shows. However, the data are regular enough to suggest a different form of strategy (McGonigle & Chalmers, 1977). Also, when combined into an overall choice matrix, it is clear that the set of items is ordered by subject (see Table 6.7). Thus we have shown an impeccable transitivity profile in a subject unable to co-ordinate the premises within the same task. Yet the set is ordered overall, and all of the characteristics of performance reported with the adult subjects emerge clearly.

To account for this performance, we have suggested (McGonigle, 1978) that the scale of values recorded in Table 6.7 can be derived from an

TABLE 6.6

Performance by Monkeys on Triadic Combinations from the Five-Term Series (% Bias)

Triads	Choice projection[a]			Obtained		
ABC	00	33	67	00	31	69
BCD	17	33	50	03	36	61
BDE	17	17	67	16	24	60
CDE	00	33	67	11	24	65
BCE	00	33	67	06	28	66
ABD	00	50	50	00	44	56
ACD	00	33	67	00	30	70
ADE	00	33	67	01	21	78
ABE	00	33	67	00	30	70
ACE	00	33	67	00	26	74
Average distribution	0.03	0.33	0.64	0.04	0.29	0.67

[a] The figures in the left-hand column are predictions based on the assumptions that the subjects are sampled equally often and that preferences are absolute within those subsets presented during original training.

information theory model based on nested set notions. On this account, the subset *AB* is seen as requiring the transmission of one bit of information (log *N* to the base 2). To select *C* on this model requires the subject to transmit more information on the grounds that *C* is derived from a larger subset (three items) and *D* from a larger subset again (two bits). While in theory *E* is the most difficult case, requiring the transmission of 2.33 bits of information, it is in fact an end value and thus has a privileged status. Thus a gradable set of values can be realised with reference to end point anchors without requiring any notions of relational co-ordination.

It would strain credulity, however, to suggest that the basis of ordering reported for monkeys is due to the accessing of a mental model or spatial image of order on which the subject maps the premises. Nevertheless, there are preliminary indications that the strategy used to establish order is very similar to that described by Trasbasso for adult human subjects. As described by Trabasso (1977, p. 394), subjects trained on a five-term series proceed by "first ordering the end pairs (1, 2) and (4, 5), entering sticks 2 and 4 into the array. Then one orders pairs (2, 3) and (3, 4), entering stick 3 into the array." In a perceptual version of the co-ordination task with monkeys, where they were required to select a middle-sized stimulus (in addition to choosing in accordance with the rules for biggest and smallest as described earlier), it was found that the decision times for this rule—take middle when all the stimuli are red—were frequently shorter than those for coding the rule for 'smallest',

This result would be anomalous had the monkeys derived the middle stimuli from a co-ordinate strategy which first required them to solve for the

TABLE 6.7
Overall Triadic Choice Matrix for Monkeys Showing Frequency of Choice Within Triads and for Individual Items

A	B	C	D	E			
0	22	48	—	—	A	B	C
—	2	25	43	—	B	C	D
—	11	—	17	42	B	D	E
—	—	8	17	45	C	D	E
—	4	20	—	46	B	C	E
0	31	—	39	—	A	B	D
0	—	21	49	—	A	C	D
1	—	—	15	54	A	D	E
0	21	—	—	49	A	B	E
0	—	18	—	52	A	C	E
1	91	140	180	288	Combined		

biggest, and then the smallest, before identifying the middle (size) value. However, preliminary analysis of their scanning strategies by means of frame-by-frame analysis on a video-recorder suggest that the monkeys were using a rule analogous to that described by Trabasso in the context of six-term series problems. It would appear to be based on the following rule: Find the most prominent end anchor stimulus in any triad (usually the biggest) and then solve 'middle' by finding the value next to the anchor. If this is the case, then monkeys might generalize this rule within an expanded set of five items as the second or fourth stimulus of the set. Experiments to determine whether or not this happens are in progress and will be reported elsewhere. It seems plausible to argue, however, following these preliminary results, that monkeys may be able to show an understanding of ordinal rules following various colour instruction codes (e.g., If red, take second biggest; if blue, take third biggest; if yellow, take fourth biggest) without any corresponding (relational) co-ordination ability whatsoever.

A related finding has been reported by Siegel (1972) in work with young children. While the end points of the set are readily detected within a size series, the middle items are much more difficult. Siegel suggests that some form of 'next to' strategy is the basis of the child's seriation rule. If so, then we have begun to identify psychological mechanisms which create order structures *prior* to the operation of co-ordinate relational skills demanded within a formal system. Certainly there is no good reason to believe that either at the time of test or prior to it does the adult subject need to use anything but a prelogical ordering resource to solve transitive inference problems of this type. In short, we suggest that the spatial image or paralogical device is not constructed by relational terms as encoded by the subject. Instead, the spatial image is used as a representational schema onto which premises are mapped.

Two main psychological implications follow from this. The first is that the schema can be used as a hypothesis prior to any input. The second is that neither linguistic nor logical indeterminacy per se need abort nor inhibit any map, image or model already established by subjects as a hypothesis concerning the putative states of affairs implied by certain premises. In the final section we offer some evidence to support both implications.

IMAGE AND INDETERMINACY

Imagine a discourse task in which the recipient is attempting to place a set of checkers in a configuration in accordance with a set of instructions. In the first case, the configuration to be achieved is essentially a random walk design; in the second, it is a simple circle—a good figure precisely because of its redundant part–whole relationships. Should knowledge of a part reveal sufficient information to allow the subject to predict the rest of the figure, then it can be seen that indeterminate input is not in itself a significant impediment towards a realization of the model in question; even determinate input, if redundant, will not be fully interrogated (or at least need not be). From this we might predict that it is the inherent structure of the referential domain, rather than the type of input per se, which determines the success (or otherwise) of the performance.

However, there appears to be a conflict in the evidence concerning adults' treatment of indeterminacy. On the one hand, Moeser and Tarrant (1977) gave subjects indeterminate relations and found that they were capable of forming 'integrated' representations of these similar to those found with determinate relations. In fact, Moeser and Tarrant (1977, p. 657) found that once they had "demonstrated how to form a visual ordering, the subjects had no difficulty constructing this type of mental representation and using this construction to answer test questions". On the other hand, Mani and Johnson-Laird (1982) claim that subjects confronted with indeterminate relations fail to develop a mental model for them; instead, they encode the statements "on a shallow linguistic level".

One of the problems with indeterminacy is that the nature of the task required of the subject is unclear in the experimental versions of the problem employed thus far. Should the subject interpret the task as one of resolution and interpretation of the premises/linguistic input, then, given the extent to which the task can suggest a strong map or characterization of a possible state of affairs, it would appear as if a meaningful interpretation could be

TABLE 6.8

Premise-Reading Time (csec) as a Function of Condition (Determinacy) and Practice

	Blocks of problems solved			
	1–8	9–16	17–24	25–32
Determinate	1375	1325	1275	1130
Indeterminate	1325	1350	1180	1090
Partially determinate	1200	1000	710	680

achieved. As one 9-year-old put it during a study using both determinate and indeterminate relations (following the problem, "Simon is bigger than Tim and Simon is bigger than Larry; Which is the smallest?"), "If someone tells me there *is* an answer, I would say Larry" (Chalmers & McGonigle, 1983). Should the task suggest, however, that the subject is to determine the extent to which any interpretation drawn is (uniquely) warranted by the statements provided, then a quite different outcome might be expected—in the case of sophisticated subjects, at least. This is because the subject is now being confronted with the uncertainties and ambiguities of the language itself as a major feature of the task.

On a mapping position, the latter perception is the more sophisticated because the subject must compute what has *not* been specified. Certainly the developmental evidence supports this interpretation, for there is a growing body of evidence to suggest that young children make inferences solely on the basis of what they already know, relying on pragmatic considerations to generate interpretations (e.g., Hidi & Hildyard, 1979). Smith (1979) has found, furthermore, that young children fail to comment on the indeterminacy of items given in class-inclusion problems. Thus, by taking a particular attitude toward the statements made—that is, "interpreting them in the light of their past personal knowledgte" (Hidi & Hildyard, 1979)—young subjects achieve a level of comprehension without realising the potential ambiguity of the language (see Robinson, 1981).

Of course, many adults also seem unaware of indeterminacy even in the context of five premise-inference problems, as McGonigle and Wright (1984) report. Using a variety of measures, they compared determinate and indeterminate conditions over a series of logical tasks, each involving five premises. Premise-reading time, solution time and protocol reports were used to monitor progress. The conditions could not be differentiated on any of the measurements of performance taken.

Table 6.8 shows premise-reading time as a function of condition and practice. This has been used successfully as a measure of semantic integration

TABLE 6.9
Percentage of Adult Subjects Reporting the Use of an Image and an Image as Hypothesis as a Function of Condition

	Image	Image as hypothesis
Determinate	87	75
Indeterminate	94	64
Partially determinate	38	33

and syntactic ambiguity in texts (Trabasso & Nicholas, 1980; Tyler & Marslen-Wilson, 1977), yet no significant differences between the conditions were observed. (In contrast, a group who were given only a constrained subset of questions differed markedly from these subjects.) Of particular interest, however, was the protocol analysis on two counts: First, the percentage of subjects reporting the formation of a spatial image was as high in the indeterminate condition as in the determinate one. This contrasts with the group who had only to answer a subset of questions; here a much lower proportion of subjects reported an image strategy. Table 6.9 summarises these results. Second, practice did not reduce the frequency of image use; instead, subjects reported using the image device in anticipation of the next task. The percentage reporting these anticipatory images is also shown in Table 6.9.

These results clearly confirm those of Moeser and Tarrant (1977) and extend them. Of particular significance for a mapping position is the finding that subjects began to anticipate the task requirements through the use of a spatial representation prior to being given the terms of relation. This finding, together with the lack of any significant difference between determinate and indeterminate test conditions, would seem to provide strong support for the idea that cognitive structures already 'archived' underwrite the ongoing comprehension of logical and linguistic information.

On this view, therefore, indeterminacy per se is not the major source of difficulty; much depends on what is being specified. If the referential domain of the premises as given is inherently lacking in redundancy or good form, then the impact of the message is reduced, whatever the form of input used.

CONCLUDING REMARKS

In this chapter we have attempted to give an account of cognitive processes which appear to underwrite solutions of transitive inference problems—at least those of a certain type. As such, the work represents a case study with respect to one narrow type of inference problem. Indeed it may well be argued that any account of such a restricted type of problem is too domain-limited to be useful within a broader context of other forms of inference, both deductive and contextual. It might also be said that in selecting both directional and spatial paralogical features, we have restricted the search even further, concentrating, perhaps, on epiphenomena (in the case of the spatial device) and strategic factors (in the case of term directionality). We would be foolish indeed not to recognise the potential force behind such arguments. However, it has to be said that much of the considerable variation in performance found in transitive inference tasks of the sort we report seems to be accounted for using the notions of congruity and distance developed within our account. More reassuring, perhaps, is the predictive power of these concepts when applied to other types of tasks.

Although indeterminate problems differ formally from those which have been conventionally used, it is interesting to note the apparent indifference of the psychological apparatus to this shift in problem type, at least under the conditions we describe. On a mapping position, this is not altogether surprising, as what is schematically represented could and should be used as part of a feed-forward system, reflecting the subject's need to be in a state of readiness for the information with which he or she will be confronted (see Bruner, 1957). This psychological invariance of procedures over task types may help to explain the somewhat paradoxical concordance between the psychological accounts of deductive inference and language understanding, even though deductive inferences per se may play a relatively minor role in linguistic comprehension.

In one critical sense, however, linguistic decoding and deductive inference tasks are highly similar. What is at issue in the deductive case is the extent to which the information processor is informed by one logical statement when interrogating another. The crucial psychological question seems to be one concerning the nature of the bridge or connectivity between these statements. The same issue seems true in the case of language understanding in one of its most critical senses, namely, intersentential bridging. In both cases, also, two radically different alternatives are offered: The first position, and the one we espouse, is that some appeal to factors quite extrinsic to the language or the logical forms of expression is necessary if the nature of the connectivity is to be understood. The second is that some intrinsic properties of language alone can be specified which can tie the elements together into a cohesive corpus. In this context, it is interesting to note Gore Vidal's comments on the current state of fiction, which seems to have polarised around these two possibilities. He states:

> Currently there are two kinds of serious novel. The first deals with the Human Condition (often confused in Manhattan with marriage) whilst the second is a word

structure that deals only with itself. Although the Human Condition novel can be read—if not fully appreciated—by any moderately competent reader of the late Dame Agatha Christie, the second cannot be read at all. (Vidal, 1982, p. 83).

ACKNOWLEDGEMENTS

Much of the research reported in this chapter has been supported by grants awarded to the first author from the Social Science Research Council (HR 5277/2 and HR 6904/1) and the Medical Research Council of Great Britain (G8314354N).

REFERENCES

Banks, W. P. Encoding and processing of symbolic information in comparative judgments. In G. H. Bower (Ed.), *The psychology of learning and motivation*, Vol. II. New York: Academic Press, 1977.

Breslow, L. Re-evaluation of the literature on the development of transitive inference. *Psychological Bulletin*, 1981, **89**(2), 325–351.

Brown, G., & Yule, G. *Discourse analysis*. Cambridge: Cambridge University Press, 1983.

Bruner, J. S. On perceptual readiness. *Psychological Review*, 1957, **64**, 123–152.

Bryant, P. E., & Trabasso, T. Transitive inferences and memory in young children. Nature, 1971, **232**, 456–458.

Chalmers, M., & McGonigle, B. O. Metamemorial strategies during problem solving by nine year olds. Paper presented at the annual meeting of the Developmental Section of the BPS, Oxford, September 1983.

Chalmers, M., & McGonigle, B. O. Are children any more logical than monkeys on the five-term series problem. *Journal of Experimental Child Psychology*, 1984, **37**, 355–377.

Clark, H. H. Linguistic processes in deductive reasoning. *Psychological Review*, 1969, **76**, 387–404.

Clark, H. H., Carpenter, P. A., & Just, M. A. On the meeting of semantics and perception. In W. G. Chase (Ed.), *Visual information processing*. New York: Academic Press, 1973.

de Soto, C. B., London, M., & Handel, S. Social reasoning and spatial paralogic. *Journal of Personality and Social Psychology*, 1965, **2**, 513–521.

Egan, D. E., & Grimes-Farrow, D. D. Individual differences in strategies for reasoning. *Memory and Cognition*, 1982, **10**(4), 297–307.

Foos, P. W. Constructing cognitive maps from sentences. *Journal of Experimental Psychology: Human Learning and Memory*, 1980, **6**(1), 25–38.

Hidi, S. E., & Hildyard, A. Four-year-olds understanding of pretend and forget: No evidence for propositional reasoning. *Journal of Child Language*, 1979, **6**, 493–510.

Holyoak, K. J., Dumais, S. T., & Moyer, R. S. Semantic association effects in a mental comparison task. *Memory and Cognition*, 1979, **7**(4), 303–313.

Huttenlocher, J. Constructing spatial images: A strategy in reasoning. *Psychological Review*, 1968, **75**, 550–560.

Hunter, I. M. L. The solving of three-term series problems. *British Journal of Psychology*, 1957, **48**, 286–298.

Inhelder, B., & Piaget, J. *The early growth of logic in the child*. London: Routledge & Kegan Paul, 1964.

Jones, S. Visual and verbal processes in problem-solving. *Cognitive Psychology*, 1970, **1**, 201–214.

Johnson-Laird, P. N. *Mental models*. Cambridge: Cambridge University Press, 1983.

Mani, K., & Johnson-Laird, P. N. The mental representation of spatial descriptions. *Memory and Cognition*, 1982, **10**(2), 181–187.

McGonigle, B. O. Inferential mechanisms in squirrel monkey. *Neuroscience Letters*, 1978, **3**, 58.

McGonigle, B. O. Sign, symbol and syntax in the language of apes. *Nature*, 1980, **286**, 761–762.

McGonigle, B. O., & Chalmers, M. Are monkeys logical. *Nature*, 1977, **267**, 694–696.

McGonigle, B. O., & Chalmers, M. On the genesis of relational terms: A comparative study of monkeys and human children. *Antropologica Contemporanea*, 1980, **3**(2), 236.

McGonigle, B. O., & Chalmers, M. The selective impact of question form and input mode on the symbolic distance effect in children. *Journal of Experimental Child Psychology*, 1984, **37**, 525–554.

McGonigle, B. O., & Wright, P. Mapping versus constructivism. Paper presented at EPS Conference, Bangor, April 1984.

Minsky, M. A framework for representing knowledge. In P. H. Winston (Ed.), *The psychology of computer vision*. New York: McGraw-Hill, 1975.

Moeser, S. D., & Tarrant, B. L. Learning a network of comparisons. *Journal of Experimental Psychology*, 1977, **3**(6), 643–659.

Moyer, R. S. Comparing objects in memory: Evidence suggesting an internal psychophysics. *Perception and Psychophysics*, 1973, **13**(2), 180–184.

Paivio, A. Perceptual comparisons through the mind's eye. *Memory and Cognition*, 1975, **3**(6), 635–647.

Paivio, A. A dual coding approach to perception and cognition. In H. L. Pick & E. Saltzmann (Eds), *Modes of perceiving and processing information*. Hillside: Erlbaum, 1978.

Potts, G. R., & Scholz, K. W. The internal representation of a three-term series problem. *Journal of Verbal Learning and Verbal Behavior*, 1975, **14**, 439–452.

Richards, M. M. Sorting out what's in a word from what's not: Evaluating Clark's semantic features acquisition theory. *Journal of Experimental Child Psychology*, 1979, **27**, 1–47.

Robinson, E. J. Conversational tactics and the advancement of the child's understanding about referential communication. In W. P. Robinson (Ed.), *Communication in development*. London: Academic Press, 1981.

Sanford, A. J., & Garrod, S. C. *Understanding natural language: Explorations of beyond the sentence*. Chichester: Wiley, 1981.

Schank, R. C. The structure of episodes in memory. In D. D. Bobrow & A. M. Collins (Eds), *Representation and understanding*. New York: Academic Press, 1975.

Siegel, L. Development of the concept of seriation. *Developmental Psychology*, 1972, **6**(1), 135–137.

Smith, C. L. Children's understanding of natural language hierarchies. *Journal of Experimental Child Psychology*, 1979, **27**, 437–458.

Trabasso, T. The role of memory as a system in making transitive inferences. In R. V. Kail & J. W. Hagen (Eds), *Perspectives on the development of memory and cognition*. Hillside, NJ: Erlbaum, 1977.

Trabasso, T., & Nicholas, D. Memory and inferences in the comprehension of narratives. In F. Wilkening, J. Becker & T. Trabasso (Eds), *Information integration by children*[2]. Hillsdale, NJ: Erlbaum, 1980.

Trabasso, T., & Riley, C. A. On the construction and use of representations involving linear order. In R. L. Solso (Ed.), *Information processing and cognition: The Loyola symposium*. Hillsdale, NJ: Erlbaum, 1975.

Tyler, L. K., & Marslen-Wilson, W. D. The on-line effects of semantic context on syntactic processing. *Journal of Verbal Learning and Verbal Behavior*, 1977, **16**, 683–692.

Vidal, G. *Pink triangle and yellow star*. London: Heinemann, 1982.

7

On Making Models: A Study of Constructive Memory

KEITH STENNING

Centre for Cognitive Science and Department of Psychology
University of Edinburgh

INTRODUCTION

It has been extensively argued (see, e.g., Johnson-Laird, 1978; Johnson-Laird & Bara, 1983; Johnson-Laird & Steedman, 1978; Stenning, 1975, 1978, 1980) that what subjects seek to represent about a text is a model of its statements—that is, a set of objects mapped onto the predicates and relations of the text. This chapter describes an experimental approach, at a rather early stage of development, to the study of the processes whereby we construct representations of models for simple texts which specify small arrays of objects differing on a few binary dimensions.

To conceive of a comprehender's goal as the representation of a model of a text, rather than as the representation of a set of propositions, forces a focus on texts which do not determine unique models stepwise (sentence by sentence). This in turn emphasises the fact that the texts used by psychologists working on this problem have almost uniformly been of the type that *do* determine unique models stepwise. Unfortunately, such texts do not allow us to distinguish between model-based and proposition-based accounts of the representational process.

This conspiracy is not without reasons. Because comprehenders are engaged in constructing representations of models of texts, and speakers are

REASONING AND DISCOURSE PROCESSES

ISBN 0-12-512320-5

engaged in supplying them with the material they require, in the order if which they require it, there are powerful conventions for text design which constrain departures from stepwise model specification (see particularly Stenning, 1978, for a discussion of these conventions).

The goal of the experiment reported here was to find a way of studying the comprehension of texts which are unusual in their transient indeterminacy in order to throw light on the processes of model construction posed by the 'garden variety' determinate text. In fact, even this program demands some base-line measurement of determinate texts, which is necessary because it is curiously absent from the literature. The reasons for this absence are of some interest themselves, but I shall first supply some examples of the type of texts used in the study before explaining the choice of task.

Following is an example of a text in which the pattern of definite and indefinite phrases determines which pieces of information apply to which objects:

> There are just two objects. One is white. The white one is large. It is square. The other is black. The black one is small. It is square.

This example can be contrasted with one in which all phrases are indefinite and it is only the predicates which permit the inferences that tell us which information applies to which objects. (In the following four examples, I shall take for granted the prefacing statement that there are just two objects in the array.)

(1) There is a small black object. There is a small white object. There is a black square. There is a white circle.

Nevertheless, the inferences, dependent as they are on supplementary assumptions about the logical relations between the predicates, are sufficient to make the text stepwise determinate of a model, namely, a model containing a small black square and a small white circle. However, this type of text, in which co-reference must be inferred, affords the possibility of texts which are temporarily indeterminate as to their co-reference relations. For example:

(2) There is a small black object. There is a small square. There is a large black object. There is a large circle.
(3) There is a small black object. There is a small square. There is a small white object. There is a white circle.
(4) There is a small black object. There is a small square. There is a small white object. There is a white square. There is a black circle.

Examples 2–4 differ in the point at which their indeterminacies are resolved. Intuitively, they are more difficult to represent than either of the previous two examples. It is important to stress that this is not because of the complexity of any of their constituent propositions. One might well suspect that at least part of the awkwardness of the last three examples is the result of their requirement that we work out the referential relations—a feature that they share with example 1. This might lead us to reject them as 'unnatural' and therefore as poor test-beds for theories of representation. The present study will address this concern.

Before entering on a detailed discussion of the study and its results, it is worth surveying some of the psychological landscape to find relevant and related studies and to motivate the choice of technique. From a theoretical perspective, some curious lacunae emerge in the psychological literature on text comprehension and memory.

The modern text comprehension literature can be seen as the heir to Bartlett's approach to the study of memory. It attempts to explain on the idea that memory is a constructive process in which the input is radically transformed. It also seeks to say something more explicit about what it is that is contructed. For example, Bransford and his colleagues (e.g., Bransford & Johnson, 1972) have performed many demonstration experiments to show that it is not sufficient for a subject to appreciate the meaning of each constituent proposition in order to be able to accrete a representation of a whole text. Relations between the propositions are crucial to our search for meaning, but such rich texts defy the formulation of parametric measures of complexity, or of general accounts of what is constructed. Theorists with greater leanings towards experimental analysis or computer simulation, such as Anderson (1976), Kintsch and Van Dijk (1978), and Rumelhart, Lindsay and Norman (1972) and their colleagues, have attempted to formulate general theories of what is constructed, but they have used texts which demand little effort after meaning, since the constituent propositions are present in the input and their referential relations explicitly provided by anaphorical devices. This choice with respect to level of tractability shifts the emphasis of the work towards memory and away from inference. This appears to have had broad ramifications for choice of paradigm.

All of these researchers' choices of task have followed Bartlett (1932) in probing complex memory structures once they have been set up. For example, Anderson (1976) gives his subjects sets of sentences as study material to be learned up to a criterion and then proceeds to relate subsequent statement verification times to the complexity of the network representations posited by his theory. (I choose this work because the present study's results will later invite comparisons.) The goal of the present study, by contrast, is to study the process of the construction of representations; some conventional verification probes were given, chiefly as a check on subjects' thoroughness, but they will not be discussed further. The most direct measure of such processes is the time a subject requires to read a portion of text and incorporate its information into a current representation. Accordingly a self-paced reading task was chosen. This task has, of course, been widely used by those interested in the processing of anaphora in text (notably Stanford & Garrod, 1980), but this work has focused on the retrievability of relations of different degrees of implicitness rather than on the nature of whole text representations.

In a self-paced reading task, one observes a reader take in a sentence, make inferences about how its information relates to that contained in the current representation, and accrete the appropriate additions. One is studying both inference and memory. Inference has, of course, been widely studied—logic problems such as conditional inferences, syllogisms both categorial and relational, and so on—but these are not the forms of inference which concern us here; they do not establish antecedents for anaphors. Johnson-Laird (1983) proposes a theory of subjects' solution processes for syllogisms which assigns a prominent role to representations which are extended forms of a model. This theory amounts to a proposal that subjects assimilate syllogisms to texts which are expository. But the relations between these model-like representations and the experimental texts he uses are much more indirect than the relations in the present task.

The inferences required to establish antecedents for anaphors have been studied under the heading of bridging inferences (see Clark, 1975), but only insofar as these relations are implicit. The inference from "There is a white object. The object is square." to "There is a white square." is an inference all the same. This inference may not be the result of an earth-shattering effort after meaning, but any study of constructive memory that does not see itself as simultaneously a study of inference does not deserve the name. The observation that one cannot study inference without memory has become a commonplace of the developmental literature (e.g., Bryant & Trabasso, 1971), though the observation that one cannot study memory without studying inference would be as apposite, both there and in the present context. Since it is correctly assumed that few subjects make substantial errors on inferences in the texts studied in text comprehension experiments, it would seem to follow that it is necessary to study the time course of the construction rather than the behaviour of the completed structure.

Bartlett (1932) stresses the heritage of meaning that a subject brings to the experimental laboratory and applies to the most impoverished of experimental materials. He points out that Ebbinghaus' attempts to study the semantically uninterpreted both failed and missed the point. What psychologists have come to call 'semantic memory' is the field of general knowledge—in particular, lexical knowledge. Many of the experiments in this field examine relations between words. This is paradoxical when we consider the logician's sense of the word 'semantics'—the study of the relations between linguistic and non-linguistic entities.

TABLE 7.1

Values of a Function Relating Objects in a Domain and Classifying Predicates to Distinct Model Types[a]

Number of classifying predicates	Number of objects in domain 1	2	3	4	5	6	7
1	2	3	4	5	6	7	8
2	4	10	20	35	56	84	—
3	8	36	120	330	792	1716	—
4	16	136	816	3876	—	—	—
5	32	—	—	—	—	—	—
6	64	—	—	—	—	—	—
7	128	—	—	—	—	—	—

[a] Underlined values indicate model sizes used in the first half of the study. The double underlined value is the model size used in the second half.

The present study examines texts which specify sets of objects and their properties. The lexical properties of the predicates that appear are of direct concern only in that they establish antonymy between pairs of predicates. This material is thoroughly episodic; we learn that the current array contains a large white square. Nevertheless the texts have a clear semantic interpretation; we know which sets of objects would make satisfactory models for them. This is semantic memory in the most direct sense. We must not, of course, lose sight of the fact that there is another level of analysis at which 'white' and 'square' may be more easily (because more habitually) conjoined by the chess player, as would 'black' and 'cross' by the practitioner of the dark arts. By judicious choice of material, we seek to minimise the effects of these other levels and concentrate on the manipulation of the meanings of logical particles. In short, the present study seeks to investigate the actual processes of construction of representations for texts by measuring the time needed for each accretion of information and, in particular, by comparing the construction of representations for texts which do (and do not) determine unique models in a stepwise fashion.

In order to begin studying subjects' capacities for constructing models, it is desirable to have some absolute metric for comparing their size and complexity. A model is a set of objects mapped onto a set of predicates and relations. The number of distinct model types of a given size is a function of the number of elements in the domain set, and of the number of predicates and relations onto which they are mapped. Table 7.1 gives values of this function for some small domains and small numbers of monadic predicates. The apparent complexity of the function arises from the fact that the objects within a model are distinguished only by their differences—a model of a

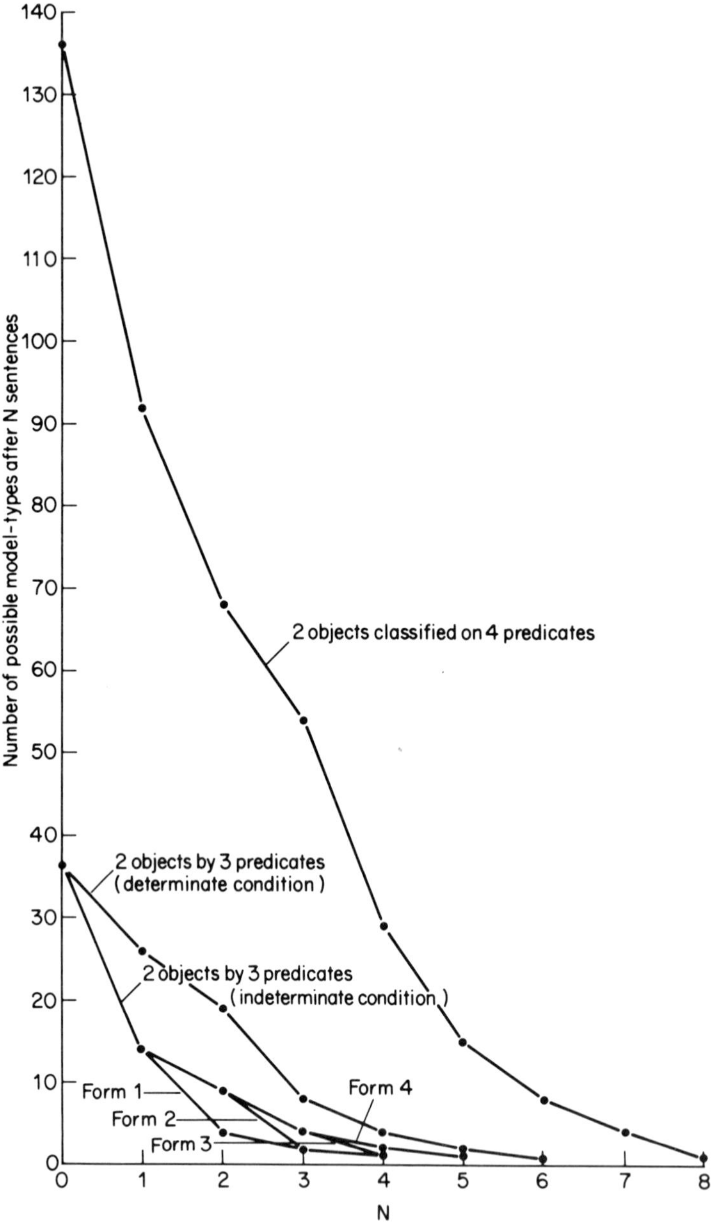

Figure 7.1. Possible model types remaining after each sentence of description.

white square and a black circle is identical to one of a black circle and a white square.

It is necessary to talk of model types (e.g., the pair of objects consisting of a small black circle and a large white square) because there may be infinitely many pairs of objects, real and imaginary, which are not discriminated by predicates. Nevertheless, the description specifies one unique model type—for example, that consisting of a small white circle and a small black square. It is possible to compute how many model types remain consistent with the information presented after each sentence of our experimental texts. Since all of these texts eventually determine a unique model, after their final sentences just one model remains consistent. The profile of the successive narrowing of possibilities for our example texts in shown in Figure 7.1.

Our initial point is that the absolute amount of indeterminacy created by the delay of model determination in examples 2 through 4 is rather slight. It is a specific type of irresolution that creates problems. The profile for a text determining a much more complex model is given for comparison.

Table 7.1 was used to select some complexities of models for our initial investigation. In order to study how models are constructed, it is necessary to study texts which delay their resolution of a model. To study such texts, however, we require base-line information about how determinate texts are processed. Accordingly, the study is divided into two parts. The first is a general exploratory investigation of the effects of the size and composition of arrays and text design on the construction of representations for determinate texts. The second part investigates the comprehension of temporarily indeterminate texts which specify a single, fixed complexity of array. The purpose of the first half is to enable interpretation of the second, a novel approach that itself raises issues of considerable interest.

STEPWISE DETERMINATE TEXTS WITH ANAPHORS

The Design of the Texts

Model Size

In order to investigate the gross effects of size, two pairs of structures were selected from Figure 7.1 which were roughly equivalent in absolute complexity. Model types with two objects classified on three predicates (36 alternatives) are closely comparable to model types of four elements classified on two predicates (35 alternatives). Likewise, model types with three elements classified on three predicates (120 alternatives) are closely comparable to those with two elements classified on four predicates (136 alternatives).

Models comprising two objects classified on three predicates were used in the second half of the study. Our choice of these four model sizes allows comparison of this basic type with models derived by adding one object or one predicate, as well as with models of comparable complexity.

Text Organisation

These simple texts can be organized in many different ways. In this exploratory study, it seemed worthwhile to contrast two main layouts which we will call 'object by object' and 'predicate by predicate'. In the first, all the predications of one object are given first, followed by all the predications of the next object, and so on. In the second, one predicate is first applied to all the objects, then the next predicate is applied, and so on. As will become evident, these two organisations are important for the representation of aspects of memory involved in model construction.

Predicate Sequencing

There is a natural sequencing of predicates within a noun phrase: We say 'a large black square' and not 'a black large square'. This order has been preserved within the noun phrases of the constituent statements in the texts used here.

Predicate Selection

We could have used predicates and their negations in the construction of the texts, but this would have meant adhering to logical theory at the price of psychological complexity. Instead, antonyms were used—black/white, smal-l/large, and so on. This decision rests on an intuitive judgement that it is easier to infer that a black object is distinct from a white one than that a black object is distinct from something which is not black. Negation, particularly explicit negation, presents notorious problems when it appears in unnatural positions in text.

There are not enough common pairs of antonyms to provide fresh lexical material in each new text. Instead, material for each text was selected from a battery of words constructed as follows: Twenty-four antonym pairs were sorted into four cohorts of six pairs, so that any word from an earlier cohort would normally precede any word from any successive cohort. The cohorts corresponded roughly to magnitudes, textures, colours and shapes.

Words were chosen that would combine with any words from other cohorts to form possible descriptions, though these would certainly vary in many relevant psychological dimensions, such as familiarity or perceptibility. Texts were constructed by randomly selecting one pair from each cohort to provide each of the predicate dimensions on which elements of the model varied. If fewer than four predicates appeared in the text, one of the pairs from the earliest three cohorts was dropped. This ensured that the most noun-like cohort was always represented, and that it was always used as the introducing dimension for an object in the anaphoric texts.

Model Structure

Quite apart from size, it would seem likely that some models are easier to represent than others. For example, a model of two elements which contrasts on all three predicates has a certain salience. This variable is not easily controlled, as the patterns vary from one model shape to another. Apart from ensuring that no models contained pairs of identical objects, the model structures were chosen randomly.

Task Details

The texts were displayed, one sentence at a time, on a computer monitor. Subjects instigated a trial by replying to a 'ready' signal with a carriage return. The first sentence then appeared and remained on the screen until the subject pressed the space bar. This action removed the sentence, returned a reading time, and displayed the next sentence in the same screen position as the last. This process continued until the subject pressed the space bar after reading the last sentence of the text. At that point a signal warned the subject of impending questions, and after a 2-second delay for finger positioning, the first question appeared. Subjects responded with 'a' for affirmative or 'n' for negative to the yes/no questions. Each response removed the question, returned a time, and displayed the next question. After the second question, a prompt for 'recall' appeared and the subject typed a description of the array. This recall was not performed against the clock. Subjects were given considerable practice with the self-paced reading task through the administration of task instructions in this same sentence-by-sentence mode.

The structure of some example texts is shown in Figure 7.2. All texts were prefaced by a setting which displayed the dimensions on which objects

Setting:	Black/white, circle/square, large/small
Number statement:	There are just two objects.
Object-by-object text body:	There is a square. The square is white. The square is large. There is a circle. The circle is black. The circle is large.
Predicate-by-predicate text body:	There is a square. There is a circle. The square is large. The circle is large. The square is white. The circle of black
Question 1:	Is there a large black object?
Question 2:	Are there two large objects?
Recall prompt:	What is there?

Figure 7.2. Determine texts specifying models of two objects classified on three dimensions.

differed in the ensuing text. A sentence then stated the number of objects in the array. The body of the text followed, sentence by sentence. The final sentence of the text body preceded a warning that questions were to come. Two yes/no questions then appeared, such as, "Is there a black circle?" or "Are there two squares?" The second question, once answered, was followed by a request for a description of the whole array. Subjects were instructed that each array was unrelated to the others and that they could rest between texts.

Results

This exploratory experiment produced some very rich data, a full treatment of which is beyond the scope of this chapter. However, certain results emerged quite systematically after just five subjects had completed the task.

Each subject's median reading time from six sessions on each text form was measured first. Figure 7.3 shows the means of five subjects' median reading times of statements of text in each of the four model sizes. The means are arranged into groups of statements applying to a specific object. The bottom half of the figure presents the data for the object-by-object texts. For these texts, the abscissa represents the temporal succession in which the sentences were presented. The top half of the figure presents the data for the predicate-by-predicate texts in which each predication applied to a given object was interrupted by predications to other objects. The first predication applied to an object was always an indefinite phrase containing only one predicate.

There is a clear tendency for sentence-reading times to increase with the successive specification of an object's properties. Upon introducing a new object, however, reading times decrease. These effects are extremely systematic across readers, texts and text positions, as well as sessions. Less easy to determine is whether the slowing of reading times is linear or exponential.

In contrast to the marked increase in reading time found with successive predications on the same object are the very slight and somewhat variable increases in reading time for successive objects. While there is some slowing, it is not uniform across text positions for different model sizes.

Interestingly, the pattern of lengthening reading times within an object's specification appears just as strongly for the predicate-by-predicate texts as for the object-by-object texts. (Remember that each successive predication to a given object was interrupted by predications to other objects.) The phenomenon of increasing times with further specification appeared to be driven by underlying features of the model under construction rather than by superficial features of the input sequence.

How are we to interpret this effect? Psychologists are accustomed to the idea that there are rhythms in reading or listening whereby information is

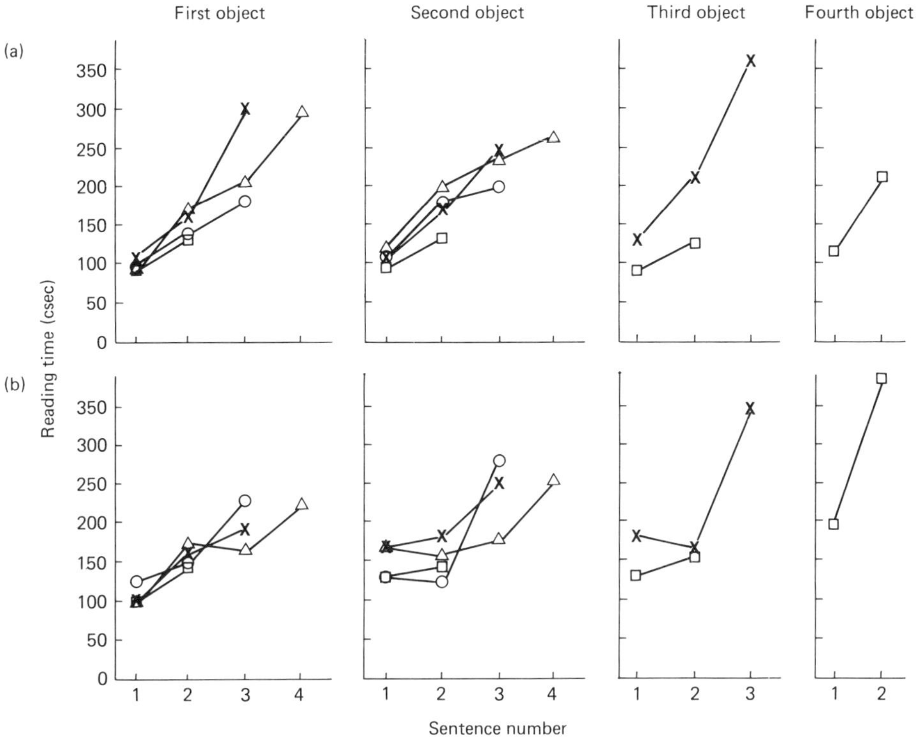

Figure 7.3. Mean Sentence-Reading Times for determinate texts specifying four model sizes. (a) Predicate-by-predicate and (b) object-by-object modes of text organization. △, two objects, four predicates; ○, two objects, three predicates; ×, three objects, three predicates; □, four objects, two predicates.

accumulated in working memory for a period and then reformulated and transferred to long-term memory in a different form. Jarvella (1971) demonstrates such a rhythm which cycles with clauses. One might suppose that we have another such rhythm here, though one which extends over several clauses. However, such an explanation sits oddly with the observation that the predicate-by-predicate texts show concurrent, interlaced rhythms, each centered on an object representation. If the size of working memory is the capacity which sets the frequency of oscillation, then this observation would indicate that there are several working memories operating in parallel during the processing of predicate-by-predicate texts.

In a spreading activation model of memory (Anderson, 1976), increasing sentence verification times as a result of increasing node specification are explained in terms of a fixed amount of activation spreading through a more ramified network. Although this 'fan effect' is reported from tasks which are probing 'ready-built' memory structures, it still might explain the current effect, since adding material to a representation presumably entails locating the node at which the addition must take place. Nevertheless, this explanation is much less natural in a context where locating the relevant node in a network does not appear to be a major part of the task. Once a node has been set up, the subject knows exactly which node will require accretion based on the information in the next sentence. Searching for the appropriate node is hardly the problem.

It may be that the present phenomenon is the result of quite different causes. In a constructive task, it may be that these are inference rather than retrieval effects. As an object's attributes are specified, it may become successively more difficult to accommodate further specification. This hypothesis is particularly plausible with regard to the abstract material used in this study. To know that something is a rod and then to be told that it is sharp requires one to find the appropriate type of sharpness to assign to the rod. Similarly, to know that something is a sharp rod and then to be told that it is dull requires that one find an appropriate type of dullness. Such searches may well take longer the more specific the constraints that have been layed down. This sort of interpretation make no claims about storage or search capacity but only about the effort of construction—thus Bartlett stalks Ebbinghaus.

The fan effect is known to disppear when dealing with overlearned material (Hayes-Roth, 1977). Speculation that the present effect may be due to semantic integration prompts the question as to whether the fan effect might not appear in sentence verification times when material has not been fully incorporated into a model representation. The present data cannot establish this explanation, but such an alternative is readily distinguishable within the paradigm. It is, of course, quite possible that the fan effect and the current phenomenon are similar results of quite disparate causes.

Even if speculation about alternative explanations seems premature with regard to the data, it serves to raise important questions about propositional network theories of representation. Because such theories assume that some semantic interpretation is achieved for the proposition related to each input sentence, and because the representations are themselves manipulated as words in expositions of the theories, there is a tendency to diminish the importance of any agglomerative operations that are not quasi-syntactic. These theories invite the notion that if we have to connect three successive predicates to a node, this operation will be comparable to conjoining three predicates applied to a common variable in some calculus.

The present suggestion assumes that while there are semantic representations for individual input propositions, there is also a level of representation of the textual model which demands that accommodations be

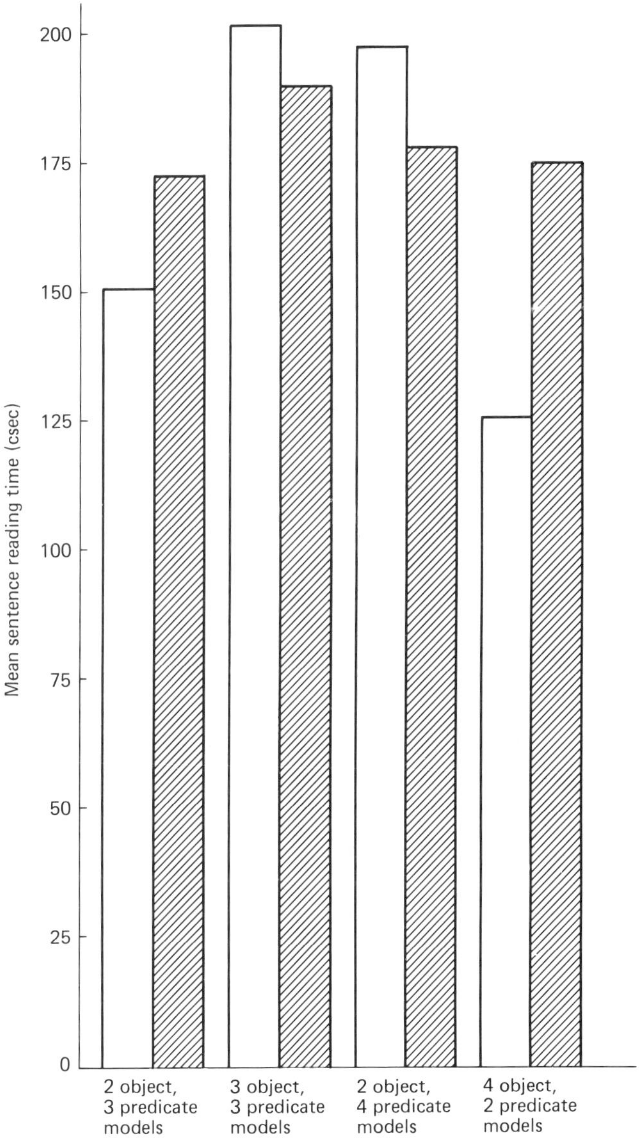

Figure 7.4. Effects of model size and text organization on mean statement-reading time. Open bars, object-by-object texts: slashed bars, predicate-by-predicate texts.

made between the conjoined predicates in inferring the properties of the object they specify. Thus it supposes that there are at least two levels of semantic representation—one rather close to the proposition of the input sentence, and the other closer to representations of the properties of non-linguistic objects. The second half of this study lends support to this idea by demonstrating that propositions containing references that cannot be resolved, and that are therefore agglomerated into the model representation, behave quite differently during the period of their irresolution.

What of size effects? Compared with the strength of the effects just described, absolute effects of size and complexity are rather slight. Figure 7.4 shows the mean reading time per statement for each of the model sizes, broken down by the two modes of text organization. The sentences specifying the two large model sizes were read more slowly than their counterparts specifying the small models, but the effects are small (about 20%). The absolute information content of the larger models is about 300% greater. This accords with the well-known behaviour of the magical number, 'seven plus or minus two'. Although the statements of the texts specifying the largest models contain up to fifteen predicate occurrences, their models may be represented by nine predicates or fewer through the expected inferences. Perhaps this exploratory experiment should have extended the size beyond this threshold.

With reference to the question of levels of encoding, it would be interesting to know whether the step from three predicates to some integrated representation of an object with three properties constitutes 'chunking'. It could be that we have a 'vocabulary' of object types that can be accessed to extend our memory capacity beyond that tested in this study.

Text organization, at least as it is expressed in the two forms here, seems to have variable effects on different model configurations. For the two smaller models, the predicate-by-predicate texts were read slightly faster, whereas for the two larger models, the object-by-object texts were easier. These effects are slight, and although they raise some interesting questions about memory encodings, they detain us here only because they complicate comparisons with the second half of the study. Since the indeterminate texts of the second half differ in organization from both of the forms used in the first half, it is not easy to know which comparison to make. We shall return to this point later.

TEXTS WITH TEMPORARY INDETERMINACY

In this condition, all texts specify models containing two objects classified on three dimensions. Each text consists of a setting sentence which lists the predicate contrasts relevant to the ensuing text, a reminder that there are two objects in the array, and a series of twin predications as in examples 2–4. In order to motivate the design of text, subjects were told to think of them as produced by a speaker who was sampling objects from an unknown array. Two of the object's properties were then glimpsed and reported and the object returned to the array. Redundant repetitions of statements were edited out by the speaker, and no array contained any indiscernibles. Subjects accepted these instructions, and all made the appropriate inferences, with few errors.

There are several thousand alternative non-redundant text forms for any selection of three predicate oppositions. All contain at least four, and at most five, statements. The problem for the present study was to select a manageable sample without allowing the subject to adopt artifactual solution heuristics. The variable of chief interest here was the amount of delay during model resolution. Four alternative forms were selected as representing this dimension. They are shown, with their interrelations, in Figure 7.5. The three predicate oppositions are represented by small/large, black/white and square/circle.

Form 1 represents a control for this novel text design, since it involves no indeterminacy. At each step it is possible to identify which object the statement applies to. Form 2 delays this identification for the second sentence until the third sentence. Form 3 delays it until the fourth sentence, and Form 4 until the fifth.

As the figure shows, the four text forms are designed to manipulate indeterminacy and its resolution. However, other dimensions of variation in text structure could result in differences in comprehensibility. In particular, it is possible to vary which predicate carries the contrast information that

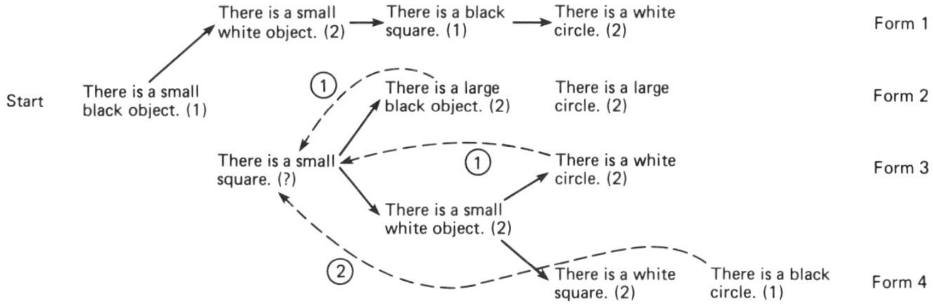

Figure 7.5. The indeterminate text forms. The solid arrows indicate the reading sequence for each text form. The numbers in parentheses refer to the objects to which the statements are resolved to apply. The dashed arrows originate from the statement that allows resolution, and are tagged with the number of the object to which they resolve that the second statement applies.

allows the references to be distinguished. For example, two alternatives for Form 1 would be (1) small black, small white, black square, white circle; and (2) small black, large black, small square, large circle. These variants are identical as far as their indeterminacy goes (in fact, since both are Form 1, neither displays any indeterminacy), but they differ in terms of which predicate opposition carries the contrast information. Since the oppositions differ in their place in the adjective ordering phenomena alluded to in the first half of this study, it is altogether possible that this variable could affect comprehensibility. Accordingly, for each of the four text forms in this condition, four variants were constructed, with their contrasts carried by different predicates.

It is important not to confuse this textual phenomenon with the phrase-internal adjective-ordering phenomena which necessitate its control. All texts

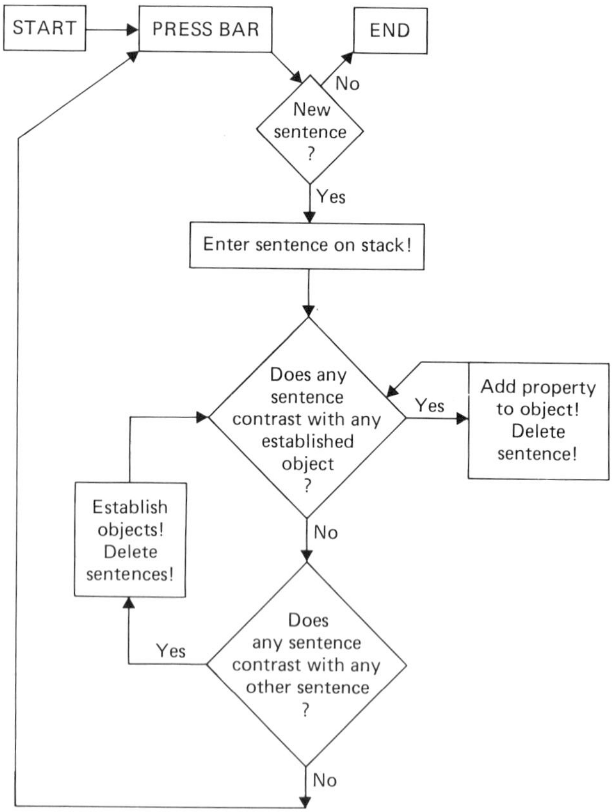

Figure 7.6. One solution process for indeterminate texts.

in this condition, as with the last, contained pairs of predicates in their natural noun-phrase order. The necessity of including these text variants notwithstanding, they turned out to have reassuringly little effect on the recorded pattern of reading times; the variants showed extremely good replication of reading-time patterns, with large differences between the text forms which were the target of the study.

It may help the reader at this point to look at a possible process for achieving a representation of these texts. Figure 7.6 shows one such process, perhaps what a programmer in search of generality might suggest rather than the most plausible psychological candidate. This process serves to highlight

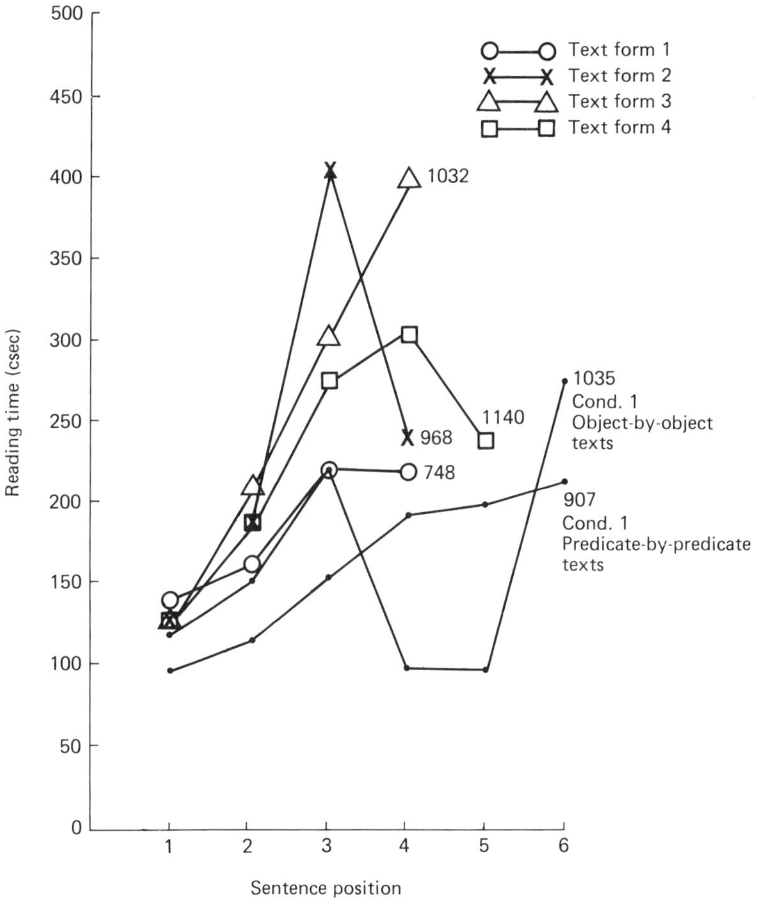

Figure 7.7. Mean reading times for four text forms of Condition 2 and two of Condition 1.

the fact that although a good deal of box-shifting could distinguish other candidate processes, the main effects in the data are assumed to reflect memory limitations, a topic on which such diagrams remain moot.

Figure 7.7 shows the means of the five subjects' median reading times for successive sentences of the four text forms and includes, for comparison, the times for the two text designs based on two objects classified on three dimensions from the determinate condition. The cumulative time for processing each text is shown to aid comparison.

It is not easy to know exactly how to compare performances on Form 1 texts of this condition with the two texts specifying the same size arrays from the first condition. The number of statements is different (four or five instead of six), and the statement sequence is not identical to either object-by-object or predicate-by-predicate layouts. In a sense, Form 1 texts are predicate-by-predicate texts, but they do not have a single predicate statement introducing them. It happens that for this size array, predicate-by-predicate texts are comprehended more quickly. It is difficult to compare texts with different numbers of sentences because we have no measure of the cost of overheads such as bar pressing and the more superficial aspects of reading. Nevertheless, it seems reasonable to say that there is little evidence that the design of texts used in this indeterminate condition is inherently difficult to understand. If anything, it is difficult to say why the latencies to read the final statements of the object-by-object texts of the first condition should be so long.

Does the effect of slow reading times in conjunction with increased object specification (the most prominent effect of the first half of this study) show up with these new texts? For the Form 1 texts it does reappear, modified, as would be expected in the changed circumstances. In these texts, the first two statements each establish their respective objects with two properties. The third and fourth statements further specify these two objects by adding one predicate to each. They are most closely homologous to statements 5 and 6 of the predicate-by-predicate texts, and the processing times are comparable (222 and 222 csecs for statements 3 and 4 of Form 1; 181 and 200 csecs for statements 5 and 6 of the anaphoric predicate-by-predicate texts). The homologous statements for the object-by-object texts are 3 and 6, and their times are 228 and 282 csecs, respectively. Thus the Form 1 data appear to offer a reasonable base line against which to interpret the effects of indeterminacy.

The three remaining forms are identical up to their second statements, and the reading times are satisfactorily similar. The second statement of these three forms introduces the indeterminacy. It is about 20% slower than sentence 2 of Form 1 ($190 = 190 = 207 > 164$).

A large difference appears with the third sentence of Form 2, which resolves that text's indeterminacy. This resolution results in a very slow time for sentence 3, followed by a time for sentence 4 which is barely slower than for the equivalent sentence in Form 1. The introduction of indeterminacy slows the reaction time slightly (20%), whereas its resolution slows reading dramatically (200%). However, this expenditure of effort then allows a resumption of processing as if nothing had happened.

When resolution is delayed further, reading times slow down. Sentence 3 of Form 3, which maintains the indeterminacy resolved at this point in Form 2, is read more slowly than its predecessor (20%) but more quickly than Form 2's resolving statement. When Form 3's resolution arrives at the next statement, it is read as slowly as that of Form 2. Unfortunately, we cannot tell whether its resolution allows a resumption of determinate speed, as this sentence ends the text.

In the results for the Form 4 texts (those which delay the resolution until a fifth sentence), this neatly interpretable pattern is disturbed. The intake of unresovable sentences continues to slow, but with resolving sentence 5, there is a slight speeding up rather than a slowing down of the latency of response to the other texts' resolving statements. The cumulative time for these texts is the longest of all four forms, but this is not a straight comparison because of the extra statement. There is little doubt that subjects regard these texts as the most difficult of the four forms, an observation supported by a higher error rate for this form. (The errors were 3.6%, 6.1%. 4.3% and 14.3%, respectively, for the four text forms.

One of Form 4's peculiarities is that the arrival of a fifth sentence cues the subject to the fact that the end of the text has been reached, regardless of whether the subject has worked this out from the incompleteness of the representation. There was a five-second delay between the final statement bar press and the arrival of the first question. This means that the subjects could well have adopted a strategy of pressing the bar before resolving all the necessary inferencing, since they expected to do so in the interval while working on a surface representation of the last sentence. It is also possible that the speeding up on the fifth sentence of Form 4 texts reflects a desperate dash for the finish on the part of subjects for whom memory for unresolved sentences was reaching an overflow—a dash that is reflected by a doubling of the error rate. This interpretation stands in need of investigation. A reduced delay of questioning and an insistence on lower error rates, or an extension of the texts, would achieve this.

Does the specification effect appear in the data for Forms 2–4? It is hard to say more than that the data are consistent with its presence. All the times for sentences after the second position are longer than the times for sentences 3 and 4 of Form 1. However, any effect would be superimposed on even more powerful effects of unresolvable information.

PROSPECTS

Constructing the referential framework of a text representation is only a small part of the construction that must be accomplished in order to represent a text. It is a part that is so basic that it easily escapes our attention, which is often focused on texts of a richness and complexity sufficient to detain our practical interest. And yet it is of great theoretical interest in that it is a general part of our representational task. It is accomplished by the deployment of, among other things, our knowledge of the logical particles of our language. What prospects do the direct methods used here provide for a detailed study of this part of our representational capacities? What have we learned from this study, and how can it be extended?

The data for the anaphoric determinate texts display a phenomenon that suspiciously resembles the fan effect, but it does so in a task of constructing representations rather than searching for them. This finding affords us the opportunity to broaden the basis of our understanding of both effects, and therefore of the nature of our representations. Perhaps the effects are merely superficially similar, or perhaps they are both manifestations of deeper processes of semantic integration or ramified search.

These same data provide the base line for our interpretation of non-anaphoric texts. They allow us to infer that subjects can process co-reference information that is implicit in the logical relations of predicates almost as quickly as when the same information is marked in the article system. This in turn allows the inference that when co-reference cannot be deduced, information must be held in some unresolved form which behaves quite differently from information that has been resolved into a model representation. Perhaps the most unexpected finding is that the large delays in processing occur not when indeterminacy is introduced, but rather at the point at which it is resolved. The limitations on the processor in dealing with unresolved information are primarily those of storage capacity. The delays are occasioned when inferences must be made which allow integration into the model. This task allows a particularly direct analysis of the processes involved.

Model representations have been employed conspicuously by Johnson-Laird and his colleagues (e.g., Johnson-Laird, 1983; Johnson-Laird & Bara, 1983; Johnson-Laird & Steedman, 1978) in analysing subjects' performance in syllogistic reasoning. This use assumes that subjects assimilate logic problem texts (prime examples of argumentation) into their experience with expository texts. Expository texts, such as those used in this study, invite the construction of a unique model; texts of argumentation do not. In adapting representations design for one task to the performance of another, extra operations such as checking must be added to normal procedures.

From one perspective, we can see the present study as a direct examination of the representations invoked as theoretical entities in the others. This perspective serves to highlight the differences between inferences that are required on the road to the representation of a text and those which are themselves topics of a text, such as those from premise to conlusion in a logic problem. Prospectively it would be most rewarding if the present approach could elucidate the part played by the same or similar representations in two different but fundamental cognitive processes.

REFERENCES

Anderson, J. R. *Language, memory and thought*. Hillsdale, NJ: Erlbaum, 1976.

Bransford, J. D., & Johnson, X. Y. Contextual prerequisites for understanding: Some investigations of comprehension and recall. *Journal of Verbal Learning*, 1972, **11**, 717–726.

Bartlett, F. C. *Remembering: A study in experimental and social psychology*. Cambridge: Cambridge University Press, 1932.

Bryant, P. E., & Trabasso, T. Transitive inferences and memory in young children. *Nature*, 1971, **232**, 456–458.

Clark, H. H. Bridging. In R. C. Schank & B. L. Nash-Weber (Eds.), *Theoretical issues in natural language processing*. Cambridge, MA: MIT Press, 1975.

Hayes-Roth, B., Evolution of cognition: Structures and processes. *Psychological Review*, 1977, **84**, 260–278.

Jarvella, R. J. Syntactic processing. *Journal of Verbal Learning and Verbal Behaviour*, 1971, **10**, 409–416.

Johnson-Laird, P. N. *Mental models: Towards a cognitive science of language, inference and consciousness*. Cambridge: Cambridge University Press, 1983.

Johnson-Laird, P. N., & Bara, B. G. Mental models and syllogistic reasoning. Unpublished manuscript, 1983.

Johnson-Laird, P. N., & Steedman, M. J. The psychology of syllogisms. *Cognitive Psychology*, 1978, **10**, 64–99.

Kintsch, W., & Van Dijk, T. A. Towards a model of text comprehension and production. *Psychological Review*, 1978, **85**, 363–394.

Rumelhart, D. E., Lindsay, P. H., & Norman, D. A. A process model of long term memory. In E. Tulving & W. Donaldson (Eds.), *Organization of memory*. New York: Academic Press, 1972.

Sandford, A. J., & Garrod, S. C. *Understanding written language: Explorations of comprehension beyond the sentence*. Chichester: Wiley, 1980.

Stenning, K. *Understanding English articles and quantifiers*. Ann Arbor, MI: University Microfilms, 1975.

Stenning, K. Anaphora as an approach to pragmatics. In M. Halle, J. Bresnon & G. A. Miller (Eds.), *Linguistic theory and psychological reality*. Cambridge, MA: MIT Press, 1978.

Stenning, K. On why making reference out of sense makes it so hard to make sense out of reference. *Linguistics*, 1980, **18**(7), 619–634.

8

Anaphora Resolution

P. A. M. SEUREN
Filosofisch Instituut
Nijmegen University

It is a remarkable fact in anaphora research that sentence-internal anaphora is dealt with almost exclusively in the linguistic literature, whereas sentence-external anaphora seems hunting ground reserved for psycholinguists. This curious division of labour is no doubt due to the fact, accidental or not, that linguists feel ill at ease outside the sentence while psycholinguists, at least until recently, tended to concentrate on experiments, eschewing the abstract formal structures needed to explain internal anaphora. In this study an attempt is made to bridge the gap by proposing an integrated theory of anaphora, at least in outline. The proposal is rooted in a psychological theory of linguistic understanding where factors of context and discourse play a decisive role. An algorithm is proposed according to which pronouns occurring in sentences can be interpreted. For internal anaphora the algorithm or Assignment Procedure (AP) can be applied to sentence-types; for external anaphora it applies to sentences in context (i.e., utterance types).

AP presupposes a grammar (i.e., a parser and a generator) relating surface structures to semantic analyses (SA) via shallow structures and syntactic deep structures. The calculus of semantic interpretation takes SA as input and delivers, in a cumulative fashion, bits of cognitive discourse representation. AP is part of the semantic calculus. It applies to fully lexicalized NP's and to pronouns. The pronominal part of AP differs from the rest of the semantics in that it can draw information from all derivational stages of sentences between SA and surface structure, though it still takes SA as input.

REASONING AND DISCOURSE PROCESSES

ISBN 0-12-512320-5

Pronouns are treated by the parser as any other NP: only morphological markings of number, gender, and case play a role there. Their specification in terms of very general lexical categories ('male', 'thing', etc.) will be largely neglected here. In SA they are represented as pronouns (the symbol "x" will be used here); when they are morphologically marked for 'reflexive' one way or another, this is indicated in SA by a subscript R: "x_R". NP's are either quantified or definite. Definite NP's are either variables (pronouns) or denoting NP's. The relation of denoting holds between denoting NP's and cognitive entities or addresses. The term "referring" is used for the relation between NP's or their corresponding addresses on the one hand and real entities on the other. Denoting NP's in false assertions or in subdomains of the cognitive discourse representation need not refer.

Three kinds of (personal or possessive) pronouns are distinguished: reflexive pronouns, bound variable pronouns, and denoting pronouns. The first and second categories are obligatorily pronominal. The third category may be represented, salva veritate, by a full noun phrase containing a predicate denoting either a very general property or expressing an evaluative judgement. Such NP's will be called *epithetic NP's*. They must always be unaccented. Only denoting pronouns (or epithetic NP's) can have a sentence-external antecedent.

The category of *reflexive pronouns* does not coincide with the class of pronouns with reflexive morphological marking (the latter will be called *marked reflexives*). A pronoun is reflexive just in case it is co-denotational with (or is the same variable as) the subject of either the same clause or of the higher clause to which its own clause is a complement, at some stage of analysis. If the pronoun is related to the subject of its own clause, it is a *directive reflexive*. If it is related to the subject of the higher clause it is an *indirect reflexive*. Languages differ considerably in the morphological marking of reflexives. In Attic Greek, for example, there is a special morphological set of indirect reflexives. Latin uses ordinary reflexive marking also for indirect reflexives:

(1) a. *Sibi* Asterigem mitti *Caesar* iussit.
(*Caesar* ordered that Asterix be sent to *him*)
b. *Caesar* Asterigi imperavit ut *sibi* nuntium mitteret.
(*Caesar* ordered Asterix that he send *him* a messenger)

Latin (like Swedish) also has a separate third person reflexive possessive pronoun *suus* (Swedish: *sin*), besides the non-reflexive personal pronoun genitive *eius* (*hans*). Dutch has three different forms for the third person reflexive: *zich*, *zichzelf*, and *hemzelf* (*haarzelf*, *henzelf*) for English *himself* (*herself*, *itself*, *themselves*). The conditions of use for the three Dutch marked reflexives differ from each other (and from English) in fairly complex ways. A few examples will suffice here:

(2) a. *Ben* toonde Josef een foto van *zichzelf.*
(*Ben* showed Josef a picture of *himself*)
b. Ben toonde *Josef* een foto van *hemzelf.*
Ben showed *Josef* a picture of *himself*)
c. *Karel* liet *zich* het pakje bezorgen.
(*Karel* let the parcel be delivered to *him*)
d. *Karel* liet Ben *hem* het pakje bezorgen.
(*Karel* let Ben deliver the parcel to *him*)
e. *Karel* liet voor *zich* werken.
(*Karel* allowed (people) to work for *him*)
f. *Karel* liet Ben voor *zich* werken.
(*Karel* let Ben work for *him*)
g. Karel liet *Ben* voor *zichzelf* werken.
(Karel let *Ben* work for *himself*)

The obvious differences between Dutch and English in this respect come about as a result of differences in the grammar of complementation (Dutch *laten* ("let") takes obligatory Predicate Raising (see Seuren, 1972), and of differences in reflexive morphology and the conditions of use of the morphology. Restrictions of space forbid an adequate discussion of the rules of Dutch grammar in this respect, so we must be content with the conclusion that, apparently, languages differ considerably in the morphological marking of reflexives. We will assume that reflexives are often not marked morphologically. Unmarked reflexives differ from denoting pronouns in their conditions of use, and also because they cannot be replaced by epithetic NP's salva veritate:

(3) a. In *his* office *Graham* writes novels.
b. !In *the man's* office *Graham* writes novels.[1]
c. !In *Graham's* office *he* writes novels.
(4) a. That *she* was clever, *Mary* knew very well.
b. !That *the old girl* was clever, *Mary* knew very well.
c. !That *Mary* was clever, *she* knew very well.

If no account were taken of reflexivity it would be difficult to explain why co-denotation is disturbed in the (b) sentences by the epithetic NP's, or why there is no co-denotation in the (c) sentences. The latter point is remarkable (see, e.g., Akmajian & Jackendoff, 1970) since one of the outstanding features of denoting pronouns is that they have no difficulty in taking *preceding* NP's as their antecedent. In fact, however, pronouns are subject to the *Reflexive Principle*:

> Whenever a *subject* is involved, at any stage of analysis, in a co-denotation (or co-variable) relation between two NP's, the subject must be the antecedent and the other NP will be reflexive,

marked if the grammar of the language requires marking, and otherwise unmarked or null, depending on the grammar of the language.

By "subject" is meant either the subject of the same clause, or the subject of the higher clause to which the clause in which the other NP occurs is a complement.[2] Furthermore, if an NP is antecedent to a pronoun, it may, of course, itself be a pronoun of any kind needing its antecedent or binder.

The phrase "at any stage of analysis" needs some comment. It has been said that a grammar establishes an identity relation between sentence representations at different levels: semantic analysis (SA), Syntactic Deep Structure, Shallow Structure, and Surface Structure. These are related by top-down (i.e., from SA to Surface Structure) transformations or bottom-up parsing rules. The parsing rules are the inverse of the transformations, so that the stages of bottom-up analysis are identical with those of the topdown generation. The Reflexive Principle applies at any stage of generation or parsing between SA and Surface Structure, not necessarily at one of the four defined levels of representation.[3] (These are defined by the kind of rules to which they are input or output.) It is thus possible to have marked reflexives that are not co-denotational with the surface subject, but with the semantic subject:

(5) a. Ben had wanted *Graham* for a long time to look after *himself.*
b. Karel gelastte *Ben* voor *zichzelf* te werken.
(Karel ordered *Ben* to work for *himself*)
c. Ben told *Graham* a story about *himself.*

In (5a) the semantic subject *Graham* of the lower clause has been raised into the main clause by a well-known transformation. In (5b) *Ben* is object to *gelasten* ("order"), causing the deletion (by the rule usually called "Equi") of the co-denotational subject of *werken* in the lower clause. In (5c) *Graham* is the subject, in SA, of the clause "Graham know a story about himself" in the overall structure "Ben caused$_S$[Graham know a story about himself]"—with the semantic presupposition that the causing was mediated by verbal communication.

It is to be noted that (5a) does not allow for a reading in which *Ben*, i.e. the surface subject, is co-denotational with *himself.* This shows that the assignment of morphological reflexive marking takes place top-down: marking is assigned at the 'earliest' opportunity in the transformational process, not in the parsing process. This has the interesting consequence for AP that a considerable amount of top-down checking is required. This is not unnatural if we consider that AP takes as input SA's of sentences plus their entire derivations to surface structures.

Bound variable pronouns are so called because they function logically and semantically as the well-known variables bound by quantifiers in predicate calculus. For a pronoun to belong to this category it is necessary that it be preceded, in its surface structure, by a quantified NP. Furthermore, it must be commanded by it, according to the traditional definition of the relation "command":

> In a constituent tree structure, a node A *commands* a node B just in case the first S-node in the tree up from A also dominates B.

If a pronoun is both preceded and commanded by a quantified NP then its preferred interpretation is that of a variable bound by the quantified NP in question. This interpretation can be overruled by context or discourse factors, in which case the pronoun will take a sentence-external antecedent and belong to the category of denoting pronouns. Consider the following examples:

(6) a. *Nobody* left because *he* was tired.
b. !*Nobody* left, because *he* was tired.
c. !Because *he* was tired, *nobody* left.
d. !Because *nobody* was tired, *he* left.

Assuming the following approximate surface structures for (6a) and (6b), respectively:

(6) a′

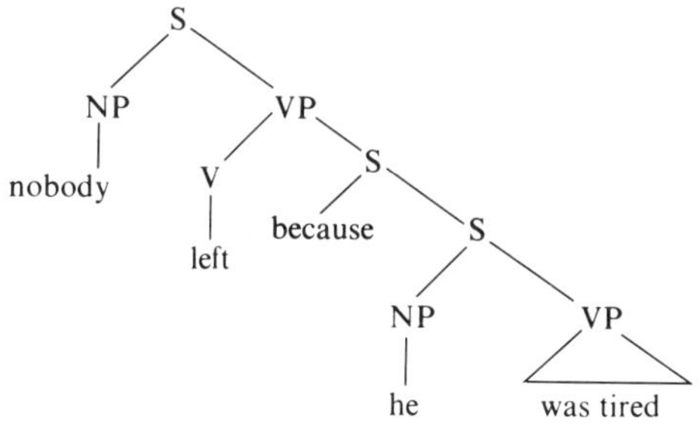

(6) b′

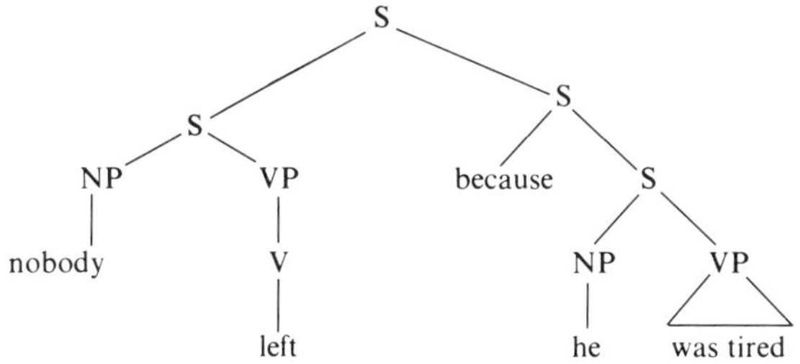

we see that only (6a)· fulfills the conditions for the pronoun *he* to be interpreted as a variable bound by *nobody* in the sense of the predicate calculus analysis:

(6) a″ $\sim\exists x[x$ left because x was tired$]$

It is, in fact, assumed that the SA of (6a) corresponds to (6a″), with the bracketed part analysed in a suitably abstract way. The first occurrence of the variable x is incorporated, by the rules of the grammar, into the quantified NP *nobody*; the second occurrence emerges in the surface structure as *he*. It is clear that in (6b–c) the pronoun *he* does not fulfill the conditions for a bound variable pronoun interpretation. In these sentences the pronoun *he* cannot but be interpreted as a denoting pronoun. Note that replacement of *he* by an epithetic NP leaves the interpretation intact:

(7) a. Nobody left, because the kid was tired.
 b. Because the little runt was tired, nobody left.
 c. Because nobody was tired, the great man left.

The third category of pronouns distinguished, the *denoting pronouns*, has attracted most attention in anaphora research. In fact, since reflexives were recognized only in so far as they are morphologically marked, and since, at least in certain quarters, there was a reluctance to recognize bound variable pronouns as a separate category, the existing literature is characterized by the phenomenon that many pronoun occurrences were taken to be of the denoting kind whereas they are not. It is hardly surprising, therefore, that attempts to account for (sentence-internal) anaphora relations with the help of only one principle had to fail. Now that the category of denoting pronouns has been severely restricted we may expect that the problem of sentence-internal anaphora resolution will be less refractory.

The ‘primordial’ principle (Langacker, 1969) for the assignment of antecedents to internally anaphoric pronouns was that the antecedent must either precede or command the pronoun. This principle could account for a large number of cases, such as:

(8) a. Since *Harry* felt unwell, *he* stayed at home.
 b. Since *he* felt unwell, *Harry* stayed at home.
 c. !*He* stayed at home, since *Harry* felt unwell.
 d. *Harry* stayed at home, since *he* felt unwell.

It was, however, unequal to substantial classes of counterexamples, such as (3) or (4c). We have now seen that these are explained by the Reflexive Principle. Likewise, apparent complications arising in connection with bound variable pronouns, as in (6), are eliminated by the recognition of that category as a separate class. Note, in particular, that the Reflexive Principle solves seemingly difficult cases like:

(9) a. !That *Mary* was clever, was something *she* knew very well.
 b. That *she* was clever, was something *Mary* knew very well.

If *she* in these sentences were indeed a denoting pronoun, then, according to the primordial principle, anaphora as indicated should be all right in (9a) and not in (9b). In fact, however, *she* is not a denoting pronoun, as appears from:

(9) c. !That *the old girl* was clever, was something *Mary* knew very well.

The strict analogy with (4) above suggests very strongly that *she* in these cases must be treated as an indirect reflexive. All that is needed to let the Reflexive Principle apply is a level or stage of representation where (9b) shares with (4a) the property that the *that*-clause is structurally a complement of the clause *Mary knew very well.* Even though present-day grammatical theory does not provide a clear account of the grammatical relations between sets of sentences like (4) and (9), it is clear that such an account must eventually be found, given the semantic properties of the sentences in question. Not all counterexamples to the primordial principle disappear, however, with the separating out of reflexives and bound variable pronouns. Consider, for example:

(10) a. The fact that *Mary* was clever made us suspect that *she* would come out first.
b. The fact that *she* was clever made us suspect that *Mary* would come out first.
c. The fact that *the old girl* was clever made us suspect that *Mary* would come out first.
d. The fact that *Mary* was clever made us suspect that *the old girl* would come out first.

Examples (10c) and (10d) show that the pronoun *she* in (10b) and (10a), respectively, is a true denoting pronoun. Although (10a) is unproblematic, in that the antecedent precedes the pronoun, (10b) should be impossible, since the antecedent *Mary* neither preceds nor commands the pronoun *she*. Quite a few more cases could be cited showing that Langacker's primordial principle is inadequate for denoting pronouns, even after the reflexives and the bound variable pronouns have been split off. How the old principle could be amended so that it covers all cases adequately, is not entirely clear.[4] It does seem, however, that internal anaphora resolution for denoting pronouns is perhaps not to be accounted for exclusively in structural terms, but also in terms of discourse phenomena such as topic and focus. We might venture the following principle:

(11) For denoting pronouns carrying sentence-internal anaphora, the antecedent may follow the pronoun only if the pronoun is in a subordinate clause and if the denotation of the antecedent is the topic of the discourse in process. Otherwise, the antecedent must precede the pronoun.

This takes care of a significant number of counterexamples, and perhaps all. It is, however, still incomplete because it fails to cover a number of relevant cases. Thus, it has been observed (e.g. Akamajian & Jackendoff, 1970) that NP's under contrastive or emphatic accent are prevented from being antecedents for any pronouns not commanded by them:

(12) a. !That *JIM* was going to be Harry's supervisor surprised *him*.
b. That JIM was going to be *Harry's* supervisor surprised *him*.
c. !That Jim was going to be *HARRY*'s supervisor surprised *him*.
d. That *Jim* was going to be HARRY's supervisor surprised *him*.
e. People dislike *JIM* because *he* is abrasive, not HARRY.

Note that *he* in (12e) is not a denoting pronoun:

(12) f. !People dislike *JIM* because *the fellow* is abrasive, not HARRY.

It is however, in (12b) and (12d):

(12) g. That JIM was going to be *Harry*'s supervisor surprised *the creep*.
h. That *Jim* was going to be HARRY's supervisor surprised *the old maniac*.

The answer to these cases would be given if it could be established that NP's under emphatic or contrastive accent function the same way the quantifiers do: they bind variables and require bound variable pronouns. This would explain why (12a) and (12c) are ruled out (the binder precedes but does not command the pronoun), while (12e) passes muster (the binder both precedes and commands the pronoun). In (12b) and (12d), on the other hand, we have to with denoting pronouns, and here there is no problem, since the antecedent precedes the pronoun. In fact, we can have the antecedent and the pronoun swop places (provided the antecedent is topic), since the pronoun will then occur in a subordinate clause:

(12) i. That JIM was going to be *his* supervisor surprised *Harry*.
j. That *he* was going to be HARRY's supervisor surprised *Jim*.

What is needed, therefore, is an analysis whereby emphatic or contrasted NP's function as quantified NP's. Such an analysis will not be attempted here.

Another class of difficult cases not covered by our analysis is provided by sentences containing anaphoric reference to an antecedent NP—not, however, taking over its denoting and/or referring function but making reference to its mere occurrence as a word:

(13) You've lived in *Dnepropetrovsk* for twenty years, and you still find *it* an impossible name to pronounce!

Note that the inverse is not possible, at least not in the same way:

(14) !"*Volapük*" means "world speak" in *it*.

Yet we do find:

(15) It's called "*punch*" because it has *it*.

I prefer not to venture an explanation for these cases. A feeble excuse might be that our main interest here is in establishing antecedent–pronoun relations, not in determining the semantic role fulfilled by the pronoun once it has found its antecedent. (The excuse is feeble since, even though that might be so, the question still remains there to be solved. Moreover, even under the excuse (14) will remain unexplained.)

The same feeble excuse might help us through the problem area of so-called 'sloppy identity', or other forms of vicarious identity:

(16) a. Harry drank *the milk*, but Leo threw *it* away.
b. *The temperature* was 50 degrees yesterday, but now *it* is much higher.
c. I used to be able to remember *the names of my students*, but nowadays I keep forgetting *them*. (De Rijk, 1974)

It is clear what the (external) antecedent is in these cases, but it is not clear how the pronoun is related semantically to the antecedent, since referential (or denotational) identity is absent (though there is some role analogy).

A much-quoted problem in philosophical circles is that of so-called 'donkey-sentences':[5]

(17) a. If Harry owns *a donkey* he beats *it*.
b. Either Harry owns *no donkey* or he beats *it*.

The problem resides in the fact that there is no straightforward relation between what must count as the antecedent on the one hand and the pronoun (*it*) on the other. The pronoun, in these cases, is clearly of the denoting kind:

(18) a. If Harry owns *a donkey* he beats *the poor animal*.
b. Either Harry owns *no donkey* or he beats *the creature*.

We should note that in our theory the question of the grammatical or external relation with an antecedent is of lesser importance than the determination of the right cognitive discourse 'address' for the pronoun to 'land at', i.e., the determination of the correct denotation relation between the denoting pronoun and an address in the discourse representation. This is especially true for external anaphora, where no (or hardly any) grammatical restrictions exist. What is needed here is a theory of discourse representations that sets up suitable addresses for the pronouns in question. It seems that this is best done by treating these cases of anaphora as being sentence-external.

Denoting pronouns, as has been said, are the only pronoun category that can take external antecedents. These are, in principle, of two kinds. First, the antecedent may be a (salient) definite NP in a preceding sentence (conjunctions counting as successive sentences). Here the pronoun (if it is of the right gender and number) takes over the denoting function of the antecedent NP,—due allowance being made for 'sloppiness' or other denoting complications. Under certain still partially unknown[6] conditions the required antecedent NP may not be overtly present in the preceding discourse but retrievable on grounds of either background or situational knowledge.[7] Secondly, the antecedent may however have just been set up in the discourse representation by an existentially quantified NP in the preceding sentence (or conjunct), as in:

(19) Harry owns *a donkey*, and he beats *it*.

In these cases the semantics must be such that a new discourse address is set up for the donkey mentioned in the first conjunct, so that the pronoun *it* in the second conjunct can denote that address.

It is not too difficult to analyse sentences of the types (18a) and (18b) as either directly involving a conjunction like (19) or invoking the first conjunct on cognitive grounds. Both (18a) and (18b) would in fact be reducible (though with minor differences) to an abstract representation of:

(20) Either Harry owns no donkey, or he owns a donkey and he beats it.

The semantics will then set up two subdomains, one for each disjunct. In the first, Harry owns no donkey, but in the second Harry both owns a donkey and beats it. It is clearly not possible to elaborate here the semantics, the lexicon and the grammar needed for such an analysis.

A final and highly relevant problem to be discussed here is that of the so-called 'Bach–Peters paradox.' This is about sentences containing one or more denoting pronouns that are distributed in such a way that a *grammatical* characterization of the antecedents results in an infinite regress:

(21) a. The girl who got them liked the flowers that were sent here.
b. The man for whom Ann bought the car he liked was not grateful.

Owing to their occurrence in relative clauses, the pronouns cannot be replaced by their antecedent NP's without recurring themselves. This apparent paradox is solved if (a) it is accepted that pronouns occur in semantic analysis as pronouns, and not as their antecedents, and (b) a procedure of tentative denotation is developed, whereby tentative or provisional denotations are confirmed if consistency is achieved.

This last point is in need of some clarification. We assume that lexical definite NP's denote addresses that have either been set up in previous discourse or can be supplied on grounds of background or situational knowledge. They select the right address on the basis of their lexical material. Thus, taking (21a) as an example, there must be a discourse address d_1 characterized by at least the predicates 'girl' and 'got the flowers that were sent her'. Likewise, there must be an address d_2 characterized at least by the predicates 'flowers' and 'were sent to d_1'. More precisely:

d_1	d_2
girl(x) be sent(d_2, to x) get(x, d_2)	flowers(x) be sent(x, to d_1) get(d_1, x)

One can imagine these addresses having been set up on the basis of some amount of preceding discourse such as: "There was a girl. She was sent flowers. She got the flowers." Neither of the two main NP's in (21a), however, matches either of the addresses completely: *the girl who got them* matches d_1 but for the pronoun *them*, which does not match d_2 in any lexical sense. However, if the pronoun can be made to denote d_2, then indeed *the girl who got them* will denote d_1. So we provisionally assign d_1 to *the girl who got them*, and likewise d_2 is provisionally assigned to *them*. Now take the other main NP, *the flowers that were sent her*. Here the same complication arises: *her* does not match d_1 lexically but could still denote d_1. Now we are in a quandary, since neither of the two NP's is assigned a definitive address. But if *them* denotes d_2 and *her* denotes d_1, all is well. Note that they may well do so, since *the flowers that were sent her* fulfills the conditions for being antecedent to *them* (though it follows the pronoun, the pronoun is in a subordinate clause), and *the girl who got them* is allowed to act as antecedent to *her*. Moreover, the assignments required have already been made provisionally, so we cut the tie and confirm the provisional assignments, a confirmation to be overruled only on grounds of discourse plausibility, in which case one or both of the pronouns take external antecedents.[8]

Before an assignment procedure (AP) can be formulated, a summary specification of the syntax of SA must be given (for further analysis, see

Seuren, 1985). SA structures can be considered as constrained by the following formation rules:

$$(1)\quad S \rightarrow \left\{ \begin{array}{l} V^1 + \left\{ \begin{array}{l} NP_s \\ S_s \end{array} \right\} \\ V^2 + \left\{ \begin{array}{l} NP_s \\ S_s \end{array} \right\} + \left\{ \begin{array}{l} NP_o \\ S_o \end{array} \right\} \\ V^3 + \left\{ \begin{array}{l} NP_s \\ S_s \end{array} \right\} + NP_i + \left\{ \begin{array}{l} NP_o \\ S_o \end{array} \right\} \end{array} \right\}$$

$$(2)\quad NP_s \rightarrow \left\{ \begin{array}{l} x \\ x: \ + S_x^{**} \\ \hat{x} + S_x \end{array} \right\}$$

$$(3)\quad NP_i \rightarrow \left\{ \begin{array}{l} x_{(R)} \\ x: + S_x^{**} \end{array} \right\}$$

$$(4)\quad NP_o \rightarrow \left\{ \begin{array}{l} x_{(R)} \\ x: \ + S_x^{**} \\ \hat{x} + S_x^{**} \end{array} \right\}$$

Subscript s stands for 'subject'; o for 'object'; i for 'indirect object'. S_x stands for S with at least one argument x. S** stands for any number of successive S's. 'x: + S_x' is to be read as 'the x such that $_S[\ldots x \ldots]$'. Definite NP's are analysed (parsed) into this form. Thus, *the rose* is analysed as 'x: Rose(x)' or 'the x such that x is a rose'. Subsequent S's after the first end up as relative clauses or adjectives in surface structure. The operator $\hat{}x$ denotes sets of potential addresses in any cognitive discourse representation: '$\hat{}x$(Rose(x))' reads 'the set of potential addresses characterized by the predicate "Rose"'.

Such set denotations are used in the grammatical and semantic analysis of quantified NP's (see Seuren, 1985 for details). The quantifiers are analysed as two-term predicates (V^2) which take set denotations as terms. The first term corresponds to the nuclear sentence, the second (object) term to the quantified NP. For example, (22a) is analysed as (22b) and reads as (22c):

(22) a. *The man drives a new car.*
b. $\exists 1\ [\hat{}x(\text{Drive}(x{:}\text{Man}(x), x)),\ \hat{}x(\text{Car}(x), \text{New}(x))]$
c. "The set of things the man drives overlaps (with an overlap of at least one element) with the set of things that are cars and are new."

The discourse increment brought about by (22) consists in the setting up of a new address characterized by the lexical material 'car(x)', 'new(x)'. and 'drive(d_n, x)', where d_n stands for the address denoted by the NP 'the man' and its semantic analysis 'x:Man(x)'. This increment value is indicated in the assignment procedure to follow as $i[S]$. Finally, the subscript R indicates morphologically marked reflexivity (the brackets indicate optionality).

Having said this, we now proceed towards a formulation of the assignment procedure (AP) proper. It starts with an initial instruction used to decide whether the lexical or the pronominal procedure is to be followed. It ends with the final instruction F assigning the proper discourse address, unless AP has blocked somewhere in mid-course, in which case no assignment is made and the term in question remains uninterpreted. Surface pronouns always end up in SA as x (or as x_R if they are marked for reflexivity). A bound variable pronoun is considered 'fixed' in SA by the operator $\hat{}x$ just in case it is an argument to the predicate of an S_x specified in the NP-rules for x. An occurrence of x in an S_x specified for the definite NP operator x: is also considered fixed by x:. Such occurrences of x only appear overtly in surface structure as reflexives (*the man who likes **himself***) or as relative pronouns (*the car **that** he bought*). Otherwise, they are not overtly present, but 'hidden' in the grammar of NP's. If more than one x occurs in an S_x, the preferred procedure is to let $AP[x_1] = AP[x_2]$. However, due to overriding cognitive factors, one x may be treated as not fixed. The notation t_f is used to indicate the NP headed by the fixer of a fixed x.

Whenever the symbol t is used in AP, it refers to the definite NP-term under treatment. The symbol d ranges over addresses, while **P**(t) stands for the lexical (predicate) material characterizing terms. The expression $d[t]$ is the denotation of a term t (i.e., its address). D stands for the domain in question, and G for the grammar of the language in question. t_s is the clause-mate subject term. The instruction → is a traffic direction of the 'go-to' kind. Provisional address assignments are marked as $d[t] =_p d_n$. Provisional address assignments are marked thus: $d[t] =_p d_n$. Provisional assignments to an address d_n are made when **P**(t) contains one or more terms t_u which do not match d_n, though all other material does. In such a case, d_n contains either an address-name d_k in the appropriate position, or x. If the latter, AP must asssign to x a defined semantic role, as in (23). If the former, AP applied to t_u may now yield $d[t_u] = d_k$. If it does, the provisional assignment of d_n to t is confirmed. If neither d_k nor any other available address either fits t_u lexically or can be expanded (because of cognitive backing) so that it will fit, and if there is no cognitive backing for the post hoc insertion of a new address, then AP blocks. If t_u is pronominal (it follows from the system that it must be a denoting pronoun) AP looks for an internal antecedent NP. AP is then let loose on the internal antecedent term t_i. If $d[t_i] = d_k$ or $d[t_i] =_p d_k$ all previous provisional assignments are confirmed and d_k is assigned to t_i.

AP applies to the terms of a sentence in a hierarchical order. That is, AP starts with the terms of the highest predicate in the order subject-object-indirect object. Track is kept of assignments made so that terms that have already been interpreted in the course of a complex-term interpretation or a pronominal interpretation can be skipped.

The *Assignment Procedure* (AP) now runs as follows:[9]

I: Check if t is *Lexical* → L-1
Pronominal → P-1

L-1: Check if some d_n (or the provisional d_n) is matched by **P**(t).
Yes → *F*
No → L-2
Tentatively → L-4

L-2: Check if for some d_n (or the provisional d_n) cognitive backing of D allows for further characterization of d_n by whatever lexical material in **P**(t) fails to match d_n.
Yes → F
No → L-3

L-3: Check if cognitive backing of D allows for the post hoc insertion of a d_n matching **P**(t).
Yes → F
No → BLOCK

L-4: Provisionally assign d_n to t. Take the uninterpreted term t_u and provisionally assign any corresponding address d_k to t_u (i.e., $d[t_u] =_p d_k$). Apply I to t_u.

P-1: Check if there is a d_n such that $d[t] =_p d_n$.
Yes → P-7
No → P-2

P-2: Check if t is reflexive. (A pronominal term t is reflexive just in case (a) t is marked for reflexivity and required to be thus marked by G if P-2 yields 'yes', or (b) t is not marked for reflexivity and not required by G to be thus marked if P-2 yields 'Yes', and if morphological, lexical,[10] and cognitive factors allow for the selection of a (direct or indirect) subject.)
If *Yes*, select the appropriate t_s. AP[t] = AP[t_s].[11] Confirm any provisional assignments made. CLOSE.
No → P-3

P-3: Check if t is fixed (i.e., if t is argument to a predicate of an S_x specified for x: or $\hat{}x$, and if there are no overriding cognitive or lexical factors blocking this path).
Yes → P-4
No → P-7

P-4: If t is fixed by x: (i.e., a denoting NP) → P-5
If t is fixed by $\hat{}x$ (i.e., a set denotation) → P-6

P-5: For any d_n such that $d[t_f] = d_n$ or $d[t_f] =_p d_n$ → F

P-6: → semantics of quantification[12]

P-7: Check if there is an internal antecedent term t_i. (A pronominal term t takes a term u as internal antecedent (t_i) just in case (a) u is of the form x or x: + S_x^{**}, (b) u either precedes t or t is in a surface structure subordinate clause and u is topic, and (c) there are no cognitive or lexical factors blocking this path.)

If *Yes*, apply *I* to t_i if necessary. If there is a d_n such that $d[t] =_p d_n$ → P-10. Otherwise, for any d_n such that $d[t_i] = d_n$ or $d[t_i] =_p d_n$ → F

If *No* → P-8

P-8: Check if there is an external antecedent term t_e. (A pronominal term t takes a term u as external antecedent (t_e) just in case (a) u is of the form x or x: + S_x^{**}, u occurs in a recent (preferably the preceding) sentence, t matches $d[u]$ lexically, and $d[u]$ is a plausible address for t.[13])

If *Yes*, then if there is a d_n such that $d[t] =_p d_n$ → P-10. Otherwise, for any d_n such that $d[t_e] = d_n$ → F

No → P-9

P-9: Check if the preceding sentence or the preceding conjunct *S* has a non-negated existential quantifier.

If *Yes*, then if there is a d_n such that $d[t] =_p d_n$ → P-10. Otherwise, for any d_n such that $i[S] = d_n$ → F

No → L-3

P-10: Check if $d[t_i] = d_n$ or $d[t_i] =_p d_n$ or $d[t_e] = d_n$ or $i[S] = d_n$

Yes → *F*

No → BLOCK

F: Assign d_n to t. Confirm any previous provisional assignments. CLOSE.

Finally, let us illustrate AP with a few examples. Consider (23a) with the SA (disregarding tense) (23b), presupposing d_1 and d_2 as given above except that at this point in the imaginary discourse, d_1 still lacks the information 'get (x, d_2)' and d_2 'get (d_1, x)':

(23) a. *The girl got the flowers that were sent to her.*
b. Get [x_1: Girl(x), x_2: Flowers (x), Be sent (x, to x_3)][14]

AP:	$t = x_1$	I:	Lexical → L-1
		L-1:	Yes (d_1) → F
		F:	$d[x_1] = d_1$ CLOSE
	$t = x_2$	I:	Lexical → L-1
		L-1:	Tentatively (d_2) → L-4
		L-4:	$d[x_2] =_p d_2$
			$d[x_3] =_p d_1$

$t = x_3$	I:	Pronominal → P-1
	P-1:	Yes → P-7
	P-7:	Yes: $t_i = x_1$; $d[t_i] = d_1$ → P-10
	P-10:	Yes → F
	F:	$d[x_3] = d_1$
		$d[x_2] = d_2$ CLOSE

Note that we have skipped the x in 'Girl(x)', in 'Flowers(x)', and in 'Be sent(x, to x_3)'. Clearly, these would be immediately revealed to be pronominal, without provisional assignment, and fixed by their fixing x_1: or x_2:. In virtue of P-5, they thus simply take over the assignment made for the whole term. Since, however, the whole term has been assigned an address already by AP, we are fully justified in ignoring these vacuous x's. Having now assigned all definite NP's in (23b) to their proper discourse addresses, the semantics now increments d_1 and d_2 as shown above. That is, d_1 is incremented with 'get(x, d_2)', and d_2 with 'get(d_1, x)'.

Let us now try the Bach–Peters paradox case (21a), based on the addresses d_1 and d_2 as given above. The SA of (21a) is

(21)a′. Like [x_1: Girl(x), Get(x, x_2), x_3: Flowers(x), Be sent(x, to x_4)]

AP:	$t = x_1$	I:	Lexical → L-1
		L-1:	Tentatively (d_1) → L-4
		L-4:	$d[x_1] =_p d_1$
			$d[x_2] =_p d_2$
	$t = x_2$	I:	Pronominal → P-1
		P-1:	Yes → P-7
		P-7:	Yes: $t_i = x_3$
	$t = x_3$	I:	Lexical → L-1
		L-1:	Tentatively (d_2) → L-4
		L-4:	$d[x_3] =_p d_2$
			$d[x_4] =_p d_1$
	$t = x_4$	I:	Pronominal → P-1
		P-1:	Yes → P-7:
		P-7:	Yes: $t_i = x_1$
			$d[t_i] = d[x_1] =_p d[x_4] =_p d_1$ → P-10
		P-10	Yes → F
		F:	$d[x_4] = d_1$ $d[x_3] = d_2$
			$d[x_2] = d_2$ $d[x_1] = d_1$ CLOSE

We try (21b) next. It presupposes the following three addresses:

d_3	d_4	d_5
man(x)	'Ann'(x)	car(x)
like(x, d_5)	buy(x, d_3, d_5)	like(d_3, x)
buy(d_4, x, d_5)		buy(d_4, d_3, x)

The SA of (21b) is:

(21)b′. ~Grateful[x_1:Man(x), Buy(x_2:'Ann'(x), x, x_3:Car(x), Like(x_4, x))]

AP:	$t = x_1$	I:	Lexical → L-1
		L-1:	Tentatively (d_3) → L-4
		L-4:	$d[x_1] =_p d_3$
			$d[x_2] =_p d_4$
			$d[x_3] =_p d_5$
	$t = x_2$	I:	Lexical → L-1
		L-1:	Yes → F
		F:	$d[x_2] = d_4$
	$t = x_3$	I:	Lexical → L-1
			L-1: Tentatively (d_5) → L-4
			L-4: $d[x_3] =_p d_5$
			$d[x_4] =_p d_3$
	$t = x_4$	I:	Pronominal → P-1
		P-1:	Yes → P-7
		P-7:	Yes: $t_i = x_1$
			$d[t_i] = d[x_1] =_p d[x_4] =_p d_3$ → P-10
		P-10:	Yes → F
		F:	$d[x_4] = d_3$
			$d[x_3] = d_5$
			$d[x_1] = d_3$ CLOSE

The following sentence contains the reflexive *himself*:

(24) a. The man who loved himself was vain.
b. Vain[x_1:Man(x), Love(x_2, x_R)]

It presupposes an address of at least the following form:

d_6
man(x)
love(x, x)

AP: $t = x_1$ I: Lexical → L-1
L-1: Tentatively (d_6) → L-4
L-4: $d[x_1] =_p d_6$
$t = x_R$ I: Pronominal → P-1
P-1: No → P-2
P-2: Yes: $t_s = x_2$; $d[x_1] = d_6$
$AP[x_R] = AP[x_2]$
$=$ address-bound x in d_6. CLOSE

Finally, let us consider a simple case of variable binding:

(25) a. Some American expects that he will win.
b. $\exists 1\ [\hat{}x(\text{Expect}(x_1\ \text{Win}(x_2))),\ \hat{}x(\text{American}(x))]$

No addresses are presupposed. The semantics for set-denotations is not given here, but for a summary indication see footnote 12. From this it follows that the semantic result of (25) consists in the setting up of an address which is characterized by the lexical material in both the subject-term and the object-term. This is unproblematic, provided the x's are fixed by the set-denoting operator. The only term which is not so fixed is x_2. We therefore need to apply AP to x_2:

AP: $t = x_2$ I: Pronominal → P-1
P-1: No → P-2
P-2: Yes (ind. refl.): $t_s = x_1$
$AP[x_2] = AP[x_1] =$ address-bound x
in new address d_7 CLOSE

This enables us to set up the new address:

d_7

American(x)
Expect(x, Win(x))

We observe that a sentence like

(26) a. Some American wants to win.

has an SA which runs exactly parallel to (25b), except that 'Expect' is replaced by 'Want', as in (26b). The difference in the surface structure is brought about by the fact that the lower subject (*he* in (25a)) has been deleted in virtue of obligatory like-subject deletion for the English verb *want*. There has been a lack of clarity in the literature on the conditions to be fulfilled by the two subjects for them to be called 'like'. The answer is now, in principle, given: the higher subject and the lower subject are 'like' just in case both have the same AP-value.

That is, either they denote the same address or they are both added as x to the same address or addresses. The parser will then have to attach to x_2 in:

(26) b. $\exists 1\ [\hat{}x(\text{Want}(x_1, \text{Win}(x_2))), \hat{}x(\text{American}(x))]$

the condition that AP[x_2] must be identical to AP[x_1], the latter being the higher subject under the verb *want*. This means that AP is to be extended with an extra proviso for P-2 to the effect that when the pronoun in question is not overtly present in surface structure, it must be an indirect reflexive. That is, condition (b) must then be fulfilled: *t* is not marked for reflexivity and not required by *G* to be thus marked, though it is a reflexive, and no morphological, lexical, or cognitive factors prevent AP-identity with a (higher) subject. P-2, therefore, has to be amended in that the answer 'No' will lead to 'BLOCK' when the pronoun is zero in surface structure, but to the instruction to go to P-3 in the other cases. These and other refinements, however, are left to a more comprehensive study.

NOTES

[1] The exclamation mark is used to indicate the impossibility of a co-denotation (or co-variable) relation between the NP's in italics.

[2] Note that morphological marking of reflexive pronouns in English is not simply conditional on a co-denotation (or co-variable) relation with the subject of the same clause. The pronoun in question must also not be in a secondary VP, as in:

(i) *Ben* wanted the parcel to be delivered to *him* before noon.

When the secondary VP is 'weakened' by the deletion of the infinitive, as in:

(ii) *Ben* had the parcel delivered to *him(self)* before noon.

morphological marking seems optional. In any case, however, the pronouns in (i) and (ii) are reflexive. Witness the impossibility of, for example,

(iii) ! *Ben* wanted the parcel to be delivered to *the old rascal* before noon.

[3] Thus, for example, in the Dutch sentence:

(1) Ik wilde *Karel* gelasten Ben voor *zich* te laten werken.
(I wanted to order *Karel* to make Ben work for *him*).

Karel is not a clause-mate subject with *zich* at any of the four levels of representation. It does, however, fulfill the condition at the stage just before the NP which is the subject of the clause $_S[_V$[laten werken] NP, Ben, voor zich] is deleted by Equi under identity with *Karel*, which is the subject of *gelasten* ("order").

[4] What *is* clear is that the introduction of the new notion of C-command ('a node A C-commands a node B just in case A's first dominating node also dominates B'), as in Reinhart (1976), is also insufficient, as is clearly demonstrated by example (10).

[5] This problem was mooted by Geach (1962, pp. 128ff.), who gives the examples:

(i) If *any man* owns a donkey, *he* beats it.
(ii) If *Smith* owns a donkey, *he* beats it.

[6] See Sanford & Garrod (1981). There seems, in any case, to be an overriding principle that external antecedents are assigned according to the greatest cognitive plausibility. Other factors, however, also play a role, such as similar syntactic function and intonation:

(i) Harry kicked *Sam* and then Bill kicked *him*.

'*Sam*' and '*him*' can only be co-denotational if '*him*' is unaccented. With accent on '*him*', '*Harry*' must be the antecedent (see also Akmajian & Jackendoff, 1970).

[7] It seems (see Tasmowski-De Rijck & Verluyten, 1982) that in these cases the suppletion is mediated through a tacit linguistic form. The evidence adduced is from French: when a person A is, for example, trying to get a heavy desk (masculine: *le bureau*) through a door, another person B might say:

(1) Tu ne *le* feras jamais passer par là.
'You will never get *it* (masc.) through there.'

However, if the object is a table (feminine: *la table*), B would say:

(2) Tu ne *la* feras jamais passer par là.

With the feminine pronoun *la* (it).

[8] In (21b) the pronoun 'he' is part of its antecedent NP. Cases of this kind must be accounted for by a refined definition of the notion 'antecedent' for denoting pronouns. Note that the pronoun is of the denoting kind:

(1) *The man* for whom Ann bought the car *the pig* liked was not grateful.

[9] I am indebted to Wietske Vonk, Leo Noordman, and Ton Weyters for a thorough discussion of AP.

[10] By 'lexical factors' is meant the very general lexical characterization of pronouns which they inevitably seem to have.

[11] The expression AP[t] is used to indicate the final semantic result of AP. This need not be an address assignment in all (successful) cases. AP[t] may consist in treatment by the semantics of quantification, as mentioned in P-6 and in note 12. It may also be the placement of a term x under a predicate P in an address d_n, as in (24).

[12] The semantics of quantification (i.e., the increment values of sentences containing quantified terms) is left out of our account. Essentially, the quantifying predicate '∃' is an instruction to set up one or more new addresses characterized by the lexical material in both of its set-denoting terms. The quantifying predicate '∀' is an instruction to add to all addresses answering the description of the object term the description of the subject term. Pronominal x's fixed by the set denotator $\hat{x}$ are taken care of by the semantics of quantification.

[13] The full set of conditions for a term to be an external antecedent is not yet known, as has been said before (note 6). 'Plausibility' includes lexical (note 10) and morphological matching, as well as cognitive congruence. As for the latter, cp:

(1) Audrey asked Sue to drive Helen to the station.
a. *She* didn't want her daughter to miss the train.
b. But if *she* didn't have time, Jeeves could do it.
c. Otherwise *she* would miss her train.

[14] The subscripts are added merely for ease of reference. They have no semantic significance. x_1 stands for the whole of x_1: Girl(x), etc.: x_n: stands for the whole denoting term fixed by x_n:. The term x_3 in the x_2 term of (23b) is singled out for separate indexing because the application of AP to x_2 yields a provisional assignment for x_3.

REFERENCES

Akmajian, A., & Jackendoff, R. Coreferentiality and stress. *Linguistic Inquiry*, 1970, *1*(1), 124–126.

De Rijk, R. P. G. A note on prelexical predicate raising. In P. A. M. Seuren (Ed.), *Semantic syntax*. Oxford: Oxford University Press, 1974.

Geach, P. T. *Reference and generality: An examination of some medieval and modern theories*. Ithaca, NY: Cornell University Press, 1962.

Langacker, R. W. On pronominalization and the chain of command. In D. A. Reibel, S. A. Schane (Eds.), *Modern studies in English*. Englewood Cliffs, NJ: Prentice-Hall, 1969.

Reinhart, T. *The syntactic domain of anaphora*. Unpublished doctoral dissertation, MIT, Cambridge, MA. 1976.

Sanford, A. J., & Garrod, S. *Understanding written language: Explorations in comprehension beyond the sentence*. Chichester: Wiley, 1981.

Seuren, P. A. M. *Predicate raising and dative in French and sundry languages*. Trier: Linguistic Agency University Trier, 1972.

Seuren, P. A. M. *Discourse semantics*. Oxford: Blackwell, 1985.

Tasmowski-De Ryck, L., & Verluyten, P. Linguistic control of pronouns. *Journal of Semantics*, 1982 *1*(4), 323–346.

9

Definite NPs and Context-Dependence: A Unified Theory of Anaphora

R. KEMPSON

Linguistics Department
School of Oriental and African Studies
London

THE PROBLEM: THE PARALLELS BETWEEN DISCOURSE ANAPHORA AND BOUND-VARIABLE ANAPHORA

This Chapter presents a data problem and a methodology problem, the first being symptomatic of the second. In addition, the solution to the first will supply a solution to the second. The methodology problem is the distinction between semantics and pragmatics. The data problem is the assumed distinction between bound-variable anaphora, as displayed in (1), and discourse anaphora, as displayed in (2):

(1) *Every female worries that she's boring.*
(2) *She's boring.*

It is almost universally agreed that these two processes have to be characterized discretely. Within the government and binding (GB) framework, as argued in Reinhart (1983), only bound-variable anaphora are characterized within the grammar, with discourse anaphora being excluded as pragmatic phenomena. Sentence 3 is treated as ambiguous between the two. Within model-theoretic semantics, bound-variable anaphora are

REASONING AND DISCOURSE PROCESSES

ISBN 0-12-512320-5

conventionally handled by a quantifying-in mechanism, whereas sentence 2 is analyzed as a directly referential expression (as in Cooper 1979) involving an unbound, pragmatically determined property variable. Sentence 3 can be analyzed either way, either by Cooper or in GB.

(3) *Sue$_i$ is convinced she$_i$'s boring.*

What is less commonly recognized is that every phenomenon which indicates the pragmatic nature of discourse anaphora is also displayed by bound-variable anaphora. There are at least four such properties:

(1) *The phenomenon of bridging coreference.* This is where the use of an anaphoric expression is licensed by a preceding, not-coreferring expression by virtue of some link between the objects those expressions describe. Thus, in sentences (4) and (5) there is no relation of identity between a car and its driver, and yet the introduction of the term *car* allows one to use a definite noun phrase (NP) by virtue of the link between cars and drivers:

(4) *John lifted a car. The driver was underneath.*
(5) *John lifted a car with the driver.*

Exactly parallel is sentence 6, except that the expression *a car* can be interpreted within the scope of the quantifying expression *everyone* and the term *the driver* is accordingly interpreted as a variable bound by the expression *a car* itself sensitive to the outermost quantifier.

(6) *Everyone who was able to lift a car found the driver underneath.*
(7) *John's house is a mess. The roof needs mending.*
(8) *Every house needs the roof mended.*

The introduction of the expression 'house' in examples (7) and (8) licenses the use of *the roof* both in examples of discourse anaphora and of bound-variable anaphora.

(2) *The use of anaphoric expressions.* These can be licensed by extra information made available by the total implicit content of the preceding sentence, and not any one constituent. Thus, (9) allows use of the term *the insult* on the basis of the assumption that calling someone a 'conservative' is an insult. This has long been recognized as a pragmatic phenomenon, but there are exactly parallel examples with bound-variable anaphora which are not recognized as pragmatic phenomena, as in (10):

(9) *Jake called Jess a conservative. The insult made him bristle.*
(10) *Everyone who called his neighbour a conservative later apologised for the insult.*

(3) *Manipulating extra premises and principles of deduction in order to establish an antecedent.* This, too, is possible with bound-variable anaphora.

The restriction is one of complexity rather than an all-or-nothing condition. Thus, in sentence 11 we have to know that Jaguars make cars and that two negatives make a positive in order to use the first disjunct to provide an antecedent for the definite NP *the car*. Exactly parallel is (12), though it manipulates the assumption that Rolls-Royce makes cars:

(11) *Either my friend hasn't bought a Jaguar, or the car'll be in the garage by now.*

(12) *Each of my millionaire friends who isn't so anti-British that they haven't bought a Rolls-Royce will soon be fed up with the car's petrol consumption.*

Moreover, the principles involved may be quite complex, yet in 13 even a mere pronoun can establish a successful antecedent from the information presented by the first (complex) disjunct.[1]

(13) *Either her father's mean and she hasn't a car, or it's in the garage.*

All we have to reconstruct is the implied relation between the subject's having (or not having) a car and her father being mean or not. I shall come back to this example in detail later on. For the present, the immediate understanding, expressed as "Either her father's mean and she hasn't a car, or he isn't mean and she has a car and it's in the garage" is at least suggestive of the point that definite NP and pronomial anaphora may depend on extra premises and principles of deduction. In the case of (12), this process is relative to some quantified expression further up the syntactic tree.

(4) *The nature of pronouns and definite NPs.* In comparison to 1–3, the phenomenon of the 'given' nature of pronouns and definite NPs, as opposed to the 'newness' of indefinite NPs, is familiar, but it is not often pointed out that this concept of picking out something already "given" or previously established is displayed equally by bound-variable anaphora. Examples (14) and (15) are straightforward cases of definite NP and pronominal anaphora, while (16) and (1) present the same phenomenon for bound-variable anaphora.

(14) *John bought a house and discovered later that the house needed damp-proofing.*

(15) *A man came in. He sat down.*

(16) *Everyone who bought a house discovered later that the house needed damp-proofing.*

In these cases, the definite NP and pronoun are licensed, and in some sense given, by the preceding quantified expression. The difference is, of course, that with a quantified antecedent, the bound-variable anaphor is in some sense given by each instantiation of the quantified expression. Notice that the converse pragmatic phenomenon of indefinite NPs, that they present a 'new' individual, is also shared by quantified expressions. Example (17) directs the hearer to construe the situation as involving more than one man while (18) directs the hearer to construe the situation as involving children having to tidy another child's work-pile (see Heim, 1982, for a detailed account):

(17) *A man came in. A man set down.*
(18) *Every child had to tidy a child's work-pile.*

(5) *The phenomenon of uniqueness associated with definite NPs and pronouns.* Referring uses of definite NPs and pronouns have classically had associated with them the property of uniqueness. This problem is widely recognized to be pragmatic, relative to the circumstances in some unanalyzed way. Thus in (2) there is only one female assumed to be under consideration, in (4) and (5) only one uniquely determined driver and in (7) one uniquely determined roof. What is less commonly recognized is that this phenomenon is displayed equally by bound-variable anaphora cases such as (1). (6). (8) and (16), though in these cases the value of the interpretation of the pronoun or definite NP is uniquely determined by each instantiation of the quantifying expression. In (1) for example, for each instantiation of the subject-quantifying expression, there is only one possible object picked out by *she*; for each instantiation of *car* in (6) there is only one possible object picked out by *the driver*; and so on. Of course, we analyze these in terms of the identity of variables, but the pretheoretic phenomenon of the anaphoric expression being uniquely identified on each interpretation is exactly parallel in both referring and bound-variable uses of definite NPs and pronouns.

Finally, it has been pointed out separately by Maclaran (1982) and Partee (1983) that directly referential expressions, almost without exception, have a corresponding bound-variable analogue. Sentence (19) is Partee's example, (20) is Maclaran's.

(19) *Everyone I play duets with seems relieved when we stop.*
(20) *Every day she woke up sweating, she knew that later that day she'd have a migraine.*

Both *we* and *that* are normally thought of as classical cases of directly referential expressions picking out a fixed set or individual from a given context. Yet (19) and (20) are instances of bound-variable interpretations, with the interpretation of *we* and *that* being dependent on the superordinate quantifying expression.

For all the listable, apparently pragmatic properties of referring, discourse-anaphoric uses of pronouns and definite NPs, there is a direct analogue for bound-variable uses. Yet it is the pragmatic properties which provide the motivation for analyzing discourse anaphora as pragmatic phenomena.

Bound-variable anaphora, by contrast, are thought to be phenomena which it is one of semantic theory's main tasks to explain. If we are to give a unitary account of problems of anaphora, we have to assume a pragmatic basis to bound-variable anaphora as well. This is what I propose. It is not, however, a wastepaper-bucket maneuvre. On the contrary, I provide a set of rules which purport to capture the phenomenon in a unitary way.

I argue that our assumptions about the concepts of semantics and pragmatics need to be altered. In particular, I propose that all that goes into the semantic component of a grammar is a set of instructions on the construction of logical forms. This constitutes the output of a grammar, with a different set of instructions defined for each sentence. It is the interaction of such instructions with well-founded pragmatic principles that determines logical forms, and it is these constructs for which an orthodox, non–context-dependent, model-theoretic interpretation is available. From this is follows that model theory is not a semantics of natural language expressions themselves, but only of the propositional objects they are used to construct.

THE SOLUTION: A RELEVANCE-BASED ACCOUNT OF ANAPHORA

The conception of linguistic semantics I defend in general, and the unitary analysis of discourse and bound-variable anaphora I defend in particular, are both dependent on the theory of utterance interpretation of Sperber and Wilson (forthcoming; see also Chapter 10, this volume). There are five main claims[2] of the theory of which I make direct use:

(1) Utterance interpretation is an inferential, and largely deductive, exercise which involves the construction by the hearer of a context set of premises which combine with the propositional form of what is heard to yield indirect implications (the implicit content of the utterance, roughly equivalent to implicatures). Thus contextual information is not in general given antecedently nor accumulated throughout a discourse; rather, the construction of the context is an essential part of utterance interpretation.

(2) The linguistic content of natural language sentences is underdetermined with respect to propositional content. The construction of a context set of premises, the decision as to the propositional content expressed by the sentence, and the consequent deduction of contextual implications are driven by a single principle, that of relevance. In particular, domain selection, reference assignment, and disambiguation are all subject to this principle.

(3) The principle of relevance is defined thus: The speaker has done his best under the circumstances to utter a sentence which is of maximal relevance to the hearer. This is the sole maxim of the theory and thus needs some explication. Relevance itself is defined as the nontrivial deduction of contextual implications from a pair comprising a context set of premises and an expressed proposition. The hearer's task is to select what the actual content of the pair should be. The principle of relevance is the guarantee that the speaker believes that the form which he or she has used makes immediately accessible to the hearer a context set and a proposition from which the hearer can derive contextual implications. Implicit in the concept of maximal relevance is a trade-off between maximum amount of information (contextual implications) for minimal processing costs. The motivation behind this is the stated aim of Sperber and Wilson to provide a theory of pragmatics which is not yet another module, but a theory of performance in which memory storage, processing costs, inferential properties of the central cognitive mechanism and information presented in a grammar all come together.

(4) The linguistic specification of elements of language may involve a dual specification: (a) their contribution to propositional content, and (b) their contribution to determining what information is made accessible for the purposes of context construction.

(5) The only factor that constrains the construction of contexts, in addition to any relevant specification of elements of the language and the principle of relevance, is the assumption that certain types of information are immediately accessible—specifically, the preceding utterance, the scenario of the utterance itself and information associated with concepts expressed by the lexical items used (this last stored in a mental lexicon of discrete concepts, with both encyclopaedic and analytic knowledge entered with them). Thus the preceding utterance U_{i-1} for some utterance U_i contributes to what is immediately accessible to U_i but by no means fully determines it, since not only may the scenario facts alter, but the concepts of U_i itself and any encyclopaedic information associated with them contribute to what is accessible in U_i.

It is this concept of accessibility that is central to my analysis of anaphora. Consider for the moment only indexical anaphora as in (2). discourse anaphora as in 3 and 15, and the bridging coreference cases in (4) and (5). I propose that the concept of definiteness associated with both pronouns and definite NPs is simply that of guaranteed accessibility. If a speaker uses a pronoun or a definite NP, then he or she is indicating to the hearer that a representation of a NP type is immediately accessible in the sense specified—either from the scenario of the utterance itself, from the preceding utterance, from preceding parts of the same utterance or from concepts expressed by what precedes the anaphor. Thus, in (2) the referent of *she* has to be accessible from the immediate context of utterance. In (15) reference is provided by the previous utterance, in (3) by some previous representation in the same utterance and in the bridging coreference cases of (4) and (5) by a premise accessible from a conceptual address associated with cars (namely, that cars normally have a driver). The bridging cases, and those were extra premises are required (see properties 1–3 listed earlier) are straightforwardly predicated on this analysis, given the Sperber–Wilson framework.

Since the content of all anaphoric expressions is a guarantee that an antecedent is immediately available, we can predict that where no antecedent is provided by the explicit content of the discourse, nor indexically, the anaphor will act as an instruction to the hearer to construct a context premise which will provide an antecedent as part of the implicit content of the discourse. Consider example (4). On this analysis, the use of an anaphoric expression is, by the principle of relevance, a guarantee of the instant accessibility of some representation of an individual described by the predicate 'driver' about which the speaker is making some assertion. But the immediately accessible environment (in this case just the preceding utterance) does not provide such a representation, although the speaker is using an anaphor as a guarantee of such a representation. He must therefore be using the anaphor as an indication to the hearer that he or she should construct a context premise such that the appropriate representation is derived as a contextual implication. In other words, the very use of the expression *the driver* indicates to the hearer that he or she should construct a context premise to the preceding utterance to the effect that a car has a driver. This will allow the hearer to deduce, as the implicit content of what he hears, that the car John lifted had a driver. This effect is directly predictable from the proposed analysis in terms of accessibility and the principle of relevance, without any further postulation.

Cases such as (9) are virtually the same. The only difference is that the contextual premise required (triggered by use of the predicate *insult*) cannot be accessed from any particular constituent of the preceding utterance. It is the whole of *Jake called Jess a conservative* that combines with 'To call someone a conservative is to insult them' to provide by deduction the contextual implication, 'Jake insulted Jess.' The only way to construe the statements in (9) so that the expression *the insult* fulfils the guarantee of accessibility of its anticedent is to construct such a context set. Hence, the account of anaphora in terms of accessibility enables us to predict that in cases where accessibility is not fulfilled by the explicit content of an utterance, the anaphor will act as a trigger for the construction of a context premise such that an antecedent is provided as part of the implicit content of what **Is** immediately accessible.

So far, I have characterized a definite NP as expressing as its intrinsic content a guarantee of instant accessibility of its antecedent. But the guarantee of immediate accessibility is simply an intrinsic part of the principle of relevance. It is this that determines the context set and the propositional content that a hearer selects. Thus, all we require of an analysis of anaphora is that an anaphor be some expression whose value is not given by the rules of grammar. All the rest will fall out from the application of the principle of relevance. And this is what my analysis provides. An anaphor will be represented as a metavariable whose value is not determined by any principle of grammar. Given my assumption of the Sperber–Wilson framework, it follows that it will have to be identified by a relevance-controlled principle of antecedent identification.

On this account, there is no stipulation of uniqueness as an intrinsic property of definiteness, for this too follows from the assumption of the principle of relevance triggering the rule. Antecedent identification is made by virtue of the guarantee that a representation of an individual is immediately, recognisably accessible to the hearer about whom he or she is to understand the speaker as making an assertion. If there is any doubt as to which individual that should be, then the hearer will have to put processing effort into deciding which individual it is. However, the speaker's utterance in that form is a guarantee that no such processing cost is necessary. Thus, if the speaker is obeying the principle of relevance, as we would assume him or her to be, there can only be one such individual.

In order to get this account to extend to sequences relative to the binding of a quantifier, as in (1), (6), (10) or (12), all we need to do is assume that we can manipulate a construct corresponding to a variable, a representation which can stand arbitrarily for any one of the individuals over which the domain of the quantifier ranges. The standard maneuvre in natural deduction systems is to assume the device of so-called arbitrary names, which do just this. As long as we have some such representation, we can apply exactly the same analysis in terms of accessibility that we had when the antecedent was a referring expression. Given that a quantifier introduces an arbitrary name, the name is accessible in just the same way as a referring expression and can enter into just the same deductive and context-specifying processes. The only difference is that its availability is restricted to the scope of the quantifier that introduced it. Thus it is not invariably available like a name. This is just the distinction we want.

I have so far been somewhat slapdash about such expressions as 'the content of the utterance' and 'identifying the referent of the pronoun'. However, the ontology of the Sperber–Wilson framework is explicitly deductive and computational in the Fodor sense, with deductions taking place by virtue of form. Thus, in talking of the principle of relevance identifying the referent of some NP, I in fact mean 'the principle of relevance identifying the representation of some reference or antecedent'. The significance of this is that the formal syntactic nature of the explanation is critical to my proposal that arbitrary names can provide an antecedent for a pronoun or definite NP, for these are syntactic, representational constructs and not genuine individuals in a semantic (set-theoretic) sense. Thus the simplicity of this analysis is made possible by the representational, deductive framework of the assumed pragmatic theory.[3]

We now come to the form of the proposal itself. The way in which the system works is really quite simple, stated in English. We assume two syntactic objects as in GB, logical form (LF) and LF′. A set of construction rules R1–5, formally defined in the next section, provide a mapping from the surface structure of a sentence onto a standard/GB style LF. From here, a set of projection rules, P1–7, also formally defined in the next section, combine with the construction rules R1–5 to provide a mapping onto an LF′, which is a standard predicate calculus formula containing no anaphors and no unbound variables (and in fact no contradictions). This second part of the mapping is compositional from bottom to top (rules P1–6). Lexical items are projected onto predicate calculus elements or configurations, and then progressively up the tree, each configuration defined at LF is projected onto the required predicate calculus configuration. This progressive projection of predicate calculus constructs up the tree interacts with a pragmatic, relevance-driven rule of antecedent identification (P7). Indeed, the rule binding variables to a quantifier (P5) depends on this interaction. The reason for this bottom-to-top projection is that in order to be able to identify the antecedent of a complex anaphoric expression such as *the man with brown hair half way down his back*, we need to have a representation of its parts which, as in this case, may itself involve identifying a pronoun. So in order for the antecedent identification rule to apply correctly, at this stage of the projection the system has to work from the representation of the elementary parts onto the representation of the whole.

Let me be more precise. What my proposal reconstructs are the two assumptions of Sperber and Wilson listed above as (2) and (5). That is, since an anaphor is under-determined with respect to its contribution to propositional form, my analysis gives a single specification of the content that a pronoun or definite article contributes to propositional forms. This specification takes the form of a metavariable, a place-holding device labelled β. I predict the various uses to which pronouns and definite NPs are put by a specified pragmatic principle of antecedent identification which interacts with the process of quantifier binding, which may follow it. The principle of antecedent identification selecting some accessible representation as antecedent applies blindly, without distinguishing between what are going to be bound-variable pronouns and what are going to be discourse-anaphoric or indexical pronouns.

In order to reconstruct Sperber and Wilson's principle (5), I specify a set of accessible concepts which any given node makes available for the rule of antecedent identification. This principle of identification then makes use of the set of accessible concepts in selecting an antecedent. In other words, each node of a tree has associated with it a pair—a structured specification of its predicate calculus form, and an unordered set of concepts which have been used up to that point in the tree. (In fact, I have three sets of stores for each node, storing separately traces, arbitrary names and untreated metavariables, and a general concept store, but this separation is merely for clarity.)

The formal framework I propose has the following seven properties:

(1) It specifies a quantifier-raised (QR) version of LF (see May, 1977) as the output of the syntactic component of the grammar. This is rule R1.

(2) It has a set of translation instructions, called projections, associated with each syntactically defined configuration which make explicit how the projected predicate-calculus parts combine to make a well-formed formula with no unbound variables. These are projections P2-6.

(3) It has a storage system which provides a history not only of what traces and unbound or metavariables are available at any stage, but also of which concepts, both simple and complex, have been used and are accessible in the required sense at any stage.

(4) It has an analysis of indefinite NPs (incorporated from Heim, 1982) in terms of an arbitrary name not so far selected, which has subsequently to be bound by a co-indexed superordinate quantifier.

(5) It has an analysis of all quantifying expressions (here, *every*) in terms of a superordinate operator, the quantifier and an arbitrary name which acts as a place-holder for the quantified variable which will eventually fill the slot in question. This separation of the quantifier from its position in the surface syntactic tree is effected by rule R2. This rule leaves an NP with a blank determiner, a configuration which, like indefinite NPs, is assigned an arbitrary name as its argument.

(6) It has an analysis of definite NPs and pronouns as metavariables, place-holders whose value is determined by the principle of antecedent identification (P7).

(7) It has the principle of antecedent identification, which can apply at any point to determine what the value of that place-holder shall be based on what is accessible to it. The latter is either the store associated with the preceding propositional constituent, or its own store as accumulated at the point at which the rule applies or from some other nonlinguistic source. In essence, I

am giving an explicit yet pragmatic mapping from LF onto LF′, both constructs construed as in GB.

THE FORMALISM

Assumptions

1. A universe containing a countably infinite set of individuals, U, to which I make no direct reference.
2. A metalanguage which contains
   a. the quantifiers, variables and operators of predicate calculus: $\forall, \exists, x, y \ldots, \&, -, \vee$;
   b. a countable set of names of individuals (assigned to some subset of U) $m_1, m_2 \ldots$, a countable set of names of subsets of U, a countable set of names of sets of ordered pairs of individual members of U, and so on. This total set is the set M.

(in other words, a set of metalinguistic names which pick out individuals, a set of one-place predicate names which pick out sets of individuals, a set of two-place predicate names, and so on);

   c. a countable set of arbitrary names, whose values range over individual members of U: $a_1, a_2, \ldots \in A$
   d. a countable set of metavariables (place-holding devices) whose value when assigned is one from either the set M or the set A. In other words, they are term variables:

$$\alpha_1, \alpha_2, \ldots, \beta_1, \beta_2, \ldots$$

   e. a set of traces, variables which take as their value the variable or constant assigned as an argument position to the projection of the NP subject to NP prefixing (QR). These therefore have to range over $\beta_1, \beta_2 \ldots$ assigned as argument positions to definite NPs and over $a_1, a_2 \ldots$ assigned as argument positions to indefinite and quantified NPs:

$$t_1, t_2, \ldots$$

Construction Rules

R1. NP-prefixing (QR): Chomsky-adjoin every NP other than pronouns and proper names to the immediately dominating S, leaving behind a co-indexed trace.

R2. Quantifier-construal: Chomsky-adjoin every Q (*a* and *the* do not have Q associated with them directly, since they are projected onto variables) to the immediately dominating S. If the quantifier is *every*, *each* or *all*, insert → between its restrictive term and nuclear scope (all quantifiers have the associated structure):

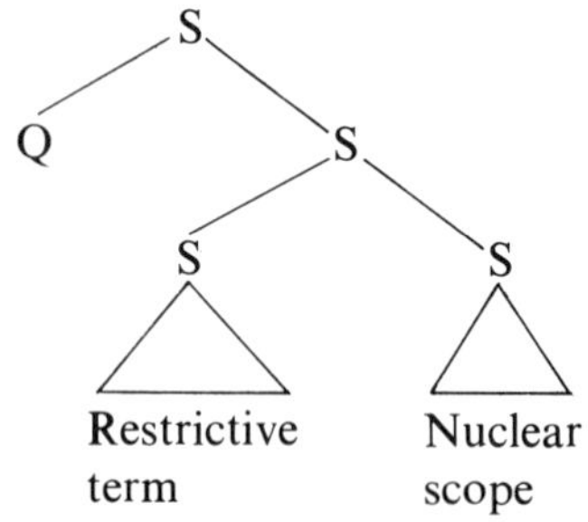

(This rule is generalized to adverbial quantifiers and negation.)

R3. Existential closer: Chomsky-adjoin a quantifier ∃ to the nuclear scope of every operator, and in the case of symmetrical connectives, & and ∨, to both conjuncts.

R3b (optional). For any sequence of S nodes where the leftmost immediately dominates an existential quantifier, Chomsky-adjoin the quantifier to the immediately superordinate *S*:

$$[_{S_m} [_{S_k} \exists x(\ldots \psi(x) \ldots)] \text{ Op } S_j] \rightarrow$$
$$[_{S_{m'}} \exists_n [_{S_m} [_{S_{k'}} \ldots \psi(a_n) \ldots] \text{ Op } S_j]]$$
$$a_n \notin \text{PST}(\text{NP}_{n-i})$$
$$\text{PST}(S_{k'}) = \text{PST}(S_k) \cup \{a_n\}$$
$$\text{ACC}(S_{k'}) = \{\text{ACC}(S_k) - \exists x(\ldots \psi(x) \ldots)\} \cup \{a_n, (\ldots \psi(x/a_n) \ldots)\}$$
$$\text{PST}(S_{k'}) = \text{PST}(S_k) \cup \{a_n\}$$
$$\text{ACC}(S_{k'}) = \{\text{ACC}(S_k) - \exists x(\ldots \psi(x) \ldots)\} \cup \{a_n, (\ldots \psi(x/a_n) \ldots)\}$$

PST(X_1): the pronoun store associated with the constituent x_i (see p. 216)

ACC(X_i): the accessibility store associated with the constituent x_i (see p. 216)

R4. The selectivity of quantifiers is guaranteed by selection indices 1, when Q moves out by R2, since it takes the referential index as a selection index, and 2, by copying the referential index of every indefinite NP as a selection index on the lowest c-commanding quantifier (so a quantifier may have more than one). I assume that every NP has assigned to it a referential index which percolates down to the head. In all cases, the index *j* assigned must not be a member of the set of indices assigned to arbitrary names in any previous constituent:

$$j \notin \{i\colon i \text{ assigned to members of PST}(X_{i-n})\} \quad n < i$$

R5. For two sister nodes of the same logical category not otherwise conjoined (i.e., quantifier-raised NP and S), insert &.

Projection Rules for Terminal Elements (TST = trace store, PST = pronoun store, ACC = accessibility store)

			TST	PST	ACC
P1.	$[t_j]_{NP_i}$	$\rightarrow t_j$	t_j	$\varnothing$	$\varnothing$
	$[\text{he}]_{NP_i}$	$\rightarrow \beta_i$	$\varnothing$	β_i	$\{\beta_i, \text{male}'(\beta_i)\}$
	$[\text{a}\_\_]_{NP_i}$	$\rightarrow \bar{N}'(a_i)$	$\varnothing$	a_i	$\{a_i, NP_i'\} \cup ACC(\bar{N})$
	$[\_\_\bar{N}]_{NP_i}$	$\rightarrow \bar{N}'(a_i)$	$\varnothing$	a_i	$\{a_i, NP_i'\} \cup ACC(\bar{N})$
	$[\text{the}\_\_]_{NP_i}$	$\rightarrow \bar{N}'(\beta_i)$	$\varnothing$	β_i	$\{\beta_i, NP_i'\} \cup ACC(\bar{N})$
	$[\text{John}]_{NP_i}$	$\rightarrow m_k$	$\varnothing$	$\varnothing$	$\{m_k, \text{John}(m_k)\}$
	every	$\rightarrow \forall$			
	hit	$\rightarrow$ hit′	$\varnothing$	$\varnothing$	hit′
	run	$\rightarrow$ run′	$\varnothing$	$\varnothing$	run′
	man	$\rightarrow$ man′	$\varnothing$	$\varnothing$	man′
	$[\ldots \text{not} \ldots]_{S_i}$	$\rightarrow -(S_i)$	$TST(S_i)$	$PST(S_i)$	$\{ACC(S_i) - S_i'\}$

(inadequate, but will not be taken up)

$$_{S_h}[S_i \text{ and } S_j] \rightarrow [S_i \,\&\, S_j]$$
$$TST(S_h) = TST(S_i) \cup TST(S_j)$$
$$PST(S_h) = PST(S_i) \cup PST(S_j)$$
$$ACC(S_h) = ACC(S_i) \cup ACC(S_j)$$
$$_{S_h}[S_i \text{ or } S_j] \rightarrow [S_i \vee S_j]$$
$$TST(S_h) = TST(S_i) \cup TST(S_j)$$
$$PST(S_h) = PST(S_i) \cup PST(S_j)$$
$$ACC(S_h) = ACC(S_i) \cap ACC(S_j)$$
$a_i \in A$ such that $a_i \notin PST(NP_{i-n})$

$m_k \in N \subset M$

α_i, β_i variables which range over $A \cup N \subset M$

For any category or expression X, X' is the metalanguage projection of X.

Projection Rules for Configurations Defined by R1–R5

P2. $[V \;\; NP]_{VP} \rightarrow V' \; (NP')$

$$TST(VP) = TST(V) \cup TST(NP)$$
$$PST(VP) = PST(V) \cup PST(NP)$$
$$ACC(VP) = ACC(V) \cup ACC(NP) \cup VP'$$

P3. $[NP \;\; VP]_S \rightarrow VP' \; (NP')$

$$TST(S) = TST(NP) \cup TST(VP)$$
$$PST(S) = PST(NP) \cup PST(VP)$$
$$ACC(S) = ACC(NP) \cup ACC(VP) \cup S'$$

P4. $[_{S_o}\mathrm{NP}_i(\mathrm{op})[_{S_p} \ldots t_i \ldots]] \rightarrow \mathrm{NP}_i(\mathrm{op})[_{S_p} \ldots t_i/\alpha_i \ldots]$
$\mathrm{TST}(S_o) = \mathrm{TST}(\mathrm{NP}_i) \cup \mathrm{TST}(S_p) - t_i$
$\mathrm{PST}(S_o) = \mathrm{PST}(\mathrm{NP}_i) \cup \mathrm{PST}(S_p)$
$\mathrm{ACC}(S_o) = \mathrm{ACC}(S_p) \cup \mathrm{ACC}(\mathrm{NP}_i)$ except that all conditions $\phi(t_i)$ are replaced by conditions $\phi(t_i/\alpha_i)$

P5. $[_{S_o}Q_j[_{S_p} \ldots a_j \ldots]] \rightarrow \mathrm{Q}(x)(\ldots a_j/x \ldots)$
$\mathrm{TST}(S_o) = \mathrm{TST}(S_p)$
$\mathrm{PST}(S_o) = \mathrm{PST}(S_p) - a_j$
$\mathrm{ACC}(S_o) = \{\mathrm{ACC}(S_p) - \psi(a_j) \text{ for arbitrary } \psi\} \cup \{\mathrm{Q}(x)(\ldots a_j/x \ldots)\}$

In the case of relative clauses, I am assuming a configuration which parallels NP-prefixing:

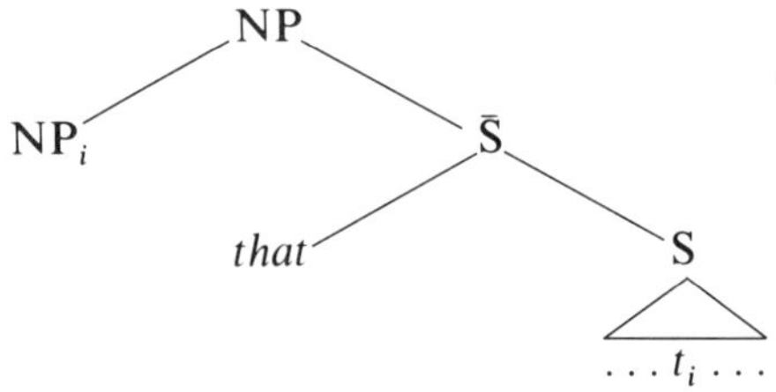

P6. $[_{\bar{S}} \text{ that } S] \rightarrow S'$ $\quad \mathrm{TST}(\bar{S}) = \mathrm{TST}(S)$
$\mathrm{PST}(\bar{S}) = \mathrm{PST}(S)$
$\mathrm{ACC}(\bar{S}) = \mathrm{ACC}(S)$

P7. Antecedent identification (F_{AI}):

$$[\ldots \beta_i \ldots]_{X_j} \rightarrow [\ldots \beta_i/\alpha_k \ldots]_{X_j}$$

where

$$\alpha_k \in \mathrm{ACC}(X_n) \cup \mathrm{PST}(X_n) \cup \mathrm{ACC}(X_j) \cup \mathrm{PST}(X_j) \cup N \subset M$$

and

X_n is left sister to X_j
$[\beta_i/\alpha_k]$ must be free in its governing category

$$\beta_i \neq \alpha_k$$

$\mathrm{TST}(F_{\mathrm{AI}}(X_j)) = \mathrm{TST}(X_j)$
$\mathrm{PST}(F_{\mathrm{AI}}(X_j)) = \mathrm{PST}(X_j) - \beta_i$
$\mathrm{ACC}(F_{\mathrm{AI}}(X_j)) = \mathrm{ACC}(X_j)$ except that all conditions $\psi(\beta_i)$ are replaced by conditions $\psi(\beta_i/\alpha_k)$

The formalism I have adopted is as close as possible to that of Heim (1982). Thus I am for the most part adopting her analysis of indefinite and definite NPs as variables, her analysis of quantification, the use of a level of LF in which QR applies to all NPs other than proper names and pronouns, her analysis of conditionals and modified versions of her set of rules of LF construction. In many ways, my analysis is simply a syntactic image of Heim (1982). One way in which the proposals obviously differ is that mine is totally syntactic, hers essentially semantic. Moreover, her concept of context change in a discourse is relentlessly incremental, whereas I am reconstructing the Sperber–Wilson concept of accessibility at any given point as in part independently selectible, and I am invoking a relevance-controlled principle of antecedent identification. Furthermore, I have accessibility stores which are modelled on Bach and Partee's (1980) storage system for pronominal anaphora. In particular, it is from Bach and Partee that I get the accumulation effect of the storage system. Though the projection of accessibility stores is normally accumulative, it involves extraction from the stores in three cases: (1) the binding of a trace by its antecedent NP (P4), (2) the binding of an arbitrary name by its associated quantifier (P5) and (3) the identification of a metavariable using the principle of antecedent identification (P7).

The immediate point of the system is that it allows us to give a unitary account of anaphora, predicting the phenomena listed at the beginning of the chapter as properties 1–5. This is demonstrated by the derivations which follow. But it also has a quite general consequence concerning the orthodox truth–theoretic interpretation of the compositionality-of-meanings requirement, which will be the conclusion of the chapter.

Consider first the simplest of the derivations, *A man came in. He sat down.* The rules of NP prefixing (R1), quantifier construal (R2), indexing (R4) and R5 give the following LF tree:

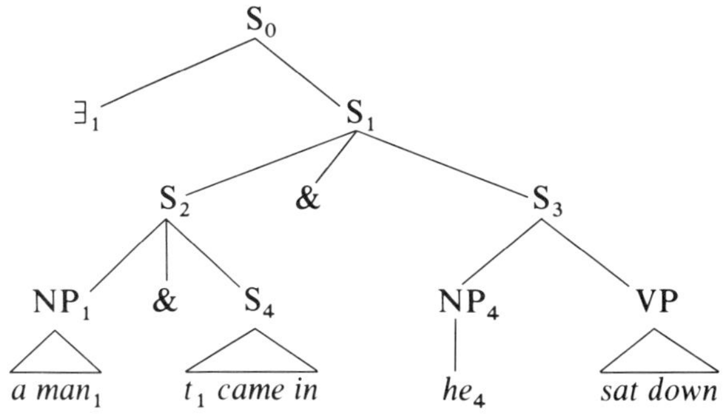

The indexing on the quantifier is given by rule R3b. The indexing of the NPs themselves is guaranteed as distinct in the normal way, which in turn guarantees that the arbitrary name associated with the indefinite article is distinct from any other arbitrary name.

The projection rules now apply as follows:

Step	Rule	Constituent	Projection	TST	PST	ACC
1	P1	a man_1	man′(a_1)		a_1	{a_1, man′, man′(a_1)}
2	P3	t_1 came in	came in′(t_1)	t_1		{came in′, came in′(t_1)}
3	P4	S_2	man′(a_1) & came in′(a_1)		a_1	{a_1, man′, man′(a_1), came in′, came in′(a_1)}
4	P1	NP_4	β_4		β_4	{β_4, male′(β_4)}
5	P3	S_3	sat down′(β_4)		β_4	{β_4, male′(β_4), sat down′, sat down′(β_4)}
6	P7	$F_{AI}(S_3)$	sat down′(a_1)			{a_1, male′(a_1), sat down′, sat down′(a_1)}
7	P1	S_1	man′(a_1) & came in′(a_1) & sat down′(a_1)			
8	P5	S_0	$\exists x$ man′(x) & came in′(x) & sat down′(x)			{man′, came in′, sat down′, $\exists x$ man′(x) & came in′(x) & sat down′(x)}

At line 1 we have the projection onto man′(a_1) where a_1 is an indexed arbitrary name, the pronoun store contains a_1, and the ACC store contains both the parts from which the projection was computed and the result. The same is true in line 2, except that I assume that traces have their own store. At line 3, the rule projecting a quantifier raised structure guarantees that the trace is removed from its store and replaced by the arbitrary name whose index it bears with the substitution of a_1 for t_1. S_3 is projected in a similar fashion (lines 4–5), but in this case the argument is a metavariable, β_4.

In computing S_1 at line 6, we find that the ACC store of S_2 contains a representation uniquely accessible, specifically a_1. If we look at the conditions on the application of antecedent identification, we see that it requires that an antecedent either be a member of the storage system of its sister node, or of its own storage system, or of some set $N \subset M$ which is a subset of the total set of names available in the metalanguage. This condition is fulfilled by a_1, a member of the ACC store of S_2. Hence the rule of antecedent identification can apply to yield as a projection of S_1 (line 7). Then at line 8, the quantifier rule has the effect of replacing all arbitrary names coindexed with the quantifier by a variable and removing all trace of the arbitrary name from the store, leaving only the concepts that did not involve the arbitrary name, together with the quantified formula itself.

The derivation of the following structure is parallel. (I ignore the existential quantifier following the connective. This is a consequence of adopting Heim's analysis of indefinites and plays no part in the derivation.)

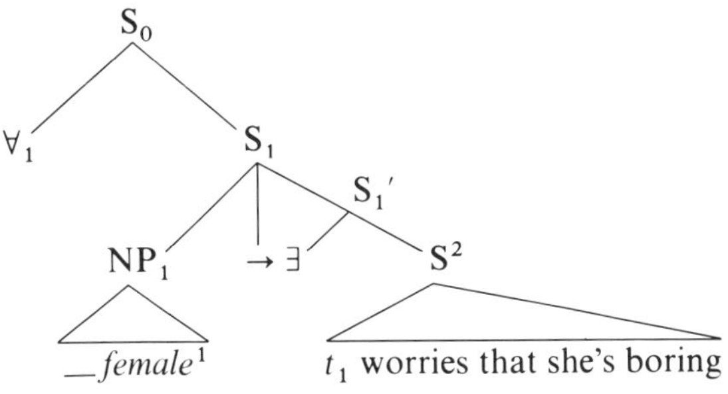

Step	Rule	Constituent	Projection	TST	PST	ACC
1		NP_1	female'(a_1)		a_1	{female', a_1, female'(a_1)}
2		S_2	t_1 worries that β_3 boring	t_1	β_3	{worries', boring', worries that β_3 boring, female'(β_3), boring'(β_3), t_1 worries that β_3 boring}
3	P4	S_1	female'$(a_1) \rightarrow a_1$ worries that β_3 boring		$\{a_1, \beta_3\}$	{a_1, female', female'(a_1), worries', boring', β_3, boring'(β_3), worries that boring(β_3), female'(β_3), a_1 worries that β_3 boring, female'$(a_1) \rightarrow a_1$ worries that β_3 boring}
4	P7	$F_{AI}(S_1)$	female'$(a_1) \rightarrow a_1$ worries that a_1 boring		a_1	{a_1, female', female'(a_1), worries', boring', boring'(a_1), worries that boring(a_1), female'$(a_1) \rightarrow a_1$ worries that a_1 boring}
5	P5	S_0	$\forall x$(female'$(x) \rightarrow x$ worries that x boring)			{female', worries', boring', $\forall x$(female'$(x) \rightarrow x$ worries that x boring)}

The extraction of the quantifier $\forall$ from NP_1 is effected by the quantifier construal rule, which also inserts $\rightarrow$. The projection of NP_1 has a_1, the arbitrary name in the PST, and the ACC store, made up of the parts of its translation. Similarly for S_2. Then at line 3, rule P4 combines the projection of NP_1 and S_2 to form the projection of S_1, and now we have a representation in store which the principle of antecedent identification (P7) can manipulate, specifically, a_1. Hence the rule applies, giving a projection of S_1 (line 4). Furthermore, the quantifier projection rule guarantees that the arbitrary name is bound as a variable, with all trace of the name removed from the stores.

Incidentally, it is this removal from the store which enables one to make correct predictions about the structural restrictions on bound-variable anaphora. Since the rule of antecedent identification (P7) depends on the content of the stores, as long as the quantifier binding has taken place, the variable will not be available as antecedent. Hence the predicted effects: (21) is acceptable on a reading with the pronoun bound by the quantified expression, but (22) is not.

(21) *A woman grinned at every man$_x$ who bought a donkey that smiled at him$_x$.*
(22) *A woman grinned at every man$_x$. *He$_x$ smiled back.*

Rather than establish this in detail, I give derivations involving the injection of extra contingent premises, since it is these my analysis particularly purports to explain. Thus example (5):

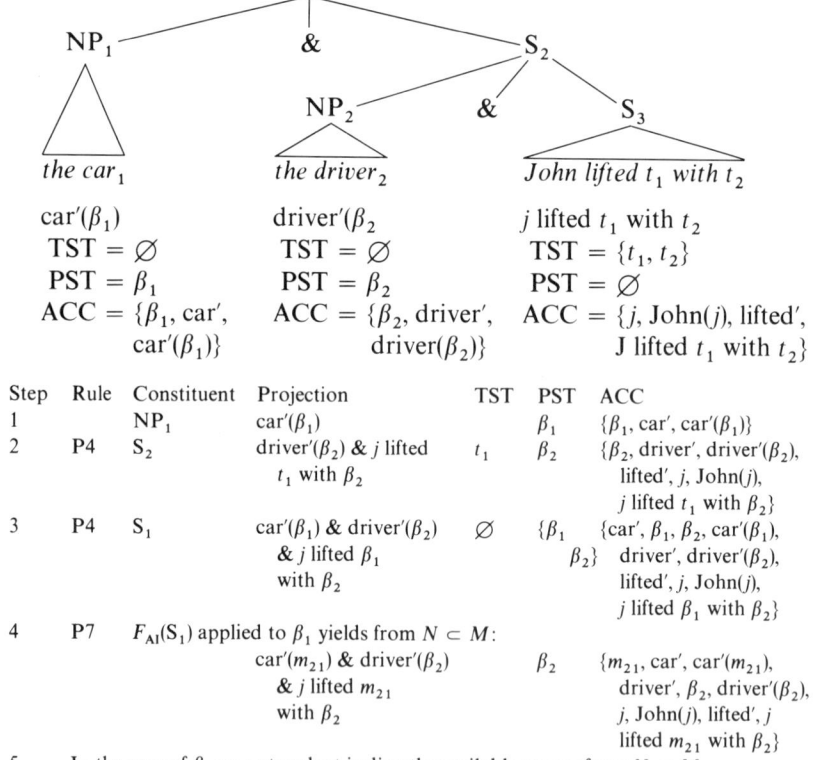

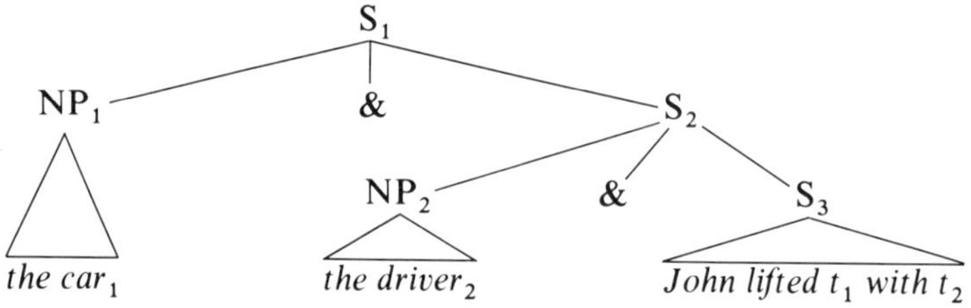

the car$_1$	the driver$_2$	John lifted t_1 with t_2
car'(β_1)	driver'(β_2	j lifted t_1 with t_2
TST = $\varnothing$	TST = $\varnothing$	TST = $\{t_1, t_2\}$
PST = β_1	PST = β_2	PST = $\varnothing$
ACC = $\{\beta_1$, car', car'(β_1)$\}$	ACC = $\{\beta_2$, driver', driver(β_2)$\}$	ACC = $\{j$, John(j), lifted', J lifted t_1 with $t_2\}$

Step	Rule	Constituent	Projection	TST	PST	ACC
1		NP$_1$	car'(β_1)		β_1	$\{\beta_1$, car', car'(β_1)$\}$
2	P4	S$_2$	driver'(β_2) & j lifted t_1 with β_2	t_1	β_2	$\{\beta_2$, driver', driver'(β_2), lifted', j, John(j), j lifted t_1 with $\beta_2\}$
3	P4	S$_1$	car'(β_1) & driver'(β_2) & j lifted β_1 with β_2	$\varnothing$	$\{\beta_1$ $\beta_2\}$	$\{$car', β_1, β_2, car'(β_1), driver', driver'(β_2), lifted', j, John(j), j lifted β_1 with $\beta_2\}$
4	P7	F_{AI}(S$_1$) applied to β_1 yields from $N \subset M$:	car'(m_{21}) & driver'(β_2) & j lifted m_{21} with β_2		β_2	$\{m_{21}$, car', car'(m_{21}), driver', β_2, driver'(β_2), j, John(j), lifted', j lifted m_{21} with $\beta_2\}$
5	In the case of β_2 no antecedent is directly available except from $N \subset M$.					

So we separate the two conjuncts by &E:

&E (1) car'(m_{21})
&E (2) driver'(β_2) & j lifted m_{21} with β_2

From car′ ∈ ACC(S_1) we obtain as context premise for NP_2' (specifically, car′(m_{21}):

	(3)	$\forall x$ (car′(x) → $\exists y$ y drive of x)
$\forall_E$	(4)	car′(m_{21}) → $\exists y$ y driver of m_{21}
MPP	(6)	$\exists y$ y driver of m_{21} (Add to ACC(S_1): $\exists y$ y driver of m_{21})
&I	(6)	car′(m_{21}) & $\exists y$ y driver of m_{21} & driver′(β_2) & j lifted m_{21} with β_2
R3b	(7)	car′(m_{21}) & $\exists_3$ [a_3 driver of m_{21} & driver′(β_2) & j lifted m_{21} with β_2] PST(S_1) = {a_3, β_2}
P7	F_{AI}(S_1)in case of β_2:	
	(8)	car′(m_{21}) & $\exists_3$ [a_3 driver of m_{21} & driver′(a_3) & j lifted m_{21} with a_3] PST(S_1) = a_3
EE	(9)	car′(m_{21}) & $\exists y$ (y driver of m_{21} & driver′(y) & j lifted m_{21} with y)

PST(S_1) = ∅
ACC(S_1) = {m_{21}, car′, car′(m_{21}), driver′, j, John(j), lifted′,
$\exists y$ (y driver of m_{21} & driver′(y) & j lifted m_{21} with y)}

ACC(S_1) was ignored in intermediate stages for the sake of simplicity. (Here and in all subsequent derivations, I omit the vacuous ∃ quantifiers.)

The projection of NP_1, S_2 and S_1 is straightforward for steps 1–3, giving both β_1 and β_2 in place of their traces by step 3. Given the configuration, the identification of the antecedent for the metavariable β_1 could only be from a source outside the sentence, and since we have no preceding utterance, we can only assume this to be from the context of utterance, here given as $N \subset M$. This is step 4. Step 5 is more complex. With respect to β_2, it is NP_1, which presents the most immediately accessible information (apart from $N \subset M$). However, the linguistic content of NP_2 guarantees that in order for some representation to be an antecedent to β_2, it must have predicated of it the predicate driver′. Moreover, the use of the definite article is a guarantee that such information is accessible. This therefore triggers the premise accessed from car′ ∈ ACC(S_1), as at 3:

$$\forall x \text{ car}'(x) \rightarrow \exists y\ y \text{ driver of } x$$

which by universal elimination, given 'car′(m_{21})', yields:

$$\text{car}'(m_{21}) \rightarrow \exists y\ y \text{ driver of } m_{21} \qquad (4)$$

and by modus ponendo ponens at 5:

$$\exists y\ y \text{ driver of } m_{21}$$

which provides an antecedent for the anaphor β_2.

This use of contingent premises, it will be recalled, is altogether predicted from the theory of relevance. All I have done is to construct as a context set for the proposition associated with NP_1 the proposition '$\forall x$ car'$(x) \rightarrow \exists y\ y$ driver of x', which combines with 'car'(m_{21})' to give as a contextual implication '$\exists y\ y$ driver of m_{21}'. It is thus the implicit content of the projection of NP_2 which in this case provides the antecedent for 'driver'(β_2)'. The only extra piece of machinery I have to assume at step 7 is the ability to extend the bracket of an existential quantifier, stated as rule R3b. This is unorthodox, but it is a phenomenon which has often been pointed out and is awkward only insofar as predicate calculus itself is awkward.[4] With a newly introduced arbitrary name, we have a boosted pronoun store (PST) and hence an introduced antecedent that enables the rule of antecedent identification (P7) to apply to β_2 at (7). All we then have to do is reintroduce the existential quantifier at line (9).

Notice the conclusion this forces on us—that the process of context construction and the deduction of contextual implications (i.e., implicit content) has to be carried out with respect to subparts of a surface sentential string. Thus the proposal that context premises be constructed and principles of deduction manipulated with respect to subparts of a sentence has motivation quite independently of the problems of quantifier binding, to which I now turn.

The derivation of example (8) exactly parallels the previous one except that the quantifier involved is $\forall$ and the connective $\rightarrow$,

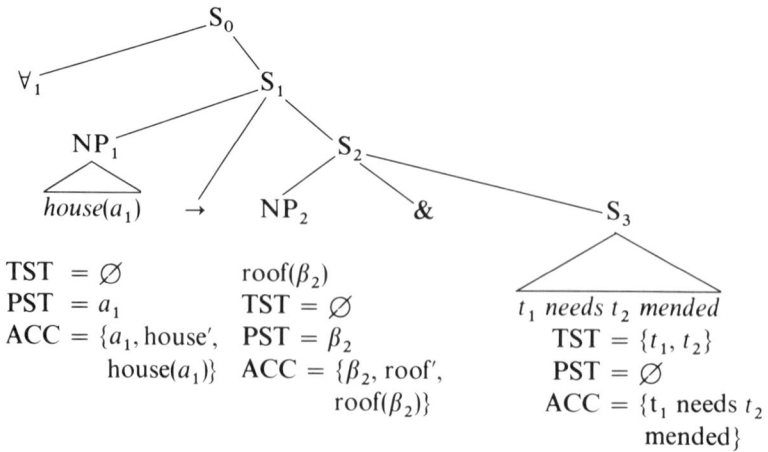

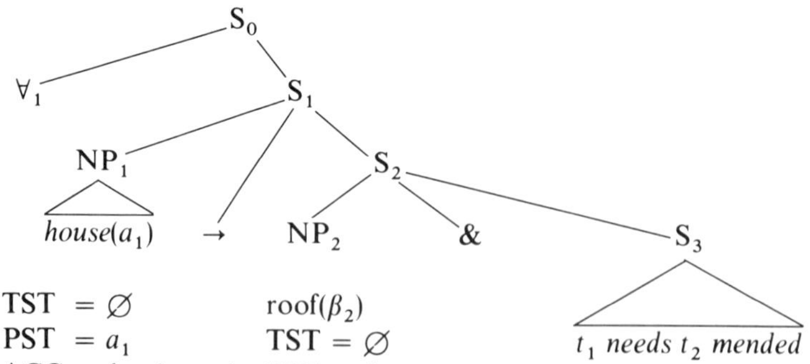

TST $= \varnothing$
PST $= a_1$
ACC $= \{a_1, \text{house}', \text{house}(a_1)\}$

roof(β_2)
TST $= \varnothing$
PST $= \beta_2$
ACC $= \{\beta_2, \text{roof}', \text{roof}(\beta_2)\}$

TST $= \{t_1, t_2\}$
PST $= \varnothing$
ACC $= \{t_1 \text{ needs } t_2 \text{ mended}\}$

Step	Rule	Constituent	Projection	TST	PST	ACC
1	P4	S_2	$\text{roof}'(\beta_2)$ & t_1 needs β_2 mended	t_1	β_2	$\{\text{roof}', \beta_2, \text{roof}'(\beta_2)$, t_1 needs β_2 mended$\}$
2		NP_1	$\text{house}'(a_1)$	$\varnothing$	a_1	$\{\text{house}', a_1, \text{house}'(a_1)\}$
3	P4	S_1	$\text{house}'(a_1) \rightarrow \text{roof}'(\beta_2)$ & a_1 needs β_2 mended		$\{\beta_2, a_1\}$	$\{a_1, \beta_2, \text{house}', \text{house}'(a_1)$, *roof′*, *roof′*$(\beta_2)$, a_1 needs β_2 mended$\}$
4	$F_{AI}(S_1)$ cannot apply directly except from $N \subset M$. However, from $\text{house}' \in \text{ACC}(S_1)$ we obtain:					
	ASS	(1)	$\forall x\ \text{house}'(x) \rightarrow \exists y\ y$ roof of x			
	$\forall$E	(2)	$\text{house}'(a_1) \rightarrow \exists y\ y$ roof of a_1			
	ASS	(3)	$\text{house}'(a_1)$			
	MPP	(4)	$\exists y\ y$ roof of a_1 (Add to $\text{ACC}(S_1)$: $\exists y\ y$ roof of a_1)			
	MPP	(5)	$\text{roof}'(\beta_2)$ & a_1 needs β_2 mended			
	&I	(6)	$\exists y(y$ roof of $a_1)$ & $\text{roof}'(\beta_2)$ & a_1 needs β_2 mended			
	R3b	(7)	$\exists_3(a_3$ roof of a_1 & $\text{roof}'(a_3)$ & a_1 needs β_2 mended$)$		PST $= \{\beta_2, a_1, a_3\}$	
	*P*7	(8)	$\exists_3(a_3$ roof of a_1 & $\text{roof}'(a_3)$ & a_1 needs a_3 mended$)$			
	$F_{AI}(S_1)$				PST $= \{a_1, a_3\}$	
	EE	(9)	$\exists y(y$ roof of a_1 & $\text{roof}'(y)$ & a_1 needs y mended$)$		PST $= a_1$	
5	P5	S_0	$\forall x(\text{house}'(x) \rightarrow \exists y(y$ roof of x & $\text{roof}'(y)$ & x needs y mended$))$ $\text{ACC}(S_0) = \{\text{house}', \text{roof}', \forall x(\text{house}'(x) \rightarrow \exists y(y$ roof of x & x needs y mended$))\}$			

As before, the projection of S_2 and NP_1 and the initial projection of S_1 are straightforward, as evidenced by steps 1–3 (i.e., all traces are removed from store). However, we cannot apply antecedent identification directly to β_2 except indexically, via $N \subset M$, for there is no representation available such that $\text{roof}'(\beta_2)$ is true, although we have the concept of house′ as a member of $\text{ACC}(S_1)$. By this, we can access the contingent premise:

$$\forall x\ \text{house}'(x) \rightarrow \exists y\ y \text{ roof of } x$$

Given the assumption of '$\text{house}'(a_1)$', we can deduce '$\exists y\ y$ roof of a_1' as the implicit content of NP_1 at 4. We therefore add this to the store. This does not have to be stipulated; it is simply that two pieces of stored information—namely 3 and 1—combine together by a process of deduction. The combination of the implicit and explicit content at line 6 then allows the bracket extension process I have stipulated as R3b at line 7, providing an interim boosting of the pronoun store, so that it now contains β_2, a_1 and a_3 at line 7. The rule of antecedent identification can now apply at line 8. Finally, the two quantifiers are introduced, and the final store has only the initial concepts and the quantified formula itself. I have had to stipulate nothing particular at all, since the accessing of contingent premises is predictable from the assumed pragmatic framework. The principle of antecedent identification and the progressive incrementation of the accessibility store all operate precisely as before. The reason for this is the assumption, as a constructive device, of the slot-filling capacities of arbitrary names, but these are orthodox representations within natural deduction systems.

I have so far dealt only with noncompond cases. But it is the compound cases, and in particular those involving *or*, which have been a stumbling block to many accounts of presupposition projection. Since it is a consequence of the proposal here that the presupposition projection phenomena require no separate stipulation, I demonstrate how this analysis handles one of the more complex cases—say, (13). This example is particularly interesting in that it stands in contrast to the logically equivalent (24), whose first disjunct fails to successfully provide an antecedent for the definite NP in the second disjunct.

(24) ?*Either it's not the case that John isn't mean or Sue has a car, or it's in the garage.*

What the analysis has to predict is why this should be so, given the manipulation of de Morgan equivalences that a Sperber–Wilson style analysis allows.

Before getting into the complexities of (13) and (24), I first demonstrate the pattern of analysis with a much simpler example, that of (23). Like (13) this structure has a first disjunct which can be construed as having some implicit relation to the second disjunct such that if the first is false, then some identifiable object is in the car. What I am going to reconstruct is a route of identification that we are forced to choose in (13), even though in (23) there is in fact a simpler direct analysis.

(23) *Either Daddy's been busy or it's in the car.*

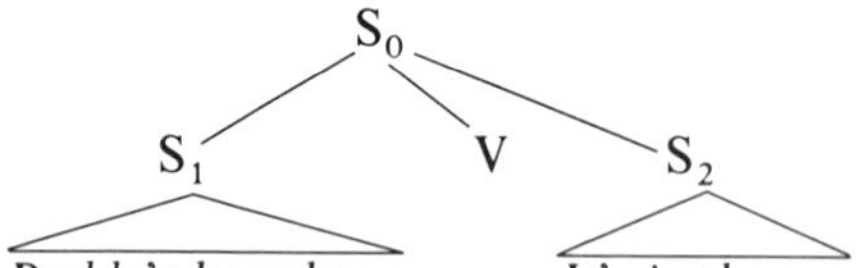

Daddy's been busy	*It's in the car*
busy′(d)	β_2 in m_{21} & car′(m_{21})
TST = $\varnothing$	TST = $\varnothing$
PST = $\varnothing$	PST = β_2
ACC = {d, busy′, busy′(d)}	ACC = {m_{21}, β_2, β_2, in m_{21}, car′, car(m_{21})}

1 $S_0 \quad S_1 \vee S_2 \equiv S_1 \vee (-S_1 \,\&\, S_2)_{S_1'}$

2 $S_0 \quad \text{busy}'(d) \vee (-\text{busy}'(d) \,\&\, \beta_2 \text{ in } m_{21} \,\&\, \text{car}'(m_{21}))_{S_1'}$

3 Assume 2nd disjunct (S_1'):

Assumption	(1)	$-\text{busy}'(d) \,\&\, \beta_2 \text{ in } m_{21} \,\&\, \text{car}'(m_{21})$	
&E	(2)	$-\text{busy}'(d)$	(isolating conjuncts)
&E	(3)	$\beta_2 \text{ in } m_{21} \,\&\, \text{car}'(m_{21})$	

Take (2) and construct context premise from $-\text{busy}(d) \in \text{ACC}(S_1')$:

MPP	(4)	$-\text{busy}'(d) \leftrightarrow \exists x\, \text{present}'(x)$	
MPP	(5)	$\exists x\, \text{present}'(x)$	(contextual implication of S_1': Add to $\text{ACC}(S_1')$)
&I	(6)	$-\text{busy}'(d) \,\&\, \exists x\, \text{present}'(x) \,\&\, \beta_2 \text{ in } m_{21} \,\&\, \text{car}'(m_{21})$	
3b	(7)	$-\text{busy}'(d) \,\&\, \exists_3[\text{present}'(a_3) \,\&\, \beta_2 \text{ in } m_{21} \,\&\, \text{car}'(m_{21})]$	$\text{PST}(S_1') = \{a_3, \beta_2\}$
P7 $F_{\text{AI}}(S_1')$	(8)	$-\text{busy}'(d) \,\&\, \exists_3[\text{present}'(a_3) \,\&\, a_3 \text{ in } m_{21} \,\&\, \text{car}'(m_{21})]$	$\text{PST} = a_3$
EE	(9)	$-\text{busy}'(d) \,\&\, \exists x\, \text{present}'(x) \,\&\, x \text{ in } m_{21} \,\&\, \text{car}'(m_{21})$	

$\text{TST} = \varnothing, \text{PST} = \varnothing$

$\text{ACC} = \{d, \text{busy}', -\text{busy}'(d), m_{21}, \text{car}', \text{car}'(m_{21}). \exists x\, \text{present}'(x) \,\&\, x \text{ in } m_{21}\}$

4 Reintroduction of disjunction:

$$\text{busy}'(d) \vee (-\text{busy}'(d) \,\&\, \exists x\, \text{present}'(x) \,\&\, x \text{ in } m_{21} \,\&\, \text{car}'(m_{21}))$$

The projection of S_1 is straightforward (I assume the identification of *Daddy* as $d \in N \subset M$ for simplicity). In the projection of S_2, I assume that the antecedent for the expression *the car* is provided only indexically from $N \subset M$, as m_{21}.

We now come to computing β_2 and S_0. I assume that a pair of disjuncts S_1, S_2 are characteristically interpreted by the hearer as '$S_1 \vee (-S_1 \,\&\, S_2)$'. In other words, I assume the analytic rule listed under '$\vee$' at line 1. Given the tendency to interpret *or* exclusively, I simply stipulate this on the basis of its intuitive plausibility, though it is in fact compatible with '$\vee$' itself. (Its justification would be on the basis of the intrinsic content of '$\vee$' and the communicative function of disjunction.) Being an equivalence rule, we can simply replace '$S_1 \vee S_2$' by '$S_1 \vee (-S_1 \,\&\, S_2)$' at line 2.

In order to process each of the disjuncts, we consider them separately, assuming each disjunct in turn. In particular, take the second disjunct at line 3. This contains a pronoun, and we know by the use of that pronoun that unless the speaker intends its identification to be made indexically, what he says in the first disjunct must combine with the use of *or* to provide an antecedent for the pronoun. Yet in order to reconstruct such an antecedent, we have to interpret the falsity of the first disjunct as providing such an antecedent. How can we do this? One obvious way is to assume a relation between the first disjunct and the assertion of such a suitable antecedent as being mutually exclusive. Thus in processing the second disjunct, now in the form '$-S_1$ & S_2', I have constructed the premise at line 4, assumed to be triggered by the pronoun and ($-$busy$'(d)$' $\in$ ACC(S_1):

$$-\text{busy}'(d) \leftrightarrow \exists x \text{ present } x$$

This yields as the implicit content of '$-$ busy$'(d)$' that there is a present (line 5) which combines with that from which it was derived to give the total content of S_1' at line 6. The bracketing is then extended as before at line (7), with the temporary addition to the pronoun store of a new arbitrary name. This term, a_3, provides the required antecedent for β_2. The only remaining steps are to reintroduce the existential quantifier and the main connective to give as the total explicit and implicit content of (23): 'Either Daddy's busy or Daddy isn't busy and there's a present and it's in the car.' (In fact, the same context premise combines with the first disjunct to give the converse contextual implication from the first disjunct—specifically, 'either Daddy's busy and there isn't a present or Daddy isn't busy and there's a present and it's in the car').

The two mechanisms I have had to assume here are (a) the equivalence rule associated with '$\vee$', and (b) the assumption that in processing a disjunction, the hearer constructs what may in principle be separate premises for each disjunct and only having done so puts the information together. Though this requires detailed pragmatic justification in terms of the theory of relevance, I assume such justification here, for the function of 'or' on an intuitive basis is to present the two disjuncts as separate, normally mutually exclusive pieces of information. Otherwise, all I have done is to assume, as before, that the use of the anaphoric expression forces the hearer to construct a context premise of a form he or she might not otherwise have had immediately accessible. In the present case, this is quite implausible, since when children are obsessed with presents they have been promised, the promised objects are invariably accessible. So any utterance of (23) in such circumstances would probably trigger the identification of the antecedent directly from $N \subset M$, rather than by the assumption of the combined communicative effect of the anaphor, the first disjunct and the particular connective *or*. However, in (13), it is precisely this effect that is achieved. In such cases we would predict that steps of deduction in deriving the antecedent by contextual implication would be involved, as indeed they are in this instance.

What the derivation of (13) does is to follow exactly the maneuvre of (23), but here the assumption of the falsity of S_1 in processing S_2 involves the falsity of a compound, and processing this compound involves steps of deduction. I assume that the initial output at LF is the tree given (ignoring the identification of *John*, *Sue* and *the garage* for simplicity).

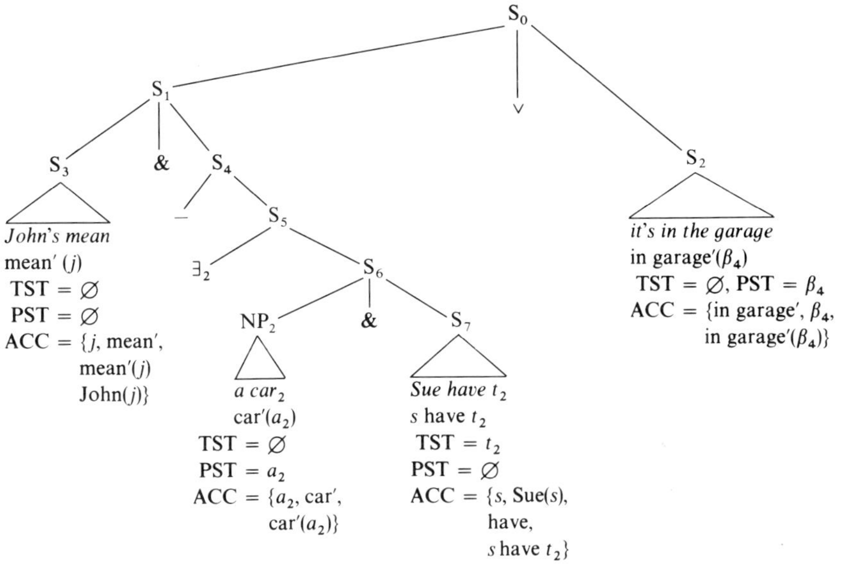

1 $S_1 \rightarrow$ mean′(*j*) & $-\exists x$ car′(*x*) & *s* have *x*
TST = ∅, PST = ∅
ACC = mean′, *j*, mean′(*j*), car′, have′, $-\exists x$(car′(*x*) & *s* have *x*), *s*, John(*j*), Sue(*s*)

By elimination rule associated with '∨':

$$S_1 \vee S_2 \equiv S_1 \vee (-S1 \,\&\, S_2)_{S_8}$$

2 $S_0 = S_1 \vee (-S_3 \,\&\, S_4) \,\&\, S_2)$
3 $\equiv S_1 \vee ((-S_3 \vee --S_5) \,\&\, S_2)$
4 $\equiv S_1 \vee ((-S_3 \vee S_5) \,\&\, S_2)_{S_8}$

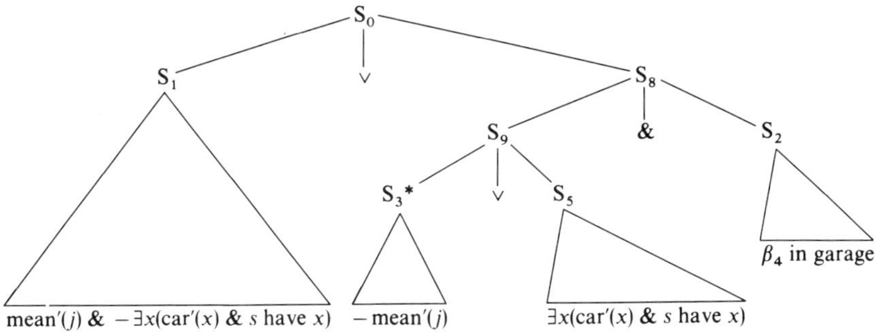

5	ASS	(1)	Assume 2nd disjunct, S_8: (− mean′(*j*) ∨ ∃*x* car′(*x*) & *s* have *x*) & β_4 in garage	
	&E	(2)	− mean′(*j*) ∨ ∃*x* car′(*x*) & *s* have *x*	
	&E	(3)	β_4 in garage	
	ASS	(4)	Assumption from ACC(S_8): − mean′(*j*)*x* ∃*x* car′(*x*) & *s* have *x*	
	ASS	(5)	Assume first disjunct of (2): − mean′(*j*)	
	MPP	(6)	∃*x* car′(*x*) & *s* have *x*	
	ASS	(7)	Assume second disjunct of (2): ∃*x* car′(*x*) & *s* have *x*	
	VE	(8)	Deduce (6) direct from (2): ∃*x* car′(*x*) & *s* have *x* (Add to ACC(S_8))	
	&I	(9)	Implicit content of S_8: ∃*x* car′(*x*) & *s* have *x* & β_4 in garage	
	R3b	(10)	$\exists_{21}$(car′(a_{21}) & *s* have a_{21} & β_4 in garage)	PST = {a_{21}, β_4}
	P7 $F_{AI}(S_8)$	(11)	$\exists_{21}$(car′(a_{21}) & *s* have a_{21} & a_{21} in garage) ACC(S_8) = {car′, a_{21}, car′(a_{21}), *s*, have′, *s* have a_{21}, garage′, a_{21} in garage}	PST = a_{21}
	EE	(12)	∃*x* car′(*x*) & *s* have *x* & *x* in garage ACC(S_8) = {car′, *s*, have′, garage′, ∃*x* car′(*x*) & *s* have *x* & *x* in garage}	PST = ∅
6	The initial disjunction is reintroduced: (mean′(*j*) & − ∃*x*(car′(*x*) & *s* have *x*)) ∨ ∃*x*(car′(*x*) & *s* have *x* & *x* in garage)			

In processing the combination of 'S_1 ∨ S_2', we move as before at line 2 to the form 'S_1 ∨ (− S_1 & S_2)'. (I need to label the introduced conjunction and do so arbitrarily as S_8.) The driving force of the derivation as before, and here critically, will be that the use of the expression *it* requires the hearer to access a contingent premise connecting information presented in the first disjunct in such a way that the assumption of its falsity in processing the second disjunct leads to establishing an implicit antecedent for the anaphor. The pragmatic motivation behind this maneuvre I have already given, and the steps in the derivation parallel the earlier example, with the only additional complexity being the number of equivalences that can be manipulated.

Since S_1 itself is compound, this leads us through steps 2 and 3 to line 4, presented also in tree diagram form. As the second disjunct, we now have a conjunction of a disjunction and 'β_4 in garage', which as before we assume at line 5(1). It is the trigger of the metavariable β_4 and the availability of the required bi-conditional premise as a member of the accessibility store for S_8 (projected from the intersection of the stores of S_3* and S_5, both '− mean′(*j*)' *and* '∃*x* car′(*x*) & *s* have *x*' having the same associated bi-conditional) which guarantees the construction of the premise, '− mean(*j*) ↔ ∃*x* car′(*x*) & *s* have *x*' at line 5(4). With this premise we can deduce '∃*x* car′(*x*) & *s* have *x*' from the two disjuncts S_3* and S_5 (where we have it direct) and thus arrive at the implicit content of S_8 at line 5(9). All the remaining moves are as in earlier derivations. The maneuvre of treating the introduced existential quantifier as an arbitrary name, a_{21}, then comes into play at 5(10). The rule of antecedent identification applies to identify β_4 with a_{21} at 5(11). We reintroduce the quantifier at 5(12) and finally reintroduce the initial disjunction at step 6.

In effect, what we have is the balancing of two simple disjuncts: *John's mean* and *The car's in the garage.* Given the premise that is required, the second conjunct of what is the actual compound disjunct is an explicit spelling out of what would otherwise be only the implicit content of the first disjunct. Since this leads to greater explicitness as to the contingent premise required, the additional complexity of processing the falsity of a compound is outweighed by the greater explicitness gained.

The difference in anaphor–antecedent linkage between (13) and its equivalent (24) (see p. 28) should now be virtually self-explanatory. The former presents information in the way most likely to lead the hearer to the interpretation intended. Even the contingent premise required is indicated by spelling out the contextual implication that should be derived from the first disjunct itself (a common use of *and*). Example (24) stands in marked contrast to this. Though the de Morgan equivalences we would need to apply to this are themselves no more complex than those required for (13), the very use of the disjunction between her father's not being mean and 'she has a car' suggests the separateness of these two pieces of information rather than their relatedness. The deliberate avoiding of the use of *and* buttresses this point. Furthermore, negation in otherwise simple clauses is known to be relatively hard to process, and double negation even more so, since processing difficulties accrue to more than one disjunction. Yet the principle of relevance is a guarantee that the speaker is attempting to express himself in a way which most efficiently indicates to the hearer what it is he is trying to say. In contrast with the logically equivalent (13), (24) fails to fulfill this requirement. Thus, (13) presents the information to be conveyed in a way that is compatible with the principle of relevance and succeeds in establishing an antecedent–anaphor linkage, while (24) does not. The style of explanation here is important. This is not merely a deductive analysis in which principles of deduction are freely available and no other criterion is applicable. On the contrary, the analysis I am proposing assumes the principle of relevance, whose operation depends on the form of presentation, the accessibility of contingent information in a specified way, and principles of deduction.

Similar arguments defuse the examples attributed to Partee which have been used against purely pragmatic analyses of anaphora:

(21) *I've dropped* 10 *marbles and found all of them except for one. It's probably under the sofa.*

(22) ?*I've dropped* 10 *marbles and found* 9 *of them. It's probably under the sofa.*

Here, the reply to the normal form of the objection that these examples are said to present (Heim, 1982) is even simpler. The standard objection is made on the assumption that the semantic explanation of the sentences is concerned solely with their set–theoretic content. This being so, the objection runs, how can a pragmatic account distinguish them? This objection does not apply at all to this account, since the linguistic content expressed by the sentences in question (which is available at the time of the application of the rule of antecedent identification) is not their set–theoretic content, but a form closely related to their surface form. In this respect, the two first sentences of the sequences differ. Only that of the first contains a representation corresponding to the one marble still lost. The second sequence not only lacks any such representation but involves deductions which are not even logical, but mathematical. Not only is this sequence therefore higher in processing cost to interpret, but it is not at all obvious that mathematical deductions have the same psychological status vis-à-vis processes of the central cognitive system such as logical deductions. Hence, if the speaker desired to direct the hearer towards a representation of that one marble as providing an antecedent for the pronoun she uses in the second sentence, then (25) is the most cost-effective way of doing so. Given the principle of relevance, that is the way she must choose.

The Consequences: The Compositionality Requirement Revisited

There was one overall purpose in constructing the framework presented in this chapter—namely, to spell out the consequences of adopting Sperber and Wilson's pragmatic theory, particularly (a) the claim that specifications within the grammar of natural language expressions are underdetermined with respect to propositional content; (b) the claim that sentences in discourse contribute to the concept of accessibility without completely determining it and (c) the claim that natural language elements may involve the specification of their contribution to processes of context construction rather than to the propositional content of sentences. The more particular purpose was to provide a unitary account of anaphora. The immediate consequence of the present proposal is that processes of context construction and the consequent deduction of contextual implication have to be postulated as part of the interpretation of even a single utterance, and not merely as a process which takes utterances as units. Put in the simplest way possible, working out the consequences of what we hear is a process which operates from the outset of an utterance, and not merely utterance by utterance.

I am painfully aware that the formalism proposed here falls far short of the ideal. I adopted a set of rules which induce predicate calculus formulae via a level of LF involving QR for two reasons: (a) to construct as close a syntactic image of Heim (1982) as possible, and (b) to manipulate a familiar deductive system. But in so doing, I have laid myself open to some easy objections. Phrasal co-ordination is problematic for any analysis of noun phrase interpretation involving the application of QR, so this system cannot account for interdependencies between phrasal conjunction and anaphora (see Rooth & Partee, 1982). This system gives no account of reflexives or of cross-over facts, and all the inadequacies of predicate calculus carry over here. But there are consequences for everyone working in semantics if the proposals of this chapter are even aimed in the right direction. One major problem which dominates work in formal semantics is the principle of compositionality, the principle that the meaning of a sentence is made up of the meaning of its parts. If the meaning of a sentence is given in terms of truth conditions directly (say, along model–theoretic lines), then the problem appears to be that the meaning of a sentence is not merely made up of its parts, but by those parts, by various hidden contextual variables, and on occasion by the incorporation of contingent information clearly not part of the linguistic information presented by the sentence. In effect, this is the core of the three problems I presented initially.

For those working in model theory, the principle of compositionality is both a central claim of the formalism and yet apparently not strictly retainable as a requirement on the surface sequences of the language. If I am right, there is a resolution to this problem. For model theory simply is not a semantics for natural language sequences directly. Rather, it provides a set–theoretic interpretation of a construct which is not the natural language itself but a metalanguage which both linguistic principles and pragmatic principles of relevance have played a part in constructing. If we apply a requirement of compositionality to this metalanguage, it can only take the form of requiring that for that language the interpretation of the whole be strictly dependent on its parts. And while the construction of the language is largely triggered by properties of the object language from which it is constructed, it is not fully determined by those properties, but rather by the combination of the properties and certain independently motivated principles of pragmatic theory. This is the reason that the compositionality requirement cannot be simultaneously applied strictly to natural language sequences and construed truth–theoretically. The correct conclusion to draw, on this view, is that the specifiable content of linguistic expressions is a set of instructions on constructing the metalanguage object, and that model theory and its associated compositionality requirement only apply to the completed construction of the metalanguage sequence (where it is applied strictly with no context-dependence). It follows that we must necessarily have two syntactic objects—let's call them LF and LF′ (though the former might only be that of surface structure)—one the output of the grammar and one the articulated metalanguage sequence. In particular, the latter is not a dispensable construct of convenience.

The lack of any application of concepts of model theory may strike some as barrenly solipsistic. But I am not in any way seeking to deny the status of model theory as a necessary part of an account of natural language. What I am denying is that it is a semantics of any such language directly. And what I am asserting is that the account of the interpretation of natural language sentences themselves—call this the semantic component of a grammar, if you like—is nothing but a set of syntactic instructions. On this view, impoverished as it may be, the semantic specifications contained within a grammar are clearly separable from and yet essential to the input to pragmatics: thus the methodology problem of what the relation between semantics and pragmatics should be is resolved. The mistake that we have made has been in thinking that real semantics, the semantics of truth conditions, was a part of grammar in any sense at all.

ACKNOWLEDGEMENTS

The first attempts towards presenting the ideás in this chapter were made in a course on context dependence at the University of Massachusetts, Amherst, in the spring of 1983. I am grateful to all those of the Linguistics Department who heard my first tentative and informal views on this subject, and to Toni Borowsky, Diane Brockway, Robyn Carston, Annabel Cormack, Wynn Chao, Hans Kamp, Craige Roberts, Mats Rooth and Deirdre Wilson for various extensive conversations leading up to the writing of this chapter. In particular, I am indebted to Deirdre Wilson for two major improvements of content on earlier versions and to Annabel Cormack for goading me into whatever degree of explicitness this chapter has achieved. This work was supported in part by SSRC research grant HR8635.

REFERENCES

Bach, E., & Partee, B. Anaphora and semantic structure. 1980, *Chicago Linguistic Society*, 1980, **16**, 1–28.

Cooper, R. The interpretation of pronouns. In F. Heny & H. Schnelle (Eds.), *Syntax and semantics*, Vol. 10.

Fine, K. A defence of arbitrary objects. *Aristotelian Society*, 1983, Suppl. Vol. LVII, 56–77.

Fine, K. Generative semantics for natural deduction. *Aristotelian Society Monograph Series*.

Heim, I. *The semantics of definite and indefinite noun phrases*. Unpublished doctoral dissertation, University of Massachusetts, Amherst, 1982.

Maclaran, R. *The semantics and pragmatics of the English demonstrative*. Unpublished doctoral dissertation, Cornell University, Ithaca, NY, 1982.

May, R. *The grammar of quantification*. Unpublished doctoral dissertation, MIT, Cambridge, MA, 1977.

Partee, B. Compositionality. In F. Landman & F. Veltman (Eds), *Varieties of formal semantics*. Foris.

Reinhart, T. Coreference and bound anaphora: A restatement of the anaphora questions. *Linguistics & Philosophy*, 1983, **6**, 47–88.
Rips, L. Cognitive processes in psychological reasoning. *Psychological Review*, 1983, **90**, 38–71.
Rooth, M., & Partee, B. Conjunction, type ambiguity, and wide scope 'or'. *West Coast Conference in Formal Linguistics*, 1982, **1**, 353–362.
Sperber, D., & Wilson, D. *Relevance: Communication and cognition.* Blackwell, Harvard University Press, 1986.

NOTES

[1] This example and (24) originated with Mats Rooth.

[2] I shall not be making use of Sperber and Wilson's claim that the logic of the central cognitive mechanism involves a restricted concept logic. Indeed, I make free use of the introduction rule of '&-Introduction' debarred by that logic. However, my use of &-Introduction is a consequence of adopting predicate calculus, which I did in order to manipulate a familiar deductive system. It remains an open question whether &-Introduction would be required in the optimal deductive system for natural language. In this connection, see Rips (1983), who advocates the use of introduction rules but restricts their use to derivations in which the form of the conclusion explicitly indicates the need to manipulate these rules.

[3] Fine (forthcoming) proposes a natural deduction system involving arbitrary names directly. Moreover, he has an associated semantics in terms of arbitrary objects (see Fine, 1983, for a defence of such constructs). Should Fine's proposals turn out to be straightforwardly applicable to the problems addressed here, we would have an explication of the phenomena both in the syntactic terms of natural deduction and in terms of the corresponding model–theoretic image.

[4] The incidental effect of this rule is to undermine Heim's claim that indefinite NPs are not quantified, since the rule attributes the scope-extending possibilities associated with indefinite NPs to the existential quantifier itself, and not to the translation from English onto the metalanguage (as Heim does). But in cases where the existential quantifier is deduced, the analogue of the Heim analysis of indefinites is not open to us, as one cannot claim that a quantifier is not really a quantifier. However I shall not draw out the consequences of this further (though see footnote 3).

10

Inference and Implicature in Utterance Interpretation

D. WILSON

Department of Phonetics and Linguistics
University College London

D. SPERBER

CNRS and Université de Paris X

THE CALCULABILITY REQUIREMENT

Grice (1975) distinguishes two main types of implicit content or implicature that an utterance can convey. Conventional implicatures are determined by particular lexical items or linguistic constructions occurring in the utterance, and fall within the domain of linguistic theory. Conversational implicatures follow from general maxims of truthfulness, informativeness, relevance and clarity that speakers are assumed to observe, and fall within the domain of a theory of communication. For Grice, the important difference between a conventional and a conversational implicature is that the conventional implicatures of an utterance are arbitrarily stipulated, whereas its conversational implicatures should be recoverable by a reasoning process: "The presence of a conversational implicature must be capable of being worked out; for even if it can in fact be intuitively grasped, unless the intuition is replaceable by an argument, the implicature (if present at all) will

REASONING AND DISCOURSE PROCESSES

ISBN 0-12-512320-5

not count as a *conversational* implicature: it will be a *conventional* implicature" (Grice, 1975, p. 50). Grice regards this calculability requirement as fundamental:

> The final test for the presence of a conversational implicature had to be, as far as I could see, a derivation of it. One has to produce an account of how it could have arisen and why it is there. And I am very much opposed to any kind of sloppy use of this philosophical tool in which this condition is not fulfilled. (Grice, 1981, p. 187)

However, his own account of the derivation process is rather sketchy, and although the idea of conversational implicature has had enormous appeal and has been used in an informal way to account for a wide range of pragmatic phenomena, little progress has been made in specifying the exact nature of the inference process by which conversational implicatures are 'worked out'. In this chapter we make some suggestions about the derivation of conversational implicatures and their role in comprehension.

Grice (1975, p. 50) suggests that the conversational implicatures of an utterance might be derived by arguments of the following form:

(1) a. He has said that *p*.
  b. There is no reason to suppose that he is not observing the maxims.
  c. He could not be doing this unless he thought that *q*.
  d. He knows (and knows that I know that he knows) that I can see that the supposition that he thinks that *q is* required.
  e. He has done nothing to stop me thinking that *q*.
  f. He intends me to think, or is at least willing to allow me to think, that *q*.
  g. And so, he has implicated that *q*.

It is unclear what sort of argument this is meant to be; it is not even clear which of (1a–g) are meant to be premises and which conclusions. What does seem clear is that (1c), in which the content of the implicature is introduced for the first time, is not directly deducible from (1a–b). Either (1c) is simply an independent premise, or it is meant to be derivable from (1a–b) with the aid of some supplementary premises whose nature has been left unspecified. What (1) really offers is not a method for working out the content of the propositions that the speaker, in producing an utterance, implicitly commits himself to, but rather a method for working out which of these commitments the speaker *meant*, in Grice's special technical sense (Grice, 1968). An adequate pragmatic theory should also provide some method of recovering the content of the implicatures themselves: that is, some method of deriving not (1g) but (1c).

It is becoming a commonplace of the pragmatic literature that deductive inference plays little if any role in the recovery of implicatures. Leech (1983, pp. 30–31) says that implicatures are 'probabilistic', and that the process by which they are recovered "is not a formalized deductive logic, but an informal rational problem-solving strategy". Levinson (1983, pp. 115–116) says that in some respects implicatures are more like inductive than deductive inferences, and that in these respects "they appear to be quite unlike logical inferences, and cannot be directly modelled in terms of some semantic relation like entailment". Bach and Harnish (1979, pp. 92–93) say that the form of inference by which implicatures are recovered "is not deductive but what might be called an inference to a plausible explanation". Brown and Yule (1983, p. 33) say that utterance comprehension rarely involves deductive processes, and that in the recovery of implicatures, "we are more likely to operate with a rather loose form of inferencing." These remarks can be taken in a number of ways.

In a sense, they follow directly from Grice's characterization of implicature, and some of these authors may be making a purely definitional point. Consider (2b), for example:

(2) a. He: *Do you want some coffee?*
b. She: *I've just had some.*

In normal circumstances, the speaker of (2b) would implicate (3):

(3) She doesn't want any more coffee.

But (3) is not deducible from the content of (2b) alone: (4) is not a contradiction:

(4) She has just had some coffee and wants some more.

Indeed, if (3) *were* deducible from (2b), it would not be an implicature in Grice's sense, since according to him, "the truth of a conversational implicature is not required by the truth of what is said (what is said may be true—what is implicated may be false)" (Grice, 1975, p. 58). If this is taken as a defining feature of implicature, no implicature will be deducible from the explicit content of an utterance alone.

However, to show that (3) is not directly deducible from (2b) is not to show that deduction plays no significant role in its derivation. Grice himself claims that background knowledge must play a role in the process by which conversational implicatures are 'worked out'. Why should the hearer not simply supply the background assumption in (5) and use it, together with the content of (2b), to deduce the conclusion in (3)?

(5) If she has just had some coffee, she doesn't want any more.

We will argue that deduction processes of this type play a central role in the recovery of implicatures. This is not, of course, to tell the whole story about how implicatures are derived. It is also necessary to show how appropriate premises for the deduction process are selected and potential conclusions evaluated: Why does the hearer of (2b) supply the background assumption (5) and accept the conclusion (3) rather than, say, supplying assumption (6) and deriving conclusion (7)?

(6) If she had just had some coffee, she wants some more.
(7) She wants some more coffee.

However, there is no reason in principle why an account of implicature in which deduction is a central element should not be adequate to deal with the interpretation of (2b) and other examples of implicature-carrying utterances.

Some of the authors cited above seem to be making not just the definitional point that implicatures cannot be deduced from the content of the utterance alone, but the stronger claim that deduction plays no significant role in their derivation, and in particular that an account like the one just suggested cannot be correct (see, e.g., Levinson, 1983, p. 116; Brown & Yule, 1983, pp. 33–35). To be able to evaluate this claim, we would have to have not only a clearer idea of the deduction-based account but also some idea of possible alternatives to it. By what non-deductive inference processes might the hearer of (2b) arrive at the conclusion in (3), and how would the alternative conclusion in (7) be ruled out?

It is now fairly widely recognized that there can be no non-demonstrative inference *rules*, in the sense that there are deductive inference rules, which given a set of premises simply enumerate a set of valid conclusions. Instead, the process of reaching valid non-demonstrative conclusions is standardly broken down into two distinct stages: hypothesis formation and hypothesis confirmation. For example, the hearer of (2b) would have first to form the hypothesis in (3), or the hypothesis that the speaker was trying to communicate (3), and, second, to confirm or disconfirm this hypothesis.

As Fodor (1983) points out, we are very far from having an adequate account of the psychology of hypothesis formation and confirmation. It is well known that from the purely logical point of view, any empirical proposition confirms or disconfirms an infinity of others. For example, (8) is logically equivalent to (9), and any proposition that confirms the latter confirms the former:

(8) All grass is green.
(9) Anything that is not green is not grass.

Proposition (9) is confirmed by anything that is not green and not grass: for example, a yellow camel. Hence, (10) confirms the claim that all grass is green:

(10) This is a yellow camel.

Someone who says (10) would not normally, of course, be construed as encouraging the hearer to derive either (8) or (9) as a conclusion. The problem is that there is as yet no principled account available of which of the infinite set of possible conclusions that the hearer of a given utterance *could* draw should actually be drawn.

Hypothesis formation, according to Fodor, is a creative process involving analogical reasoning, about which virtually nothing is known. Once formed, a given hypothesis will be accepted or rejected on a basis which is again very little understood. As Fodor sees it, the difficulties with hypothesis formation and confirmation arise from the fact that they are *global*, as oppose to *local*, processes. The distinction between global and local processes corresponds roughly to a distinction between processes in which contextual information plays a significant role and those in which it does not. A global process is one in which any item of information, however remote and unrelated to the information being processed, may legitimately be used. So, for example, in creating a scientific hypothesis to account for a certain range of data, it is legitimate to rely on analogies with other domains of knowledge, seemingly random associations of ideas, and any other source of inspiration that comes to mind. Once a hypothesis has been formed, the extent to which it is regarded as confirmed will depend on how well it fits not only with neighbouring domains of knowledge but with one's overall conception of the world. A local process, by contrast, is one which needs to take nothing into account apart from the information actually being processed. For example, given a set of premises, deduction is a purely local process in which no attention need be paid to information not contained in the premises themselves. Fodor's argument is that although we have a fair understanding of a variety of local processes, the working of global processes remains a mystery.

Given the haziness of our understanding both of the psychology of hypothesis formation and confirmation and of the effects of context on information processing, it is perhaps not surprising that pragmatists who express scepticism about the role of deductive reasoning in comprehension have said little about the processes by which implicatures are recovered. Bach and Harnish (1979, p. 83), after establishing that the working out schema is not deductive, add:

> Our empirical thinking in general is rife with generalizations and inference principles that we are not conscious of when we use them, if we are conscious of them at all. It would take us well beyond present-day cognitive psychology to speculate on the details of any of this . . . Whatever these processes are, whatever activates them, whatever principles or strategies are involved, they work, and work well.

But the fact that these processes work well enough in everyday utterance comprehension does not absolve us from saying what they are. If anything, the lack of any existing framework for describing them should make us more, not less, interested in their nature. Given the 'probabilistic' nature of implicatures, as illustrated in (2b) above, an adequate theory of how implicatures are recovered might shed light not just on utterance comprehension but on the more general psychological problem of hypothesis formation and confirmation which, for the reasons Fodor has given, has proved to be so intractable.

The claim that pragmatics must be based on *either* deductive *or* non-demonstrative systems, or that the adoption of one type of system must inevitably lead to the rejection of the other, seems to us to be unfounded. For the last few years, we have been working on a theory of hypothesis formation and confirmation, designed to apply to utterance comprehension, in which deductive processing plays a central role. In previously published work (see, e.g., Sperber & Wilson, 1982; Wilson & Sperber, 1986), we have concentrated on the central, deductive element of the theory, which will be outlined briefly in the next section. In the remainder of this chapter we will sketch in some of the broader background against which this central deductive element is set and show how 'probabilistic' implicatures would be handled in this framework.

RELEVANCE THEORY

Grice's work can be seen as providing the elements of a pragmatic hypothesis confirmation system. Given (a) a source of hypotheses about the speaker's communicative intentions and (b) an adequate account of what it is for a speaker to observe the conversational maxims, it seems reasonable to claim that the most favoured hypothesis, the one the hearer should choose, would be the one which best satisfies the maxims. In at least a few cases, it is easy to see how this proposal might work. Consider disambiguation, for example. Here the source of hypotheses is the grammar, which assigns a range of possible senses to an utterance. On the approach now being considered, the sense the hearer should assume that the speaker wanted to communicate is the one which best accords with the assumption that Grice's maxims have been observed.

Or consider how a hearer might decide which of the deductive consequences of an utterance the speaker wanted to communicate. Here the source of hypotheses is the deductive inference rules. On the approach now being considered, the hearer should assume that the speaker wanted to communicate any subset of these needed to satisfy him that the maxims have been observed. Consider, for example, the exchange in (11):

(11) a. He: *Is Bill an extrovert?*
b. She: *He's an actor, and all actors are extroverts.*

Here, in order to satisfy himself that the speaker of (11b) is observing the maxims of relevance and informativeness, the hearer must assume that she wanted him to deduce from her utterance the conclusion in (12):

(12) Bill is an extrovert.

In these two types of case, Grice's maxims can thus be used, if not to generate a set of hypotheses about the speaker's communicative intentions, at least to choose among them.

To provide an adequate account of implicature along these lines, two questions have to be answered. First, what is the source of hypotheses about the possible implicatures of an utterance? Second, is it possible to show more precisely what it is for a speaker to observe Grice's maxims? In previously published work (e.g., Wilson & Sperber, 1981; Wilson & Sperber, 1986), we have offered, in outline, an answer to the second of these questions. We have proposed a definition of relevance and suggested what factors might be involved in judgements on degrees of relevance. We have also argued that all of Grice's maxims can be replaced by a single principle of relevance—the speaker tries to be as relevant as possible in the circumstances—which, when suitably elaborated, can handle the full range of data that Grice's maxims were designed to explain.

We treat relevance as a relation between a proposition P and a set of contextual assumptions $C_1 \ldots C_n$. In previously published work we have made the simplifying assumption that the only propositions used in the comprehension process are those believed to be true. On the basis of this assumption, we have defined relevance as follows:

(13) A proposition P is relevant in a context $C_1 \ldots C_n$ if and only if P has at least one contextual implication in $C_1 \ldots C_n$.

A contextual implication is a special type of logical implication, derived by the use of a restricted set of deductive rules which derive at most a finite set of conclusions from any finite set of premises. (The details of this system will not concern us here; see Wilson & Sperber, 1986, and Sperber & Wilson, 1986, for discussion). The contextual implications of a proposition P in a context $C_1 \ldots C_n$ are all of the conclusions deducible from the union of P with $C_1 \ldots C_n$ but from neither P alone nor $C_1 \ldots C_n$ alone. For example, (2b) above contextually implies (3) in a context containing (5), and contextually implies (7) in a context containing (6); it would thus, by our definitions, be relevant in a context containing either (5) or (6).

The intuitive idea behind these definitions is that relevance is achieved when the addition of a proposition to a context modifies the context in a way that goes beyond the mere incrementation of that context with the proposition itself and all its logical implications. As we will show, the production of contextual implications is a special case of a more general notion of contextual modification which emerges once we drop the assumption that the only propositions used in comprehension are those believed to be true. For the moment, we will continue to assume that a hearer who wants to establish an utterance as relevant should be looking for a context with which it will interact to yield contextual implications.

Consider, in this framework, how a hearer might set about processing the information in (14):

(14) She: *Susan can drive any car.*

One possible line of interpretation would be to think of the names of some cars, as in (15), and conclude that Susan can drive them, as in (16):

(15) a. A Volkswagen is a car.
b. A Mercedes is a car.
c. A Buick is a car.

(16) a. Susan can drive a Volkswagen.
b. Susan can drive a Mercedes.
c. Susan can drive a Buick.

One of the conclusions in (16) might in turn combine with further contextual assumptions to yield a range of further contextual implications, which could in turn combine with further contextual assumptions, and so on indefinitely.

Another line of interpretation would be to think of conditional premises with (14) as antecedent and derive their consequents as conclusions:

(17) a. If Susan can drive any car, she is probably a good driver.
b. If Susan can drive any car, she is probably interested in cars.
c. If Susan can drive any car, she may be able fix an engine.

(18) a. Susan is probably a good driver.
b. Susan is probably interested in cars.
c. Susan may be able to fix an engine.

Again, one of the conclusions in (18) may combine with further contextual assumptions to yield further contextual implications, and so on indefinitely.

We assume that in processing a proposition, the hearer begins by systematically searching for contextual implications in a small, immediately accessible context consisting of the propositions that have most recently been processed. To these, further assumptions may be added subject to the

Parallel processing?

following constraint. We assume that information is stored in memory in encyclopaedic entries attached to concepts, and that the information in a given encyclopaedic entry can only be accessed via the presence in the set of propositions currently being processed of the concept to which it is attached. For example, an utterance mentioning cars makes accessible (to varying degrees) the set of propositions in the encyclopaedic entry attached to the concept *car*; these in turn give access to the encyclopaedic entries attached to the concepts they contain, and so on indefinitely.

It can be seen that in this framework, not all of the contextual implications of a given proposition will be equally easy to obtain. Those derived from small, easily accessible contexts will be relatively cheap in processing terms. By contrast, those derived from larger, less easily accessible contexts will be relatively expensive in processing terms, because of the additional effort required to access the contexts needed to derive them and to search these contexts systematically for contextual implications. We assume that the universal aim in processing is to obtain the maximum number of contextual implications in return for any processing effort expended. However, at a certain point in processing—which will vary from person to person and situation to situation—the cost of obtaining any further contextual implications will become too high, and processing will stop.

Let us say that, other things being equal, the relevance of a proposition increases with the number of contextual implications it yields and decreases as the amount of processing needed to obtain them increases. Maximizing the relevance of a proposition is thus a matter of accessing, as quickly as possible, a context in which it will yield the maximum number of contextual implications in return for the available processing effort. The most relevant propositions will be those which yield a wide range of contextual implications in a small, immediately accessible context.

We assume that the universal goal in cognition is to acquire relevant information, and the more relevant the better. We also assume that a speaker who thinks it worth speaking at all will try to make his utterance as relevant as possible. A hearer should therefore bring to the processing of every utterance the standing assumption that the speaker has tried to be as relevant as possible in the circumstances. It is this assumption that we call the principle of relevance.

A speaker cannot observe the principle of relevance without believing that his utterance will convey some relevant information to the hearer. Sometimes, he may have only the most general grounds for thinking so. For example, if I know you follow the pop music charts, I can reasonably assume that it will be relevant to you to know the name of the new number one hit, even though I may have no idea what implications this information will have for you. At other times, however, a speaker may have a much more specific idea of the sort of context that will be brought to bear and the sort of conclusions derived. It is in situations like this that we believe implicatures arise.

Consider, for example, the exchange in (19):

(19) a. He: *Can Susan drive a Buick?*
b. She: *She can drive* **any** *car.*

On what grounds might the speaker of (19a) have thought her utterance would be relevant to the hearer? What sort of context might she have expected him to supply that would be both accessible enough and rich enough in contextual implications for it to be worth his while to process her utterance? The answer is clear. He has just asked her whether Susan can drive a Buick. In our framework, he would not have asked this question if he had not had immediately accessible a context in which the information that she could (or could not) drive a Buick would be relevant—and indeed more relevant than any other information he thinks she will be able to provide. By providing this information directly, she would therefore be sure of satisfying the principal of relevance.

In fact, her utterance does not provide the information directly; the hearer has first to supply the contextual assumption in (15c) and then to derive the conclusion in (16c):

(15) c. A Buick is a car.
(16) c. Susan can drive a Buick.

However, the speaker can reasonably expect him to do this. On the one hand, her utterance gives him immediate access to his encyclopaedic entry for *car*, which should in turn provide access to propositions of the form (15a–c). On the other hand, on normal assumptions about the organization of memory. the immediately preceding mention of a Buick should act as a prompt, making (15c) more accessible than other propositions of this form. It would therefore be reasonable to assume that one of the grounds on which the speaker of (19b) thought her utterance would be relevant was that she expected it to be processed in a context which contained (15c) as an assumption and yielded (16c) as a contextual implication.

We want to say that the speaker of (19b) implicates both (15c) and (16c). On this approach, the implicatures of an utterance are those contextual assumptions and implications which the hearer has to recover in order to satisfy himself that the speaker has observed the principle of relevance. Here, (15c) is a necessary precondition on the recovery of (16c), and (16c) is a necessary precondition on the recovery of the whole range of contextual implications on which the main relevance of (19b) depends. We will call (15c) an *implicated assumption* and (16c) an *implicated conclusion* of (19b).

In fact, as we have described it, the interpretation of (19b) does not conform to the principle of relevance. The speaker could have conveyed the whole of this interpretation more economically by producing the direct answer in (16c). Instead, she has forced the hearer to process the proposition expressed by (19b), to access (15c) and deduce (16c) as a contextual implication, each step requiring some processing effort which would not have been required by the direct answer (16c).

Suppose the hearer asks himself why she might have thought that the indirect answer (19b) would be more relevant to him than a direct answer. The only possible explanation is that she must have expected it to yield some additional contextual implications not derivable from the direct answer (16c), which would more than compensate for the extra processing cost. In other words, the only possible explanation is that she believed that the surplus of information she was providing had some relevance in its own right.

As always, the speaker must have some reason for thinking that this surplus of information will be relevant, and more relevant than any alternative information she could provide. She may know, for example, that Susan has asked the hearer to lend her his Buick, and that he is wondering whether he can trust her with it or not. In these circumstances, her response in (19b) would encourage him to derive conclusions along the lines of (18): that Susan is an experienced driver, that she will look after his car, that he can safely lend it to her, and so on.

Grice (1975, p. 58) suggests that many implicatures are indeterminate:

> Since, to calculate a conversational implicature is to calculate what has to be supposed in order to preserve the supposition that the Co-Operative Principle is being observed, and since there may be various possible specific explanations, a list of which may be open, the conversational implicatum in such cases will be a disjunction of such specific explanations; and if the list of these is open, the implicatum will have just the kind of indeterminacy that many actual implicata do in fact seem to possess.

Grice's commentators have been divided in their reaction to this suggestion. Some, realizing the difficulty of providing an explicit treatment of indeterminacy, have largely ignored it. Gazdar (1979, p. 40), for example, notes the existence of indeterminacy but adds, "Because indeterminacy is hard to handle formally, I shall mostly ignore it in the discussion that follows. A fuller treatment of implicatures would not be guilty of this omission, which is really only defensible on formal grounds." Others, less interested in an explicit treatment of the processes by which implicatures arise, tend to use the indeterminacy of implicatures as an argument against deductive models of the recovery process and in favour of 'informal', 'loose' or 'probabilistic' models (see, e.g., Leech, 1983, Chaps. 2, 7). In our framework, the indeterminacy of implicatures can be dealt with without losing the explicitness of the deductive approach.

Sometimes, as we have shown, a speaker can observe the principle of relevance without having any idea of the sort of context in which the utterance will be processed, or the sort of conclusions that will be derived. In these cases, the utterance will have no implicatures at all. In other cases, as with (19b) and its implicatures (15c) and (16c), it is impossible to see how the speaker could have observed the principle of relevance without expecting a specific contextual assumption to be supplied and a specific conclusion derived. In these cases the utterance will have fully determinate implicatures. However, between these two extremes lie a whole range of intermediate cases. We have discussed a situation where the indirect answer (19b) would encourage the hearer to think of assumptions along the lines of (17) and to derive conclusions along the lines of (18). Here, the speaker has a general idea of the type of assumption to be supplied and the type of conclusion to be derived but may not know or care which specific assumptions and conclusions will be supplied. The clearer an idea the speaker must have had of the specific assumptions and conclusions to be supplied, the more determinate the implicatures will be; the vaguer an idea he could have had while still observing the principle of relevance, the less determinate the implicatures will be, up to the point where they vanish altogether and the choice of contexts and conclusions is left solely up to the hearer.

In every case, the method of processing is the same. The hearer supplies specific contextual assumptions and derives specific contextual implications. What varies is not the specificity of the assumptions and conclusions derived, or the formality of the reasoning processes involved, but simply the amount of foreknowledge the speaker must be assumed to have had of the way the utterance would be processed, and with it, the degree of responsibility he must take for the particular conclusions derived. Suppose, for example, that I could not have observed the principle of relevance without expecting you to supply a certain assumption and derive a certain conclusion in processing my utterance. Then by encouraging you to supply them, I take as much responsibility for their truth as for the truth of the proposition I have explicitly expressed.

Suppose, for example, that after the exchange in (19), it turns out that Susan cannot drive a Buick. Although (19b) does not *entail* that Susan can drive a Buick, the speaker could be quite rightly accused of having misled the hearer by allowing him to suppose that she could. Similarly, a speaker who secretly believed that the Buick was only a make of tractor could be accused of at least having *tried* to mislead the hearer by uttering (19b), thus encouraging him to suppose that the Buick was a make of car. In other words, the speaker is committed to the truth of all determinate implicatures conveyed by her utterance, just as if she had expressed them directly.

With less determinate implicatures, the speaker cannot be held solely responsible for their truth. Suppose, for example, that the exchange in (19) takes place in the circumstances described above, where the speaker of (19a) is wondering whether to lend Susan his Buick. Here, (19b) would clearly carry implicatures to the effect that Susan is a good driver, interested in cars, a suitable person to lend a car to, and so on. However, it would be a little strong to say that the speaker of (19b) had specifically indicated that the hearer could safely lend Susan his car. This is only one among a range of roughly equivalent conclusions that the hearer could have drawn, any of which would have satisfied him that the speaker had observed the principle of relevance. The weaker the implicature—that is, the wider the range of roughly equivalent alternative assumptions and conclusions would have satisfied the hearer that the speaker has observed the principle of relevance—the weaker the speaker's responsibility for its truth, up to the point where the implicature disappears altogether and the responsibility for the assumptions used and the conclusions drawn lies solely on the side of the hearer.

Talk of degrees of responsibility for the truth of implicated assumptions and conclusions takes us outside the simplified framework we have been assuming so far—a framework which abstracts away from the fact that a proposition can be expressed by the speaker with a stronger or weaker guarantee of truth, and that this guarantee may be more or less trusted by the hearer. The full framework is presented in detail in Sperber & Wilson (1986). In the next section we will outline only as much as is needed to account for the 'probabilistic' nature of implicatures.

AN EXTENSION TO THE THEORY

What would happen, in our simplified framework, if the hearer of (20) tried to process it in a context such as (21a–d), which directly contradicts it?

(20) She: *Peter is not coming to the party.*

(21) a. Peter is coming to the party.
b. If Peter is coming to the party, Jane will come.
c. Jane will come to the party.
d. If Peter is not coming to the party, Harry will not come.

We assume that no contextual implications at all are derivable from a contradictory set of assumptions (see Sperber & Wilson, 1986, for discussion). The hearer of (20) must therefore either reject the utterance as irrelevant or modify his assumptions in (21). By eliminating (21a) he could, in the simplified system outlined above, establish the relevance of (20) in a context consisting of the remaining assumptions (21b–d), deriving (22) as a contextual implication:

(22) Harry will not come to the party.

However, this is a rather unsatisfactory account, for two reasons. First, it implies that if (21d) had not been present in the context to enable (22) to be derived, (20) could not have been relevant at all. Yet intuitively, it is always relevant to discover that one has been mistaken. In such cases, our original intuition that a proposition achieves relevance by interacting with or modifying the context in which it is processed is not matched by our formal definition. Second, it is clear that a hearer in real life might neither reject (20) and retain (21a) nor accept (20) and reject (21a). He might decide that on the whole, (20) is more likely to be true than (21a), or that (21a) is more likely to be true than (20), or that he has no idea which of (20) and (21a) is true. To account for these facts, we must abandon the assumption that the only way a proposition can modify a context is by yielding contextual implications, and that the only propositions which play a role in processing are those regarded as certainly true.

Let us say that when a proposition is processed, it is assigned a subjective probability value representing its estimated likelihood of being true. (For reasons discussed in Sperber & Wilson, 1986, we do not regard these as numerical values.) Positive values represent the estimate that it is more likely to be true than false; the highest positive value, 'true', represents it as certainly true. Negative values represent the estimate that it is more likely to be false than true; the lowest negative value, 'false', represents it as certainly false. The absence of a value represents the absence of an opinion either way. When (20) is added to the context in (21), some complementary assignment of values to (20) and (21a) must be achieved—for example, by giving (20) the value 'true' and (21a) the value 'false', or by giving (20) some positive value less than 'true' and (21a) some negative value greater than 'false'. The greatest possible effect that (20) could have would be to make the hearer abandon entirely his former assumption (21a), assigning (20) the value 'true' and (21a) the value 'false'. Let us assume that this readjustment takes place.

The deductive rules must now be applied to a context in which one premise, (21a), is false. Moreover, (21a) combines with (21b) to yield (21c) as a conclusion. What happens to this conclusion now that one of the premises used to derive it is false? Let us say that only conclusions based on premises with positive probability values can have probability values of their own, so that once (21a) is assigned the value 'false', (21c) automatically loses its own value. Any further conclusions involving (21c) will in turn be affected. Let us also assume that (21d) has some positive value less than 'true'. How does this affect the value of (22), a contextual implication based on (20) and (21d) as premises? Let us say that a conclusion based on a mixture of premises with positive values will inherit at most the lowest value of any premise used in deriving it. Thus (22) will inherit at most the value of (21d).

The total effect of a proposition on a context can now be assessed by answering the following questions. First, did it directly affect the value of any proposition already present in the context, as (20) affected the value of (21a)? If so, how large was the change? Second, did it indirectly affect the value of any proposition already present in the context, as the modification of (21a) indirectly affected the value of (21c)? If so, how many propositions were affected, and how large was the change? Third, did its addition to the context yield any new contextual implications, as (20) yielded (22)? If so, how many were there, and how high were their values? We assume that the higher the value of any new contextual implication, the greater the modification to the context, and that a new contextual implication which lacks a probability value does not modify the context at all. With this extension to the framework, the recovery of contextual implications becomes just a special case of a more general notion of contextual modification in terms of which relevance can be redefined.

Let us say, then, that a proposition *P* is relevant in a context $C_1 \ldots C_n$ if and only if it modifies $C_1 \ldots C_n$ in one of the ways described above. Let us say that other things being equal, the more *P* modifies the context, the more relevant it is, but that other things being equal, the greater the amount of processing it requires, the *less* relevant it is. As before, the aim of the hearer in processing *P* will be to access a context which makes the best possible use of the available processing resources—that is, a context that maximizes the relevance of *P*.

From this very brief account, one or two general principles emerge. In particular, the only new contextual implications worth deriving will be those based on assumptions with positive values, the higher the better. The use of other assumptions will incur processing costs, but without leading to any reward in terms of contextual modification, since no new contextual implication based on them will be assigned a probability value. The use of such assumptions will thus detract from the relevance of any proposition being processed. Retrieval strategies geared to the maximization of relevance should therefore be aimed at retrieving, as quickly as possible, assumptions with positive probability values (the higher the better), and this fact should be known to any speaker. The hearer should also be able to infer, from the fact that the speaker is observing the principle of relevance, that he must have believed that all implicated conclusions, and all assumptions needed to derive them, had positive probability values, even if the hearer, of his own knowledge, would have been inclined to treat them as false.

Let us return, in the light of this discussion, to (2b) and its implicature, (3):

(2) a. He: *Do you want some coffee?*
b. She: *I've just had some.*
(3) She doesn't want any more coffee.

We can now answer the two questions raised in the first section: How is (3) derived, and how is the alternative derivation of (7) ruled out?

(7) She wants some more coffee.

The answer to the first question is that (3) is a contextual implication of (2b) in a context containing (5):

(5) If she has just had some coffee, she doesn't want any more.

Moreover, (5) is a implicated assumption and (3) an implicated conclusion. By parallel arguments to those used in the second section, the hearer knows that a speaker observing the principle of relevance must have expected him to supply the assumption in (5) and derive the conclusion in (3). A question we have not yet considered is what probability value the speaker expects the hearer to assign to the implicated assumption and conclusion.

The hearer could no doubt, of his own knowledge, assign some positive probability value less than 'true' to (3) and (5). Under normal assumptions, it would be no more than a probability that someone who had just had some coffee does not want any more. In these circumstances, however, the information that the speaker probably doesn't want any more coffee would not be relevant enough. In the first place, she ought to know whether she does or does not want any coffee, and if she knows, she should have told him, since he has indicated that this information would be relevant to him. In the second place, she must realize that the hearer would have been aware that she *might* not want any coffee when he asked his question. What he indicated by asking it was that a categorical answer would be relevant to him. Therefore, if she has this information and is observing the principle of relevance, she ought to have given it. Is there any way of construing (2b) as giving a categorical answer to the question in (2a)? Certainly. All the hearer has to do is upgrade the values of (3) and (5) to 'true'. To preserve the assumption that the speaker has observed the principle of relevance, this is what he must do. By the arguments of of our second section, the speaker, who has encouraged him to do this, will be held just as responsible for the truth of (3) and (5) as if she had expressed these propositions directly.

To complete the interpretation, some justification has to be found for the fact that the speaker has chosen an indirect rather than a direct form of answer. Failure to find such a justification would be prima facie evidence that this line of interpretation was not correct. Here, at least on an informal level, the reason is easy to see. A direct refusal, with no explanation, would be likely to raise all sorts of questions in the hearer's mind about why his offer has been refused. The indirect answer (2b) simultaneously refuses the offer of coffee and explains the refusal, thus saving the hearer the time he might have spent speculating on the reasons behind it. This line of interpretation is thus confirmed as satisfying the principle of relevance.

By contrast, an interpretation based on the contextual assumption in (6) and the conclusion in (7) is unlikely to be considered at all. If considered, it should be rejected as not conforming to the principle of relevance:

(6) If she has just had some coffee, she wants some more.
(7) She wants some more coffee.

The hearer of (2b) would no doubt, of his own knowledge, assign a lower probability value to (6) than to (5). On the assumption that retrieval strategies give preferential access to higher valued assumptions, (5) should be retrieved before (6); and since it gives rise to a satisfactory interpretation, there is no reason why (6) should be considered at all. However, suppose it is. The resulting interpretation should still be rejected as not conforming to the principle of relevance. There is no reason why a speaker observing the principle of relevance should have preferred the indirect answer (2b), construed in this way, to the direct answer that she wants some more coffee. An acceptance, unlike a refusal, normally needs no justification; it normally raises no questions in a hearer's mind about the reasons behind it. Moreover, if a speaker attempted to justify her acceptance on the ground that she had just had some coffee, she *would* raise a number of questions in her hearer's mind, and cost him valuable processing time if she did not go on immediately to answer them. Hence, the line of interpretation based on (6) and (7) is ruled out at a number of points as failing to conform to the principle of relevance.

Many standard examples of implicature fit straightforwardly into this framework. For example, Clark (1977) discusses a class of 'bridging' implicatures needed to establish the reference of the referring expressions in (23b)–(25b):

(23) She: a. *I went into the room.* b. *The window was open.*
(24) She: a. *I went into the room.* b. *Both windows were open.*
(25) She: a. *I went into the room.* b. *All three windows were open.*

As Clark points out, in normal circumstances the hearer of these utterances would supply assumptions (26)–(28), respectively, even if there had been no previous mention of the number of windows in the room.

(26) The room had a window.
(27) The room had two windows.
(28) The room had three windows.

Consider how this might happen in the case of (24b). Given the immediately preceding mention of a room, the hearer of (24b) would no doubt, of his own knowledge, have relatively easy access to each of the assumptions in (26)–(28) and be able to assign each of them some probability value less than 'true'. On the assumption that the speaker has observed the principle of relevance, he will take it that he must upgrade the value of (27) to 'true' and use it to establish the reference of the referring expression 'both windows' in (24b). As long as this assignment leads to a satisfactory range of contextual implications, he will accept it as correct. The role of the implicated assumption here is not to yield any particular contextual implication but to establish the referential content of the utterance, which is a necessary precondition to recovering any contextual implications at all.

There may, of course, be many other logically possible assumptions that the hearer of (24b) could have used—for example, the windows might have been in the house opposite, or mentioned in a letter the speaker found in the room. However, in normal circumstances, unless the existence of these windows had already been established, these assumptions would be much less accessible than those in (26)–(28), and a speaker observing the principle of relevance could not normally have expected the hearer to supply them. The general principle, for bridging implicatures as for all other implicated assumptions, is that they should—at least in the estimation of the speaker—be virtually instantaneously accessible, and more accessible than any alternative assumption likely to lead to an acceptable interpretation. If they are not, a speaker observing the principle of relevance should do something to increase their accessibility—such as directly mentioning them in the utterance—thus saving the hearer some unnecessary processing costs.

Grice (1975, p. 51) is unsure whether the implicatures carried by (29b) would be categorical or merely probable:

(29) a. A: *I am out of petrol.*
 b. B. *There is a garage round the corner.*

> B would be infringing the maxim "Be relevant" unless he thinks, or thinks it possible, the garage is open, and has petrol to sell; so he implicates that the garage is, or at least may be open, etc.

We can shed some light on Grice's uncertainty. A speaker observing the principle of relevance should expect the hearer, among other things, to supply the contextual assumption in (30) and derive the conclusion in (31):

(30) If there's a garage round the corner, I can get some petrol there.
(31) I can get some petrol round the corner.

However, if it occurs to the hearer that garages may be closed or out of petrol, he will be unable of his own knowledge to assign more than a fairly high degree of probability to (30) or (31). In other words, he will only be able to derive the conclusion that he *may* be able to get some petrol round the corner. So far, the case is exactly like the two previous ones discussed in this section. The difference is that in this case, even the information that he *may* be able to get petrol round the corner might be relevant enough for a speaker who could not make a more categorical claim to think this information worth offering.

More precisely, what the speaker of (29b) indicates is that *as far as he knows*, (30) and (31) are true, and therefore that *as far as he knows*, the garage is open and selling petrol. In some circumstances—for example if the speaker was coming from the direction of the garage with a full petrol can in his hand—the hearer would be justified in assuming that he was certain, and in this case the implicatures (30) and (31), and their necessary conditions that the garage is open and selling petrol, would be regarded as categorical. In different circumstances only a weaker attribution of probability values would be justified. The general principle is thus that when a less-than-categorical implicature would conform to the principle of relevance, the hearer is not entitled to assume that the speaker expects a categorical implicature to be supplied.

All the implicatures considered so far have arisen in processing the explicit content of the utterance, or, in Grice's terms, "what was strictly speaking said". As Grice points out, many implicatures arise not so much from the content of what was said as from the saying of it, in those circumstances, to that audience, and so on. Consider (32), for example:

(32) a. A: *Where does C live?*
b. B: *Somewhere in the South of France.*

In normal circumstances, B would implicate that he does not know more precisely where C lives. We would analyze this implicature as resulting, not from the explicit content of (32b), but from the fact, which the hearer is expected to notice and process, that the speaker has failed to give more precise information when, in the circumstances, more precise information would have been more relevant. To reconcile this fact with the assumption that the speaker has observed the principle of relevance, the hearer would have to access the contextual assumption in (33) and derive the conclusion in (34):

(33) If B has failed to give more precise information on C's whereabouts, he has no more precise information to give.

(34) B has no more precise information to give.

Here, (34) is a contextual implication, not of the content of (32b), but of (35):

(35) B has failed to give more precise information on C's whereabouts.

This is a proposition which may, and in this case clearly does, have some relevance in its own right. It would therefore be a mistake to think of a speaker as providing relevant information only through the explicit content of his utterance. An act of utterance may draw the hearer's attention to a number of propositions other than the one explicitly expressed, and these may contribute to the overall relevance of the utterance.

Grice analyzes (32b) as involving a clash between the maxims of informativeness and truthfulness, the desire to give precise information about C's whereabouts being sacrificed to the demands of truthfulness. He says little to explain why the supposed clash is not resolved in the opposite direction, which is a weakness of his system. Any system with more than one pragmatic principle must provide some account of their interaction—an account which is rarely provided. In our framework, with its single principle, there is no possibility of clashes. Notice, too, that there is no appeal to a violation of the principle of relevance, real or apparent, in our account of (32b). The speaker has been as relevant as he can in the circumstances—more relevant, for example, than if he had merely said, "I don't know." His failure to provide more detailed information is simply explained by the assumption that he did not have it to provide.

We would like to make the more general claim that the recovery of implicatures *never* involves an appeal to the deliberate violation of the principle of relevance. Grice (1975, p. 54) himself remarks that it is hard to find cases in which his maxim of relevance is deliberately violated, but offers the following as a candidate example:

> At a genteel tea party, A says "Mrs X is an old bag." There is a moment of appalled silence, and then B says "The weather has been quite delightful this summer, hasn't it?" B has blatantly refused to make what *he* says relevant to A's preceding remark. He therefore implicates that A's remark should not be discussed and, perhaps more specifically, that A has committed a social gaffe.

However, the fact that B's utterance is not relevant to the immediately preceding remark does not mean that it is not relevant at all. Most of its relevance would be achieved, not through its content, but by drawing the hearers' attention to the fact that B is deliberately ignoring A's remark. To reconcile this with the assumption that the principle of relevance has been observed, they would have to access assumptions along the lines of (36a–b) and derive conclusions along the lines of (37a–b):

(36) a. If B is deliberately ignoring A's remark, he believes it should not be discussed.
b. If B believes A's remark should not be discussed, he believes it was a social gaffe.

(37) a. B believes A's remark should not be discussed.
b. B believes A's remark was a social gaffe.

In our framework, these would be implicatures, since they are needed to reconcile the fact that B is deliberately ignoring A's remark with the assumption that he is being as relevant as he can. They would, however, be relatively weak implicatures, since a variety of roughly equivalent assumptions could be made, all of which would reconcile B's behaviour with the assumption that he is observing the principle of relevance. By the arguments of our second section, the speaker could therefore not be held solely responsible for their truth.

Relevance theory thus makes a number of specific claims about the role of implicatures in comprehension and the processes by which they are recovered. First, they are either contextual assumptions or contextual implications that the hearer is expected to supply in satisfying himself that the speaker has observed the principle of relevance. Implicated assumptions are recovered by the same processes used to retrieve other contextual assumptions, with ease of accessibility playing a decisive role; implicated conclusions are recovered by deduction. Second, the hearer may be expected to upgrade the probability value of an implicated assumption to the point where the conclusions it yields conform to the principle of relevance. The speaker is held responsible for the truth (or probability) of any assumptions and conclusions upgraded in this way. The hearer may thus acquire new information, not only from the explicit content of an utterance and its implicated conclusions, but also from its implicated assumptions. Third, implicatures may be recovered either in the course of processing the explicit content of an utterance or in the course of processing some higher level description of it which the hearer is expected to construct. It is important, therefore, that relevance is defined not as a relation between utterances but as a relation between propositions or sets of propositions. Fourth, there is no essential connection between the recovery of an implicature and the assumption that the speaker has deliberately violated the principle of relevance. On the contrary: In this aspect of comprehension, as in every other, it is the assumption that the speaker has *not* violated the principle of relevance that makes all the differences between processing an item of information that has been deliberately communicated and one that has not.

Within this framework, utterance comprehension is ultimately a matter of hypothesis formation and confirmation; the best hypothesis about the speaker's communicative intentions and expectations is the one that best satisfies the principle of relevance. However, it does not follow that deductive inference plays no role in the formation and confirmation of pragmatic hypotheses. On the contrary, because relevance is itself defined in partly deductive terms, the description of pragmatic hypothesis formation and confirmation makes essential reference to deductive processing. In particular, the class of possible implicated assumptions must be of a form capable of combining with information derived from the utterance to undergo deductive inference rules, and the class of possible implicated conclusions is itself deductively determined. The assumption that the overall framework in which comprehension takes place is ultimately a non-demonstrative one is not incompatible with the assumption that deductive processing plays a central role in comprehension.

CONCLUDING REMARKS

As we have described them, the processes of pragmatic hypothesis formation and confirmation are clearly context-dependent. But to what extent are they global processes in Fodor's sense? They are in principle because, as we have shown, the interpretation of a given utterance can proceed, in ever-expanding contexts, as long as the hearer thinks that the rewards are likely to outweigh the processing costs. With certain types of utterance—for example, a sacred text or a fortune-teller's prophecy—a hearer might be willing to devote a lifetime's effort to the interpretation process. In practice, however, expectations of relevance are generally much lower, there are other demands on the hearer's processing time, and he generally satisfies himself with establishing relevance in the most immediately accessible context and leaves it at that.

The same point applies to the formation and confirmation of scientific hypotheses. At one extreme are major theories, which may take a lifetime to develop and confirm. At the other extreme are such minor hypotheses as that there is a bird on the grass, or that spring is on the way, which are formulated in passing, processed in the most immediately accessible context and either abandoned or stored for future use.

We see little reason to think that there are differences of principle between what might be called the macro- and micro-processes of either pragmatic hypothesis formation and confirmation or scientific hypothesis formation and confirmation. In particular, the role of context and the goal of maximizing relevance seem to us to remain the same, although the principle of relevance of course applies only to deliberately communicated information. What distinguishes the two types of process is simply that the micro-processes draw on only the smallest and most immediately accessible contexts, whereas the macro-processes relax both size and accessibility constraints. We therefore suggest that the most useful way of gaining insight into global processes in Fodor's sense is to look at the micro-processes of everyday utterance interpretation and the interpretation of everyday sights and sounds, and to work on the assumption that the macro-processes involve the same cognitive principles and goals.

Academic text an intermediate type context?

REFERENCES

Bach, K., & Harnish, R. M. *Linguistic communication and speech acts*. Cambridge, MA: MIT Press, 1979.

Brown, G., & Yule, G. *Discourse analysis*. Cambridge: Cambridge University Press, 1983.

Clark, H. H. Bridging. In P. N. Johnson-Laird & P. C. Wason (Eds.), *Thinking: Readings in cognitive science*. Cambridge: Cambridge University Press, 1977.

Fodor, J. *The modularity of mind*. Cambridge, MA: MIT Press, 1983.

Gazdar, G. *Pragmatics: Implicature, presupposition and logical form*. New York: Academic Press, 1979.

Grice, H. P. Utterer's meaning, sentence meaning and word meaning. *Foundations of Language*, 1968, **4**, 225–2421.

Grice, H. P. Logic and conversation. In P. Cole & J. Morgan (Eds.), *Syntax and semantics 3: Speech acts*. New York: Academic Press, 1975.

Grice, H. P. Presupposition and conversational implicature. In P. Cole (Ed.), *Radical pragmatics*. New York: Academic Press, 1981.

Leech, G. N. *Principles of pragmatics*. London: Longman, 1983.

Levinson, S. C. *Pragmatics*. Cambridge: Cambridge University Press, 1983.

Sperber, D., & Wilson, D. Mutual knowledge and relevance in theories of comprehension. In N. V. Smith (Ed.), *Mutual knowledge*. London: Academic Press, 1982.

Sperber, D., & Wilson, D. *Relevance: Communication and Cognition*. Cambridge, MA: Harvard University Press, and Oxford: Basil Blackwell, 1986.

Wilson, D., & Sperber, D. On Grice's theory of conversation. In P. Werth (Ed.), *Conversation and discourse*. London: Croom Helm, 1981.

Wilson, D., & Sperber, D. On defining relevance. In R. Grandy & R. Warner (Eds.), *Philosophical grounds of rationality: Intentions, categories, ends*. (Festschrift for Paul Grice.)

11

Relevance and Beliefs*

Y. WILKS

Computing Research Laboratory
New Mexico State University

INTRODUCTION

This chapter compares two approaches to the modelling of human discourse and, more particularly, dialogue. Both place themselves within a general information processing paradigm, and both descend from the insight of Grice (1975) that understanding is a matter of inference from what is said and what is assumed. So general is that assumption now, and so widespread are the disciplines that draw upon it—philosophy, pscyhology, linguistics and artificial intelligence—that it is hard to capture briefly, except in opposition to the transformational–generative paradigm of language, with its notions of the primacy and autonomy of syntax and the theoretical primacy of explications of competence over those of performance. The generative semanticists attempted to merge the two traditions, and their failure has made it easier to separate out and clarify the work under discussion here.

The two pieces of work to be compared are the work on relevance logic by Sperber and Wilson (1982) and that on points of view and environments by Wilks and Bien (1979, 1983). The last is a much fuller account than appears

* This research is currently supported by the (UK) Science and Engineering Research Council contract GR/C/44938.

ISBN 0-12-512320-5

here, and the reader is referred to it for more detail. Similarly, the present critique of Sperber and Wilson will be found in a fuller form in Wilks and Cunningham (1983). Both seek to show how one might repair the major lacunae in the work of Grice: Exactly what information is to be assumed in the inference processes associated with dialogue, and how it is accessed and manipulated? Sperber and Wilson (1982) make strong claims concerning these, and we shall argue that their claims are misleading or false. We shall then seek to show that our own approach, for all its shortcomings, addresses the problems more directly. One aspect of the comparison we shall offer will be that Sperber and Wilson's system remains, at bottom, a process-free linguistic approach, best seen as maintaining certain Chomskyan principles in a plainly pragmatic area, whereas what we offer is a process-oriented account, firmly within the AI-psychology tradition.

It may be necessary to make clear that, in making the last distinction, no suggestion is intended that the existence of actual programs is of any theoretical significance in itself. In fact, the work described in the last part of the chapter is being programmed (under a SERC research grant), but no conclusions can be drawn from that. Indeed, it would be wrong to do so because there is much work, in psychology for example, firmly within the information-processing paradigm which does not have programs, as well as work within AI itself where no programs are written, although important points about representation are nevertheless made. In separating out Sperber and Wilson from other work in this way, it is not the existence or absence of programs that is at issue when one refers to the information-processing paradigm.

Within the broad paradigm of work on discourse understanding as a function of inference and a base of knowledge, belief or assumption lies a great deal of research in four neighbouring fields, as we have noted. We shall greatly narrow that scope here by restricting our attention to work which offers some explication of the key notion of an individual's beliefs, and hence some way of distinguishing formally between what one participant in a dialogue believes and what another does, where those two may be quite different, even though the two people communicate perfectly well. The need for that can be seen very easily: Suppose a doctor is talking to a patient and says:

(1) *Where in your stomach is that pain, Mr. Smith?*

indicating, as he says it, an area of the lower belly. The doctor accepts, by his statement, a lay representation of where the stomach is (i.e., some good way below its actual location). In order to communicate satisfactorily with Mr. Smith, he assumes the false belief that he believes Mr. Smith to have, although he does not himself hold or assert that belief.

Attempts have been made to describe such phenomena within an informal logic of presupposition, but the above is not an example of presupposition on any strict definition of the term and, in any case, the delimitation of that notion is beside the point if what is essential to the example is capturing some notion of "belief space", or partitioning of the assumptions to a discourse, so one can say whose they are.

The need for such a representational facility has long been recognized in philosophy (e.g., Donnellan, 1966), psychology (e.g., Johnson-Laird, 1980), linguistics (Levy, 1977; Shadbolt, 1983), and in AI particularly in the pioneering work of Perrault and Allen (1980). There has not been such recognition in all AI work on inference and understanding of the last ten years, and our case will be that, whatever the plausibility and sophistication of its claims, there is not that recognition in Sperber and Wilson (1982), and it is a fatal drawback.

We shall refer to that representational requirement as 'recursive cognitive solipsism' (to use an old philosophical term that Fodor, 1980, has deployed for other purposes): the requirement that a model of discourse understanding is solipsistic in the sense of modelling only some particular entity's understanding. Hence, the simultaneous modelling of the beliefs of others must be the principal entity's beliefs about those beliefs. Moreover, it must be possible to model the "belief of" operator recursively and applied as deeply as is needed for a particular example. In the second section of this chapter, we offer some suggestions as to how this might be done.

MUTUAL KNOWLEDGE

One type of psychological–linguistic account, also descending from the work of Grice (1975) must be mentioned: the 'mutual knowledge' approach of Schiffer (1972) and Clark and Carlson (1982). This approach accepts much of what has been set out so far and seeks to explicate a formal notion of "A and B mutually know P". Although a great deal is idiosyncratically known or believed by individuals, communication is as successful as it is because we not only believe many things in common with other beings, but believe ourselves to do so. The work of Clark and Carlson thus forms a middle case between Sperber and Wilson's (1982) "uniform assumption space" approach, which does not attribute ownership of beliefs to individuals (see below), and our own attempt to characterize beliefs more generally than by restricting attention to what can be "mutually known". Clark and Carlson's (1982) work has been discussed in Smith (1983), by Sperber and Wilson (1982) and ourselves, and is not central to the concerns of this chapter, but it may be worth recapitulating briefly why that is so.

Clark and Carlson's (1982) analysis is essentially of situations of actual or potential co-presence, as when two people observe an object lying between them or go to a cinema together. It is not only that each believes the other to have had such and such an experience, but that each believes (probably truly) that the other believes it of the first person, and so on, indefinitely. Infinite numbers of steps like

A believes B believes A believes. . .

are possible, and it is not important for the sake of illustration which of the predicates "believe" or "know" are used here. Clark and Carlson (1982) have been misunderstood (not only through the faults of their commentators) as implying that understanders sometimes go through an infinite number of such steps. Of course, they do not, and the authors did not intend that, claiming instead that to know "A and B mutually know P" is to have the ability to apply a rule as often as is required in a particular case.

We believe that only very special cases can fall under this description, and that not much communication requires assumptions about real co-presence. For all other cases, belief is a matter of cognitive solipism: I truly believe that you believe the world is *round* (rather than flat) just as I do. But this is *my* belief, not *yours*, and I am unlikely to have or have ever had any direct evidence of the matter. Even in cases of true co-presence, as when two people went together to a cinema the night before and refer to the matter later in conversation, the ability to infer infinitely many propositions is either vacuous (in that there is a rule producing as many as are required for a case, and no evidence is relevant) or, in real cases, the evidence is relevant at each stage and may fail (e.g., on the sixth recursive application of the rule). It is hard to see that real inference is much aided by the application of the trivial rule, though it might be handy to have available for special cases, even though the mutual knowledge literature gives no clear guide as to which situations allow its application.

In the case of real, fallible, applications, storage and effort considerations make it almost impossible that a truth value can reverse after a small number of consistent results (Steele, 1981, personal communication). In sum, then, we find Clark and Carlson's (1982) analysis highly ingenious for extraordinary cases but little help in the everyday solipsistic world, where we have no guarantees of what it is both people know, and know each other to know, outside of intensive psychological experiment. As we shall see, understanding does require assumptions about the knowledge of the other partner, but they are always fallible and hence, ex hypothesi, are not "mutual knowledge".

SPERBER AND WILSON'S RELEVANCE ACCOUNT OF UNDERSTANDING

Sperber and Wilson (1982) set out a more general account of reasoning than that of "mutual knowledge". They call it a theory of relevance, and its starting point is Grice's four maxims of communication. The authors argue that these four maxims can be reduced to one, that of relation or "being relevant", and their theory is intended to give content to that rather bare injunction.

The aim of Sperber and Wilson's analysis can be stated as one of making explicit the appropriate inferences so as to show, within a single logical space, what is said by a speaker, what additional implicit items of information must be brought to bear by a hearer, and what inferences follow from the above, including those which Grice would have called implicatures. A key term for Sperber and Wilson (1982) is "contextual implications". These are non-trivial inferences that can be drawn from context and utterance combined, for "having contextual implications in a given context is a necessary and sufficient condition for relevance" (Sperber and Wilson, 1982, p. 73), and deriving the contextual implications is, in effect, establishing the relevance of an utterance. A key requirement will be a procedure for establishing what the context (in the sense of a set of propositions as input to an inference procedure) is for a given utterance.

Things get interesting when claims move to a quantitative stage and specify the inferences appropriate for understanding in terms of the processing resources available, or when they offer quantitative selection of the most appropriate inference or inferences. This has been done within AI/psychology under the term "resource limited processing" (e.g., Norman & Bobrow, 1975) and, as a special case, within the field of natural language processing as "least effort" or "preference" theories (e.g., Bien, 1980; Wilks, 1975).

Sperber and Wilson's version starts with their principle of relevance (p. 75), which is "the single principle governing every aspect of comprehension": "The speaker tries to express the proposition which is the most relevant one possible to the hearer." This is a counsel of perfection, of course, and, like all such principles, may not be adhered to by the speaker. Here we shall understand it in reverse, as it were, in keeping with the hearer-orientated aspect of Sperber and Wilson, as a principle that the hearer is well advised to believe that the speaker is observing. But the reader should note in passing that this is not a trivial gloss, since this principle, unlike the authors' treatment of other examples, refers only to the speaker's intentions. It is one of the continuing themes of this chapter that such perspective-switching by Sperber and Wilson leads to muddle throughout.

We shall call the content of this principle "the claim": "Of two utterances that take the same amount of processing, it is the one with the most contextual implications that will be the more relevant; and, of two utterances which have the same number of contextual implications, it is the one which takes the least amount of processing that will be the more relevant."

Some care is needed now in interpreting this claim in terms of processing by a hearer, (and Sperber and Wilson seem to intend this: "the hearer has to supply" (p. 73)), since "relevant" in the claim and the principle may not refer to the same items. This is a problem for the authors, one which we will not attempt to solve for them here, The real origin of the problem is the ultimate incompatibility of a Gricean speaker's-intention approach and one based on hearer's information processing, let alone with an abstract, non-directional model based on notions of Chomskyan competence, although Sperber and Wilson preserve elements of all of these.

The Thalassemia Example

Let us set out the authors' principal illustrative example for their case: the thalassemia example (Sperber & Wilson, 1982, pp. 74–75):

> Compare utterances (19)–(21) in a context consisting of (22a–c):
>
> (19) Susan, who has thalassemia, is getting married to Bill.
> (20) Susan is getting married to Bill, who has thalassemia.
> (21) Susan, who has thalassemia, is getting married to Bill, and 1967 was a very good year for Bordeaux wine.
> (22) a. People who are getting married should consult a doctor about the possible hereditary risks to their children.
> b. Two people both of whom have thalassemia should be warned against having children.
> c. Susan has thalassemia.
>
> In this context both (19) and (20) carry the contextual implication that Susan and Bill should consult a doctor, but (20) also carries the implication that Susan and Bill should be warned against having children. The sentences in (19) and (20) are almost identical in linguistic and lexical structure. Suppose that processing involves identifying the propositions expressed by the utterance, computing its non-trivial implications, and matching each of these against the propositions in the context to see if further non-trivial implications can be derived. Then (19) and (20) should take roughly equal amounts of processing. In this context since (20) yields more contextual implications than (19), with the same amount of processing, it should be more relevant than (19), and this seems intuitively correct. By contrast, (19) and (21) have the single contextual implication that Susan and Bill should consult a doctor. (21) is linguistically more

complex than (19). On the above assumptions about processing, (21) will thus require more processing and be predicted as less relevant in context; again, this prediction seems to be intuitively correct.

Let us put four immediate considerations against this:

1. What serious quantitative information processing comparison can be going on in which a hearer can be considered as comparing the relevance of two different utterances (outside explicit psychological laboratory tests, that is) as distinct from a realistic situation where a hearer compares two alternative interpretations of a single utterance so as to select the more relevant? A hearer is normally offered an utterance, not several between which to choose, so what are the consequences for the information process?

2. It is true, as Sperber and Wilson note, that (20) produces the (undoubtedly nontrivial) implication that the couple should consult a doctor, but surely that must have required a great deal of processing to obtain: the location and application of an *and* rule, and the location and application of some form of *modus ponens* to (20) + (22b) and (22c)? Or do the authors somehow imagine that the actual inference itself, normally set out as explicit steps, does not require processing effort? If they believe that, they should not use the metaphor at all, but rather leave it in the hands of others. If the processing required by inferencing is taken into account, as they seem to intend, then the assumption of equal processing effort required by (19) and (20) is plainly ludicrous, since the accessing of a rule of conjunction and its application is a clear quantifiable cost. In general, the safe assumption, other matters being equal (which, of course, they are not), is that more implications will require more processing effort—exactly the opposite of what the claim suggests.

3. The real issue has been ignored until now: What basis can there possibly be for assuming, as Sperber and Wilson still do at this point in their account, that (19), (20) and (21) all access the same context, and that access will require the same effort in all three cases (for, if it does not, then the comparisons drawn so far fall to pieces)? Since (22c) is already explicitly part of (19), the context invoked by (19) cannot include (22c), as it does here. (Or, if it does, then other parts of utterances can occur explicitly in contexts, which will have other disastrous consequences for the claim). Hence the assumption that (19) and (20) "require the same processing effort" will be quite false if that effort includes context location (and in the next section the authors concede that it does). If the effort is not the same, then we have another case where the claim fails to apply, since neither equality is satisfied, although that, too, can give no comfort to the authors.

Again, (21) with its mention of Bordeaux must draw into the context propositions about wine? They can only be kept out by the indefensible assumption that this simply *is* the context, achieved cost-free, and declining to discuss the matter futher. If the mention of Burgundy did draw in that wider context, at correspondingly greater effort than those drawn in by (19) and (20), then again the whole comparative farrago would fall to bits, since the assumption that (21) will yield the same number of contextual implications as (19) may well turn out to be false. Some ingenuity with replying to what one hears could certainly produce a context for, and a reply to, (21). Gazdar and Good (1982) have pointed out that if a hearer has additional or idosyncratic information about, or interest in, a topic mentioned, then this may well give rise to a great number of non-trivial implications. Had the speaker said, in place of (21), "Susan, who has thalassemia, is getting married to Bill, who is a wine expert", then a wine expert hearer could have correctly inferred a great deal about Bill. Sperber and Wilson, lacking any clear notion of what a hearer or speaker believe, separately or about each other, have no defence to this and make none in their reply to Gazdar and Good in Smith (1982). In a properly founded theory, of course, it would be a requirement that the inferencing was constrained to a sub-space of assumptions that was the hearer's view of what the speaker believed the hearer believed (and the proposals of the last part of this chapter are intended to be such). That would meet Gazdar and Good's point, for a hearer behaving appropriately would not draw such "expertise" inferences if he believed the speaker did not know he was in possession of such information. Only in that way can context finding deal with apparently irrelevant input (and real errors by speakers and hearers can, of course, occur concerning such information.)

(4) The conclusions drawn by Sperber and Wilson (1982) depend crucially on the context containing the particular premises cited and not others, equally likely to be postulated by a hearer. (22b′) is as plausible to a layperson as (22b), and (22d) may be widely believed by normal (selfish) individuals (and in their study, Sperber and Wilson produce a context with a similar selfish belief about the function of charities):

(22b′) Thalassemia is a form of bone cancer.

(22d) It is unwise to marry a woman with diagnosed cancer, since she would need too much attention.

From the whole context (22a), (22b′), (22c) and (22d), (19) now has the implications that the couple should consult a doctor and that it is unwise of them to marry. Sentence (20) also has the same two implications from that context, whereas in Sperber and Wilson's context, (20) carried one more implication. It is obvious that the number depends crucially on the context located, and nothing general or significant follows, as the authors believe, from the particular examples they have chosen.

Locating the Context

At this point in the exposition, Sperber and Wilson (1982) introduce a principle that draws the whole theory closer to reality but has the effect of vitiating much of what has gone before. They now face up to the consequences of the fact that locating contexts is a matter of processing effort: "We want to argue . . . that the search for the interpretation on which an utterance will be most relevant involves a search for the context which will make this interpretation possible. In other words, determination of the context is not a prerequisite to the comprehension process, but a part of it" (p. 76).

But are we faced at this point by the withdrawal of a minor simplifying assumption, one which can now be withdrawn without ill effect, or is it rather that the recognition that context-finding costs processing effort (one accepted ab initio by all those in the AI psychology tradition who have discussed the issue) makes nonsense of the claim and everything based on it? The following definitions would at least remove the obvious absurdities in Sperber and Wilson's position:

New principles for hearers (and assumed by speakers to be in use by hearers):

1. Maximize the number of contextual implications drawn for some total given processing effort (up to some arbitrary maximum per unit time, say, one to be empirically determined) for interpretation of input, location of context and drawing of implications.
2. Minimize the amount of processing for context-finding so as to leave more available for drawing contextual implications under 1.

These proposals, too, may well not stand up to any detailed examination, but they are at least procedurally plausible and not self-evidently self-contradictory (though they are not independent). On Sperber and Wilson's account, by contrast, the hearer is under an injunction simultaneously to maximize and minimize the same sort of thing, in that the hearer is to minimize effort overall, while at the same time maximizing the number of contextual implications, whose production must require effort! Our hunch, for what it is worth, is that the authors should simply go for a least-processing-effort theory (as we have ourselves), for it is not clear what help having more contextual implications is. The number of implications can vary unpredictably with contexts, however chosen, and we believe that their addiction to the notion comes from a false view of maximizing information in communication.

In their reply to Gazdar and Good (1982), Sperber and Wilson (1982, p. 106) deny that they assume that "processing speed is constant". Thus, they argue, processing-per-unit time considerations are not relevant. They also claim that context-finding processing is non-inferential, as distinct from the inferential processing that draws implications, and so no considerations drawn from summing processing capacities are appropriate in a discussion of their system. This is, we believe, the merest obfuscation, and nothing that they write gives any support to the view that there are separate processing capacities that cannot be added. It is certainly possible that the brain does have separate capacities for the two processes, ones that cannot be added, but claiming that would require some shred of physiological evidence above and beyond the undoubted convenience to Sperber and Wilson. Moreover, such a concession would be quite at variance with the discovery that the "determination of context is not a prerequisite to the comprehension process but a part of it" (1982. p. 76).

Given (1) and (2) above, some version of Sperber and Wilson's claim could now be reinstated, and they might well feel that these new principles are just what they intended and have expressed ("We would suggest that the amount of processing tends to remain roughly constant throughout a stretch of discourse" (1982. p. 77)), if that is taken to mean processing per unit time, but they certainly have not, and indeed are unable to, because the claim was stated on the basis of false assumptions about cost-free syntactic processing which is a matter of complete irrelevance to logical complexity and inferential effort. It would be hard to find in the recent linguistic literature a clearer example of the bad effects of the hangover of beliefs in the autonomy and primacy and syntax.

Cognitive Solipsism

We drew attention earlier to the fact that Sperber and Wilson have no clear or consistent appreciation of the fact that real inference must go on somewhere and, in a model of human communication, that it must be in a hearer model or a speaker model (where each may, and must, contain models of the other). This lack surfaces in their study at intervals, as when they discuss the "common ground", which is their version of "mutual knowledge": the set of facts, serving as potential contexts, that both conversational participants know.

On Sperber and Wilson's account, there is no method or theory to explain the differences among

1. premises/beliefs believed by the hearer to be held by the speaker when speaking;

2. general knowledge known by the hearer and believed by him or her to be imputed by the speaker; and
3. enthymemic beliefs, not retrieved by the hearer from anywhere, but constructed by him or her as part of a context, and imputed to the speaker on the basis only of what is said (i.e., not believed previously by the hearer, nor previously believed by him or her to be held by the speaker).

Enthymemic constructions are beliefs attributed to the speaker so as to make the implications follow from what is already in the inference space (e.g., the current utterance). In writing this chapter, we produced, out of the blue, more or less plausible sets (22b′) and (22d), but as to how that process can be modelled algorithmically, no one has much to say. It is the great problem in Sperber and Wilson's theory and for all those working in this area.

No theory that fails to reflect these distinctions in some well-motivated way can be taken seriously in this area. Investigations that do make them are the very stuff of much recent work in AI, both logical-theoretical (e.g., Moore, 1975) and programmed/applied (e.g., Perrault & Allen, 1980). In the important latter series of papers, the notions of belief, speech acts, plans, reference, inference and models of the other were ingeniously explored, and the above distinctions were fundamental. A crucial advantage of work like the latter type is that it can show the contiguity of relevance and inference with human plans and goals with what it is someone is talking *for*. There is no way this can be done with Sperber and Wilson's work, and that must be a serious shortcoming in a general theory of pragmatics.

More relevant to the matter in hand is the series of papers by Wilks and Bien (1979, 1983) on the procedural location and manipulation of belief spaces or environments in which such inferences can go on, and which simultaneously constrain relevance, inference and the beliefs of the other. This work is very elementary as yet, and nothing whatever follows from it, but it makes none of the elementary errors of Sperber and Wilson (1982). In such a system, one can actually compute (albeit by naive algorithms) the appropriate environment for inference. We turn now to a more detailed description of that process.

This work is set within a general claim about least-effort human processing of language. It goes right back to earlier work (Wilks, 1975) on inference chaining in utterance interpretation in which programs interpreted utterances by establishing the shortest possible chain of inferences from context to utterance. This, as we said, was elementary stuff, but at least it was not incoherent; it was a wholly plausible assumption that locating and applying a shorter chain of inference would require less processing effort. The greatest lacuna in the list above is (3), and it is, at the moment, no more than an aspiration for all research workers. However, Sperber and Wilson do not see this, because they have no procedural grasp of what can and cannot be done, so for them the very difficult is all one with the well understood.

Let us summarize our objections to Sperber and Wilson's (1982) theory. Their errors all stem from their conviction that there is an objectively "right" context set of propositions, one that can be assumed independently of how it is located, and independently of what individuals may in fact believe. Let us now summarize an alternative account of these matters in which those features are built in from the very beginning.

AN ALTERNATIVE ACCOUNT: POINTS OF VIEW AND BELIEF ENVIRONMENTS

The following dialogue is perfectly natural and is assumed to take place between a (human) user and a system (that may or may not be human):

User: *Frank is coming tomorrow, I think*
System: *Perhaps I should leave* (I).
User: *Why?*
System: *Coming from you, that is a warning.*
User: *Does Frank dislike you?*
System: *I don't know* (II), *but you think he does, and that is what is important now.*

It is clear that, to understand this dialogue, it is necessary to distinguish the user's beliefs about Frank's beliefs from the system's beliefs about Frank's beliefs, and from Frank's actual beliefs. Such a situation is common enough to deserve special attention.

We want to tackle the issue generally (as a representational problem) and to ask the question, "What is it to maintain a structure, not only of one's beliefs about the inanimate world, but about beliefs about other individuals and their beliefs?" The argument here will be that there can be a very general algorithm for the construction of beliefs about beliefs or, if you wish, models of models of models, or points of view of points of view of points of view. The system has produced replies at the points marked (I) and (II) in the dialogue above, and the initial question we ask is why the system should say these different things at these different times, and what structure of knowledge, inference and beliefs about the user and Frank should be postulated in order to produce a dialogue of this type. We shall describe this by saying that the system is "running its knowledge about individuals in different environments at points (I) and (II)," and the difference between them will be crucial for us. One could assimilate our account to the most general form of description and say that the system in the dialogue above is interpreting the same utterance (namely, the user's first utterance) differently in the two contexts I and II, where the two contexts are, respectively, the belief space or environment of the system's view of the user's view of Frank's view of himself (the system) at I; and at II the space or environment of the system's view of Frank's view of the system.

The essence of what we shall described will be how one can express and manipulate such contexts, expressed, as in Sperber and Wilson, as sets of propositions, but now corresponding to the beliefs of individuals and their beliefs about each other's beliefs. These belief spaces or environments are temporary structures, created in real time during human communication, and not maintained permanently. The reason for that is both a processing and a storage one: There would be no argument for storing A's view of B permanently after computing it, unless it was striking and important or something we knew we would need again in the near future. Such structures would be too vast and too many to keep around in any kind of permanent memory as a general feature. We shall suggest that any natural language processing system committed to a least-possible-effort view of the process should act in the way described.

The system described has been developed (Wilks & Bien, 1979, 1983) with a view to connecting at some point with the literature on speech act phenomena, and so the computational treatment of the example above would be expected to lead to a discussion of whether anything concerning the notion of a warning was needed to model such a dialogue. Here, however, we shall direct the form of our examples towards the type chosen by Sperber and Wilson, so that points of contrast can be made.

We can use the above dialogue in order to illustrate the shorthand we shall use in the discussion.

$$\begin{matrix}[\text{Frank}]\\ \text{System}\end{matrix}$$

will be used to represent in a schematic form what the bearer of the outer name believes about the bearer of the inner name—that is to say, what the system believes about Frank. Structures like this can be nested so that the following structure

$$\begin{matrix}\begin{bmatrix}[\text{User}]\\ \text{Frank}\end{bmatrix}\\ \text{System}\end{matrix}$$

is intended to be shorthand for what the system believes about what Frank believes about the user. We shall refer to this as a nested environment, and every such structure is considered to be (trivially) inside the system, for it knows everything there is to be known about the individuals mentioned. The first important question is, "What are the structures that this shorthand represents?" For the moment, the simplest form of what the system believes about Frank—that is,

$$\begin{array}{c}[\text{Frank}]\\ \text{System}\end{array}$$

could simply be thought of as a less permanent version of a "frame" (Minsky, 1975; Charniak, 1978), or, more suitably, in the terms of Wilks (1977) as a "pseudo-text", or, if you prefer, any knowledge structure whatever about the individual named inside. In this brief discussion, we shall refer to them as pseudo-texts, but since we avoid all questions of semantic representation, they can be thought of as sets of sentences or propositions just like Sperber and Wilson's contexts. The essence of our method is to evaluate and compare two perspectives or environments (i.e., nested pseudo-texts), and they will be the ones which are created by the system at points I and II in the dialogue above. "Evaluate" here is intended to have a standard computer science meaning, one we could put more adventurously as "running structural descriptions in given environments" (Wilks & Bien, 1979). What this will mean in concrete terms is that we can draw plausible pragmatic inferences.

At (I) in the dialogue, the system is evaluating the user's initial remark, "Frank is coming tomorrow, I think" in the following nested environment:

$$\begin{array}{c}\begin{bmatrix}\begin{bmatrix}[\text{System}]\\ \text{Frank}\end{bmatrix}\\ \text{User}\end{bmatrix}\\ \text{System}\end{array}$$

At point (II) in the conversation, the system has evaluated only Frank's view of himself—that is, he has run the user's first sentence in the simpler environment

$$\begin{array}{c}\begin{bmatrix}[\text{System}]\\ \text{Frank}\end{bmatrix}\\ \text{System}\end{array}$$

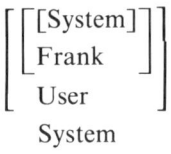

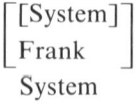

where he discovers that he has no such information on what Frank thinks of him. In doing this, the system takes no account of the speaker/user's beliefs or motives. Notice that the pseudo-texts are general items and will not be stored only for individual human beings but also for groups of humans, objects, substances, classes, my car, a jury, a professor, a salesman, sulphur and Germany. In Wilks (1977), their hierarchical relations and inheritance relations were discussed, and here we may assume these are standard.

When we consider nested environments, pseudo-texts for agents will be the only ones that can be outer environments in nesting diagrams, because we can consider, for example, Jim's view of the oil crisis but we cannot consider the view the oil crisis has of Jim. The principal algorithm computes the set of sentences corresponding to, or included in, a particular nested environment. The form of this can be put very simply: What is in an "inner pseudo-text" survives unless explicitly contradicted by an "outer pseudo-text". Thus, what I believe A believes about B will be what I believe about B (the "inner pseudo-text"), except where the "outer pseudo-text" in a nesting (in this case, what I believe about A and his beliefs about B) differs. I may believe B is a thief, but I know A does not; hence, the final inner resulting set of sentences will not assume B to be a thief and will thus differ from my own beliefs.

We describe metaphorically the process corresponding to the above in two ways: a "push down" of one pseudo-text inside another, corresponding to the nesting diagrams above, and the "percolation" of beliefs from an outer to an inner pseudo-text environment. In practice, that consists in computing the union of the beliefs in the inner pseudo-text and the relevant ones in the outer pseudo-text, and then reducing this to a consistent set by, in the case of contradiction, including only the outer belief in the result. This is a recursive process and can be applied to a nesting of any depth. The key word "relevant" in interpreted as follows: The beliefs in the outer pseudo-text deemed relevant are those explicitly containing the name of the inner pseudo-text (e.g., those beliefs in the pseudo-text for A containing the name B, in the above example). This is a highly oversimplified method, particularly because it ignores the issues of the identity of individual names and descriptions and whether or not such identities are known by the participants. But, primitive as it is, this "relevance heuristic" is just that, rather than the mystical retrieval procedure envisaged by Sperber and Wilson (1982).

The issue of identity of individuals within knowledge and belief contexts is, of course, a central issue in intensional logic, and a method for dealing with it more fully has been developed by Maida (1983). Our rule above is a particular case of what is normally called "default reasoning". The reader is referred to Wilks and Bien (1983) for a detailed working through of an example of this rule. As we noted earlier, the process assumes not only the default rule but also that belief pseudo-texts are *normally* stored only at the bottom level: One does not seek to compute and store full representations of A's beliefs about B, but only beliefs concerning A and concerning B.

Before proceeding to the core of this part of the chapter, we should mention briefly, and in turn, limitations to this "bottom-level" assumption and to the "default rule".

Limitations on Bottom-Level Beliefs: Beliefs of and about

There is already some partitioning in the pseudo-texts, corresponding to the distinction between someone's beliefs about someone and his or her beliefs about the beliefs of that individual. To put it simply, we can have beliefs about Smith, that he is male, 45, and so on. We can also have beliefs about his beliefs: that Smith believes that, say, Vitamin C cures colds. On one general view of belief, these are all properties of Smith, but they are, of course, importantly different sorts of properties.

By representing both these sets of beliefs within the system's pseudo-text for Smith, we violate the pure bottom-level view, for the representation of Smith's own beliefs is already within the nesting

$$\left[\begin{array}{l}[\text{Smith}]\\ \text{Smith}\end{array}\right]_{\text{System}}$$

As a form of diagrammatic representation, we shall put a horizontal line across a pseudo-text, with the beliefs above the line being those the system believes the individual to hold, while those below are the system's beliefs about Smith, with no commitment as to whether or not he holds them. Thus

$$\left[\begin{array}{l}\text{Smith}\\ \qquad \dfrac{\text{Smith is an alcoholic}}{\text{Smith is an alcoholic}}\\ \qquad \text{Smith likes Jones}\end{array}\right]_{\text{System}}$$

is not a redundant representation. Moreover, in actual processes we shall make use of "promotion heuristics" for certain predicates like "like" but not for those like "is-an-alcoholic", where "Smith likes Jones" as a lower belief could be promoted to the corresponding upper half of the pseudo-text containing it, on the grounds that individuals invariably know whom they like. One could express this "promotion heuristic" as a set of rules:

$$X \text{ dislikes } Y \Rightarrow X \text{ believes } (X \text{ dislikes } Y)$$

A natural additional inference (for inserting incoming dialogue into pseudo-texts) would be:

$$X \text{ assert } P \Rightarrow X \text{ believe } P$$

unless there was any indication of, or reason to suspect, lying by X. Let us turn now to limitations on the principle of default belief.

Limitations on Default Belief: Expert and Self-knowledge

A topic that has not yet been confronted is that of an individual's view of himself, which does not conform to our general heuristics for the computation of points of view. Someone else's view of X is my view except where I believe that not to be the case. No problem arises with the system's self-model. The pseudo-text:

$$\begin{matrix}[\text{System}] \\ \text{System}\end{matrix}$$

has all its content above the line (to continue the demarcation line metaphor). There are no beliefs the system has about the system that are not its own beliefs. In fact, all information in the whole system is (trivially) indexed from this pseudo-text.

More interesting cases arise when the system wishes to compute, say, Frank's view of himself or Frank's view of the system:

$$\underset{\text{System}}{\begin{bmatrix}[\text{Frank}] \\ \text{Frank}\end{bmatrix}} \quad \text{or} \quad \underset{\text{System}}{\begin{bmatrix}[\text{System}] \\ \text{Frank}\end{bmatrix}}$$

It might be reasonable to assume that Frank's view of himself is, in general, the same as my view of him, except where I have evidence to the contrary. The default heuristic would create an environment in which Frank believes his address (which I happen to know) to be what I believe it to be; his number of eyes to be what I believe it to be; but his number of teeth must be the value of what he believes it to be (and not the unevaluable function that I have), and so on.

Frank may well have beliefs, concrete and abstract, that I know nothing about, but given the limitations on my beliefs, my best construction is still to believe that his beliefs are as mine (except for the exceptions of which I am aware). The normal method of treatment here would be a lambda expression that the system cannot in general evaluate:

(the (lambda (x)(cardinality-of-Frank's-teeth x)))

The situation described so far is not different in principle from that of expert knowledge, for each individual is an expert concerning himself. So the general analysis we have given of Frank's "self-embedding" may well hold for any other case of expert knowledge that the system does not share. Suppose Frank is a doctor, but the system has no medical expertise. It may know leukemia is a disease but not its nature, diagnosis or cure, and yet it may believe that Frank does know these things. Hence, in an embedding like:

$$\begin{bmatrix}\text{[Leukemia]} \\ \text{Frank}\end{bmatrix}_{\text{System}}$$

an application of the default rule will not yield much content but will also not be misleading. The inner environment there can be seen as a general "disease pseudo-text", or frame, in which there are many empty slots (or alternatively, as a large number of lambda expressions, unevaluable by the system, of the form (knows the (x) cure-of) and so on. In situations where the system represents an average man, or non-expert, constructing the belief environment of an expert by the default rule will not mislead if the system contains the appropriate pseudo-text in a general form. Naturally, it remains a possibility that the environment so constructed is, in reality, hopelessly wrong as to the facts; the system might believe leukemia is a psychiatric condition, for example.

Let us turn to the second case—the computation of Frank's view of the system. On one hand, the general default heuristic must surely break down here, because the system cannot assume that Frank has access to all the beliefs about itself that it has. If we applied the general heuristic to a system that believed itself to be human and have 20 teeth, it would construct an inner environment in which Frank also would have the system's own beliefs about its number of teeth, which is not plausible. One simply knows oneself better than others do.

On the other hand, the method of unevaluable expressions used in the first case ought to be equally applicable here, and it ought to be possible for the system to ask and answer the question, "What is Frank's view of me?", if only because this is a common but answerable question in everyday life. One natural solution may be found (in the sense of a psychologically plausible solution) via a special pseudo-text for the system's view of its "public self" (i.e., what it believes to be the average man's view of it). That would be the entity:

$$\begin{bmatrix}\text{[System]} \\ \text{Average man}\end{bmatrix}_{\text{System}}$$

but that, while perhaps solving the defect in the default heuristic, does so at the expense of yet more belief partitioning—more beliefs in subsets whose immediate believer was not the system itself. A way of avoiding this would be for there to be beliefs in the lower half of

[System]
System

and for them to be the system's beliefs about the average man's view of the system's self. If these were present, then the general heuristic would run properly. Clearly, the bottom-half beliefs will not necessarily be any subset of those in the corresponding upper half (the system's actual beliefs about itself).

As before, we can look at this issue more generally as one of expertise and consider the case inverse to the earlier one—namely, where the system has expert knowledge that the average man does not, as in (1) if the system had medical expertise. The system should then have a belief set corresponding to the environment:

$$\left[\begin{array}{l}\text{[Leukemia]}\\ \text{Average man}\end{array}\right]$$
System

and the set of beliefs so represented would not necessarily be any computable subset of the system's own (expert) beliefs about the disease.

In this case, no solution is available in terms of a "lower half" of beliefs about a inanimate entity (since the upper–lower distinction cannot be made for non-believers). Hence, a general solution must be the first of the two considered above for the system's view of its own public self—namely, the storing of the average man's views, not only of the system itself, but of all areas for which the system considers itself to have expert knowledge, and for which there is plausible, public "non-expert" view, This could, of course, lead to a great proliferation of pseudo-texts that were not at the "bottom level" in our earlier terminology (i.e., did not have the system as the bottom-level believer), and hence to an increase in permanent belief set partitioning. Some economy would be gained from the ability to store these hierarchically, as for pseudo-texts in general (Wilks, 1977), under such nodes as

[Average Western man]
System .

Where topics such as semantic definition are concerned, the possibility would correspond precisely to what Putnam (1975) called the "division of linguistic labour" between experts and average people.

Another Point of View of Medical Examples

Let us now set out as briefly as possible our principal example, making use of the above techniques and retaining the spirit, though not at all the letter, of Sperber and Wilson's (1982) thalassemia example. The personae will be a doctor (an expert), of whom we will suppose the system to be a model. There will be a fiancée, who knows the broad facts about the disease, and a fiancé who does not, beyond that it is a disease. The doctor believes them both to carry the disease and is aware of their different degrees of informedness. Let us also suppose that they meet the doctor separately on this matter, and that the following dialogue takes place with the male partner:

He: My fiancée believes I have thalassemia.
Doctor: You do, and so does she.

at which point the doctor knows that nothing important (i.e., about children) follows for the patient, and he must now break the bad news in detail. Had he been talking to the other partner:

Doctor: You have thalassemia.
She: Does he have it too?
Doctor: Yes.

At this point, the doctor knows exactly what follows for the patient and can behave appropriately. It cannot be argued that these distinctions are unimportant, at least not by anyone who subscribes to any degree to the fundamental Gricean insights about human communication. But as we have seen in the first part of the chapter, Sperber and Wilson cannot possibly distinguish these situations with their limited theoretical mechanisms. It will be pretty clear how the environments we have described (contents in Sperber and Wilson's sense) can be constructed to correspond to the doctor/system's views of his two patients. Using the notations above, we can suppose the following pseudo-text structures:

$$\left[\begin{array}{l}\text{THALASSEMIA}\\ \text{Thalassemia is a genetic disorder.}\\ \text{Carriers should be warned against having children.}\end{array}\right]_{\text{SYSTEM}}$$

$$\left[\begin{array}{l}\text{THALASSEMIA}\\ \text{Thalassemia is a disease.}\\ \text{AVERAGE MAN}\end{array}\right]$$

(we shall write this pseudo-text as THALASSEMIA*)

$$\begin{bmatrix} \text{SHE} \\ \text{She has thalassemia.} \\ \text{He has thalassemia.} \\ \text{Intends to marry him and have children.} \\ \underline{\text{Has expert knowledge about thalassemia.}} \\ \text{She has thalassemia.} \\ \text{She believes he knows nothing about the disease.} \end{bmatrix}$$
SYSTEM

$$\begin{bmatrix} \text{HE} \\ \text{She believes he has thalassemia.} \\ \text{Intends to marry her and have children.} \\ \text{She knows about thalassemia.} \\ \underline{\text{He has thalassemia.}} \\ \text{He is average man about disease.} \\ \text{He has thalassemia.} \end{bmatrix}$$
SYSTEM

We can further suppse that "he" and "she" as variables cause no problems in this limited world, and that the states of the pseudo-texts above are after the first few dialogues. We can then consider what follows in the following environments (that the doctor/system constructs by push-down of pseudo-texts at the appropriate moment), using ordinary inference rules:

$$\begin{bmatrix} [\text{Thalassemia}] \\ \text{She} \end{bmatrix}$$
System

Implies: They should not have children, they both have the same disease.

$$\begin{bmatrix} [\text{Thalassemia*}] \\ \text{He} \end{bmatrix}$$
System

Implies: They both have same disease. She has expert knowledge of the disease they both have.

$$\begin{bmatrix}\begin{bmatrix}[\text{Thalassemia*}]\\ \text{He}\end{bmatrix}\\ \\ \text{She}\end{bmatrix}$$
$$\text{System}$$

Implies: Nothing.

$$\begin{bmatrix}\begin{bmatrix}[\text{Thalassemia*}]\\ \text{She}\end{bmatrix}\\ \\ \text{He}\end{bmatrix}$$
$$\text{System}$$

This environment contains "He has thalassemia," but no additional consequences follow. Notice that this nesting uses Thalassemia*, the average man's view of the disease, because although she does know about the disease, he does not know what it is she does know, though we should really add some unevaluable cure (and diagnosis) functions here from his general pseudo-text for disease. Even after:

> He: Does she know she has it too?
> Doctor: Yes.

nothing beyond the conclusion that they both have it follows, because he cannot compute the key fact about the disease that she knows. It is the main submission of this chapter that the above method is rather more realistic than Sperber and Wilson's (1982) proposals, and it is worth noting that it has nothing at all to do with the number of propositions that follow within any context/environment. Only some method like this can explain how a doctor treats patients differently in a way that no impersonal "heuristic of relevance" could possibly do alone.

THE CORRECT ROLE OF MUTUAL KNOWLEDGE

An issue discussed at the beginning of the chapter—that of mutual knowledge—can now be seen to be taken care of automatically by the procedures suggested here, and without the need for any special attention. If, in the pseudo-text for *X*'s beliefs there is a proposition *p*, where

$$p\text{: } X \text{ and } Y \text{ both see a candle between than at } t_n$$

then when any "push-down" of the pseudo-text for *Y* into that of *X* is made (to construct the system's beliefs about *X*'s beliefs about *Y* and his beliefs) to any required depth, that belief *p* will always move to the next inner environment, given the crude relevance heuristic proposed earlier. This transfer of beliefs, without any direct supporting evidence, which we have called the *percolation of belief*, is equivalent to the establishment of a series of propositions:

(the system believes) *X* believes *Y* believes *p*

As a result of recursive nesting, the iterative percolation will produce, in principle, the infinite belief set found in the mutual knowledge literature. In other related papers (e.g., Wilks & Bien, 1983), we have emphasized that it is just such recursive (let alone infinitely recursive) push-downs that any system based on a principle of least effort will seek to minimize. By contrast, for a "lower half" or "aboutness" belief (believed by the system), such as

X and *Y* are mafiosi

we would expect promotion to the inner belief set, and so as a candidate for iterative percolation, only if the predicate were appropriate (and "is a mafioso" presumably is such a predicate, since if you are one, you know it!), but then only for the half of the conjunction drawn in by relevance: e.g., there is no reason why *Y*'s being a mafioso should be promoted to the self-beliefs of *X*, just because that is entertained as a conjunction by the system. It would clearly be a delicate issue to settle just which predicates were so "promotable", but that is equally a problem for Clark and his collaborators.

Given any such typing of predicates, the general inference rule of the system does the rest without there being any special consideration at all of mutual knowledge phenomena. They have no privileged place but are mere epiphenomena that have arisen in the literature because of an inadequate general characterization of beliefs about beliefs and their computation. Wilks and Bien (1983) argued that some such percolations of unsupported belief into inner environments might be expected to have psychological consequences analogous to the so-called "sleeper effect". It would be interesting if that occurred as the side-effect of the operation of a very general rule for constructing nested environments.

CONCLUSION

It is hoped that the reader will be able, from this brief sketch, to assess and compare the two approaches discussed here, and to decide which offers a more realistic account of the pragmatic inferences individuals make on the basis of their actual beliefs, including their beliefs about others' beliefs. Finally, some brief note should be made of the differences between this work and similar work on speech acts and plans done at Toronto by Perrault and Allen, and by Cohen (see Perrault & Allen, 1978; Cohen, 1978). One is their emphasis on plans, which are not of central concern here. A second, and fundamental difference is that in the Toronto systems, all possible perspectives on beliefs *are already considered as computed*. That is to say, if, in a Toronto system, you want to know what the system believes the user's belief about Frank's belief about the system is, then you can simply examine an inner partition of a set of beliefs that has already been constructed, where it is already explicitly stored. This is the exact opposite point of view to that adopted in this chapter, which is that such inner environments are not stored already, and previously computed, but are constructed when needed and then, as it were, taken apart again, subject to percolated beliefs remaining behind, with the effect that the nested environment so constructed is lost when the need for it is gone. It is this that keeps belief structures stored as much as possible at what we have been calling the "bottom level".

You can see the difference by asking yourself if you already know what Reagan thinks Gorbachev thinks of Gaddafi. If you think you *already* know without calculation, then you will be inclined towards the Toronto view that such inner belief partitions are already constructed. If you think that in some sense, consciously or unconsciously, you have to think it out, you will lean towards a constructivist hypothesis, like the one advanced in this chapter.

REFERENCES

Bien, J. Proceedings of the IJCA, 1980, 675–677.

Charniak, E. On the use of knowledge in language comprehension. *Artificial Intelligence*, 1978, **11**, 225–265.

Clarke, H., & Carlson, T. Speech acts and hearers' beliefs. In N. Smith (Ed.), *Mutual knowledge*. London: Academic, 1982.

Cohen, P. R. *Journal of Personality and Social Psychology*, 1978, **36**, 1061–1074.

Donnellan, K. Reference and definite description. *Philosophical Review*, 1966, **75**, 281–304.

Fodor, J. A. Methodological solipsism. *Behavioral and Brain Sciences*, 1980, **3**, 63–73.

Gazdar, G., & Good, D. On a notion of relevance. In N. Smith (Ed.), *Mutual knowledge*. London: Academic, 1982.

Grice, H. In P. Cole & J. Morgan (Eds.), *Syntax and semantics: Speech acts*, Vol. 3. London: Academic, 1975.

Johnson-Laird, P. The meaning of modality. *Cognitive Science*, 1980, 4, 71–115.

Levinson, S. *Pragmatics*. Cambridge: Cambridge University Press, 1983.

Levy, D. Communicative goals and strategies. In T. Givon (Ed.), *Syntax and semantics*, Vol. 12. New York: Academic Press, 1979.

Maida, A. Knowing intensional individuals. Proceeding of the IJACI, 1983, 179–183.

Minsky, M. A framework for representing knowledge. In P. Winston (Ed.), *The psychology of computer vision*. New York: McGraw-Hill, 1975.

Moore, R. *Reasoning from incomplete knowledge in a procedural deduction system.* Technical report, MIT-AI Lab., AI-TR-347.

Moore, R., & Hendrix, G. *Computational models of belief and the semantics of belief sentences.* SRI Technical Note No. 187, 1979.

Perrault, R., & Allen, J. *American Journal of Computational Linguistics.* 1980, **6**, 167–182.

Putnam, H. In *Mind, language and reality.* Cambridge, 1975.

Schiffer, S. *Meaning.* Oxford: Clarendon Press, 1972.

Shadbolt, N. Processing reference. *Journal of Semantics*, 1983, **2**, 63–98.

Schiffer, S. *Meaning*, Oxford: Clarendon Press, 1972.

Shadbolt, N. Title. *Journal of Semantics*, 1983, **2**, 63–98.

Smith, N. (Ed.). *Mutual knowledge.* London: Academic, 1982.

Sperber, D., & Wilson, D. Mutual relevance and knowledge in theories of comprehension. In N. Smith (Ed.), *Mutual knowledge.* London: Academic, 1982.

Wilks, Y. A preferential, pattern-seeking, semantics for natural language inference. *Artificial Intelligence*, 1975, **6**, 88–111.

Wilks, Y. Making preferences more active. *Artificial Intelligence*, 1977, **8**, 75–97.

Wilks, Y., & Bien, J. Speech acts and multiple environments. *Proceeding of the IJCAI*, 1979, 451–455.

Wilks, Y., & Bien, J. Beliefs, environments and points of view. *Cognitive Science*, 1983, **8**, 120–146.

Wilks, Y., & Cunningham, C. *A purported account of semantic relevance.* Essex University Cognitive Studies Memorandum, No. 16.

Index